HRM

NELSON SERIES IN HUMAN RESOURCES MANAGEMENT

Managing Performance Through Training and Development

THIRD EDITION

NELSON SERIES IN HUMAN RESOURCES MANAGEMENT

Managing Performance Through Training and Development

THIRD EDITION

ALAN M. SAKS
UNIVERSITY OF TORONTO

ROBERT R. HACCOUN
UNIVERSITÉ DE MONTRÉAL

SERIES EDITOR:
MONICA BELCOURT
YORK UNIVERSITY

THOMSON

NELSON

Australia   Canada   Mexico   Singapore   Spain   United Kingdom   United States

THOMSON

NELSON

**Managing Performance Through
Training and Development**
Third Edition

Alan M. Saks and Robert R. Haccoun

Editorial Director and Publisher:
Evelyn Veitch

Executive Editor:
Anthony Rezek

Marketing Manager:
Don Thompson

Senior Developmental Editor:
Karina Hope

Production Editor:
Julie van Veen

Production Coordinator:
Renate McCloy

Copy Editor and Proofreader:
Erin Moore

Permissions Researcher:
Krista Alexander

Creative Director:
Angela Cluer

**Cover Design and Interior Design
Modifications:**
Sarah Battersby

Compositor:
Janet Zanette

Indexer:
Jin Tan

Printer:
Transcontinental

**National Library of Canada
Cataloguing in Publication Data**

Saks, Alan M. (Alan Michael),
1960-
   Managing performance through
training & development / Alan M.
Saks, Robert R. Haccoun. — 3rd ed.

(Nelson Canada series in human
resources management)
Previous ed. written by: Monica
Belcourt, Phil[l]ip C. Wright, Alan
M. Saks.

Includes bibliographical references
and index.

ISBN 0-17-622460-2

   1. Employees—Training of. I.
Haccoun, Robert R. II. Title. III.
Title: Managing performance
through training and
development. IV. Series.

HF5549.5.T7S23 2003   658.3'124
C2003-904773-3

To Kelly and Justin, my best friends

Alan Saks

To Jennifer, my superb daughter and a terrific person

Robert Haccoun

Brief Contents

Detailed Contents

About the Series

More than ever, HRM professionals need the knowledge and skills to design HRM practices that not only meet legal requirements but also are effective in supporting organizational strategy. Increasingly, these professionals turn to published research and best practices for assistance in the development of effective HR policies and practices. The books in the *Nelson Series in Human Resources Management* are the best source in Canada for reliable, valid, and current knowledge about practices in HRM.

The texts in this series include

- *Managing Performance through Training and Development*
- *Management of Occupational Health and Safety*
- *Recruitment and Selection in Canada*
- *Strategic Compensation in Canada*
- *Strategic Human Resources Planning*
- *An Introduction to the Canadian Labour Market*
- *Research, Measurement, and Evaluation of Human Resources*

The *Nelson Series in Human Resources Management* represents a significant development in the field of HRM for many reasons. Each book in the series (except for *Strategic Compensation in Canada*) is the first Canadian text in its area of specialization. HR professionals in Canada must work with Canadian laws, statistics, policies, and values. This series serves their needs. It also represents the first time that students and practitioners have had access to a complete set of HRM books, standardized in presentation, that enables them to access information quickly across many HRM disciplines. The books are essential sources of information that meet the requirements for the knowledge exam for the academic portion of the HR certification process. This one-stop resource will prove useful to anyone looking for solutions for the effective management of people.

The publication of this series signals that the field of human resources management has advanced to the stage where theory and applied research guide practice. The books in the series present the best and most current research in the functional areas of HRM. Research is supplemented with examples of the best practices used by Canadian companies that are leaders in HRM. Each text begins with a general model of the discipline, then describes the implementation of effective strategies. Thus the books serve as an introduction to the functional area for the new student of HR and as a validation source for the more experienced HRM practitioner. Cases, exercises, and references provide opportunities for further discussion and analysis.

As you read and consult the books in this series, I hope you share my excitement in being involved in the development of a profession that has such a significant impact on the workforce and our professional lives.

Monica Belcourt
Series Editor
July 2003

About the Authors

Alan M. Saks

Alan M. Saks, Ph.D. is a Professor of Organizational Behaviour and Human Resources Management at the University of Toronto, where he holds a joint appointment in the Division of Management–UTSC and the Joseph L. Rotman School of Management. Prior to joining the University of Toronto, Professor Saks was a member of the Department of Management in the Faculty of Commerce and Administration at Concordia University and in the School of Administrative Studies at York University.

Professor Saks earned an H.B.A. in Psychology from the University of Western Ontario, an M.A.Sc. in Industrial-Organizational Psychology from the University of Waterloo, and a Ph.D. in Organizational Behaviour and Human Resources from the University of Toronto. He conducts research on a number of topics in human resources management and organizational behaviour including recruitment, selection, job search, training, absenteeism, and the socialization and work adjustment of new employees. His research has been published in refereed journals such as the *Journal of Applied Psychology*, *Personnel Psychology*, *Academy of Management Journal*, *Journal of Organizational Behavior*, *Journal of Vocational Behavior*, and *Human Resource Development Quarterly*, as well as in professional journals such as the *HR Professional Magazine*, *The Training Report*, *The Learning Journal*, *Canadian HR Reporter*, and the *HRM Research Quarterly*. In addition to this text, he is also the author of *Research, Measurement, and Evaluation of Human Resources* and a co-author of *Organizational Behaviour: Understanding and Managing Life at Work*.

Professor Saks is currently on the editorial boards of the *Academy of Management Journal*, *Journal of Organizational Behavior*, and *Journal of Vocational Behavior*. He regularly speaks to the media and organizations on human resources management and work-related issues.

Robert R. Haccoun

Educated at McGill University (B.A. 1969) and the Ohio State University (M.A. 1970; Ph.D. 1973), Robert R. Haccoun is currently Professor of Psychology at the Université de Montréal. Prior to returning to academia in 1978, Professor Haccoun was a research scientist for Bell Canada in Montreal. He is a founding member and past President of the Industrial-Organizational Psychology section of the Canadian Psychological Association.

He has delivered papers at scientific conferences and published scholarly articles in French and in English in a number of areas including training, absenteeism, gender issues, and research methodology. He has published in many journals including *Personnel Psychology*, the *Journal of Applied Psychology*, *Journal of Organizational Behaviour*, *Applied Psychology: An International Review*, *Canadian Psychologist*, *Revue Gestion*, and *Canadian Journal of Administrative Studies*. His research book *Comprendre l'organisation: Approches de recherches*, co-authored in 1982, has been translated into Spanish.

In addition to serving as a reviewer for many scientific journals and research funding agencies, he is Associate Editor of *Applied Psychology: An International Review*.

Active in the transfer of knowledge from academia to applied settings, he has lectured to practitioner audiences and written many professional articles. He has also provided consulting services to a number of leading organizations in Canada, the U.S., and Europe.

Preface

In order to adapt, compete, and survive in today's frequently changing and uncertain environment, organizations must have the capacity for continuous learning and improvement. Continuous learning and improvement, however, depends in large part on the effectiveness of an organization's training and development programs—the focus of this textbook.

Since the second edition of this text was published, the field of training and development has experienced continued growth and development in terms of both the science and practice of training. In fact, while this book was being written, a new national association for training and development professionals called the Canadian Society for Training and Development (CSTD—www.cstd.ca) was established, making it the first national organization of training and development professionals in Canada.

In addition, there has also been a great deal of new and exciting practices and research in training and development. The increasing use of technology-based training methods, the emphasis on blended approaches to training delivery, team task analysis, just-in-time learning, and new approaches for improving the transfer of training are just a few examples of the exciting changes that have been happening in the training and development field. The third edition of *Managing Performance Through Training and Development* reflects these changes and represents an extensive and thorough revision.

First, we are thrilled to welcome a new co-author, Robert R. Haccoun, who has an excellent reputation as a scholar and researcher in industrial/organizational psychology and human resources management, and who is one of Canada's leading experts on training and development. Robert brings considerable research breadth and practical experience to the text. As well, Alan M. Saks has taken over as the lead author of the third edition.

Second, the third edition includes three new chapters: Learning and Motivation (Chapter 3), Technology-Based Training Methods (Chapter 8), and Challenges and Best Practices (Chapter 14). These chapters represent important additions to the text. Since training is ultimately about learning and the motivation to learn, we felt that students should have a solid grounding and understanding of the theories, principles, and concepts of learning and motivation. We also added a new chapter devoted to technology-based training given the dramatic rise in the use of technology for learning and training in recent years. A new concluding chapter has also been added to describe the challenges that organizations face today, and the implications, trends, and best practices for training and development.

In addition to these new chapters, several chapters have been substantially revised. In particular, Chapters 9 (Transfer of Training), 10 (Training Evaluation), 11 (The Costs and Benefits of Training Programs), and 13 (Management Development) have been almost completely rewritten. Furthermore, every chapter in the text contains new content. Here are some examples to look for:

Chapter 1: The instructional systems design (ISD) model of training and development

Chapter 2: Learning organizations in Canada

Chapter 3: David Kolb's learning cycle model and learning styles

Chapter 4: Cognitive task analysis and a team task analysis

Chapter 5: Prepractice conditions for learning

Chapter 6: Physical and psychological fidelity

Chapter 7: Off-the-job versus on-the-job training methods

Chapter 8: Asynchronous and synchronous training

Chapter 9: Baldwin and Ford's model of the transfer of training process

Chapter 10: Kurt Kraiger's decision-based evaluation model

Chapter 11: Cost effectiveness and cost-benefit evaluation

Chapter 12: How to design an effective diversity training program

Chapter 13: Models of management skill development

Chapter 14: Ethical guidelines for trainers

In addition to these changes in content, we have also added the following new pedagogical features: chapter-opening vignettes; The Trainer's Notebook boxes; Weblinks; RPC (Required Professional Capabilities) icon; Discussion Questions; Using the Internet exercises; and a case in every chapter.

First, every chapter in the text begins with a chapter-opening vignette. The vignettes tell the story of an actual training program in an organization that is of relevance to the material covered in the chapter. The vignette sets the stage for each chapter. The majority of these vignettes feature Canadian organizations.

Also new to this edition is a feature called "The Trainer's Notebook." This feature presents practical hands-on information for the practising trainer (e.g., facilitating learning in organizations). Weblinks have also been added to each chapter for students who want to learn more about an organization or association mentioned in the text. A Weblink icon appears in the margin of the text and the Web addresses can be found at the end of each chapter. Also new to the third edition is the RPC icon, which represents the learning objectives in the area of Organizational Learning, Development, and Training for the new national Certified Human Resources Professional (CHRP) designation. The icon's appearance in the text signals RPC-relevant content to students.

A number of "end-of-chapter" features have also been added. Several discussion questions can be found in every chapter for instructors who wish to focus on particular issues for class discussion. As well, Internet exercises called "Using the Internet" have been added to each chapter. These exercises require students to visit a website and to gather information to answer a question(s) or to prepare a brief report on what they have found. As well, we have added many new exercises and have made sure to include two general kinds of exercises in each chapter. Some of the exercises can be done in class and do not require any preclass preparation, while others must be done outside of class and require preclass preparation. These exercises can also be used as projects and assignments. In addition to the exercises, we have added seven new cases and unlike the previous edition, every chapter in the third edition now includes a case.

We have also retained those features that appeared in the second edition. Learning Objectives appear at the beginning of every chapter. Key Terms are highlighted in the text in bold and in the margins, and are also listed at the end of each chapter. Training Today boxes feature current events, stories, and examples that pertain to material presented in the chapter. Chapter-ending summaries review the main content of each chapter. And the Vandalais Department Stores running case appears in Chapters 5, 6, 7, 8, 9, 10, 11, and 14.

For instructors, new to this edition are an Instructor's Manual and Microsoft™ PowerPoint™ slides that can be downloaded directly from **www.hrm.nelson.com**.

We hope that students and instructors find these changes as exciting as we do and that they facilitate and maximize learning.

Structure of the Book

The text begins with an overview of the training and development process. In addition to presenting training and development within the larger context of the organization and the human resources management system, Chapter 1 also describes the instructional systems design (ISD) model of the training and development process, which sets the stage for many of the subsequent chapters in the text.

Chapters 2 and 3 focus on learning, which is first and foremost what training is all about. We feel that it is important that students first understand learning at both the organizational and individual level before they begin to learn about the role of training and development in the learning process. Therefore, Chapter 2 describes organizational learning, the learning organization, types of knowledge and intellectual capital, and knowledge management practices. The chapter concludes with a multilevel systems model of organizational learning that shows how learning at the organizational, group, and individual level are interrelated, as well as a model that shows how training is related to individual and organizational learning.

Chapter 3 focuses on how individuals learn and their motivation to learn. The major theories of learning, adult learning theory, and theories of motivation are presented along with their implications for training and development. The chapter concludes with a model of training effectiveness, which shows the different variables that influence learning and retention and how learning and retention are related to individual behaviour and performance and organizational effectiveness. The training effectiveness model is further developed in Chapters 5 and 9.

The training and development process begins with needs analysis, the focus of Chapter 4. Chapter 4 describes the needs analysis process with particular emphasis on the three levels of needs analysis (organizational, task, and person) and how to determine solutions to performance problems. The chapter also describes the methods of needs analysis and some of the obstacles to conducting a needs analysis.

Chapter 5 describes how to design and deliver a training program. The chapter begins with an overview of the importance of training objectives and how to write good training objectives. The chapter then proceeds to cover the main steps involved in the design and delivery of training programs, including whether to purchase or design a training program; the training content; training methods; active practice and conditions of learning; characteristics of good trainers; the selection of trainees; training materials and equipment; the training site; scheduling training programs; preparing a lesson plan; and delivering the training program.

One of the most important steps in the design of a training program is choosing training methods. Given the vast array of training methods and instructional techniques available, Chapters 6, 7, and 8 are devoted to this topic. Chapter 6 describes the most frequently used off-the-job training methods including the lecture, discussion, audio-visual methods, case study, case incident, behaviour modelling, role plays, games, simulations, and action learning. Each training method is defined and described along with tips for trainers. The chapter concludes with a discussion of the factors to consider when choosing training methods and the importance of a blended approach.

In Chapter 7, we turn to on-the-job training methods including job instruction training, performance aids, job rotation, apprenticeship programs, coaching, and mentoring. As in Chapter 6, we define and describe each method and provide tips for trainers. The chapter concludes with a discussion of the advantages and disadvantages of off-the-job and on-the-job training methods.

Chapter 8 is devoted to technology-based training methods. The chapter begins with a definition and a list of the different types of technology-based training. Particular emphasis is given to self-directed learning, computer-based training and e-learning, asynchronous and synchronous training, distance learning, electronic performance support systems, and video conferencing. The chapter also describes the advantages, disadvantages, effectiveness, and design of technology-based training methods, and concludes with a discussion of the future of technology-based training.

One of the biggest problems facing trainers is how to ensure that trainees apply what they learn in training on the job. This is known as the transfer of training and it is the focus of Chapter 9. The chapter begins with a review of the transfer problem and barriers to transfer followed by a description of Baldwin and Ford's (1988) model of the transfer process. The chapter then describes the different practices that can be undertaken by management, trainers, and trainees for improving the transfer of training before, during, and after training.

Once a training program has been designed and delivered, it needs to be evaluated. Chapters 10 and 11 are devoted to training evaluation. In Chapter 10, we first describe the purpose and difficulties of training evaluation, and then discuss several training evaluation models. The chapter also describes how to measure key variables for training evaluation and the different types of training evaluation designs.

The topic of training evaluation continues in Chapter 11, where the focus shifts to the costs and benefits of training programs. Chapter 11 describes how to calculate the costs and benefits of training programs, as well as the calculation of the net benefit and return on investment. The importance of the credibility of estimates is also discussed, as well as the use of utility analysis for determining the financial benefits of training programs. The chapter concludes with a discussion of the activities that support the costing function.

In Chapters 12 and 13 we turn to a consideration of the types of training programs that are provided by organizations. Chapter 12 describes some of the most common forms of training that employees receive including orientation training, basic-skills training, technical skills training, information technology training, health and safety training, quality training, team training, sales training, customer service training, sexual harassment training, diversity training, and cross-cultural training. Descriptions of each type of training program are provided as well as statistics on their use by organizations in Canada and the United States.

Chapter 13 is devoted entirely to management development. This reflects both the importance of management development to organizations and the large investments made by organizations in the development of their managers. The chapter begins with a definition of management development and management, and then describes the core functions, roles, and skills of management. The chapter describes models of management development as well as the content of management development programs. It concludes with an overview of the types of management development programs with particular emphasis on outdoor wilderness training and coaching.

Chapter 14 concludes the text with a discussion of training challenges and best practices. First, we discuss how the role of the trainer is changing to reflect a greater focus on managing learning and performance rather than simply providing training. We then discuss the role of ethics in training and development and how trainers must adhere to ethical guidelines and standards. Next, we discuss a number of challenges facing organizations today and the implications and trends for training and development. The chapter and text conclude with a review of the main reasons why training programs fail and best practices to make them highly effective.

Throughout the text we have tried to maintain a balance between theory and research on the one hand, and practice and application on the other. We have also tried to provide examples of the concepts and principles presented in the text by showcasing organizations, many of them Canadian, that have successfully designed and delivered effective training programs. We hope that the combination of text material as well as the pedagogical features will motivate students to learn about the science and practice of training and development.

Acknowledgments

Writing a textbook requires the support and assistance of many people who either directly or indirectly make important contributions to the process and outcome. We wish to thank all of those who have played important roles in our lives and in writing this text.

First, we thank the reviewers who provided us with insightful and constructive feedback that led to many changes and improvements: John Bratton,

University College of the Cariboo; Sarah Cunningham, Sheridan Institute of Technology and Advanced Learning; Tony Dearness, Memorial University; Alec J. Lee, Camuson College; Steve Robinson, Georgian College; Wendy Vermeersch, Sheridan Institute of Technology and Advanced Learning; Linda Yates Cameron, Seneca College; and Diane White, Seneca College. Each one contributed to this text by lending us their expertise and by taking the time to share experiences and to make insightful comments. The feedback provided by these reviewers led to some major changes in this edition and we thank them for the time and effort they devoted to reading the manuscript and providing us with excellent feedback and suggestions.

Second, we would like to express our appreciation to our many colleagues who have helped us formulate our ideas, who provided us with their own ideas and insights, or who were always available to lend a sympathetic ear.

Special thanks go to past co-author and series editor Monica Belcourt for her commitment to and support for this project. Monica was not only instrumental in the development of the *Nelson Series in Human Resources Management*, but she was also the lead author of the previous two editions of this text. We thank her for giving us the opportunity to revise her "baby." We also wish to acknowledge the contributions of our past co-author, Philip C. Wright.

Third, we wish to express our gratitude to the team at Nelson that helped us develop and produce this text. We are especially thankful to our Executive Editor, Anthony Rezek, who has been highly committed to this project and very supportive of our ideas and aspirations for this text. We also wish to thank our Senior Developmental Editor, Karina Hope, who has done a great job managing this project and keeping us on track. We are grateful for her assistance and her patience and understanding each time we missed a deadline. We also thank our Production Editor, Julie van Veen, for her professionalism and dedication to this project.

Finally, we also wish to thank our families who have had to endure the burden of living with tired and overworked authors who sometimes don't have time to play or sleep! Alan Saks is grateful to Kelly and Justin for making it all worthwhile, and Renee and Simon for being such good "trainers." Robert Haccoun thanks his daughter Jennifer, who has provided him, as the Yiddish expression goes, much in the way of "nachas."

Alan M. Saks
University of Toronto

Robert R. Haccoun
Université de Montréal

Chapter 1

The Training and Development Process

Chapter Learning Objectives

After reading this chapter, you should be able to:

- understand the meaning of the terms performance management, training, and development
- describe the organizational, employee, and societal benefits of training and development
- discuss training and development in Canada
- understand and explain the role of the environmental and organizational context of training and development
- understand the meaning of strategic human resources management (SHRM) and what makes training and development strategic
- discuss the instructional systems design (ISD) model of training and development

QUEBECOR WORLD INC.

Quebecor World Inc. is the world's largest printing company. Based in Montreal, it has 160 printing plants located in 14 countries and employs 43 000 people. In 1998 the company embarked on the largest training initiative the organization ever attempted. After extensive research and a year-long assessment, the company identified some strategic and pressing business realities. The printing industry had undergone some dramatic changes in a short period of time. Gaining a competitive advantage was no longer measured in months and weeks, but in hours and minutes and the company was no longer able to compete on price and quality alone.

As a result of the assessment process, the company determined that customer service was the most important issue to focus on and the key to gaining a competitive advantage and differentiating themselves from their competitors. This led to the development of the company's ALLSTAR customer service training program. The goal of the program was to educate the firm's customer-service and account representatives from its North American operations in world-class skills. Some of the program's objectives included improving understanding of customers' needs; improving account-management skills; and achieving a high performance, team-based, customer-oriented culture.

The nine-day program consists of three intensive sessions of three days each with no more than 25 participants per session. During one of the sessions, employees participate in a team-building cooking exercise in which customer-service representatives must design, prepare, and serve a banquet meal within two hours without any instruction. The exercise forces employees to work together to come up with focused solutions in a short time.

The program also includes role-play situations between plant and customer partnerships. A low-ropes exercise requires trainees to climb over a 15-foot wall and navigate other challenges. Trainees must also make presentations to senior managers about what they have learned and how they will apply it back on the job. Upon completion of the program, trainees evaluate the program and receive a certificate for completing it.

The results have been no less than remarkable. The training program helped Quebecor World Inc. gain a competitive advantage over its competitors by achieving world-class customer-service skills that have increased customer satisfaction, decreased turnaround time, lowered the cost of errors, and improved internal and external communications. It has received superb feedback within the company and is now receiving national recognition in the United States. In 2001, *Workforce Magazine* awarded the company its Optimas Award in the Competitive Advantage category.[1]

Quebecor World Inc. is a shining example of the importance of training and development for an organization's success and competitiveness. The company's ALLSTAR customer service training program was a critical factor in helping the organization achieve its strategic objective of excellent customer service and in gaining a competitive advantage. It is also an excellent example of how to design and implement effective training and development programs.

It is not hard to understand how investments in human capital and training can improve an organization's success and competitiveness. But have you ever considered how the training of employees can impact your life? Consider the emergency landing of an Air Transat Airbus on an island in the Atlantic Ocean several years ago. With both engines dead and the lives of 291 passengers and 13 crew at stake, the pilots successfully made an emergency landing without power.

The loss of power was due to a fuel leak in the right engine that caused it to shut down. A chafing fuel line on the right engine, which had recently been replaced, leaked during the flight. Although there was a leak in the right engine causing a loss of fuel, the left engine should have been sufficient to keep the plane in the air. However, fuel from the undamaged left engine tanks was pumped to the leaking right side where it was dumped overboard. This led to a loss of fuel in the left-side engine, which then caused it to lose power. The Airbus would have been able to fly safely with just the left-engine operating had its fuel not been pumped to the leaking right side.

According to Airbus, the maker of the twin-engine A330, Air Transat improperly reconnected the main fuel line to the aircraft's right-side engine when it was changed four days before the near-disaster. The fuel line to the right-side engine chafed against a hydraulic pipe that eventually cracked and created the fuel leak. Air-safety investigators also blamed faulty mechanical work by Air Transat mechanics as the cause of the fuel leak that led to the near-catastrophic emergency landing.

The near-disaster was averted only by the skilled emergency landing by the pilots, who were hailed as heroes for safely landing the plane. However, one of the pilots, Captain Piché, denied being a hero, stating that landing a plane with no engines is "what you train for."

Transport Canada ordered the airline to provide pilots and flight crews with special training on fuel management and emergency landings. Senior Transport Canada officials and Air Transat top management agreed that the airline's pilots would take special training sessions. Air Transat also provided Transport Canada with a corrective-action plan to improve the performance of maintenance that included human-factors training for all technical personnel.[2]

Although we can not say that inadequate training was the cause of this near-disaster, we do know that training was required in order to prevent a similar incident from happening again. We also know that experience and training had a lot to do with the pilot's ability to safely land the plane.

There are dozens of examples of how the training of employees affects our lives in ways that we are unaware of and seldom if ever think about. Did you know, for example, that aircraft flying over Canada have nearly collided or come too close to each other at least four times since 1997? Reports indicate that, besides failing to go through the proper checklists before ending their shifts, air traffic controllers are not adequately trained.[3] And do you remember the worst subway accident in Canadian history in which three people were killed and dozens more were injured in Toronto when two trains collided? The subway operator, who was only on his second shift, admitted that he wasn't ready to operate the train. Although he had successfully completed the 12-day subway training course, he had wished for more instruction behind the controls and was not sure if he was ready to operate the train. At an inquest into the accident, he said "I really didn't understand a lot of this stuff, I really didn't understand the mechanics of the train."[4]

As these examples demonstrate, employees who are poorly trained can make mistakes and cause accidents that threaten the public's safety and well-being. And while these examples are among the most extreme, it is important to note that poorly trained employees also produce poor products and provide us with bad service. Thus, training is of vital concern not just to employees and their organizations, but for all of us who purchase goods and services every day of our lives.

For organizations, their success and competitiveness is highly dependent on continuous learning and education. In fact, continuous learning and education have become key to the success of individuals and organizations. Whether an organization is adopting new technology, improving quality, or simply trying to remain competitive, training and development is a critical and necessary part of the process. Training and development is also a fundamental component of one's career development and advancement. Not surprisingly, education and training is one of the distinguishing characteristics of the best companies to work for in Canada.

Therefore, it should not surprise you that organizations today invest millions of dollars each year on training and development. This book will teach you about the exciting world of training and development and how to design, deliver, and evaluate training programs. In this chapter, we introduce you to the topic of training and development and describe the training and development process. We begin with a discussion of performance management since training and development is first and foremost all about managing performance in organizations.

Performance Management

Performance management

The process of establishing performance expectations with employees, designing interventions and programs to improve performance, and monitoring the success of interventions and programs

As the title of the text indicates, training and development is all about managing performance. Performance management is the process of establishing performance expectations with employees, designing interventions and programs to improve that performance, and monitoring the success of interventions and programs. This process signals to employees what is really important in the organization, ensures accountability for behaviour and results, and helps to improve performance.[5] Performance management is not a single event, such as a performance appraisal or a training program; rather it is a comprehensive process that involves various activities and programs designed to improve performance.

Training is one of the most important ways that performance can be improved. Training refers to the acquisition of knowledge, skills, and abilities to improve performance on one's current job. Training usually consists of a short-term focus on acquiring skills to perform one's job. Most of you have experienced this type of training, such as when your company sends you to a workshop to learn a software package like Excel or to learn how to deal with hostile customers. The goal is to help you learn to do your current job better.

Development refers to the acquisition of knowledge, skills, and abilities required to perform future job responsibilities and for the long-term achievement of individual career goals and organizational objectives. The goal is to prepare individuals for promotions and future jobs as well as additional job responsibilities. This process might consist of extensive programs such as leadership development, and might include seminars and workshops, job rotation, coaching, and other assignments. The goal is usually to prepare employees for managerial careers. You can read more about management development in Chapter 13.

Training and development is part of a larger human resources system that plays a role in the performance management process. The creation of an organizational environment conducive to optimum performance is a fundamental first step in the process of a performance management system. All systems are concerned with the goal of improving organizational effectiveness through the improvement of human resources. Key to the achievement of this goal is training and development that has benefits for organizations, employees, and society at large.

The Benefits of Training and Development

Organizations that invest in the training and development of their employees reap many benefits. But so do employees and the society in which they live. In this section, we describe some of the benefits of training and development.

Organizational Benefits

Organizations that invest in training and development benefit in many ways that ultimately help an organization obtain a sustained competitive advantage. Training and development can facilitate the strategy of an organization, increase effectiveness, and improve employee recruitment and retention.

1. Organizational Strategy

The goal of all organizations is to survive and prosper. Training and development can help organizations achieve these goals. Organizations can be successful by training employees so that they have the knowledge and skills necessary to help organizations achieve their goals and objectives. By linking training to an organization's strategy, training becomes a strategic activity that operates in concert with other programs and activities to achieve an organization's strategy.

For example, at Space Systems/Loral, a company in the United States that designs and manufactures satellites and satellite systems, training is aligned with the company's strategic goals. The learning and development group meets with the company's executives on a regular basis to plan training and development programs to support the company's strategic goals.[6]

In the service sector, Alimentation Couche Tard Inc., Canada's second-largest convenience-store operator, uses training as a strategic tool to grow its stores under company labels such as Provi-soir, Winks, and Red Rooster. Couche Tard invests twice as much as the national average in training its employees in customer service, management, and merchandising.[7] And as indicated in the chapter-opening vignette, training was a key factor for Quebecor World Inc. in achieving its customer-service strategy, which helped the firm gain a competitive advantage.

2. Increase Organizational Effectiveness

There is a calculable benefit in training employees. Trained employees can do more work, make fewer errors, require less supervision, have higher loyalty and morale, and have lower rates of attrition.[8] These improvements all have a positive effect on an organization's effectiveness.

For example, a survey conducted by the American Management Association found that companies that expanded their training programs showed gains in productivity and larger operating profits.[9] In another study, a 10 percent increase in training produced a 3 percent increase in productivity over two years.[10] Those companies that invest more heavily in training ($900 per employee versus $275 per employee) are more successful and more profitable. These companies spend up to 6 percent of payroll on training, but they achieve 57 percent higher sales per employee, 37 percent higher gross profits per employee, and a 20 percent higher ratio in market-to-book values.

The link between training and an organization's effectiveness is strongly supported by research. Study after study has found that companies with a strong commitment to training have higher revenues, profits, and productivity growth than firms that carry out less training.[11] A recent review of research on training and organizational effectiveness concluded that training improves organizational productivity, quality, and customer service.[12]

3. Employee Recruitment and Retention

Training can be used by organizations to increase their attractiveness to prospective employees and to retain their current employees. For many organizations today, training is the number one attraction and retention tool. An organization that fails to provide training opportunities to its employees will find itself increasingly dependent on the external labour market to fill positions. In one study, 99 percent of the respondents said that there are job areas in which training would be useful to them, and in which training decreases their willingness to move to another company.[13]

Many organizations offer extensive training and development opportunities to retain employees. For example, at Delta Hotels and Resorts, employees are guaranteed ongoing training. If an employee does not receive proper training, he or she can claim an extra week's salary. About 30 employees a year receive an extra week's salary. Not surprisingly, Delta has an employee retention rate of 89 percent, which is considered one of the best in the hospitality industry. In addition, hotel-school graduates are attracted to Delta because of the training they will receive.[14]

Employee Benefits

Training and development also has benefits to employees. The benefits to employees can be categorized as those that exist within an individual, such as knowledge and attitudes or intrinsic benefits, and those that exist outside or that are external to an individual and are extrinsic benefits.

1. Intrinsic Benefits

Employees who are trained benefit by acquiring greater knowledge and skills that enable them to perform their jobs better. In addition to improving their knowledge and skills, trained employees also develop higher confidence or self-efficacy (see Chapter 3 for a discussion of self-efficacy) in their ability to perform their job. They describe feelings of increased usefulness and belonging in the organization, and they seek out opportunities to fully exploit their new skills and abilities.[15] Trained employees also have more positive attitudes toward their job and organization.[16]

2. Extrinsic Benefits

In addition to the intrinsic benefits that reside within employees, there are also extrinsic benefits associated with training. Extrinsic benefits include things such as higher earnings as a result of increased knowledge and skills, improved marketability, greater security of employment, and enhanced promotion prospects. A number of studies have found that company-sponsored training programs increase workers' wages by 4 to 11 percent.[17]

Clearly, employees who have greater knowledge and skills as a result of training will have more and better work-related opportunities, and those who work for organizations that provide extensive training are at an advantage compared to those who work for organizations that do not provide very much training.

Societal Benefits

Training and development also has benefits for society that extend beyond the workplace. The training and development with which organizations provide their employees also help to create an educated and skilled population that benefits the economy and our standard of living.

1. Educated Population

The knowledge and skills that employees receive through workplace training help to create an educated and skilled workforce. For example, some organizations offer literacy and numeracy training for employees who did not obtain them through regular educational channels but who require them to perform their jobs. This training also enables employees to function more effectively in their daily lives and therefore has a number of societal benefits.

Employees who have participated in organization-sponsored training programs report using their new skills to better manage their personal lives. They are more likely to be able to read instructions for assembling various products and to be able to calculate bills and expenses. They are also more likely to be able to find employment if they are laid off or their employer closes a plant.

2. Standard of Living

The key to a country's standard of living, incomes, and overall prosperity is its productivity and productivity growth. Canada currently lags behind the United States in its productivity performance. There are a number of ways to improve productivity, and one of them is by improving the education and skills of the workforce.[18] An improvement in Canada's productivity will have a positive effect on the economy and our standard of living.

The federal government spends more than $11 billion annually on education and training because it sees a strong link between an educated workforce and a high-wage economy. In Quebec, employers are required to invest 1 percent of all payroll on training (see Training Today). Higher corporate training investments also leads to the creation of more jobs.[19]

Given the benefits of training and development, you might now be wondering to what extent Canadians are realizing these benefits. Obviously, this depends on the extent to which Canadian organizations invest in training and development, the topic of the next section.

Training and Development in Canada

In order to reap the benefits described in the previous section, companies must invest in training and development. So how much do you think Canadian organizations invest in training their employees?

Although data exists on the amount spent by organizations, such data do not exist for the country as a whole. In the United States, however, it has been reported that organizations spend in the range of $54 billion a year on formal training programs. Most of this cost goes towards paying the training staff salaries.[20]

It is tempting to use the U.S. statistics and apply the one-tenth rule (our population of 30 million is about one-tenth of the American population of about 300 million) to determine spending in Canada (i.e., $5.4 billion a year). However, we know from previous surveys that Canadian organizations spend less (maybe about half) of what U.S. firms spend.[21] We also know that the U.S. estimate includes only organizations with more than 100 employees, calculates formal training, and does not include the cost of employee time off the job. So even the U.S. figure of $54 billion might be an underestimation. Given all these cautions, we think a reasonable estimate of the amount spent by Canadian organizations on training and development is about $5 billion a year.

Training Today

Legislating Training Investments: Does it Make a Difference?

It is generally recognized that training and development is essential to maintaining and fostering organizational competitiveness. As a result, many societies have enacted laws that require organizations to invest in employee training and development. This is a common practice in Europe but it is not the norm in North America. In Canada, Quebec is the only province that has payroll training tax legislation.

In Quebec, companies with payrolls that exceed $250,000 are required by Law 90 to invest an amount equal to 1 percent of their payroll on training or to remit an equivalent amount in additional taxes. Haccoun and Saks reported a study that investigated the impact of this legislation on firm training using information obtained from Statistics Canada's Work and Employment Survey—a very large-scale survey that included more than 6,000 Canadian companies. This research compared data available from over 3,000 firms in Quebec and Ontario—Canada's two largest provinces—to address three questions: Do firms in these two jurisdictions differ with respect to a) training investments? or b) training programs offered? and c) do these affect bottom-line profits?

The research compared Quebec firms exempted or not exempted from the law with Ontario firms of equivalent size. Since firms in Ontario are not required to invest in training, it is possible to determine the potential impact of the legislation in Quebec by comparing it to training investments made by firms in Ontario.

The results of the study showed that: a) Quebec firms that are subject to Law 90 invest considerably more in training than firms that are exempted from the law; b)

firms in Quebec spend more on training than do firms in Ontario. In fact, the average firm in Quebec spends considerably more than the minimal 1 percent required by law; c) firms in Quebec tend to emphasize technical (hard skills) training to a larger degree than do firms in Ontario; and d) the larger investment in training did not lead to significant differences in the level of profitability of the firms.

Clearly, the legislation does stimulate greater proportional training investments and it does affect the type of training that is offered. The evidence shows that on average, Quebec companies not only meet but also they significantly exceed the 1-percent minimal investment required by the law while Ontario firms spend proportionally less. Thus, legislating training investments is a step in the right direction and firms are abiding not only by the letter of the law but also the spirit of it.

However, there is no clear evidence to show that such investments are necessarily rewarded by greater profits. Simply "throwing money" at training may not be sufficient to guarantee increased profitability. Indeed, it is important for organizations to offer effective training programs to their employees by ensuring that training needs are adequately identified, by implementing training programs that are well designed and delivered, and by ensuring that the use of new skills is properly supported once employees return to work.

Source: Haccoun, R. R, & Saks, A. M. (2002). Legislating Company Investments in Training: Does it Make a Difference? Paper presented at the annual conference of the Society of Industrial and Organizational Psychology, Toronto.

Many Canadian organizations do in fact invest heavily in training and development. Scotiabank, for example, invested $47 million in training and education in the last fiscal year. Employees can receive tuition assistance, language training, and on-line programs for upgrading their skills. In addition, managers receive training on leadership skills and coaching techniques.[22] At Labatt Brewing Co. Ltd., employees from all areas attend beer school to learn how beer is made and to gain a greater knowledge of and appreciation for the company's products. Company president Bruce Elliot intends to position Labatt as a leader in training and development.[23]

Unfortunately, as a whole, Canada is not keeping up with the United States when it comes to total training expenditures. In the United States, organizational spending per employee on training and development has increased from $1,072 (Cdn) in 1999 to $1,115 in 2000. This compares to $859 per employee spent by Canadian organizations in 2000, which is a negligible increase from what it was in 1993. Training and development investments by Canadian organizations have remained stable and the lag between Canadian and U.S. organizations appears to be increasing.[24]

One notable exception, however, is the training provided to IT workers. Companies in the U.S. have cut back on the hours of training provided to IT workers in recent years and as a result, IT workers in Canada now receive more hours of training per year than those in the U.S. This might explain why Canadian IT workers are among the most productive in the world even though they are paid less than their counterparts in the U.S.[25]

Overall, however, Canadian organizations spend less on training than organizations in the U.S., Europe, Asia, and the Pacific Rim. A report by The Conference Board of Canada found that Canadian organizations spend an average of 1.8 percent of their payroll on training and development and provide an average of 30 hours of training per employee. The report concluded that this underinvestment in training and development might lead to a gap in essential knowledge and skills, and if Canadian organizations are going to be able to compete effectively, they must increase their investments in the development of human capital.[26] Canada currently ranks 12th out of 49 countries in its ranking of employee training as a high priority in organizations.[27]

Information about training and development in Canada is summarized in Table 1.1. This information will enable you to compare your organization and experience against others. This information also highlights some differences in training across industries. For example, a quick glance shows that those with advanced skills and positions receive the most training. Canadian organizations in the technology/communications and financial services sectors are among the top investors in training and development. Organizations in the health and education sector as well as wholesale/retail report the lowest investment in training per employee.

TABLE 1.1

Training and Development in Canada

Individual Training and Development

- 5.8 million Canadian adults are enrolled in education and training activities
- men spend about 108 hours per year on learning; women spend about 98 hours per year on learning
- about 37 percent of Canadians between the ages of 25 and 44 are engaged in learning activities
- 57 percent are studying for career reasons, 29 percent for personal reasons, and 14 percent for both

TABLE 1.1 *(continued)*

- 66 percent of learners are employed full-time, 12 percent work part-time, and 21 percent are unemployed
- 59 percent of those studying earn more than $60,000 annually compared with 21 percent who earn less than $21,000

Organizational Training and Development

- the average expenditure on training and development is 1.8 percent of payroll (note that the benchmark for highly productive companies is 6 percent of payroll)
- $859 is spent per employee
- organizations provide an average of 30 hours of training per employee
- technical employees receive the most training hours (37 hours) and clerical/support staff receive the least (16 hours)
- training is provided to roughly three-quarters (72 percent) of all employees
- average days on training per management employee: 4.4; for sales, 3.3; for clerical, 2.8; for production, 5.1; for service, 3.7; and for trades, 5.3
- on average, 564 employees are served by one full-time staff trainer
- organizations invest the largest proportion of their training expenditures in management/supervisory skills, technical processes, information technology skills, and professional skills, and the least in basic skills
- the transportation, communication, public utilities, and oil and gas sectors spend the most on training and development, and the health and education sectors spend the least
- older and senior people get more training while younger people get less
- management, professional, and technical staff receive more training and development opportunities than others do and their training is more costly
- 95 percent of employees with a university degree received formal training from their employer, while 66 percent of those with high school or less received formal training
- a significantly smaller proportion of employees in small organizations receive training compared to larger firms
- the two most widely used training practices are tuition reimbursement and employer-supported conference attendance
- above-average performing organizations have higher total training expenditures both on a per capita basis and as a percentage of payroll compared to below-average performing organizations
- organizations rated as one of the 100 best companies to work for in Canada spend the most on training per employee

Sources: Human Resources Development Canada. (1998). *Canada's adult learners and learning technologies.* Ottawa: Office of Learning Technologies, Author; Beach, B.K. (1998). The Canadians are training, the Canadians are training. *Training & Development 52* (2); Little, B. (1997, June 13). Training splits into haves and have-nots. *The Globe and Mail*, p. B9; MacDonald, G. (1997, February 13). Growth prompts more training. *The Globe and Mail*, p. 4; Betcherman, G., Leckie, N., & McMullen, K. (1997). *Training for the new economy.* Ottawa: Canadian Policy Research Networks, www.cprn.com; Saigue, J.P. (1996). Focus on competencies: Training and development practices, expenditures, and trends (Report 177–96). *The Conference Board of Canada.* Ottawa; Harris-Lalonde, S. (2001). Training & Development Outlook. *The Conference Board of Canada.* Ottawa.

The Context of Training and Development

Although we have been discussing training and development as an independent activity, the reality is that training and development are imbedded within a larger environmental and organizational context that influences the amount, type, and nature of training in organizations. Thus, training and development are not isolated activities independent of the surrounding environment and organization. As shown in Figure 1.1, training and development is a subsystem that is influenced by environmental and organizational factors.

Environmental factors such as legislation, the economic climate, demographics, and social values have an impact on organizations. For example, if a competitor introduces a lower-priced product, the organization will have to decide whether to match the competitor's actions or compete in other ways, such as providing superior service. This strategic decision will in turn affect costs, the ability to pay employees, or the necessity to train and reward employees for effective performance.

Sometimes sudden and unexpected changes in the environment can lead to changes in organizations and human resources policies and practices. For example, consider how the terrorist attacks of September 11, 2001, in the United States affected airport and flight security and the need for training. The Transportation Security Administration in the United States developed new guidelines for the training of baggage screeners and flight crews that will make airport security fully federalized.

The training of baggage screeners will include technical training on metal detectors, X-ray scanners, bag searching, and how to deal with difficult passengers and manage stress. Their training will increase to 40 hours of classroom training and 60 hours of on-the-job training. Pilots and flight attendants will receive training on how to assess and react to dangerous situations.[28] This is a good example of how changes in the environment can have a direct effect on the training of employees. Below we discuss how changes in specific environmental and organizational factors can impact training and development.

The Environmental Context of Training and Development

Some of the key environmental factors that drive human resources and training and development are global competition, technology, the labour market, and change.

Global Competition

Increasing global competition has forced organizations to improve their productivity and the quality of goods and services. Improvements in the production process and quality initiatives almost always require employees to learn new skills. Furthermore, when Canadian organizations need to send workers on assignments in foreign countries, they need to provide them with cross-cultural training so that they will be able to adapt and function in a different culture.

FIGURE 1.1

Training and Development as a Subsystem

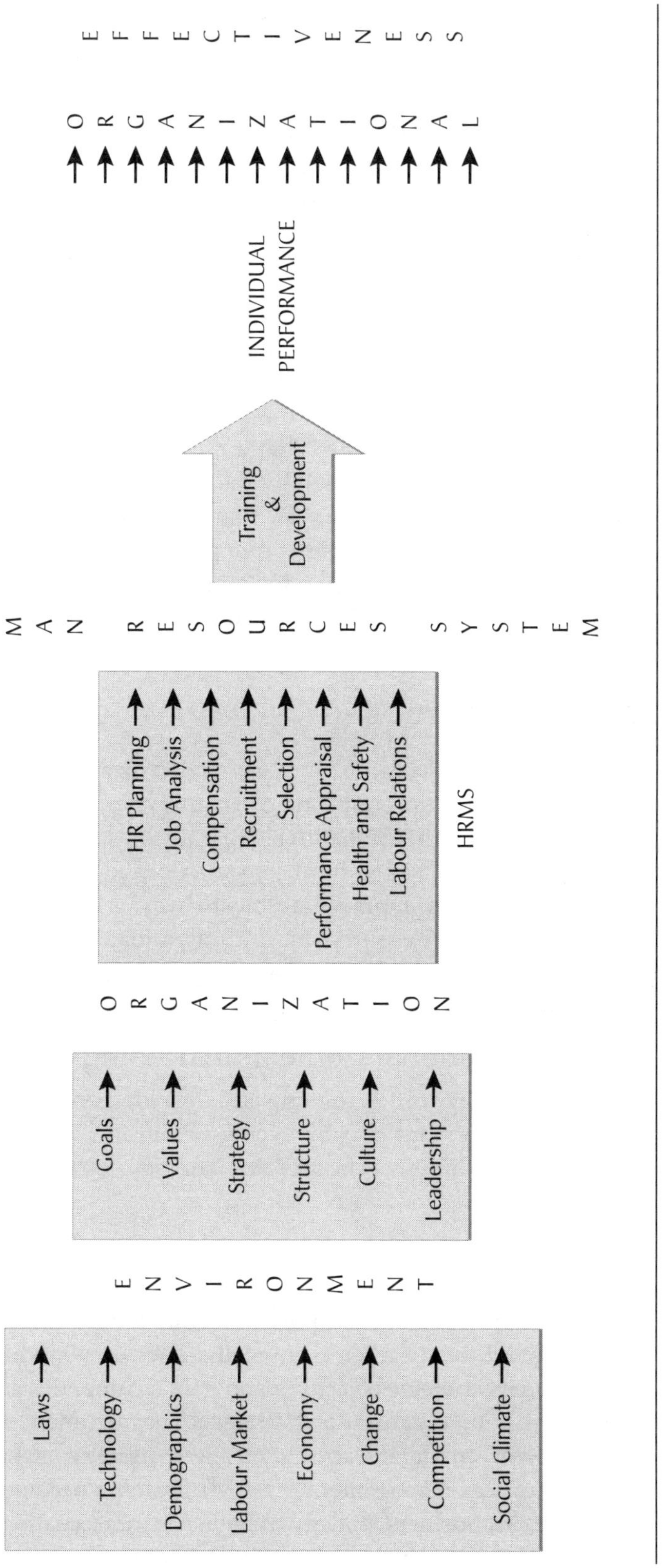

ENVIRONMENT

- Laws
- Technology
- Demographics
- Labour Market
- Economy
- Change
- Competition
- Social Climate

ORGANIZATION

- Goals
- Values
- Strategy
- Structure
- Culture
- Leadership

HUMAN RESOURCES SYSTEM

- HR Planning
- Job Analysis
- Compensation
- Recruitment
- Selection
- Performance Appraisal
- Health and Safety
- Labour Relations

HRMS

Training & Development

INDIVIDUAL PERFORMANCE

ORGANIZATIONAL EFFECTIVENESS

Technology

Technology has had a profound effect on the way organizations operate and compete. New technologies can provide organizations with improvements in productivity and a competitive advantage. However, such improvements depend on the training that employees receive. Technology will only lead to productivity gains when employees receive the necessary training to exploit the technology.[29] Thus, the adoption of new technologies will have a direct impact on the training needs of employees who will be required to use the technology.

The Labour Market

Changes in the labour market can have a major effect on training and development. For example, consider the impending shortage of skilled labour in Canada. It has been estimated that a critical shortage of skilled workers in Canada could reach one million by the year 2020. To deal with this looming crisis, the country will have to change its approach to education and training.[30] If organizations cannot hire people with the necessary knowledge and skills, they will have to provide more training if they are to compete and survive. Changes in the labour market require changes in the amount and type of training.

Change

The technological revolution, increasing globalization, and competition have resulted in a highly uncertain and constantly changing environment. In order to survive and remain competitive, organizations must adapt and change. As a result, managing change has become a normal part of organizational life, and training and development is almost always a key part of the process. The Minister of Human Resources has indicated that both the provinces and the private sector must prepare workers for a rapidly changing work world.[31]

The Organizational Context of Training and Development

As indicated in Figure 1.1, training and development are influenced not only by external factors but also by events within the organization. Among the most important internal factors are strategy, structure, and the human resources system.

Strategy

Strategic human resources management (SHRM)

The alignment of human resources practices with an organization's business strategy

Strategy is one of the most important factors influencing training and development. As indicated earlier, training and development can help an organization achieve its strategic objectives and gain a competitive advantage when it is aligned with an organization's strategy. The alignment of human resources practices with an organization's business strategy is known as **strategic human resources management (SHRM)**. Training becomes strategic when it is aligned with business strategy. Whether an organization has a strategy for quality, innovation, or customer service, training as well as other human resources practices must be designed to reinforce and support the strategy.

For example, if an organization decides to improve customer service or perhaps product quality, then employees will most likely require training in order to learn how to provide better service or improve product quality. If an organization's strategy is to grow as rapidly as possible, then employees need to be trained in the management of mergers, acquisitions, joint ventures, and international ventures. All these growth components necessitate the building of new skills and training is required to do this. As already noted, Quebecor World Inc. determined that customer service was a key strategy and this led to the ALLSTAR training program, which was a critical factor for implementing their strategy.

Thus, strategy is often a key factor driving the need for and nature of training and development in organizations. By linking training to business strategy, training becomes strategic rather than an isolated and independent activity and as a result, it is more likely to be effective. In fact, there is some evidence that training can lower an organization's market value when it is not strategically focused.[32]

Structure

The structure of an organization also affects training and development activities. Organizations are increasingly becoming flatter with fewer levels of management. Employees are expected to perform tasks that were once considered managerial tasks and so they must be trained in traditional managerial activities such as problem solving, decision making, team work, and so on. Many organizations have experienced dramatic structural changes such as downsizing and reengineering in an effort to survive. These changes to an organization's structure often lead to changes in employees' tasks and responsibilities and necessitate the need for training.

Human Resources System

The human resources system and other human resources functions also influence training. In fact, in addition to being linked to business strategy, human resources practices should also be aligned and linked to each other. Thus, strategic human resources management involves two kinds of links. First, human resources practices should be linked to business strategy as discussed earlier. Second, human resources practices should be linked to each other so that they work together to achieve an organization's strategy.

The objective of human resources management is to attract, motivate, develop, and retain employees whose performance is necessary for the organization to achieve its strategic objectives. The human resources system accomplishes this through the provision of policies, guidelines, and practices such as HR planning, recruitment and selection, orientation, training and development, performance appraisal, compensation and benefits, health and safety, employment equity, and so on.

Each function should be aligned with the others so that they work in concert towards the organization's strategic objectives. For example, if an organization's strategy is to provide excellent customer service then they will need to hire employees who have the skills required to interact with customers; they will need to train employees on how to provide excellent customer service; they will need to evaluate employees' customer service behaviour and performance; and they will need to reward employees for providing excellent customer service.

Training and development must be closely aligned with other HRM activities for several reasons. First, there is a need for every unit to do more with less and this efficiency can be achieved by eliminating redundancies. For example, there should not be separate systems for recording information about performance evaluations and attendance at training programs. Second, each area must be more strategic and business oriented. This means that the focus has to be on the whole system rather than its parts. Performance problems may be the result of poor selection, bad job design, the wrong incentives, or a lack of skills. It is important for training professionals to work with other HR professionals to determine the most appropriate solution to performance problems.

Monitoring the flow of HR also provides information for training purposes. Increases in turnover, hiring, transfers, and promotions often precipitate training programs. HR planning is the process of anticipating the need for employees with particular skills for expected jobs. By linking training plans with HR plans, organizations can prepare employees for new assignments, promotions, and so on to meet the organization's needs.

In summary, external factors influence an organization's strategy, structure, and the way human resources are managed, and these factors in turn influence the design and delivery of training programs. Training and development should be tightly aligned with an organization's strategy and the human resources system. In other words, there should be a good fit between strategy and training and between training and other HR practices. In this way, effective training programs can improve individual performance and ultimately organizational effectiveness. Thus, the model in Figure 1.1 not only explains the context of training and development, but it also helps to understand the link between training and development and organizational effectiveness.

The Instructional Systems Design (ISD) Model of Training and Development

Instructional systems design model

A rational and scientific model of the training and development process that consists of a needs analysis, training design and delivery, and training evaluation

In the previous section, we described how training and development is a subsystem that is embedded within a larger context. In this section, we will focus on the training and development subsystem. In particular, we will describe a systems approach to training and development that is known as the instructional systems design (ISD) model.

The instructional systems design model of training and development depicts training as a rational and scientific process that consists of three major steps: a training needs analysis, training design and delivery, and training evaluation. The process consists of an analysis of current performance and ends with improved performance.[33]

The process begins with a performance gap or an *itch*. An *itch* is something in the organization that is not quite right or is of concern to someone. Perhaps customer complaints are too high, quality is low, market share is being lost, or employees are frustrated by management or technology. Or perhaps there is a performance problem that is making it difficult for employees or departments to achieve its goals or meet standards. If some part of the organization itches, or is not satisfied with the performance of individual employees or departments, then the problem needs to be analyzed.

A critical first step in the instructional systems design model is a needs analysis to determine the nature of the problem and if training is the best solution. A needs analysis is performed to determine the difference or gap between the way things are and the way things should be.

Needs analysis consists of three levels known as an organizational analysis, a task analysis, and a person analysis. Each level of needs analysis is conducted to gather important information about problems and the need for training. An organizational analysis gathers information on where training is needed in an organization; a task analysis indicates what training is required; and a person analysis identifies who in the organization needs to be trained.

Based on the data collected from managers, employees, customers, and/or corporate documents, strategies for closing the gap are determined. Before training is determined to be the best solution to the problem, alternatives must be assessed. The solution to the performance gap might be feedback, incentives, or other human resource interventions. If training is determined to be the best solution, then objectives—or measurable goals—are written to improve the situation and reduce the gap. The needs analysis, the consideration of alternative strategies, and the setting of objectives force trainers to focus on performance improvement, not the delivery of a training program. Training is only one solution—and not necessarily the best one—to performance problems.

If training is the solution to a performance problem, a number of factors must be considered in the design and delivery of a training program. The needs analysis information and training objectives are used to determine the content of a training program. Then the best training methods for achieving the objectives and for learning the training content must be identified. Other design factors such as learning principles, which are described in Chapter 5, must also be considered in the design and delivery of a training program in order to maximize trainees' learning.

After a training program has been designed and delivered, the next stage is training evaluation. The needs analysis and training objectives provide important clues regarding what should be evaluated in order to determine if a training program has been effective. Some of the critical evaluation questions include: Did the training program achieve its objectives? What did employees learn? Did employees' job performance improve? Is the organization more effective? Was it worth the cost?

The purpose of all training and development efforts is ultimately to improve employee performance and organizational effectiveness. Thus, it is important to know if employee job performance has changed and if the organization has improved following a training program. In this stage, the trainer has to decide what to measure as part of the evaluation of a training program as well as how to design an evaluation study. On the basis of a training evaluation, decisions can be made about what aspects of a training program should be retained, modified, or discarded.

Figure 1.2 presents a simplified version of the instructional systems design model of training and development. As we have described, each stage leads into the subsequent stage with needs analysis being the first critical step that sets the stage for the design/delivery and evaluation stages. Also notice that there are feedback loops from evaluation to needs analysis and training design/delivery. This indicates that the process is a closed-loop system in which evaluation feeds back into needs analysis and training design/delivery. In this way, it is possible to know if performance gaps identified in the needs analysis stage have been closed, and if changes are required in the design and delivery of a training program in order to make it more effective. Thus, training programs are continuously modified and improved on the basis of training evaluation.

To understand how the ISD model can be applied in an actual organization, let's return to the chapter-opening vignette on Quebecor World Inc. First, the company conducted an extensive needs analysis that identified customer service as a key strategy for differentiating the company from its competitors and for gaining a competitive advantage. It also identified the firm's customer-service and account representatives from its North American operations as the employees that required customer-service skills training. The company had learned from its customers that employees in the company's plants were so different that each plant was like a different company. This information led to the formation of program objectives (e.g., improving understanding of customers' needs). The program objectives then formed the basis for the design of a training program including the content of the program (e.g., team-building skills), training methods (role-play situations), as well as issues related to the scheduling of the program (e.g., three-day intensive sessions away from the workplace). And in order to ensure that

FIGURE 1.2

The Instructional Systems Design Model of Training and Development

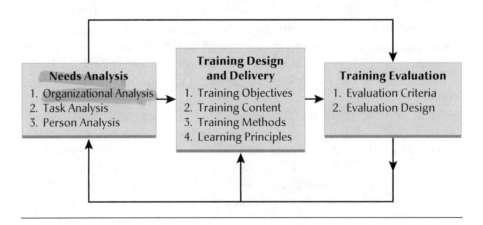

employees would apply what they learned in training on the job (i.e., transfer of training), senior management reinforced the goals of training and in the last session of the program, trainees made presentations in which they described what they had learned and how they will apply it back on the job. Once the program was completed, participants evaluated the program and the company also evaluated the program in terms of its effect on the organization (e.g., customer satisfaction).

Although the ISD model is considered to be the best approach for managing the training and development process and Quebecor World Inc.'s ALL-STAR customer-service training program is an excellent example of how to apply it, in reality many organizations do not follow all of the steps of the ISD model. In other words, many organizations do not conduct a needs analysis, they implement training programs that are not well designed, and they do not evaluate their training programs. There has also been some criticism waged against the ISD model in recent years among professionals in the training industry who have seriously challenged its usefulness. However, if used correctly it remains the best approach for managing the training and development process.[34] Training programs often fail because they have ignored an important step in the process such as conducting a thorough needs analysis.

We will have more to say about each of the stages of the training and development process as they are covered in their respective chapters in the remainder of the text. For now, you should understand the ISD model and the sequence of activities that are involved in the training and development process. To learn more about how to apply the ISD model, see The Trainer's Notebook below.

The Trainer's Notebook

The Application of the ISD Model

The instructional systems design model begins when somebody identifies a performance gap in the organization. According to the ISD model, the recognition of a performance gap should lead to the following sequence of activities:

1. Conduct an organizational analysis to investigate the performance gap and determine if training is a possible solution (when the cause of the problem is a lack of knowledge or skills).

2. If training is a possible solution, conduct a task analysis in order to determine how the job or jobs in question should be performed and the things that a skilled employee must know and be able to do.

3. Conduct a person analysis to determine how employees currently perform the job compared to how they should perform and how best to train them (e.g., training methods).

4. Design a training program using those methods and approaches that will be most effective to train employees who require training. Include specialists in various media and methods to assist in developing training material.

5. Develop and fine-tune the program. Pilot test it and revise as needed.

6. Deliver the program to its intended audience.

7. Monitor and evaluate the program and its results on an ongoing basis. The program is considered a success if the original performance gap is closed or reduced and if correcting the problem costs less than the cost of not correcting it.

Sources: Gordon, J., & Zemke, R. (2000, April). The attack on ISD. *Training*, 42–53; Zemke, R., & Rossett, A. (2002, February). A hard look at ISD. *Training*, 26–34.

Summary

This introductory chapter has introduced you to the training and development process and emphasized the important role that training and development plays in the effectiveness and competitiveness of organizations. We also stressed the importance of viewing training and development as an investment in human capital, an investment that Canadian organizations must increase. The organizational, individual, and societal benefits of training were described as well as the status of training and development in Canada. We also described training and development as a subsystem that is embedded within the environmental and organizational context. In particular, we noted that in order for training to be most effective, it should be strategic. That is, it should be tied to an organization's business strategy and aligned with other HR practices. Finally, we described the instructional systems design model of training and development that sets the stage for the remainder of the text.

Key Terms

development (page 5)
instructional systems design model (page 16)
performance management (page 4)

strategic human resources management (SHRM) (page 14)
training (page 5)

Weblinks

Delta Hotels and Resorts: www.deltahotels.com (page 6)
Labatt Brewing Co. Ltd.: www.labatt.com (page 9)
Scotiabank: www.scotiabank.com (page 9)

Discussion Questions

1. Refer to Training Today, "Legislating Training Investments: Does it Make a Difference?" and consider the following questions: Do you think that the rest of Canada should also legislate training and development? Why do you think there was not a relationship between training investments and firm profits? Does this mean that training is not important?

2. Studies comparing the competitive performance of Canadian corporations indicate that among the countries in the "G7" (Canada, United States, Japan, Germany, France, Italy, and the United Kingdom), Canada ranks last. Do you think that training and development in Canada has anything to do with this and if so, what should Canada and Canadian business firms do?

3. Discuss some of the reasons why organizations often fail to fully implement the instructional systems design model of training and development. Why do you think the ISD model has come under attack in recent years and been seriously challenged and criticized?

Using the Internet

1. There are a number of training associations that provide useful information about training and development. To learn more about some of these associations, visit the following websites:
    www.cstd.ca (Canadian Society for Training & Development)
    www.astd.org (American Society for Training & Development)
    Write a brief report in which you describe the association and indicate what information can be obtained from the site about training and development.
2. Go to **www.cstd.ca/resources/tca.html** (Canadian Society for Training & Development) to find out about the Training Competency Architecture (TCA). What is the TCA and what are the five competency categories defined by the TCA?

Exercises

1. There are three sources of funding for training and education: the public sector (governments using taxpayers' dollars), the private sector (businesses using shareholders' money) or you, using your after-tax dollars. Who should pay for training? Debate this question with two other students, each taking a different position and defending that perspective. Try to support your points by quoting surveys, which you can find by accessing the following databases: CBCA and ABI Inform from your university or college electronic library.
2. Private organizations are said to benefit from training because trained employees give them a competitive advantage and even make the companies more innovative. How does this apply to the public sector? What do you think are the organizational benefits to a public company or a volunteer organization?
3. Review the training and development facts in Table 1.1. Benchmark your organization against the statistics in the table. If you are currently employed, conduct an interview with a member of the human resources staff. If you are not currently employed, contact the human resources department of an organization you are familiar with and ask if you can speak to them about their training and development programs. Based on the statistics in the table, you might consider things such as: How does your organization compare to the Canadian averages in areas such as the amount of training hours employees receive a year; the amount of training received by different job groups; the percentage of employees that receive training; the use of different training practices; the amount spent per employee on training; etc. Does your organization fair better or worse than the average Canadian organization? What do the results tell you about your organization?
4. Consider how training and development is influenced by and in turn can influence other HR functions. In particular, give an example of how

training and development can influence and is influenced by activities within each of the following HR areas: Recruitment and Selection; HR Planning; Performance Appraisals; Compensation; and Health and Safety.

5. Using the ISD model of training and development, dissect the class your instructor has delivered to you today. In other words, what did your instructor have to do in terms of a needs analysis? How did he or she design and deliver the class? And how should the class be evaluated?

6. Assume that you are a director of training and development in a small organization. In order to reduce expenses, the company president has decided to cut the training budget in half and reduce the amount of training provided to employees. The president has asked to meet with you to discuss these plans. Your job is to prepare a short presentation to try to persuade the president to change his or her mind. What will you say and what can you do to convince the president of the importance and need for more not less training?

7. Recall the last time you attended an organization-sponsored training program. Describe the objectives and content of the training program and whether or not you think the program was strategic. In other words, was it an example of strategic training? Be specific in terms of why you think it was or was not a good example of strategic training. What would have made it more strategic?

Case

FLOTATION LTD.

"Great course, Sam!" they chorused as they trooped out the door and headed for the parking lot. Just like the others. Sam Harris, a veteran trainer with Flotation Ltd., a manufacturer of life jackets and other flotation devices, smiled as he gathered his notes together.

He had just finished two hours of wisecracking and slightly off-colour storytelling as he worked his way through the third session of a human relations' course for supervisors. "Keep 'em happy" was Sam's motto. Give the troops what they want, keep your enrolments up, and no one will complain.

Sam was good at it, too! For 20 years, he had earned an easy living, working the politics, producing good numbers (of trainees) for the top brass to brag about ("we give each employee up to 26 hours of training every year!"), and generally promoting his small training group as a beehive of activity.

Everybody knew Sam and everybody liked him. His courses were such fun. He had no trouble convincing managers to send their people. He put out a little catalogue with his course list every year in January. He hadn't had a cancellation in more than 10 years. Some managers said that training was the best reward they had. Now, only three years from retirement, Sam intended to coast comfortably into pension land. All his favourite courses had long been prepared; all he had to do was to make adjustments here and there and create some trendy titles.

But times were changing. Elsewhere, the company president was thinking differently. "I need somebody to take a close look at our training function," he said. Sitting in the president's office, Jenny Stoppard, the newly hired vice president of human resources, wondered what he meant. Flotation Ltd. had a reputation as a company with a well-trained workforce.

"We need to increase our productivity per person by 50 percent over the next three years," the president continued. "And you are going to spearhead that effort. Yes, we spend a lot on training. Yes, we cycle people through a lot of courses. But I'm not satisfied with the bottom line. I know that while Dad was president he swore by old Sam—said he was the greatest. I don't know anymore. Maybe a whole new approach is needed. Anyway, I want you to take a close look at Sam's operation."

Later in the day, the president called Sam into his office. "Sam, I want you to meet Jenny Stoppard. I've just hired her as vice president of human resources. She's your new boss. I think the next three years are going to be very exciting around here, and Jenny is going to be a key player in the drive to increase our competitiveness. I want you to do everything in your power to cooperate with her."

Questions

1. Comment on Sam's approach to training. Would you want him working for your company? Why, or why not?
2. To what extent has Sam made use of the instructional systems design model of training and development? If he were to more fully use the ISD model, what would he have to do? Comment on each of the steps of the ISD model.
3. How does Sam currently evaluate his training programs? Compare Sam's measures of training effectiveness to the president's objectives. If Sam were to evaluate his training programs based on the president's objectives, what would he have to do?
4. The president has asked Jenny to "take a close look at Sam's operation." What should she do and what should she report back to the president?

References

[1]Based on: Laabs, J. K. (2001, March). Serving up a new level of customer service at Quebecor. *Workforce Magazine*, 40–41; Quebecor World Inc. (December 19, 2000). Quebecor World Inc. Human Resources Function Wins "Workforce Optimas Award." From: www.quebecorworld.com; Lake Forest Graduate School of Management. "Lake Forest GSM Corporate Education Client Wins Workforce Magazine Optimas Award." From: www.ifgsm.edu.

[2]Norris, A. (2001, September 1). Transat work faulted. *The Gazette*, A1. Koring, P. (2001, August 31). Transat faces safety crackdown. *The Globe and Mail*, A1. Koring, P. (2002, August 30). Jet crew's handling of fuel leak questioned. *The Globe and Mail*, A1. Brazao, D. (2001, August 29). We had no second chance, pilot in jet emergency says. *The Toronto Star*, A1. Taylor, A., & Verma, S. (2002, August 31). Air Transat told to improve training on fuel handling. *The Toronto Star*, A1.

[3]Auld, A. (2002, August 6). Air traffic controller neglect cited in near-misses. *The Toronto Star*, A6.

[4]Campion-Smith, B. (1996, January 24). Rookie driver sorry for crash. *The Toronto Star*, A1, A22.

[5]Gosselin, A., Werner, J., & Hall, N. (1997). Ratee preferences concerning performance management and appraisal. *Human Resource Development Quarterly, 8* (4), 315–33.

[6]Barbian, J. (2002, March). Training top 100: Space Systems/Loral. *Training, 39*(3), p. 66.

[7]Millan, L. (1997, September 26). King of the corner store. *Canadian Business*, pp. 101–04.

[8]Bowsher, J. (1990, May). Making the call on the CEO. *Training and Development Journal*, 65–66.

[9]Adams, M. (1999). Training employees as partners. *HR Magazine, 44* (2), pp. 64–70.

[10]Bernstein, A., & Magnusson, P. (1993, February 22). How much good will training do? *Business Week*, p. 76–77.

[11]Betcherman, G., Leckie, N., & McMullen, K. (1997). *Developing skills in the Canadian workplace*. Ottawa: Canadian Policy Research Networks.

[12]Tharenou, P. (2000). *Does training improve organizational effectiveness?* Paper presented at the Academy of Management Meetings, Toronto, Canada.

[13]Schaaf, D. (1998). What workers really think about training. *Training, 35* (9), 59–66.

[14]Roseman, E. (2001, August 29). Delta Hotels knows how to keep workers. *The Toronto Star*, E2.

[15]Garavan, T.N., Costine, P., & Heraty, N. (1995). *Training and development in Ireland: Context policy and practice.* Dublin: Oak Tree Press.

[16]Schaaf, D. (1998).

[17]Bernstein, A., & Magnusson, P. (1993).

[18]Crane, D. (2002, October 27). Innovation means productivity gains. *The Toronto Star*, C2.

[19]Bernstein, A., & Magnusson, P. (1993).

[20]Galvin, T. (2002, October). 2002 Industry report. *Training, 39* (10). 24–73.

[21]Larson, P.E., & Blue, M.W. (1991). *Training and development 1990: Expenditures and policies* (Report 67–91). Ottawa: Conference Board of Canada.

[22]Galt, V. (2002, June 5). Putting the human back into resources. *The Globe and Mail*, C1.

[23]Galt, V. (2002, November 20). Training on tap. *The Globe and Mail*, C1.

[24]Tomlinson, A. (2002, March 25). T & D spending up in U.S. as Canada lags behind. *Canadian HR Reporter*.

[25](May/June 1999). Canucks lead in IT training. Training Report, www.trainingreport.ca.

[26]Harris-Lalonde, S. (2001). Training and development outlook. *The Conference Board of Canada*. Ottawa.

[27]Cooney, J. (2003, Spring). Under-Investment Continues in Training and Development. *InsideEdge*. The Conference Board of Canada. Ottawa.

[28](2002, April). Airport Training Ready to Take Off. *Training and Development*, pp. 17–18.

[29]Crane, D. (1998, March 28). Time to take worker training seriously. *The Toronto Star*, B2.

[30]McCarthy, S. (2001, February, 27). Skilled-worker shortage could reach one million. *The Globe and Mail*, A1.

[31]McCarthy, S. (2001, February, 27).

[32]Gibb-Clark, M. (2000, February 11). Employee training can backfire on firms: survey. *The Globe and Mail*, B10.

[33]Dipboye, R. L. (1997). Organizational barriers to implementing a rational model of training. In M. A. Quinones and A. Ehrenstein (Eds.), *Training for a Rapidly Changing Workplace*, Washington, DC: American Psychological Association.

[34]Gordon, J., & Zemke, R. (2000, April). The attack on ISD. *Training, 37* (4), 42–53; Zemke, R., & Rossett, A. (2002, February). A hard look at ISD. *Training, 39* (2), 26–34.

Chapter 2

Organizational Learning

Chapter Learning Objectives

After reading this chapter, you should be able to:

- define organizational learning and describe a learning organization
- explain the five disciplines and the principles of a learning organization
- discuss the four key dimensions that are critical for creating and sustaining a learning organization
- explain what knowledge is and give examples of explicit and tacit knowledge
- describe the meaning and types of intellectual capital
- define knowledge management and discuss four knowledge management practices
- describe the multilevel systems model of organizational learning
- explain how organizational learning and training are related

www.dofasco.ca

DOFASCO

Dofasco is Canada's most successful steel producer and the most profitable steelmaker, per tonne in North America. Dofasco produces high quality flat rolled and tubular steels and laser welded blanks in facilities in Canada, the United States, and Mexico. Dofasco's many steel products are sold to customers throughout North America and in many industries including the automotive, construction, energy, manufacturing, pipe and tube, appliance, packaging, and steel distribution industries.

Dofasco is known for its highly motivated and skilled workforce and its commitment to product quality and customer service. Dofasco is also a good example of a learning organization. In fact, at Dofasco, it is said, "You are going to learn a living as much as you earn a living." Top management at Dofasco is committed to becoming a learning organization and demonstrates their commitment by providing support and resources.

The learning begins as soon as new hires join the organization. New hires attend a four-day orientation program in which they learn about Dofasco's culture, strategy, values, and competencies. This, however, is just the beginning. All employees at Dofasco have a learning and development plan. Employees are empowered to take responsibility for their own learning and managers are encouraged to facilitate employees' learning.

Employees have many opportunities to learn at Dofasco including job skills training at their technical training centre, informal trainers located throughout the plant, and apprenticeship programs conducted in partnership with local community colleges. As well, informal trainers are available to assist employees who are learning on the job.

Dofasco also has a formal mentorship program for new hires and apprentices who are hired right out of college or university. The new hires are assigned a mentor to consult with and ask questions. The program has been so successful that they are considering expanding it to all new employees.

Another successful program at Dofasco is the Essential Skills program, which includes training in literacy, numeracy, and basic computer skills. The program has been so successful that it is considered a benchmark for other organizations.

Employees at Dofasco also have the opportunity to continue their formal education. The company reimburses employees for programs completed at high school, college, or university. Lifestyle programs that address employees' needs such as stress management are also available as well as lunch time programs in yoga, tai chi, and aerobics. Two gymnasiums are also available to employees 24 hours a day.

Because Dofasco is a team-based organization in which various kinds of teams play a central role, team learning is also important. Before the company became a team-based organization, a team of employees from different levels in the organization studied teams in other organizations in order to find out how teams would work best at Dofasco. And to encourage team learning, everyone at Dofasco was required to attend a four-day team-building training program.

The importance of learning at Dofasco also extends to the company's customers. The company has developed learning alliances with their customers through a program called "Solutions in Steel." One example of such a program involved a team of Dofasco employees showing an automobile manufacturer how to build a car with fewer welds and save a significant amount of money.

Learning at Dofasco also extends beyond one's job to understanding the organization and how one's job fits into the big picture. A tool called the "organizational system framework" is used to help employees understand the whole organization and how its various elements and systems are interrelated and fit together. Learning maps are also used to help employees better understand how the organization makes money.

At Dofasco, learning is seen as an investment in its employees and the organization's future.[1]

Dofasco is a good example of a "learning organization." Although this book is about training and development, training is just one way that employees in organizations learn. Furthermore, the extent to which employees learn has a lot to do with the way an organization learns. In organizations like Dofasco, learning is considered an important investment and receives a great deal of commitment and support from top management. As a result, employees have access to many opportunities for formal and informal learning.

In this chapter, we describe how organizations learn and how learning occurs at all levels of an organization. Training and development are an important part of the learning system in organizations so you should understand how it fits into the larger picture of organizational learning.

What is Organizational Learning?

A smart organization knows how to create new knowledge and disseminate it throughout the organization. In other words, it knows how to learn. **Organizational learning** refers to the process of creating, sharing, diffusing, and applying knowledge. However, organizational learning is not simply the sum of individual employee learning nor is performance management limited

Organizational learning
The process of creating, sharing, diffusing, and applying knowledge in organizations

to a training system that enables employees to learn and apply that learning. Organizational learning focuses on the systems used to create and distribute new knowledge on an organization-wide basis of which training and development is one component. Simply put, organizational learning is a dynamic process of creating and sharing knowledge.

The traditional perspective of learning has always been strongly associated with training and development. The goals of training have been viewed from a traditional perspective that focuses on developing and improving employees' knowledge, skills, and abilities (KSAs). This is, of course, key for organizational learning because an organization can't learn unless individual employees learn. As noted by Senge, the originator of the concept of the learning organization, "Organizations learn only through individuals who learn. Individual learning does not guarantee organization learning. But without it, no organizational learning occurs" (p. 139).[2]

The training of employees usually focuses on current needs or deficiencies and is most effective when the future is relatively stable and predictable. However, in today's turbulent environment, organizations have realized the need to do more than just train employees for the current state of affairs. In a learning organization, employees learn through a variety of methods and processes, and they also learn how to continuously learn.

To survive and develop, organizations must learn to manage by managing learning—the capacity to learn and change, consciously, continually, and quickly. A company's knowledge, including that contained in its employees' minds, has always been a source of competitive advantage. The ability to learn faster than the competition is a source of sustainable advantage.

For many organizations, creating learning systems and processes requires that they transform themselves into learning organizations. As you will learn in the next section, becoming a learning organization does not represent the latest management fad. It represents a strategic shift and orientation in how organizations learn that can make an organization more competitive and effective.

The Learning Organization

In 1990, Peter Senge published a book called *The Fifth Discipline: The Art and Practice of the Learning Organization*, which set in motion a whole new approach to organizations that focuses on learning and in particular, the "learning organization."

Learning organization

An organization that acquires, organizes, and shares information and knowledge, and uses new information and knowledge to change its behaviour in order to achieve its objectives and improve its effectiveness

A **learning organization** is an organization that acquires, organizes, and shares information and knowledge, and uses new information and knowledge to change its behaviour in order to achieve its objectives and improve its effectiveness. Learning organizations have established systems and structures to acquire, code, store, and distribute important information and knowledge so that it is available to those who need it and when they need it.

As a result, a learning organization is able to transform itself by acquiring and disseminating new knowledge and skills throughout the organization. Thus, it has an enhanced capacity to learn, adapt, and change its culture.[3]

Embedded in this concept is the ability to make sense of and respond to the surrounding environment. Organizational values, policies, systems, and structures support and accelerate learning for all employees. This learning results in continual improvements in work systems, products, services, teamwork, management practices—a more successful organization. Organizational learning is learning that actually results in improvements.

In his groundbreaking book, Senge identified five "disciplines" that he regarded as guiding principles to becoming a learning organization. The five disciplines are:[4]

1. *Personal mastery*. Individuals have to be open to others and willing to learn on a continual basis. People with personal mastery are always in a learning mode. This is fundamental for a learning organization because organizations only learn if the individuals in them learn. If individuals do not learn, then organizational learning will not be possible.
2. *Building a shared vision*. This involves the development of a picture and vision of the future that everyone can agree to and are committed to.
3. *Mental models*. Mental models refer to the images and assumptions that people have about themselves and the world. People need to be able to examine their mental models and be aware of how they influence their behaviour. Because such models can thwart or inhibit learning, people must understand them and hold them up to scrutiny.
4. *Team learning*. Learning takes place in teams through dialogue, discussion, and "thinking together." People need to be able to learn and act together.
5. *Systems thinking*. This discipline integrates the others and has to do with viewing the organization as a whole and being able to see and understand how its parts are interrelated.

Learning organizations have a number of important principles. First, in a learning organization everybody is considered to be a learner. Employees recognize the need for learning and are actively involved in both formal and informal learning programs.

Second, in a learning organization, employees do not learn just by attending formal training programs. They also learn through informal means such as listening and observing others. People learn from each other in a learning organization.

Third, learning is part of a change process and in fact enables change. When people are open to learning, they are able to recognize the need for change and learning is an important part of any change program. Thus, learning and change are closely related.

Fourth, continuous learning is considered to be a hallmark of learning organizations. Formal and informal learning are considered to be a regular part of every employee's job.

Fifth, learning organizations recognize that learning is an investment in the future of employees and the organization rather than an expense. Just as expenditures on plants and equipment are viewed as long-term capital investments, expenditures on learning are viewed as long-term investments in human capital.[5]

While some people might find the notion of a learning organization somewhat of a fad, there is some evidence that learning organizations are highly effective. Research conducted by The Conference Board of Canada has found that learning organizations are almost 50 percent more likely to have higher overall levels of profitability than those organizations not rated as learning organizations.[6] In addition, a recent study found a positive relationship between learning organization practices and a firm's financial performance.[7] To find out more about the study and the linkages between a learning organization and firm performance, see Training Today, "Organizational Learning and Firm Performance."

In the next section, we consider learning organizations in Canada.

Training Today

Organizational Learning and Firm Performance

Although it is widely believed that organizations that have systems and processes consistent with a learning organization will be better performers, few studies have actually tested the relationship between organizational learning and firm performance. An exception is a study by Andrea Ellinger, Alexander Ellinger, Baiyin Yang, and Shelly Howton.

Managers from 208 U.S. manufacturing firms completed a survey that measured their perceptions of their organization along the following six learning organization dimensions:

1. Create continuous learning opportunities.
2. Promote inquiry and dialogue.
3. Encourage collaboration and team learning.
4. Empower people toward a collective vision.
5. Connect the organization to its environment.
6. Use leaders who model and support learning at the individual, team, and organizational levels.

The managers also completed two perceptual outcome measures in which they indicated their organization's current performance compared to the previous year in terms of financial performance and knowledge performance. In addition, objective accounting and return on investment ratios were also used to measure each firm's financial performance including ROE (the return on shareholder investment), ROA (the return available to shareholders from the investment of all the firm's capital), Tobin's q (the value added by management above the value of the firm's assets), and MVA (the difference between the money invested in the firm and the present value of the cash flows expected to be generated by this capital).

The results indicated that there was a significant relationship between the six dimensions of the learning organization and the two perceptual outcomes (financial performance and knowledge performance). The six dimensions of a learning organization were also significantly related to the four objective measures of financial performance.

These results suggest that there is a positive association between a learning organization and an organization's financial performance. Thus, creating a learning organization has important implications for an organization's profitability and financial success. These findings provide a strong business case for the development of a learning organization.

Source: Ellinger, A. D., Ellinger, A. E., Baiyin, Y., & Howton, S. W. (2002). The relationship between the learning organization concept and firms' financial performance: An empirical assessment. *Human Resource Development Quarterly, 13,* 5–21.

Learning Organizations in Canada

As already noted, Dofasco is a good example of a Canadian company that can be described as a learning organization. But to what extent are other organizations in Canada learning organizations? The Conference Board of Canada recently examined this as part of their survey on Training and Development.[8]

They asked Canadian organizations to rate the extent to which they see themselves as learning organizations. What do you think they found?

As it turns out, not very many Canadian organizations see themselves as learning organizations. In fact, the average respondent rated their organization as "somewhat" of a learning organization, and only 15 percent rated themselves highly as learning organizations. Approximately 30 percent of the respondents rated themselves as very low.

The Conference Board also identified key dimensions of learning organizations: 1. Vision/support, 2. Culture, 3. Learning systems/dynamics, and 4. Knowledge management/infrastructure. Table 2.1 provides a description of each dimension.

The survey also found that Canadian organizations need to improve on a number of these key dimensions. For example, it was recommended that senior management be more explicit in terms of the type of knowledge that is important in their organization, and that they serve as learning role models to the rest of the organization (vision/support). Canadian organizations can also improve by creating a more positive learning culture and by encouraging and rewarding experimentation and risk taking. As well, innovation, knowledge sharing, and productivity improvements should be a more frequent part of organizational life. In the area of learning, Canadian organizations can also

TABLE 2.1

Key Dimensions of Learning Organizations

The Conference Board of Canada has identified the following four dimensions as critical in creating and sustaining a learning organization.

1. Vision/support. A clear vision of the organization's strategy and goals in which learning is a critical part and key to organizational success.

2. Culture. A learning organization has a culture that supports learning. Knowledge, information sharing, and continuous learning are considered to be a regular part of organizational life and the responsibility of everybody in the organization.

3. Learning systems/dynamics. Employees are challenged to think and act according to a systems approach by considering patterns of interdependencies when problem solving.

4. Knowledge management/infrastructure. Learning organizations have established systems and structures to acquire, code, store, and distribute important information and knowledge so that it is available to those who need it and when they need it.

Source: Harris-Lalonde, S. (2001). Training and development outlook. Reprinted by permission of *The Conference Board of Canada*. Ottawa.

improve by providing employees with more opportunities for formal and informal learning and by supporting and developing managers in their roles as coaches, mentors, and facilitators of learning (learning systems/dynamics).

Finally, Canadian organizations have to develop knowledge management systems and practices so that important information and knowledge can be stored and made available to those who need it whenever it is needed.[9]

Developing a learning organization is a time-consuming and resource-intensive change process. Thus, it represents a significant transformation for most organizations. Given that the very idea of a learning organization is a relatively recent phenomenon, it should not be surprising that only a small percentage of Canadian organizations are learning organizations.

What is most important is that organizations understand the value and importance of becoming a learning organization, and that by focusing on the four critical dimensions they can make changes that ultimately lead to the creation of a learning organization.

Becoming a learning organization involves understanding the importance of knowledge and knowing how to manage it. In the following sections, we focus on knowledge management and intellectual capital.

The Meaning and Types of Knowledge

Knowledge has become a critical resource for organizations in the information economy and is the main resource used to perform work in organizations. Employees require new knowledge in order to improve the products and services that their organizations provide, and organizations require knowledge in order to change and remain competitive in today's increasingly competitive and turbulent environment.[10]

Employee knowledge is a synthesis of information: all the facts, theories, and mental representations employees know about the world and, in the context of work, about their jobs and organization. **Knowledge** is the sum of what is known: a body of truths, information, and principles. Knowledge can be found in the minds of employees or transferred and stored in systems in the organization.

Knowledge is more than information, which we have in abundance, represented by dusty books filling shelves and facts floating across the Internet. Knowledge, on the other hand, is information that has been edited, put into context, and analyzed in a way that makes it meaningful, and therefore valuable to an organization.[11] This knowledge can be grouped in two ways: explicit knowledge and tacit knowledge.

Explicit knowledge refers to those things that you can buy or trade, such as patents or copyrights and other forms of intellectual property. The formula for making Coca-Cola and the brand name Coke are examples of intellectual properties that are extremely valuable. These tangible assets can normally be codified or formalized. Explicit knowledge can be written into procedures or coded into databases and is transferred fairly accurately. However, less than 20 percent of corporate knowledge is explicit.[12]

Knowledge

The sum of what is known; a body of truths, information, and principles

Explicit knowledge

Those things that you can buy or trade, such as patents or copyrights and other forms of intellectual property

The other 80 percent of corporate knowledge is implicit and is difficult to quantify or even describe accurately.[13] Implicit or **tacit knowledge** refers to the valuable wisdom learned from experience and insight, and has been defined as intuition, know-how, little tricks, and judgment. (Seasoned executives with tacit knowledge of a situation make million-dollar decisions.)

Tacit knowledge is used by employees but is almost impossible to transfer. To grasp the concept of explicit knowledge and tacit knowledge, imagine describing the physical characteristics of your best friend; now try to describe the methods your friend would use to influence a supervisor. The former involves explicit knowledge while the latter involves your tacit knowledge of your friend.

A well-known example of tacit knowledge is that of the decision-making behaviour of dealers in financial markets. That behaviour appears to be instinctual, but it is based on their past experience, what they read and hear, and the climate of the market. Extracting this knowledge from these dealers and then training others in this winning behaviour is extremely difficult.[14] The transfer of tacit knowledge requires personal contact. The personal contact must be extensive and built on trust and can include partnerships, apprenticeships, and mentoring.

The Meaning and Types of Intellectual Capital

Intellectual capital is more than knowledge; intellectual capital is more like intelligence. Intelligence is the ability to create knowledge and includes the ability to learn, to reason, to imagine, to find new insights, to generate alternatives, and to make wise decisions.[15] By increasing the general level of intelligence of employees, organizations hope to create new knowledge that will result in new products, services, and processes.

Intellectual capital refers to an organization's knowledge, experience, relationships, process discoveries, innovations, market presence, and community influence. Intellectual capital is the source of innovation and wealth production—it is knowledge of value.[16] Intellectual capital has to be formalized, captured, and leveraged to produce a more highly valued asset.[17]

Intellectual capital is not like other assets; it grows with use. When an employee learns and uses that learning, he/she usually learns even more, and is motivated to learn again. He/she can share the learning and not deplete it or use it up, like other assets. Sharing results in the acquisition of even more knowledge, as you probably learned when you worked on projects with other people.

Many organizations today realize the value of intellectual capital and are willing to purchase it. For example, Nortel paid $450 million for a company that had never produced a single product; they bought brainpower (i.e., 150 telecommunication specialists in high-speed networking equipment at Cambridge Systems Corporation, in Kanata, Ontario). They paid $3 million per brain.[18]

Microsoft is a good example of a company in which investors are putting a price tag on intellectual capital, because the total market value of the company

Tacit knowledge
Wisdom that is learned from experience and insight, and has been defined as intuition, know-how, little tricks, and judgment

Intellectual capital
An organization's knowledge, experience, relationships, process discoveries, innovations, market presence, and community influence

exceeds its book value. Investors must believe in the future earnings potential, based not just on goodwill, but on the intellectual potential of the company.

Intellectual capital is often divided into four types: human capital, renewal capital, structural capital, and relationship capital.

Human Capital

Human capital is the knowledge, skills, and abilities of employees. Included in this type of capital are some basic components of intelligence, such as the ability to learn, to reason, to analyze. Interpersonal skills, such as the ability to communicate with others and work in teams to generate better work methods, would also be part of an organization's human capital.

Renewal Capital

Renewal capital refers to what we have labelled intellectual property, which consists of patents, licences, copyrights, and marketable innovations including products, services, and technologies.

Structural Capital

Organizations are not amoebas; they need a skeleton or structure to function. Although the organizational chart captures some of the concept of **structural capital**, what we really mean are the formal systems and informal relationships that allow employees to communicate, solve problems, and make decisions. Structural capital is the set of structures, routines, and information systems that stay behind when employees go home. Sometimes these structures are represented by policies and procedures. For example, a company might require you to obtain the approval of the vice president of marketing before launching an innovative but costly advertising campaign. Another part of structural capital can be stored in databases and knowledge documents.

For example, a consultant at IBM developed a high-quality analysis of the forest industry, which predicted nearly perfectly the rise and fall of timber prices. A consultant in the same firm, but located in Japan, had access to this document to prepare an impressive bid for a contract for a Thai forestry company.[19]

Relationship Capital

Organizations, like individual employees, do not exist as islands. **Relationship capital** refers to an organization's relationship with suppliers, customers, and even competitors that influence how they do business. These relationships, particularly if they are based on trust and integrity, can be a source of competitive advantage.

Customer capital is a subset of relationship capital. **Customer capital** is the value of an organization's relationships with its customers. For example, many small businesses enjoy high degrees of customer capital. Neighbours will shop at the local milk store even though the milk is more expensive because they know the owner and his/her family. In larger organizations, customer capital refers to all the efforts that a company makes to keep customers returning to buy their products or services.

Human capital

The knowledge, skills, and abilities of employees

Renewal capital

Intellectual property, which consists of patents, licences, copyrights, and marketable innovations including products, services, and technologies

Structural capital

Formal systems and informal relationships that allow employees to communicate, solve problems, and make decisions

Relationship capital

An organization's relationships with suppliers, customers, and competitors that influence how they do business

Customer capital

The value of an organization's relationships with its customers

---

The four types of intellectual capital work in a cycle to increase intellectual capital. As more investments are made in human capital, the employees are more capable and committed to increasing renewal and structural capital, leading to more productive relationship capital, resulting in better financial performance. The money can then be recycled to increase intellectual capital.

In this chapter, we focus on human capital: the sum and synergy of employee knowledge. Organizations want to develop their intellectual capital, and one way to do it is to create an environment in which learning is valued and actively managed. The term "learning organization" refers to the programs and culture required to increase an organization's capacity to learn and to create intellectual capital. Creating and leveraging that knowledge has become a goal of many organizations. Training and performance specialists must understand that the creation and transfer of knowledge are strategic imperatives. Learning organizations have to actively manage this knowledge.

In the next section, we discuss the different ways to acquire, interpret, disseminate, and store knowledge.

Knowledge Management Practices

Knowledge management involves the creation, collection, storage, distribution, and application of compiled "know what" and "know-how."[20] The value of knowledge occurs when it is available to those who need it, when they need it, and when it is put into action. Many companies today have realized the importance of knowledge management.

Skandia, the Swedish insurance company, reports that by managing knowledge, they were able to reduce start-up time for launching a new facility from seven years (the industry average) to three years.[21] Other companies followed Skandia's lead and express the value of knowledge management through anecdotes and stories.

For example, at one automotive supplier, 30 percent of the design engineers' time was wasted solving problems that had already been solved in the company.[22] Companies know that knowledge isn't being shared when work is duplicated, or expertise was available but hidden in the company and opportunities were lost, or needless staffing took place. Platinum Technology saw a $6 million return on an investment of $750,000 in a Web system that allows its sales staff to find product data.[23]

Knowledge at Dow Chemical is managed like a hard asset. Dow Chemical tries to assess the hidden value of patents and licences that have not been used. Dow manages its portfolio of more than 30 000 patents by assigning them to individual managers who are then responsible for converting them into profitable businesses.[24] CIBC tracks the number of new ideas generated, new products created, and percentage of income from new revenue streams.

Recall from our earlier discussion of a learning organization that knowledge management/infrastructure is one of the four critical dimensions of a learning organization. Knowledge management/infrastructure refers to systems and structures that integrate people, processes, and technology so that

Knowledge management
The creation, collection, storage, distribution, and application of compiled "know what" and "know-how"

important knowledge is coded, stored, and made available to members of an organization when they need it. Thus, in a learning organization, knowledge must be shared and distributed so that the organization can benefit from the cumulative knowledge of all employees.[25]

According to research conducted by The Conference Board of Canada, less than 25 percent of the respondents indicated that systems and structures exist within their organization to ensure that important knowledge is coded, stored, and made available to others, and less than 50 percent indicated that their organization continues to develop new strategies and mechanisms for sharing and learning throughout the organization. As noted earlier, Canadian organizations need to develop knowledge management systems and practices to ensure that important information is coded, stored, and made available for use throughout the organization. This is an important element of becoming a learning organization and for improving organizational learning.[26]

In the remainder of this section, we will focus on four processes through which organizations manage knowledge—acquisition, interpretation, dissemination, and retention.[27] The ability to create and use knowledge is what characterizes a learning organization, and the practices in which organizations engage to actively manage knowledge are a critical part of knowledge management.

Knowledge Acquisition

Companies acquire or create new knowledge in many ways. Some focus on well-respected creative processes such as brainstorming. Others may benchmark competitors or the best companies in the world. Others engage in simulations or scenario planning to stimulate new ideas. Most scan the environment looking for new ideas or changing conditions and provide formal training to their employees.

Environmental Scanning

One of the most important ways for organizations to acquire information and knowledge is by scanning the environment. This involves tapping into both internal and external sources of information and establishing internal and external connections.

External sources of information include other organizations, customers, industry watchers, and the marketplace. These sources of information can provide an organization with information on how to improve their practices, services, and products. Internal sources of information include individuals, teams, and departments throughout an organization that might have information and knowledge that would be useful for others in the organization.

Learning organizations establish external connections through partnerships that involve the exchange of information. Internal connections might include the formation of cross-functional teams that meet to discuss changes in the industry and marketplace. Individual members form external connections through participation in professional associations, supplier forums, and through contacts with customers and others in the industry. The cross-functional team is therefore able to keep abreast of industry trends, tactics, and techniques. The key is for the organization to establish both internal and external connections and relationships in order to acquire and share information and knowledge.[28]

Formal Training and Development

One of the most formal and traditional ways to increase the acquisition of new knowledge in an organization and the focus of this book is formal training and development programs. Training and development is an integral and key part of the knowledge-acquisition process.

Xerox, one of the first companies to transform itself into a learning organization, trains all of its employees in a six-step problem-solving process that must be used at all meetings and that is used for virtually all decisions. Royal Bank has established a worldwide network of self-development programs, easily accessed from home or work, and promotes a philosophy of lifelong learning. Royal Bank's learning centre manager believes that access to learning is the first step in creating a learning organization.[29]

Informal Learning

In addition to formal training and development programs, employees also learn through informal means. In fact, it has been reported that as much as 70 percent of what employees learn and know about their jobs is learned through informal processes rather than through more formal programs that are structured or sponsored by their organization. This means that only 30 percent of what employees learn is actually acquired through formal training programs sponsored by their organization.[30]

This should not be all that surprising. Employees are often the most knowledgeable persons when it comes to performing their job, and they are also often the best informed in terms of how to improve it. For example, employees know a lot about customers' current problems and emerging needs. Customers are demanding increased responsiveness and shorter turn-around times. Employees who work daily with customers might have developed ways to be responsive. Organizations need to tap into that deep knowledge in a systematic way.

Employees have always learned without being formally trained. Many employees learn how to handle client problems by trial and error. Some learn by being taught but not in a formal (i.e., classroom) setting. For example, an employee might show co-workers a way to save time by combining two steps in handling customer complaints. Employees learn how to work together effectively, perhaps by learning meeting rules, or how to deal with conflicting points of view. Sometimes learning occurs when an employee returns from a formal training session and teaches others what he or she has learned.

When a research team studied informal training at Motorola, they discovered that every hour of formal training yielded four hours of informal training.[31] Learning often takes place informally in organizations, and managers who value learning must encourage and facilitate it.

Knowledge Interpretation

Learning occurs when individual employees form their views of the organization and its environment. These views are often called mental models. Peter Senge describes **mental models** as "deeply ingrained assumptions, generalizations, or images that influence how we understand the world and how we take action" (p. 8).[32]

For example, if we have a mental model of managers as manipulators, then we will see all their actions as politically motivated and act accordingly. New knowledge will not be accepted because we cannot recognize and change our mental models. As one researcher noted, the acceptance of new knowledge can be likened to an organ transplant—the possibility of rejection is highly probable.[33] Even when employees are aware of best practices in other companies or units, it might take more than two years for the information to be understood in a way that can be acted on.

An effective way to develop shared mental models is to establish teams. The most valuable and innovative work-related learning occurs in work teams, solving real problems.[34] At Chevron Corporation, based in San Francisco, best-practice teams save the company millions of dollars annually by improving processes. [35] These groups, learning by doing, are sometimes given a formal name of "communities of practice." **Communities of practice** are networks of people who work together and regularly share information and knowledge.

Knowledge cannot be valued unless there is a shared understanding of its importance. Learning is social, and as teams work together, they not only learn, but they develop a common way of thinking about things and a common identity emerges. These common perspectives are termed mental maps and are vitally important to the interpretation of the work environment and any lessons it contains. New learning is difficult to accept and apply without this shared perspective.

The creation and sharing of knowledge often occurs when people are given the opportunity to talk with each other, and over time, develop a relationship. As we noted earlier, these long-term relationships, such as those that occur with apprentices or protégés, are excellent vehicles for the transfer of knowledge. North Americans generally do not appreciate the importance of the social and emotional context of learning. We see learning as information transfer. Yet, even the youngest student will tell you that he or she learns more from a teacher he or she likes.

The higher your position in an organization, the more likely you are to learn about events in face-to-face conversations. Chief executives spend about 95 percent of their time in conversations and discussions. Workers at the entry level spend less time, but still need to interface to solve problems. For example, employees working on the assembly line at Motorola had no chance to even talk with co-workers—they discussed work problems and solutions as the shifts changed.[36] Perhaps a good way to start creating a learning organization is to build on what is already working at the grassroots level.

Mental models

Deeply ingrained assumptions, generalizations, or images that influence how we understand the world and how we take action

Communities of practice

Networks of people who work together and regularly share information and knowledge

Organizations can help employees interpret knowledge by creating networks in which individual learners and teams can share information and insight. For example, at one of the world's top luxury hotels, employees who refine a unique practice for improving reliable and superior customer service, are given the opportunity to be an internal consultant by sharing the information with other hotels in the chain. This includes a site visit to ensure that the innovation has been duplicated. If successful, employees are rewarded with assistance in their next career move in the organization.[37]

Knowledge Dissemination

Moving products, services, and money through and between organizations is a standard process for most organizations. Moving ideas requires a different set of skills and even different norms. At times, it feels like capturing a snowflake and passing it to a friend.

Companies must design systems or ways of sharing knowledge so that others can improve their work practices. You might say that information has always been shared between employees, and knowledge management is just a new way of describing communication. Although employees have always passed on new ideas by talking with each other, the difference is that these informal systems can be replaced by formal mechanisms grounded in technology.

Information and communication technologies (ICTs) allow for increased codification of knowledge; that is, its transformation into information that can easily be transmitted. Today, most organizations have electronic bulletin boards, libraries, virtual conference rooms, or connected knowledge bases. Through technology, employees can exchange proposals, presentations, spreadsheets, specifications, and so on.

For example, the CEO of Memphis-based Buckman Laboratories, a manufacturer of industrial chemicals, noticed informal sharing when he toured the plants and labs in 20 countries. He and his executive team accumulated case histories of best practices developed in one country, and passed on this information in the next country. Obviously, some dilution of information occurred at each stop, because the executive team did not actually do the work.

This experience led Buckman Laboratories to ask "How can we transfer our company's best practices in a better way?" They actually set up a knowledge transfer department, with more than 40 employees in information management and training. As early as 1988, Buckman Laboratories, the winner of the Optimas award for competitive advantage had established a series of private forums in which employees could share their insights 24 hours a day. Buckman Laboratories credits these online forums with an increase of $300 million in revenues, because they reduced the amount of time it takes for new ideas to reach the marketplace.[38]

There is a growth in benchmarking best practices. Normally, benchmarking implies that organizations study the best in the field and then attempt to replicate the best practices in their own companies. But as seen with the Buckman Laboratories example, benchmarking can also occur within organizations. For example, the branch in Regina may have the lowest rate of returns and it would benefit other branches to understand why.

An Intranet is a critical component for managing knowledge. An employee who posts a question or seeks advice can receive that information in hours, not weeks. Just as we use the little help icons (or wizards) for our software, we could use a company expert or subject-matter specialist who would pop up on the monitor while we are working on a new project—an instant coach!

Knowledge Retention

As noted earlier, knowledge resides in the minds of employees or in systems created to store that knowledge. To capitalize on these sources of knowledge, organizations must build tools to quickly compile, store, and retrieve this knowledge, a kind of intellectual inventory. These are called knowledge repositories. Knowledge repositories should not be seen as sacred libraries in which great books are stored and never read. The system has to be designed to encourage its use, to facilitate interaction. One reason for the growth of interest in this area is that the cost of managing it has been significantly lowered through technology.

There are ways to capture and store knowledge in information systems for later use. Some of these are highly structured databases. Digitalized knowledge can be more easily and cheaply processed, indexed, searched, converted, and transmitted.

Some knowledge repositories are more informal lists of lessons learned, white papers, presentations, and so on. Others are more actively stored in discussion groups. Most have links to the originators of the documents or at least to those who tend to access the repositories, thus signalling who is actively interested in that area. These collaborative filters monitor databases and Intranet sites, and can tell you which sites others with interests similar to yours have found useful.

Another useful idea is that of online mentors. Hughes Space & Communications Co. share knowledge and best practices using just-in-time mentoring. Hughes has an index of mentors who can be called for advice on various aspects of any project. For example, a mentor with experience preparing a business case for a project might be asked to coach an employee who is facing a similar task.[39] For more examples of online mentoring, see Training Today in Chapter 7.

Not all knowledge repositories are based on computer technology. Some knowledge is tacit and not easily codified. Some more traditional means of storing knowledge might include transcripts or audiocassettes from strategic planning sessions, consultants' reports in text or multimedia formats, videotaped presentations, market-trend analyses, and any number of information-rich resources.

IBM, whose core competence is knowledge, maintains dozens of knowledge repositories that consist of project proposals, work papers, presentations, and reports. IBM says that these repositories have reduced project time by as much as two thirds.[40]

Oral histories are another way to capture knowledge, particularly when organizations suffer the memory loss associated with departures and downsizing. For example, in the United Kingdom, Rothschild PLC used an exit interview to capture the vast amount of knowledge that its departing head of public relations held. A professional with HR and PR experience interviewed the executive, for an entire afternoon, and the conversation was recorded. Information that would not normally be transmitted to the successor was uncovered, edited, and indexed.[41] Other companies record oral histories of retiring managers.

At Kraft General Foods, the brand manager of Cracker Barrel Cheese was facing declining sales. She consulted the archives where the interview transcripts with the manager who had launched the brand were recorded. Based on these insights into the original goals for the cheese, the current brand manager was able to re-invigorate the brand.

You have just read descriptions of the various practices used by some companies to manage the acquisition, interpretation, dissemination, and retention of knowledge. A survey of knowledge management practices found that the most frequently used method was the Intranet. See Table 2.2 for a list of other common methods used.

Few organizations engage in the management of knowledge in a systematic way using all the practices outlined in Table 2.2. Those that do practise knowledge management typically formalize the job by appointing a senior executive who is responsible for this important work. This formalization signals the importance of knowledge management to the success of the organization. To learn more about how an organization can improve the management of knowledge, see The Trainer's Notebook 1, "Improving Knowledge Management."

TABLE 2.2

Knowledge Management Practices

Practice	Percentage Using
Creating an Intranet	47
Repositories	33
Decision support tools	33
Groupware to support collaboration	33
Networks of knowledge workers	24
Mapping sources of internal expertise	18
Establishing new knowledge roles	15

Source: Executive perspectives of knowledge in the organization. Ernst & Young Center for Business Intelligence [as cited in] Bassi, L., Cheney, S., & Lewis, E. (1998). Trends in workplace learning: Supply and demand in interesting times. *Training and Development* (November). Copyright 1998, adapted from *Training & Development* magazine, American Society for Training & Development. Reprinted with permission. All rights reserved.

A Multilevel Systems Approach to Organizational Learning

Although the emphasis of this chapter has been on organizational learning and the learning organization, it is important to understand that learning in organizations requires a multilevel and integrated systems approach. This means that we have to acknowledge and understand the linkages between the organization, groups, and individuals.

Figure 2.1 presents a multilevel systems approach to organizational learning. The model shows that there are three levels of learning in organizations: the organizational level, the group level, and the individual level. Each level is connected to the levels above and below it. The organizational level consists of the organization's leadership, culture, vision, strategy, and structure. Leadership is extremely important because top management needs to articulate a vision for learning and must support it and devote resources and time into the development of a learning organization. The organization must also develop and implement strategies for knowledge management and learning.

Organizational systems are necessary for the organization to acquire information and to distribute it throughout the organization. Thus, an organization must create processes, practices, policies, and structures that enable the acquisition, exchange, and distribution of information and knowledge throughout the organization. As well, the organization's culture for learning will influence the extent to which teams and individuals seek out new information and learning opportunities, and transfer new knowledge and skills on the job. There must be a culture that supports and encourages continuous learning.

Important factors at the group level include group climate, culture, norms, group dynamics, and processes, as well as the nature of the group task in terms of its complexity and task interdependence. Learning at the group level will be influenced by these factors. For example, the extent to which informal learning occurs will be influenced by the group's culture and norms for learning, and the extent to which it is rewarded will be influenced by the group's climate. The nature of the group's tasks will also influence learning. Groups that perform more complex tasks are more likely to realize the benefits of training and learning. When the tasks that group members perform are interdependent, there will be a greater need for the group to interact and share information. Thus, these group level factors will influence the extent to which learning occurs at the group level.

At the individual level, employees must also have both formal and informal opportunities to learn. This means that the organization needs to provide structured and formal training and development programs in order for employees to acquire new knowledge and skills, as well as opportunities to share and exchange information. In addition, employees must also be rewarded for learning and applying what they learn on the job.

In addition to recognizing the importance of each level for learning in organizations, the model also shows how each level is connected to the next level above and/or below it. For example, the systems and processes that exist at the organizational level will influence the extent to which learning occurs at the group level, and group level factors will influence learning at the

FIGURE 2.1

A Multilevel Systems Model of Organizational Learning

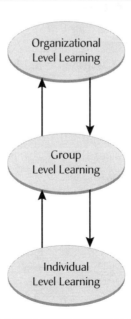

An environment for learning and the acquisition and exchange of knowledge and information.
— Organizational Level Learning

The opportunity for groups to interact, communicate, and share information.
— Group Level Learning

Individuals must have formal and informal opportunities for learning. Learning and the transfer of knowledge and information must be rewarded.
— Individual Level Learning

individual level. In addition, individual learning will influence group learning, and group learning will influence organizational learning.[42]

In summary, the multilevel systems approach to organizational learning demonstrates the importance of each level of the organization for learning. In order for organizations to learn, systems and processes must be in place at each level. After all, organizations cannot learn if individuals and groups do not learn, and individuals and groups cannot learn if organizational level factors do not provide them with opportunities to learn and exchange information.

In order to better understand what organizations can do at all levels to create a learning organization, see The Trainer's Notebook 2, "Facilitating Learning in Organizations."

Organizational Learning and Training

In this chapter, we have focused on learning in organizations, the learning organization, and knowledge management. Thus, the emphasis has been on the organizational level, although the focus of this text is on training and development at the individual and group level.

At this point, you might be asking yourself, "What is the connection between organizational learning and training?" Based on the previous section, you know that training is an important element of learning in organizations and a learning organization. In fact, research conducted by The Conference Board of Canada found a positive relationship between a learning organization and an organization's expenditures on formal training programs. In other words, learning organizations invest more in training and

---

The Trainer's Notebook 2

Facilitating Learning in Organizations

Here are 10 strategies for creating a learning system in organizations and facilitating learning in organizations:

1. Develop action learning programs throughout the organization by utilizing learning activities and by creating action learning teams with a facilitator.
2. Increase individuals' abilities to learn how to learn by teaching them how to ask questions that provide new information, how to break up complex ideas and large tasks into smaller parts, how to measure learning, and how to direct learning to meet specific goals.
3. Develop the discipline of dialogue in the organization.
4. Develop career-pathing plans for employability.
5. Establish a budget for self-development programs.
6. Build team learning skills.
7. Encourage and practise systems thinking.
8. Use scanning (of the environment to be prepared for future changes) and scenario planning (strategic and contingency planning) for anticipatory learning.
9. Encourage and expand diversity, multicultural, and global mindsets and learning by opening minds to the ideas of others.
10. Change the mental model to be consistent with learning through a paradigm shift.

Source: Sigler, J. (1999). Best practices and guiding principles: A training guide to successful development of a learning organization. *Futurics*, 23(1&2), 67–73.

development compared to organizations that do not consider themselves to be learning organizations (see Table 2.3 for more information about training in learning organizations). Furthermore, learning organizations had higher performance ratings in terms of their overall profitability and ability to retain essential employees.[43]

These results clearly indicate that there is a very close connection between training and development and organizational learning. Learning organizations exceed other organizations in terms of both training practices and expenditures. Furthermore, learning organizations not only provide more formal training, they are also more profitable than other organizations.

In summary, it should now be clear to you how important formal training programs are for organizational learning. While we have focused on learning at the organizational level, the fact of the matter is that organizational learning only occurs if individuals learn, and one of the major ways that individuals learn is through training and development.

In the next chapter, we shift our focus to individual learning. For now, we leave you with the following simple model that connects training and development to individual learning and organizational learning:

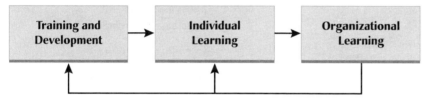

The model shows how the design and delivery of training programs influence individual learning, and how individual learning leads to organizational learning. The feedback loops also show that organizational learning influences training and development as well as individual learning.

TABLE 2.3

Training in Learning Organizations

Research conducted by The Conference Board of Canada found that learning organizations invest more in training and development in the following ways:

1. Learning organizations spend more on training per employee.
2. Learning organizations provide more hours of training per employee.
3. The percentage of employees who received training in the year 2000 was higher in learning organizations.
4. Learning organizations are more likely to use various training practices and programs such as mandatory annual training and mentoring programs.
5. Learning organizations deliver a significantly higher percentage of training time via learning technologies.

Source: Harris-Lalonde, S. (2001). Training and development outlook. Reprinted by permission of *The Conference Board of Canada*. Ottawa.

Summary

In this chapter, we described the meaning and importance of learning in organizations, a learning organization, and knowledge management. The five disciplines and the principles of a learning organization were described as well as four dimensions that are critical for creating and sustaining a learning organization. We also discussed the meaning and types of knowledge management and intellectual capital. The methods organizations use to acquire, interpret, disseminate, and retain knowledge were also described. The chapter concluded with a multilevel systems model of organizational learning that shows how organizational learning is connected to group and individual learning. The connection between training and development, individual learning, and organizational learning was also discussed. In the next chapter, we focus on learning at the individual level.

Key Terms

communities of practice (page 38)

customer capital (page 34)

explicit knowledge (page 32)

human capital (page 34)

intellectual capital (page 33)

knowledge (page 32)

knowledge management (page 35)

learning organization (page 28)

mental models (page 38)

organizational learning (page 27)

relationship capital (page 34)

renewal capital (page 34)

structural capital (page 34)

tacit knowledge (page 33)

Weblinks

CIBC: www.cibc.com (page 35)

Dow Chemical: www.dow.com (page 35)

IBM: www.ibm.com/ca (page 34)

Kraft General Foods: www.kraftfoods.com (page 41)

Microsoft: www.microsoft.com (page 33)

Nortel: www.nortelnetworks.com (page 33)

Royal Bank: www.royalbank.com (page 37)

Discussion Questions

1. Discuss the role of teams and leaders in a learning organization. How do teams and leaders contribute to a learning organization and what are some of the tasks and activities that they should perform?
2. Discuss the importance and relevance of technology for a learning organization and knowledge management. How important is technology and how should it be used in a learning organization and for knowledge management?
3. Discuss the role of the training function and the role of the trainer in a learning organization. How will these roles change in a learning organi-

zation? What knowledge and skills will a trainer in a learning organization require?

4. Discuss the multilevel systems model of organizational learning. How are the three levels related and what should organizations do for learning to occur at each level?

5. Why do you think there are not more learning organizations in Canada? What do Canadian organizations have to do to become learning organizations?

Using the Internet

1. Review the chapter-opening vignette on Dofasco and also visit their website at **www.dofasco.ca**. What are some of the things that make Dofasco a learning organization? Discuss Dofasco in terms of Senge's five disciplines, the principles of a learning organization, and the four key dimensions that are critical for creating and sustaining a learning organization. What can other organizations learn from Dofasco if they want to become a learning organization?

2. To learn more about organizational learning and the learning organization, go to: **www.brint.com/papers/orglrng.htm** and find answers to the following questions:

   1. What is organizational learning?
   2. What is a learning organization?
   3. What is the difference between organizational learning and a learning organization?
   4. What is adaptive learning vs. generative learning?
   5. What's the manager's role in the learning organization?
   6. What's the relationship between strategy and organizational learning?
   7. What is the role of information systems in the learning organization?
   8. Does IT impose any constraints on organizational learning?

Exercises

1. Contact the human resources department of an organization and ask them if you can talk about their attempts to become a learning organization. Ask them if they are a learning organization and what they have done in order to become a learning organization. Do you think they are a learning organization? What do they still have to do in order to become a learning organization?

2. Using the information in this chapter, develop a checklist to determine if the organization in which you work is a learning organization. How many of the four critical elements and principles of a learning organization are characteristic of your organization? What does your organization have to do to become a learning organization?

3. Contact the human resources department of an organization and ask them if you can talk about how they manage knowledge and information in the organization. Ask them about their knowledge management practices and what they do to acquire, interpret, disseminate, and retain knowledge. Use Table 2.2 to find out what knowledge management practices they have in place. How can the organization improve its management of knowledge?

4. Conduct an interview with several people you know who are currently employed. Interview them about how they learn in their organization. Ask them questions about how and what they have learned through formal and informal learning opportunities. Based on their responses, answer the following questions:

    a. Did they learn more or less from formal or informal learning?

    b. Did they have more or less formal or informal opportunities for learning?

    c. Which type of learning was most effective for them: formal or informal learning?

    d. What did they learn from formal and informal learning? Did they learn similar or different things from each?

    e. What kinds of practices were used in their organization for formal and informal learning?

5. Reflect on a previous or current job in terms of what you have learned and how it was learned. Make a list of all the things you learned on your job. Once you have made your learning list, indicate how each item on your list was learned. Was it through formal or informal means? Be specific in terms of the formal or informal activity that contributed to your learning. What does your list tell you about learning in organizations? What should you do if you want to improve your learning?

6. Imagine that you are a director of training in an organization and the company president wants to meet with you to discuss becoming a learning organization. What will you tell him or her about learning organizations and what the organization must do to become one? Prepare a short presentation in which you present your main ideas and suggestions for becoming a learning organization. Once complete, pair up with another member of the class and take turns presenting and evaluating each other's presentation. If time permits, presentations to the class can also be made.

7. Imagine that you are a director of training in an organization and the company president wants to meet with you to discuss how the organization can improve its management of knowledge. What will you tell him or her about knowledge management and what the organization must do to improve its management of knowledge? Prepare a short presentation in which you present your main ideas and suggestions for knowledge management. Once complete, pair up with another member of the class and take turns presenting and evaluating each other's presentation. If time permits, presentations to the class can also be made.

8. As a student, you spend a great deal of your time learning. But how exactly do you learn? Make a list of the formal and informal ways that you learn. Do you learn more from formal or informal methods? If you want to improve your learning, what are some of the things you might do? Be specific in terms of both formal and informal ways to improve your learning.

Case

FROZEN ROCK-SOLID

At General Motors of Canada Ltd., Nick Vanderstoop is in charge of implementing a system that he created to prevent the "erosion of knowledge." He loves to scare the daylights out of GM executives and managers by telling them a true story about the company.

The story goes something like this: Several years ago a worker at the head office of General Motors of Canada Ltd. in Oshawa retired. Among the many tasks that were performed by him, one was particularly important. Every fall he would spend about an hour sending messages to inform others that certain freezable chemicals like upholstery cleaners must be shipped in heated trucks during the winter.

A few months after he retired, the parts distribution centre in Woodstock, Ontario, began to receive calls from angry customers across Canada who were upset because the chemicals that they were receiving were frozen rock-solid. The reason: nobody in the company knew enough about the retiree's job to make sure that the chemicals were properly transported during the winter.

A minor oversight? Not quite. It cost the company $1.5 million. Other incidents at GM have also been reported. For example, 400 perfectly good carburetors were accidentally destroyed at a cost of $300,000 because the worker who kept them off the scrap list retired. It has also been reported that a $250,000 car prototype was crushed into scrap metal because the employee who was responsible for it was transferred. Incidents like these are known to occur at other companies.

Source: Livesey, B. (1997, November). Glitch doctor. *Report on Business Magazine*, pp. 96–102. Reprinted by permission of Bruce Livesey.

Questions

1. Why do you think this is an important story to tell company executives and managers? What is the main point of the story?
2. What kind of knowledge is most relevant for understanding the incidents mentioned in the case? What does the case tell us about the role of knowledge in organizations?

3. Organization mishaps like those reported in the case appear to be common occurrences. A traditional organization might blame or attribute the causes of them to a number of different sources. What reasons might be given for such mishaps?
4. What could GM and other companies do to solve the problems reported in the case? What knowledge management practices would you recommend and why?
5. What would a learning organization do to identify and solve the types of incidents described in the case?

References

[1]Geary, S. (2002). What does it take to implement the learning organization? *The Canadian Learning Journal, 6*(2), 27–30. www.dofasco.ca Dofasco Inc.; Iron Age New Steel; Dofasco: A Company Overview.

[2]Senge, P. M. (1990). *The fifth discipline: The art and practice of the learning organization.* New York: Doubleday.

[3]Bennet, J.K., & O'Brien, M.J. (1994, June). The building blocks of the learning organization. *Training, 31(6),* 41–49.

[4]Senge, P. M. (1990).

[5]Sigler, J. (1999). Best practices and guiding principles: A training guide to successful development of a learning organization. *Futurics, 23*(1&2), 67–73.

[6]Harris-Lalonde, S. (2001). Training and development outlook. *The Conference Board of Canada.* Ottawa.

[7]Ellinger, A. D., Ellinger, A. E., Baiyin, Y., & Howton, S. W. (2002). The relationship between the learning organization concept and firms' financial performance: An empirical assessment. *Human Resource Development Quarterly, 13,* 5–21.

[8]Harris-Lalonde, S. (2001).

[9]Harris-Lalonde, S. (2001).

[10]Sigler, J. (1999).

[11]Tapscott, D. (1998). Make knowledge an asset for the whole company. *Computerworld, 32,* (51), p. 32.

[12]Stamps, D. (1998). Learning ecologies. *Training, 35* (1), pp. 32–38.

Communities of practice: Learning is social, training is irrelevant? *Training, 3* (2), 34–42.

[13]Stamps, D. (1999). Is knowledge management a fad? *Training, 36* (3), 36–42.

[14]Baets, W.R.J. (1998). *Organizational learning and knowledge technologies in a dynamic environment.* Boston: Kluwer Academic Publishers.

[15]Miller, W. (1999, January). Building the ultimate resource. *Management Review,* 42–45.

[15]Miller, W. (1999, January).

[17]Stewart, T. (1994, October 3). Intellectual capital. *Fortune,* pp. 68–74.

[18]Pezim, S. (1999, January 11). Fishing in the knowledge pond. *Canadian HR Reporter,* pp. 15–16.

[19]Tapscott, D. (1998).

[20]Miller, W. (1999, January).

[21]Bassi, L., Cheney, S., & Lewis, E. (1998, November). Trends in workplace learning: Supply and demand in interesting times. *Training and Development,* 51–77.

[22]Kransdorff, A. (1997, September). Fight organizational memory loss. *Workforce,* 34–39.

[23]Stahl, S. (1999, April 5). Knowledge yields impressive returns. *Information Week,* p. 115.

[24]Neely Martinez, M. (1998, February). The collective power. *HRM magazine,* pp. 88–94.

[25]Sigler, J. (1999).

[26]Harris-Lalonde, S. (2001).

[27]Garvin, D.A. (1998). The processes of organization and management. *Sloan Management Review,* 39(4), 33–50.

[28]Jeppesen, J. C. (2002). Creating and maintaining the learning organization. In K. Kraiger's (Ed.), *Creating, implementing, and managing effective training and development: State-of-the-art lessons for practice,* (pp. 302–30). San Francisco. CA: Jossey-Bass.

[29]Trainor, N.L. (1998, April 20). Learning creates value for organizations. *Canadian HR Reporter,* p. 9.

[30]Harris-Lalonde, S. (2001).

[31]Stamps, D. (1998).

[32]Senge, P. M. (1990).

[33]Stamps, D. (1999).

[34]Stamps, D. (1997). Communities of practice: Learning is social, training is irrelevant? *Training, 3* (2), 34–42.

[35]Neely Martinez, M. (1998, February).

[36]Stamps, D. (1998).

[37]Jeppesen, J. C. (2002).

[38]Sunoo, B.P. (1999). How HR supports knowledge sharing. *Workforce, 78* (3), 30–34.

[39]Stuller, J. (1998). Chief of corporate smarts. *Training, 35* (4), 28–37.

[40]Tapscott, D. (1998).

[41]Kransdorff, A. (1997, September).

[42]Kozlowski, S. W. J., & Salas, E. (1997). A Multilevel Organizational Systems Approach for the Implementation and Transfer of Training. In J. Kevin Ford, Steve W. J. Kozlowski, Kurt Kraiger, Eduardo Salas, and Mark S. Teachout (Eds.), *Improving Training Effectiveness in Work Organizations*. Mahwah, N.J.: Lawrence Erlbaum Associates.

[43]Harris-Lalonde, S. (2001).

Chapter 3

Learning and Motivation

Chapter Learning Objectives

After reading this chapter, you should be able to:

- define learning and describe Gagne's five learning outcomes
- describe the three stages of learning
- describe conditioning theory and social learning theory and their implications for training and development
- describe adult learning theory, Kolb's learning styles, and accelerated learning and their implications for training and development
- define motivation and describe need and process theories of motivation and their implications for training and development
- define training motivation and discuss its predictors and consequences

www.fairmont.com

FAIRMONT HOTELS AND RESORTS

At the Toronto-based hotel chain Fairmont Hotels and Resorts, new employees have a lot to learn. Prior to their first day on the job, new employees receive an invitation to the hotel. They are asked to arrive at the front door where a valet waits to park the car. They are then greeted by senior hotel management and taken to an elegant dining room for coffee, breakfast, and an informal discussion about the hotel. Once treated to a meal or given vouchers for an overnight stay at the hotel, they view a short video message from the members of the corporate executive team welcoming them and letting them know where to go for further assistance.

The second day of orientation includes more presentations and role-playing activities that simulate encounters with guests. Trainers don't just tell new employees how customers should be treated, they show them. Trainers model customer service by treating new employees as special guests.

Each hotel has its own creative way of showing the property to new employees. Some hotels have scavenger hunts, creating a fun competition among teams of new hires. Others have developed celebrity tours, showing new employees where, for example, John Lennon and Yoko Ono had their Love-In at the Montreal hotel.

One resort in Banff Springs takes employees on a tour of rooms believed to be haunted by ghosts. These stories not only share the history and culture of the luxury hotels, but they also prepare new employees for success.

A third day of orientation takes place once employees have been on the job 60 to 90 days. During this time, employees are paired with a mentor of their choosing as a way to receive extra help and build relationships with co-workers. Supervisors also guide new employees through a personal development interview identifying goals and providing informal feedback.

The Fairmont orientation program attempts to strike the same passion in its employees as the hotel hopes to create for its guests. By experiencing the hotel as guests and hearing the stories along with corporate strategy, employees are better able to take ownership of their jobs and where they work.[1]

Training is first and foremost about learning and at Fairmont Hotels and Resorts, new employees are trained so that they learn about the company, the art of customer service, the building of relationships, and how to perform their new jobs and roles.

In Chapter 2, we discussed organizational learning and the learning organization. However, in order for organizations to learn and to become learning organizations, the people in them must learn. In this chapter, we focus on how people learn and their motivation to learn. First, we define what we mean by learning and describe learning outcomes. We then discuss the stages of learning followed by a review of learning and motivation theories. We conclude the chapter with a model that links training to learning, behaviour, and organizational outcomes.

What is Learning?

Although training is the focus of this book, it is important to keep in mind that what we are really trying to accomplish through the process of training and development is learning. In other words, training is simply the means for accomplishing the goal or end, which is learning.

Learning is the process of acquiring knowledge and skills. It is a process in which an individual's behaviour is changed through experience.[2] For our purposes, that experience is training and development. Learning occurs "when one experiences a new way of acting, thinking, or feeling, finds the new pattern gratifying or useful, and incorporates it into the repertoire of behaviours" (p. 833).[3] When a behaviour has been learned, it can be thought of as a skill.

Learning

The process of acquiring knowledge and skills and a change in individual behaviour as a result of some experience

Learning Outcomes

Learning can be described in terms of a number of domains of learning or outcomes. Robert Gagne developed the best known classification of learning outcomes. According to Gagne, skills or learning outcomes can be classified according to five general categories:[4]

1. *Verbal information* refers to facts, knowledge, principles, and information or what is known as declarative knowledge.
2. *Intellectual skills* involve the learning of concepts, rules, and procedures and are sometimes referred to as procedural knowledge.
3. *Cognitive strategies* refer to the application of information and techniques and understanding how and when to use the information.
4. *Motor skills* involve the coordination and execution of physical movements that involve the use of muscles such as learning to swim.
5. *Attitudes* refer to preferences and internal states associated with one's beliefs and feelings. Attitudes are learned and can be changed, however, they are considered to be the most difficult domain to influence through training.[5]

A training program can focus on one or more of these learning outcomes. The important thing to realize is that different training methods might be more or less effective depending on the learning outcome that a training program was designed to influence. According to Gagne, different instructional events and conditions of learning are required for each of the learning outcomes. However, regardless of the learning outcome, learning generally occurs over a period of time and progresses through a series of stages as described in the next section.

Stages of Learning

Learning and the acquisition of new knowledge and skills occur over a period of time. A theory developed by John Anderson, which he calls the Adaptive Character of Thought theory or ACT theory, describes the learning process as it unfolds over three stages.[6]

According to ACT theory, learning takes place in three stages that are known as declarative knowledge, knowledge compilation, and procedural knowledge or proceduralization.

The first stage of learning involves learning knowledge, facts, and information or what is known as **declarative knowledge**. For example, think of what it was like when you learned how to drive a car. At first, you acquired a great deal of information such as what to do when you get into the car, how to start the car and put it in gear, how to change gears if it is a standard shift and so on. These pieces of information or units are called chunks.

During this first stage of learning one must devote all of their attention and cognitive resources to the task of learning. In other words, it is not likely that you could make a phone call, listen to the radio, or carry on a conversation during this period of learning to drive a car. This is because all of your attention and cognitive resources are required to learn the task of driving. Furthermore, your driving performance at this stage is slow and prone to errors and mistakes.

During the declarative stage of learning, performance is resource dependent because all of one's attention and cognitive resources are required to learn the task. Any diversion of attention is likely to affect your learning and lower performance. Just think of what it is like when you are in class and somebody starts talking to you. Your learning is seriously affected because you need all of your attention and cognitive resources for the task of learning. Listening or talking to somebody during class will require your attention and your learning will suffer.

The second stage of learning is called **knowledge compilation**. Knowledge compilation involves integrating tasks into sequences to simplify and streamline the task. The learner acquires the ability to translate the declarative knowledge acquired in the first stage into action. During this stage, performance becomes faster and more accurate. For example, when learning how to drive a car, you are able to get into the car and begin to drive without having to carefully think about every single thing you must do. In other words, what was many single tasks or units and chunks during the declarative stage (e.g., put your seatbelt on, lock the car, adjust the seat, adjust the mirror, start the car, etc.), is now one smooth sequence of tasks. You get into the car and do all of the tasks as part of an integrated sequence.

Although the attention requirements during the knowledge compilation stage are lower than the declarative stage, performance is still somewhat fragmented and piecemeal. So when you are learning to drive a car, this

Declarative knowledge

Learning knowledge, facts, and information

Knowledge compilation

Integrating tasks into sequences to simplify and streamline the task might mean popping the clutch from time to time and occasionally rolling backwards when on an incline, stalling the car, and so on.

The final stage of learning is called **procedural knowledge** or proceduralization. During this stage, the learner has mastered the task and performance is automatized and habitual. In other words, the task can now be performed without much thought. The transition from knowledge acquisition to application is complete. This is what most of us experience when we drive. We simply get into a car and drive without giving much thought to what we are doing. The task of driving becomes habitual and automatic.

Because tasks at this stage can be performed with relatively little attention, it is possible to divert one's attention and cognitive resources to other tasks such as conversing with passengers or talking on the phone. Performance at this stage is fast and accurate and the task can be performed with little impairment even when attention is devoted to another task. At this stage, performance is said to be resource insensitive because changes in attention will not have much of an impact on performance.

ACT theory has some important implications for learning and training. First, it recognizes the fact that learning is a stage-like process that involves three important stages. Second, it indicates that different types of learning take place at different stages. And third, motivational interventions might be more or less effective depending on the stage of learning. As you will learn later in the chapter, goal setting is a motivational theory with implications for training and development. However, research has shown that goal setting can be harmful to learning during the early stages of learning when all of one's attention and cognitive resources must be devoted to learning the task. During the early stages of learning, cognitive ability is more important than motivational strategies.

However, when goals are set during the later stages of learning (i.e., procedural knowledge), they have a positive effect on learning and performance and cognitive ability is less important than it was during the declarative stage of learning. Thus, the effects of both cognitive ability and motivational interventions such as goal setting on learning and performance depends on the stage of learning.[7]

Learning Theories

Researchers have studied learning and have developed a body of knowledge and theories about the learning process. Theories are very important because they help us understand how something works or why it happens. Theories represent an attempt to organize knowledge so that we can use it in a variety of situations.

Intuitively, most trainers use some guidelines derived from learning theories. For example, the value of rewarding good performance and providing positive feedback is well known as is the importance of confidence for learning and performing a task. In this section, we describe two theories of learning that have important implications for the design and effectiveness of training and development: conditioning theory and social learning theory.

Procedural knowledge

The learner has mastered the task and performance is automatized and habitual

Conditioning Theory

The famous psychologist B.F. Skinner defined learning as a relatively permanent change in behaviour in response to a particular stimulus or set of stimuli.[8] Skinner and the behaviourist school of psychology believe that learning is a result of reward and punishment contingencies that follow a response to a stimulus.

The basic idea is that a stimulus or cue would be followed by a response, which is then reinforced. This in turn strengthens the likelihood that the response will occur again and that learning will result.

For example, behaviourists argue that similar principles are at work when an adult submits an innovative proposal and is praised, and when a pigeon pecks a red dot and is given a pellet of food. When a response is reinforced through food, money, attention, or anything pleasurable, then the response is more likely to be repeated. If there is no reinforcement, then, over time, the response will cease. If the response is punished, then it will not be repeated. The conditioning process is illustrated in Figure 3.1.

Negative reinforcement is the removal of a negative outcome after an act. To illustrate this concept, think of an alarm clock ringing. When you turn it off, the noise stops (the negative consequence is removed). Similarly, think of your course instructor chewing out the class for not participating and threatening to start picking students at random to answer questions. When students begin to participate, the instructor stops chewing them out and threatening to choose students at random (the negative consequence is removed).

It is important to realize that this is not the same as punishment in which one receives a negative consequence for doing something undesirable. In the example above, a desirable behaviour is being learned and increased (i.e., class participation) by a negative reinforcer that is removed when the desirable behaviour occurs.

Managers and trainers use conditioning theory principles when they attempt to influence employee behaviour. For example, at Capital One, a financial services company in the United States, new hires attend monthly reinforcement sessions in which they discuss what they did on the job that directly relates to the skills being developed. Once the skills are mastered

FIGURE 3.1

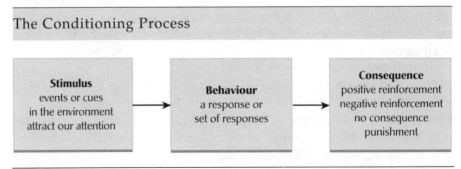

The Conditioning Process

Stimulus events or cues in the environment attract our attention	**Behaviour** a response or set of responses	**Consequence** positive reinforcement negative reinforcement no consequence punishment

they are taught new skills and the reinforcement cycle continues.[9] Linking desired complex behaviour to pleasurable consequences is based on three connected concepts: *shaping, chaining,* and *generalization.*

Shaping refers to the reinforcement of each step in the process until it is mastered, and then withdrawing the reinforcer until the next step is mastered. Shaping is extremely important for learning complex behaviour. Behaviour modelling (see Chapter 6) makes extensive use of this concept, rewarding trainees for the acquisition of separate skills performed sequentially.

Chaining is the second important concept and involves the reinforcement of entire sequences of a task. During shaping, an individual learns each separate step of a task and is reinforced for each successive step. The goal, however, is to learn to combine each step and perform the entire response. This combination is what chaining involves, and it is accomplished by reinforcing entire sequences of the task and eventually reinforcing only the complete task after each of the steps have been learned.

The third important concept is **generalization**, which means that the conditioned response occurs in circumstances different from those during learning.[10] Thus, while a trainee might have learned a task through shaping and chaining, he or she might not be able to perform the task in a different situation or outside of the classroom. To achieve generalization, the trainer must provide trainees with opportunities to perform the task in a variety of situations. For example, the trainer can change a role play script from negotiating with one's supervisor on the deadline of a project to negotiating the starting salary with a new employer. As a result, the trainee learns to generalize the skill from a simple, controlled environment to a different, more difficult one. This is a goal of training—that learning acquired during training will be generalized to and used in different situations and contexts.

When applied to training, conditioning theory suggests that trainees should be encouraged and reinforced throughout the training process. In other words, they should be reinforced for attending training, learning the training material, and applying it on the job. Based on conditioning theory, we would expect training to be more effective to the extent that trainees are reinforced for learning and the successful performance of training tasks.

Social Learning Theory

According to social learning theory, people learn by observing the behaviour of others, making choices about different courses of action to pursue, and by managing their own behaviour in the process of learning.[11] Thus, learning does not just occur as a result of reward and punishment contingencies. Learning also occurs through cognitive processes such as imitation and modelling. We observe the actions of others and make note of the reinforcing or punishing outcomes of their behaviour. We then imitate observed behaviour and expect certain consequences to follow.

For example, as part of the new employee orientation and training program at Fairmont Hotels, trainers model customer service and new employees participate in role-playing activities that simulate encounters with

Shaping

The reinforcement of each step in a process until it is mastered

Chaining

The reinforcement of entire sequences of a task

Generalization

The conditioned response occurs in circumstances different from those during learning guests. This is a good example of the process of learning through observation and imitation. Considerable research has demonstrated that people observe and reproduce the actions and attitudes of others.[12]

Social learning theory involves three key components: observation, self-efficacy, and self-management. First, as already indicated, people learn by **observation**. They observe the actions of others and the consequences of those actions. If the person being observed (the role model) is credible and knowledgeable, their behaviour is more likely to be imitated. The imitation will occur particularly if the role model is reinforced for the behaviour. New recruits watch the intense work hours of the senior staff. They then work the same long hours, in the expectation that they too will be rewarded with promotions.

There are four key elements that are critical for observational learning to take place: attention, retention, reproduction, and reinforcement. Learners must first attend to the behaviour (i.e., must be aware of the skills that are observable). Second, they must remember what they observed and encode it in their own repertoire so that they can recall the skills. Third, they must then try out the skill (i.e., try to reproduce it) through practice and rehearsal. Fourth, if the reproduction results in positive outcomes (i.e., it is reinforced), then the learner is likely to continue to reproduce the behaviour and retain the new skills.

Many training programs use social learning theory concepts to model desired behaviour that is then followed by opportunities for practice and reinforcement. At Fairmont Hotels and Resorts, trainers show new hires how customers should be treated. They model customer service by treating new employees as special guests. Some organizations assign new recruits to mentors or senior co-workers so that they can learn by observing them. At Fairmont Hotels and Resorts, new employees are paired with a mentor of their choosing. The financial services firm Edward Jones has a mentoring program in which new investment representatives are paired with more established ones. New employees shadow their mentor for three weeks to learn about the company and how things are done.[13]

While observation may provide the observer with information necessary to imitate the modelled behaviour, we know that people do not always attempt to do the things that they observe other people doing. For example, a novice skier might watch his friends skillfully make their way down a steep hill but refuse to follow suit. This is because he or she might not have the confidence or the belief that he or she will be able to do it. Such beliefs are known as self-efficacy.

Self-efficacy refers to judgments that people have about their ability to successfully perform a specific task. Self-efficacy is a cognitive belief that is task specific, as in the example of the skier's confidence that he or she can ski down a steep hill. The novice skier might have low self-efficacy to ski down the hill but very high self-efficacy that he or she can get an "A" in a training course!

Self-efficacy is influenced by four sources of information. In order of importance they are: task performance outcomes, observation, verbal persuasion and social influence, and one's physiological or emotional state.[14] The

Observation

Learning by observing the actions of others and the consequences

Self-efficacy

Judgments that people have about their ability to successfully perform a specific task self-efficacy of the skier can be strengthened not only by observing his or her friends' behaviour, but also by their encouragement that he or she can make it down the hill, his or her feelings of comfort and relaxation rather than fear and anxiety, and most important, his or her own successful attempts at skiing down the hill.

Self-efficacy has been shown to have a strong effect on people's attitudes, emotions, and behaviour in many areas of human behaviour. Self-efficacy influences the activities people choose to perform, the amount of effort and persistence they devote to a task, affective and stress reactions, and performance outcomes.[15]

Self-efficacy is also a key factor in training. Research has shown that the effectiveness of many training programs is partly due to the strengthening of trainees' self-efficacy to perform the training task. In other words, training increases trainees' self-efficacy to perform a task, and self-efficacy is related to improved task performance.[16]

The third component of social learning theory is self-management. **Self-management** refers to a process in which one manages their own behaviour through a series of internal processes.

Conditioning theory takes the position that an individual's behaviour is regulated by external factors such as rewards and punishments. However, self-management suggests that people can control and manage their own behaviour through a series of internal processes that enable them to structure and motivate their behaviour. These internal processes involve observing one's own behaviour as well as the behaviour of others, setting performance goals, practising new and desired behaviours, keeping track of one's progress, and rewarding oneself for goal achievement.[17]

Self-management has been found to be related to cognitive, affective, and behavioural outcomes and to be an important method of training. For example, one study showed that self-management training increased the job attendance of employees with above average absenteeism. The results indicated that, compared to a group that did not receive the training, employees who received self-management training had higher self-efficacy for attending work and increased job attendance. In a follow-up study, the authors found that these benefits continued up to nine months after training.[18] Several other studies have also demonstrated that self-management training leads to improvements in skill acquisition, maintenance, and performance.[19]

Social learning theory has important implications for the design of training programs. In particular, trainee learning can be improved by providing trainees with models who demonstrate how to perform a training task; by strengthening trainee self-efficacy for successfully learning and performing the task; and by teaching trainees to regulate and manage their own behaviour and performance.

Adult Learning Theory

Consider the learning environment most people have experienced throughout their lives. As students, we are told what, when, and how to learn. Learning is

Self-management

Managing one's own behaviour through a series of internal processes supposed to pay off in some unknown way in the distant future. The question is whether this is an appropriate way to educate and train adults given that adults differ from children in a number of important ways.

First, unlike children, adults have acquired a great deal of knowledge and work-related experiences that they bring with them to a training program. Adults also like to know why they are learning something, the practical implications of what they are learning, and its relevance to their problems and needs. Adults are also problem-centred in their approach to learning and prefer to be self-directed. They like to learn independently and they are motivated to learn by both extrinsic and intrinsic factors. Other contrasts between the learning needs of children and adults are highlighted in Table 3.1.

These differences have led to the development of an adult learning theory known as andragogy. **Andragogy** is a term coined by adult learning theorist Malcolm Knowles and refers to an adult-oriented approach to learning that takes into account the differences between adult and child learners. By contrast, the term **pedagogy** refers to the more traditional approach of learning used to educate children and youth.[20]

Andragogy involves making the learning experience of adults self-directed and problem-centred, and takes into account the learner's existing knowledge and experience. Using the principles of adult learning, McMaster University in Hamilton, Ontario, redesigned its medical degree program. Instead of teaching medicine by subject matter (chemistry, physiology), they created a problem-centred curriculum. After identifying about 200 of the most common medical problems faced by physicians, McMaster developed learning modules containing everything a doctor needs to know about anatomy, pharmacology, and so on to solve the problem.

Andragogy

An adult-oriented approach to learning that takes into account the differences between adult and child learners

Pedagogy

The traditional approach to learning used to educate children and youth

TABLE 3.1

Teaching Children Versus Adults

Factor	Children	Adults
Personality	Dependent	Independent
Motivation	Extrinsic	Intrinsic
Roles	Student	Employee
	Child	Parent, volunteer, spouse, citizen
Openness to change	Keen	Ingrained habits and attitudes
Barriers to change	Few	Negative self-concept
		Limited opportunities
		Time
		Inappropriate teaching methods
Experience	Limited	Vast
Orientation to learning	Subject-centred	Problem-centred

Managing Performance Through Training and Development

Adult learning theory has important implications for trainers at every stage of the training process including needs analysis, training design and delivery, and evaluation. The design and instruction of training programs and learning should be the joint responsibility of the trainer and trainees.

See The Trainer's Notebook, "Implications of Adult Learning Theory for Training" to learn more about the practical implications of adult learning theory for training and development.

Another approach to adult learning was developed by David Kolb. According to Kolb, individuals differ in terms of how they prefer to learn or what are known as learning styles. A **learning style** is the way in which an individual gathers information and processes and acts on it during the learning process.[21]

An individual's learning style is a function of the way an individual gathers and processes information or what is known as a learning mode. According to Kolb, there are four learning modes: 1. Concrete experience (CE), 2. Abstract conceptualization (AC), 3. Reflective observation (RO), and 4. Active experimentation (AE).

People who prefer to learn through direct experience and involvement as opposed to thinking are CE types. Those who prefer to learn by thinking about issues, ideas, and concepts are AC types. If you prefer to learn by observing and reflecting on information and different points of view you are an RO type. Finally, people who prefer to learn by acting on information and actually doing something to see its practical value are AE types.[22]

An individual's learning style is a function of two of the modes of learning. For example, a convergent learning style combines abstract conceptualization and active experimentation (thinking and doing). People with this learning style focus on problem solving and the practical application of ideas and theories. A divergent learning style combines concrete experience and reflective observation (feeling and watching). People with this orientation

Learning style

The way in which an individual gathers information and processes and evaluates it during the learning process

The Trainer's Notebook

Implications of Adult Learning Theory for Training

- Adults need to know why they are learning.
- Adults should have some input into the planning and instruction of training programs.
- Adults should be involved in the needs analysis and have input into things such as training content and methods.
- The designers of training programs should consider the needs and interests of trainees.
- The training content should be meaningful and relevant to trainees' work-related needs and problems.

- Trainers should be aware of trainees' experiences and use them as examples.
- Adults can learn independently, and may prefer to do so.
- Adults are motivated by both intrinsic and extrinsic rewards.
- Adults should be given safe practice opportunities.

view concrete situations from different points of view and generate alternative courses of action. An assimilation style combines abstract conceptualization and reflective observation (thinking and watching). These people like to process and integrate information and ideas into logical forms and theoretical models. Finally, an accommodative learning style combines concrete experience and active experimentation (feeling and doing). People with this learning style prefer hands-on experience and like to learn by being involved in new and challenging experiences.[23]

Kolb's theory has several implications for adult learning. First, it recognizes that people differ in how they prefer to learn. This means that a person's comfort and success in training will depend on how well the training approach matches their learning style. Thus, trainers need to be aware of these differences and design training programs to appeal to people's different learning styles.

Second, although people might prefer a particular learning style, ideally people can learn best by using all four styles. In fact, Kolb notes the importance of a learning cycle in which people use each of the four modes of learning in a sequence. The learning cycle begins with concrete experience (learning by experience), followed by reflective observation (learning by reflecting), then abstract conceptualization (learning by thinking), and finally active experimentation (learning by doing). This kind of learning cycle has been shown to improve learning and retention as well as the development of behavioural skills. Learning is most effective when all four steps in the learning cycle are part of the learning experience.[24] Thus, training programs should be designed with each learning mode as part of a sequence of learning experiences.

Kolb's learning cycle and learning styles are factored into the training process at some companies. For example, at Capital One Financial Corp., after employees are taught a new set of skills they are given work projects to implement the skills and then they must report on the experience. The approach closely mirrors Kolb's learning cycle.[25] To find out how another company applies Kolb's learning cycle and also matches trainees' learning style to training, see Training Today, "Learning Styles and Training at AmeriCredit."

A final example of adult learning is a learning approach known as accelerated learning. **Accelerated learning** is a results-oriented process that tailors the content and delivery of training to match the needs and preferences of individuals. With accelerated learning, the learner's needs and preferences are key to the content and delivery of the training.[26]

Accelerated learning is based on a scientific understanding of how the brain and senses work. The idea is to stimulate all of the senses instead of just a learner's ability to think and to memorize, as is the case with traditional approaches to learning.

The basic premise behind accelerated learning is that each person has a preferred learning style and they will learn best when the trainer's approach and methods match the person's learning style. In other words, learning will be accelerated when the learning approach is consistent with individuals' learning preferences.

Accelerated learning

A results-oriented process that customizes the content and delivery of training to match the needs and preferences of individuals

Learning Styles and Training at AmeriCredit

AmeriCredit is an auto finance company in Fort Worth, Texas. The company has a very unique approach to training that has its basis in David Kolb's learning cycle model and learning styles. The company has developed an instrument called the I-Opt Learning Style Rollout to measure employees' learning style.

The company's vision is to measure the preferred learning styles of all the company's 4,800 employees from the CEO to janitors and then log it into a database where course content will be tailored to the individual, the facilitator, and the design of the course.

Before a training program begins, the company runs an I-Opt group profile on all trainees as well as a motivation questionnaire. Data analysis then yields data on an employee's likelihood of success in learning from the course based on course design, their motivation to attend, and the style of the facilitator.

Course facilitators receive a report prior to a training session that allows them to adjust course delivery, content, and design based on the learning styles of the trainees. Facilitators can then make any necessary changes to the content of a program. They must also be fluid in each of the different learning styles so that they can shift their methods to match the styles of trainees.

In addition, employees are given cards that indicate their personal learning style. Before and after a training session, they can give the cards to the instructor for an instant "style" check, allowing the instructor to fine-tune his or her delivery on the fly.

Source: Barbian, J. (2002, March). Training top 100: AmeriCredit. *Training, 39*(3), 46–47.

Preferred learning styles refer to distinct perceptual tendencies such as logical-mathematical, visual-spatial, musical, linguistic, and so on. Accelerated learning involves identifying an individual's preferred learning style and then tailoring the learning experience around it. This might involve the use of pictures, music, and/or physical activities to stimulate learning. And as is typical of adult learning, accelerated learning takes into account what the learner already knows and if they prefer to learn individually or in groups.[27]

In summary, how people learn and the success of their learning experiences depends in part on their learning styles and preferences as well as the nature of their learning experiences. Learning and the success of a training program is also a function of people's motivation, a topic that we will focus on in the remainder of this chapter.

Theories of Motivation

Motivation is an important predictor of performance and as you will learn shortly, it is also a key factor for learning and training. Therefore, it is important to first understand what motivation is, the major theories of motivation, and the implications for training and development.

Motivation refers to the degree of persistent effort that one directs toward a goal. Therefore, motivation has to do with effort or how hard one works; persistence or the extent to which one keeps at a task; and direction,

Motivation

The degree of persistent effort that one directs toward a goal or the extent to which one applies their effort and persistence towards a meaningful goal. In organizations, this usually means that one directs their effort and persistence towards organization goals or in a manner that benefits the organization such as high productivity or excellent customer service.

There are two forms of motivation: extrinsic and intrinsic motivation. **Extrinsic motivation** is associated with factors in the external environment such as pay, fringe benefits, and company policies. These are motivators that are applied by somebody in the work environment such as a supervisor. **Intrinsic motivation** is the result of a direct relationship between a worker and the task. Unlike extrinsic motivation, it is self-applied and includes feelings of achievement, accomplishment, challenge, and competence that are the result of performing a task or one's job.

Theories of motivation can be described as need theories or process theories. Need theories have to do with the things that motivate people and the conditions in which they will be motivated to satisfy them.

Process theories of motivation address the process of motivation and how motivation occurs. In the remainder of this section, we will describe need theories of motivation as well as two process theories of motivation (expectancy theory and goal setting theory).

Need Theories

Need theories of motivation are concerned with the needs people have and the conditions in which they will be motivated to satisfy them. Needs refer to physiological and psychological desires. In organizations, individuals can satisfy their needs by obtaining incentives such as money to satisfy physiological needs, or by challenging work that allows them to fulfill higher-level psychological needs. Therefore, needs are motivational to the extent that people are motivated to obtain things that will satisfy their needs.

The best known need theory of motivation is Abraham Maslow's need hierarchy. According to Maslow, humans have five sets of needs that are arranged in a hierarchy with the most basic needs at the bottom of the hierarchy and higher order needs at the upper levels of the hierarchy. The five needs from lowest to highest are physiological, security, belongingness, esteem, and self-actualization needs.[28]

Physiological needs are needs that people must satisfy to survive and include things such as food, water, and shelter. Physiological needs can usually be satisfied with pay. Safety needs refer to needs for security, stability, and freedom from anxiety. Safe working conditions and job security can satisfy safety needs. Belongingness needs have to do with the need for social interaction, companionship, and friendship. The opportunity to interact with others at work and friendly and supportive co-workers and supervision can satisfy belongingness needs. Esteem needs have to do with feelings of competence and appreciation and recognition by others. The opportunity to learn new things and challenging work can satisfy esteem needs.

Extrinsic motivation

Motivation that stems from factors in the external environment such as pay, fringe benefits, and company policies

Intrinsic motivation

Motivation that stems from a direct relationship between a worker and the task

The highest need in Maslow's hierarchy is self-actualization needs. Self-actualization involves developing one's true potential as an individual and experiencing personal fulfillment. This can be fulfilled by work experiences that involve opportunities for creativity, growth, and self-development.

According to Maslow, people are motivated to satisfy their lowest level unsatisfied need. If one's physiological need is unsatisfied, then they will be motivated to satisfy it. The basic premise is that the lowest level unsatisfied need has the greatest motivating potential, which means that motivation depends on one's position in the need hierarchy. Once a need has been satisfied it will no longer be motivational and the next highest need in the hierarchy will become motivational. The one exception to this is the self-actualization need, which becomes stronger.[29]

Another need theory of motivation was developed by Clayton Alderfer. Alderfer's ERG theory consists of three needs. Existence needs are similar to Maslow's physiological and security needs. Relatedness needs are similar to Maslow's belongingness need. And growth needs are similar to Maslow's esteem and self-actualization needs. [30]

Alderfer's ERG theory differs from Maslow's need theory in a number of ways. To begin with, ERG theory is not a rigid hierarchy of needs in which one must move up the hierarchy in a lock-step fashion. Although both theories argue that once a lower-level need is satisfied the desire for higher level needs will increase, ERG theory does not state that a lower-level need must be gratified before a higher level need becomes motivational. Thus, one can be motivated to fulfill relatedness or growth needs even if they have not fulfilled their existence needs. Maslow, however, would argue that a lower need must first be satisfied before a higher level need will become motivational.

Another difference is that ERG theory states that if individuals are unable to satisfy a higher level need, the desire to satisfy a lower level need will increase. Maslow of course would say that this is not possible because once a need has been satisfied it is no longer motivational.

Regardless of their differences, both Maslow's and Alderfer's need theories have important implications for training and development. They highlight the fact that employees' needs must be considered in the design of a training program. For example, if trainees' needs are not being fulfilled on the job then their behaviour and performance is not likely to change as a result of a training program unless the training program leads to need fulfillment. Improving employees' knowledge and skill through training and development will be most effective when employees are motivated on the job.

Another implication of need theories for training and development has to do with employees' motivation to attend a training program, to learn the training material, and to apply it on the job. Employees are not likely to be motivated to attend training or to learn and apply the training material if doing so does not fulfill their needs. Therefore, trainers and managers should be aware of trainees' needs and ensure that training programs are designed in part to fulfill them.

Expectancy Theory

Expectancy theory is a process theory of motivation. According to expectancy theory, the energy or force that a person directs toward an activity is a direct result of a number of factors. These factors are known as expectancy, instrumentality, and valence:[31]

1. Expectancy refers to an individual's subjective probability that they can achieve a particular level of performance on a task. For example, what is the probability that you can get an "A" in this course? What is the probability that you can get a "C" in this course? These outcomes are referred to as first level outcomes since they are a direct result of one's effort or motivational force.

2. Instrumentality refers to the subjective likelihood that attainment of a first level outcome such as an "A" or "C" in this course will lead to attractive consequences that are known as second level outcomes. The consequences can be either intrinsic or extrinsic outcomes. For example, what is the probability that an "A" in this course will result in a job offer or a sense of accomplishment? What is the probability that a "C" will result in a job offer or a sense of accomplishment?

3. Valence refers to the attractiveness of the first and second level outcomes. The attractiveness of a second level outcome such as a job offer or a sense of accomplishment is simply one's subjective ratings. For example, on a scale of 1 to 10 with 10 being the most attractive, how attractive would you rate receiving a job offer? The valence or attractiveness of a first level outcome (an "A" or "C" grade in this course) is a result of the instrumentalities multiplied by the valence of each second level outcome ($I \times V$). For example, the attractiveness of receiving an "A" in this course would be a function of:

Instrumentality (the probability of receiving a job offer) $\times$ the valence of receiving a job offer + Instrumentality (the probability of experiencing a sense of fulfillment) $\times$ the valence of experiencing a sense of fulfillment.

This calculation will determine the valence or attractiveness of the first level outcome (receiving an "A" in this course). The same calculation would also be done to determine the valence of receiving a grade of "C" in the course.

To determine one's motivation or effort, the expectancy or probability of receiving an "A" or "C" grade must be multiplied by the valence of the first level outcomes. This would result in a force or motivational value for pursuing an "A" and a "C" grade. In other words, it will indicate what grade you are most motivated to attain. If you feel that you can put in the effort and time required to obtain an "A" (i.e., your expectancy), and you believe that obtaining an "A" will result in a high probability of getting a job offer and experiencing a sense of accomplishment (instrumentality), then chances are you will be motivated to get an "A" in the course.

The expectancy theory linkages can be written as the following equation:

$$\text{Effort} = \text{Expectancy} \times (\text{Instrumentality} \times \text{Valence})$$

In effect, what all this means is that one's effort or motivation is a function of people's beliefs that they can achieve a particular level of performance (first level outcome), and that this will lead to consequences that are attractive to them (the valence of the first level outcome). The attractiveness of a first level outcome is simply the probability that it will lead to attractive consequences (e.g., the probability that getting an "A" in the course will result in a job offer and a sense of fulfillment). Thus, you are likely to be motivated to obtain an "A" in this course if you believe that there is a high probability that you can get an "A" and if you believe that getting an "A" will lead to consequences that are attractive to you.

There are a number of implications of expectancy theory for training and development. First, trainees must believe that there is a high probability that they will be able to learn the training material and fulfill the training objective(s) (high expectancy). Second, learning the training material and fulfilling the training objectives must result in consequences (high instrumentality) that are attractive to trainees (high valence of second level outcomes). Simply put, you are more likely to learn something if you believe that you can in fact learn it and that you will be rewarded with something that is attractive to you once it has been learned.

The major implication of expectancy theory for training revolves around trainees' motivation to attend a training program, to learn, and to apply what is learned on the job. Along these lines, trainees must believe that there is a high probability that they will be able to learn and apply the training material, and that doing so will result in a number of attractive consequences for them.

Goal-Setting Theory

Another process theory of motivation with implications for training and development is goal-setting theory. Goal-setting theory is based on the idea that people's intentions are a good predictor of their behaviour.

According to the theory, goals are motivational because they direct people's efforts and energies and lead to the development of strategies to help them reach their goals. For goals to be motivational, however, they must have a number of characteristics.

First, goals must be *specific* in terms of their level and time frame. General goals that lack specificity tend not to be motivational. Second, goals must be *challenging* to be motivational. Goals should not be so easy that they require little effort to achieve, and they should not be so difficult that they are impossible to reach. Third, goals must be accompanied by *feedback* so that it is possible to know how well one is doing and how close one is to goal accomplishment. Finally, for goals to be motivational, people must accept them and be *committed* to them. [32]

Research on goal-setting theory has provided strong support for the motivational effects of goals. Studies across a wide variety of settings have consistently shown that challenging and specific goals that are accompanied with performance feedback result in higher levels of individual and group performance.[33]

Chapter 3: Learning and Motivation

Another important characteristic of goals that is particularly important for learning and training is the type of goal or what is known as goal orientation. There are two general types of goal orientations—a learning goal and a performance goal orientation.

Learning goals are process-oriented and focus on the learning process. They enhance understanding of the task and the use of task strategies. **Performance goals** are outcome-oriented goals that focus attention on the achievement of specific performance outcomes.

Goal orientation is important because it can influence task performance as well as cognitive, affective, and motivational processes. There is evidence that the type of goal set (i.e., learning versus performance) affects skill acquisition and self-efficacy. Learning goals appear to lead to faster skill acquisition and task self-efficacy.[34]

There is also evidence that individuals differ with respect to their goal orientation or goal preference. In other words, goal orientation has been found to be a stable individual difference such that some individuals have a preference for learning goals while others have a preference for performance goals. Individuals with a learning goal orientation are concerned more about developing competence by acquiring new skills and mastering new situations. Individuals with a performance goal orientation are more concerned about demonstrating their competence by seeking favourable judgments and avoiding negative judgments.

Research has found that a learning goal orientation is especially important for performance and leads to higher performance compared to a performance goal orientation. One study on the salespeople of a medical supplies distributor found that a learning goal orientation was positively related to sales performance but a performance goal orientation was not. A learning goal orientation has also been found to be positively related to effort, self-efficacy, and goal-setting level. Thus, learning goals appear to be important for motivation and learning outcomes.[35]

Goal-setting theory has a number of implications for training. For example, before training begins trainees should have specific and challenging goals for learning, and they should be provided with feedback during and after the training program so that they know if they have accomplished their learning goals. Setting specific and challenging goals should improve trainees' motivation to learn as well as their performance on the training task.

In addition to setting specific and challenging goals and providing feedback, trainers must also consider the goal orientation of trainees and the type of goals that are set for training. Learning goals that focus on skill development appear to be particularly important for learning, especially for individuals who have a performance goal orientation and need to be given learning goals for training. Although individuals tend to differ in their preference for a learning or performance goal, it is possible to influence goal orientation. Therefore, trainers should emphasize the importance and need to focus on learning goals during training. High learning goals appear to be especially important for challenging tasks and when new skills must be learned.[36]

Learning goals

Process-oriented goals that focus on the learning process

Performance goals

Outcome-oriented goals that focus attention on the achievement of specific performance outcomes

Training Motivation

In the previous section, we described a number of theories of motivation and their implications for training and development. In this section, we will focus more specifically on the role of motivation in training. In particular, we will introduce the concept of *training motivation* and describe both the predictors and consequences of trainees' motivation to learn.

Training motivation or motivation to learn refers to the direction, intensity, and persistence of learning-directed behaviour in training contexts. Research has found that training motivation predicts learning and training outcomes and is influenced by individual and situational factors.[37]

Among the individual factors that predict training motivation, personality variables as well as factors associated with one's job and career are important. Personality variables that predict training motivation include locus of control, achievement motivation, anxiety, and conscientiousness.

Locus of control refers to people's beliefs about whether their behaviour is controlled mainly by internal or external forces. Persons with an internal locus of control believe that the opportunity to control their own behaviour resides within themselves. Persons with an external locus of control believe that external forces determine their behaviour. Thus, internals perceive stronger links between the effort they put into something and the outcome or performance level they achieve. Persons with an internal locus of control tend to have higher levels of training motivation.

In addition, persons who are high in achievement motivation or the desire to perform challenging tasks and high on conscientiousness also tend to have high training motivation. Persons with higher anxiety, however, tend to have lower training motivation. Self-efficacy is also positively related to training motivation.

Several job and career variables are related to training motivation as well. For example, employees with higher job involvement or the degree to which an individual identifies psychologically with work and the importance of work to their self-image have higher training motivation. Organizational commitment and career planning and exploration are also associated with higher training motivation. Organizational variables such as supervisor support, peer support, and a positive climate also predict training motivation.

Training motivation is important because it is related to a number of training outcomes. For example, training motivation is positively related to declarative knowledge and skill acquisition. It is also related to trainees' reactions to training and the likelihood that trainees apply what they learn in training on the job.

There are at least two things a trainer can do to ensure that trainees' motivation to learn is high. First, they can assess trainee motivation prior to a training program. In fact, this is what the auto finance company, AmeriCredit does. Employees complete a motivation questionnaire that is used to predict their likelihood of success in learning from a training program.[38] Second, trainers and managers can try to increase trainees' motivation to learn by demonstrating the importance and relevance of training for their job performance.

Training motivation

The direction, intensity, and persistence of learning-directed behaviour in training contexts

Locus of control

People's beliefs about whether their behaviour is controlled mainly by internal or external forces

In summary, training motivation or trainees' motivation to learn is an important factor in the training process. Training is more likely to be effective and result in learning, skill acquisition, and improved job performance when trainees are motivated to learn.[39] Thus, it is important that trainers understand the importance of training motivation and increase trainees' motivation to learn early in the training process.

A Model of Training Effectiveness

In this final section of the chapter, we present a model of training effectiveness that highlights the linkages between training and learning as well as between learning and individual and organizational performance.

Figure 3.2 presents the model. Recall from Chapter 1 that training involves the acquisition of knowledge, skills, and abilities to improve performance on one's current job, and development refers to the acquisition of knowledge, skills, and abilities required to perform future job responsibilities. Thus, the first important link in the model is a path from training to learning and retention. In other words, training leads to declarative knowledge and the acquisition of skills and abilities and the retention of them over time.

In addition to training, we also know that there are personal factors that influence learning. Among the most important is cognitive ability, which is one of the most often examined individual characteristics in training research. Cognitive or mental ability is similar to intelligence. It reflects an individual's basic information processing capacities and cognitive resources. It generally refers to the knowledge and skills an individual possesses and may include cognitive skills and psychomotor skills. Examples of cognitive skills include basic numeracy and literacy, the intelligence to learn complex rules and procedures, and so on. Cognitive ability (verbal comprehension, quantitative ability, and reasoning ability) is related to the ability to learn and to succeed on the job.

Recall the earlier discussion of ACT theory in which it was noted that cognitive ability is particularly important during the early stages of learning. In fact, research has consistently shown that general cognitive ability is a strong predictor of learning, training success, and job performance. It is an especially good predictor of job performance on complex jobs. In training research, cognitive ability has been found to predict declarative knowledge, skill acquisition, and transfer.[40]

In addition to cognitive ability, training motivation is also a strong predictor of learning and training outcomes. Like cognitive ability, training motivation predicts declarative knowledge, skill acquisition, and the application of trained skills on the job. Self-efficacy and personality characteristics also have an effect on learning. Trainees with higher self-efficacy are more likely to learn during training. In addition, trainees with an internal locus of control and a high need for achievement also learn more during training.

An additional factor that can influence learning is trainees' attitudes. Three attitudinal variables that are important for learning are job involvement, job satisfaction, and organizational commitment. Employees with

Managing Performance Through Training and Development

FIGURE 3.2

Model of Training Effectiveness

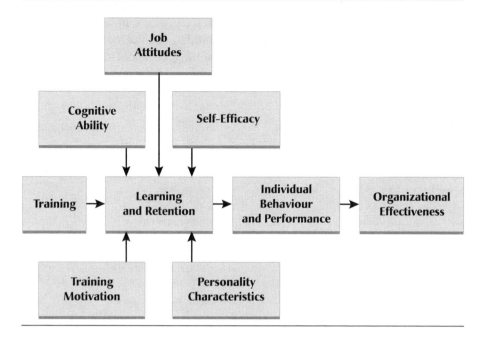

higher job involvement, job satisfaction, and organizational commitment are more likely to learn and apply what they learn on the job.[41]

The model also shows a path from learning to individual behaviour and performance. This is called transfer of training and refers to the application of learning on the job. Learning and retention are a necessary condition for changes in behaviour and job performance.

The final path in the model is between individual behaviour and performance and organizational effectiveness. This path indicates that changes in employees' behaviour and job performance will have an effect on organizational effectiveness.

In summary, the model of training effectiveness shows how training and personal factors influence learning and retention. We will further develop the model in Chapter 5 when we discuss training design, and again in Chapter 9 when we discuss the transfer of training.

Summary

We began this chapter by stating that a major goal of all training and development programs is learning. We also described five learning outcomes that can result from training and development programs. The learning process was described in terms of three stages (declarative, knowledge compilation, and procedural knowledge), and two major theories of learning (conditioning theory and social learning theory) were presented. We also discussed adult learning theory and learning styles and their implications for training and development.

This chapter also described several need theories and process theories of motivation along with their implications for the design of training programs. Training motivation was also discussed with particular emphasis on its predictors and consequences. The chapter concluded with a model of training effectiveness that shows the links between training, personal factors, and attitudes with learning and retention.

Key Terms

accelerated learning (page 64)

andragogy (page 62)

chaining (page 59)

declarative knowledge (page 56)

extrinsic motivation (page 66)

generalization (page 59)

intrinsic motivation (page 66)

knowledge compilation (page 56)

learning (page 55)

learning goals (page 70)

learning style (page 63)

locus of control (page 71)

motivation (page 65)

observation (page 60)

pedagogy (page 62)

performance goals (page 70)

procedural knowledge (page 57)

self-efficacy (page 60)

self-management (page 61)

shaping (page 59)

training motivation (page 71)

Weblinks

Capital One: www.capitalone.com (page 58)

Edward Jones: www.edwardjones.com (page 60)

McMaster University: www.mcmaster.ca (page 62)

Discussion Questions

1. Given the importance of training motivation for learning and other training outcomes, what should trainers do to ensure that trainees are motivated to learn? Discuss the pros and cons of different approaches.
2. Debate the following: Given that cognitive ability is a strong predictor of learning, only trainees with high cognitive ability should be allowed to attend training since those with low cognitive ability are not likely to learn and benefit from costly training programs.
3. What are the differences between pedagogy and andragogy and what are the implications of adult learning theory for the design of training programs?
4. Discuss Kolb's four learning styles and the implications of them for the design of training programs. How should training programs be designed if people differ in their learning style?

Using the Internet

1. Learn about your learning and motivation styles, by visiting the Learnativity website at **www.learnativity.com**. To find out your preferred learning style, click on "Learning Styles Assessment" and complete the assessment. To find out about your motivation style, click on "Motivation Styles Assessment" and complete the assessment. Write a brief report in which you indicate your primary and auxiliary learning style, and your primary and auxiliary motivation style. What do your results say about your learning and motivation preferences, and what are the implications of this for your learning? What can you do with this information to improve your learning?

Exercises

1. If you had a friend who was about to attend a training program on how to use computers and she has very low self-efficacy about her ability to learn and use a computer, what would you do to increase her self-efficacy? Describe some of the things you might do prior to the training program to increase your friend's self-efficacy to learn how to use a computer.
2. Consider Kolb's four learning modes and how they might apply to your course on training and development or another course you are taking. How might you structure the course so that students' learning occurs in the following sequence of experiences: concrete experience, reflective observation, abstract conceptualization, and active experimentation. Be specific in terms of what the instructor will have students do at each stage of the learning cycle.
3. Using the material on goal setting theory, set a goal for your training and development course. That is, set a specific and challenging goal that you will be committed to. In addition, determine how and when you will be able to obtain feedback. Be sure to also set a learning goal and a performance goal. Once you have set your goals, meet with another member of the class and review and evaluate each other's goals for the course.
4. Consider a course you are currently taking and examine it in terms of adult learning theory. To what extent does your course incorporate the principles of adult learning theory? What aspects of the course incorporate adult learning theory and what aspects do not? If you were to redesign the course to make it more consistent with adult learning theory, what are some of the things you would change and do?
5. Training motivation is an important predictor of training outcomes so it is important that trainers ensure that trainees' motivation to learn is high. You might have noticed how your own motivation to learn influences your performance in a course or training program. Using each of

the theories of motivation (Maslow, Alderfer, expectancy, and goal setting), describe what a course instructor or trainer might do to increase students' or trainees' motivation to learn. Be specific in describing the techniques that follow from each theory.

6. Review the model of training effectiveness in Figure 3.2. Assess your potential learning and retention of a course you are currently taking by evaluating yourself as best you can on each of the predictors in the model (i.e., cognitive ability, attitudes, self-efficacy, personality characteristics, and training motivation). Based on your assessment, how successful will your learning and retention of the course material be? What predictors can you try to change in order to enhance your potential learning and retention of the course material?

7. Review the material on self-management in the chapter and then design a self-management program to help you learn and improve a skill or behaviour that you want to improve (e.g., making presentations, time management, exercise program, quit smoking, etc.). Once you have chosen a skill or behaviour, prepare a self-management program. Be specific in terms of what exactly you are going to do at each step in the process (i.e., how and when you will observe and keep track of your behaviour and observe the behaviour of others; set specific performance goals; when you will practise and rehearse the desired behaviours; how you will keep track of your progress; and how you will reward yourself for goal achievement). Once you have prepared your program, meet with another member of the class to review and evaluate each other's self-management program.

Case

THE PERFORMANCE APPRAISAL TRAINING PROGRAM

The performance appraisal process is an important part of employee evaluation and development. It not only allows an organization to keep track of employee performance, but it also provides employees' with performance feedback and a chance to develop an action plan to improve performance. Unfortunately, many organizations do not conduct performance appraisals and managers tend to not like doing them.

This was the case at a large hospital where nurse supervisors seldom met with nurses to review and discuss their performance. At the same time, the administration was introducing a new model of nursing that required the nurses to perform certain key behaviours when interacting with and counseling patients and their families. It was therefore imperative that performance appraisals be conducted to ensure that nurses were implementing the new model of nursing.

The administration decided to hire a performance management consultant to provide a one-day workshop on how to conduct performance appraisals for all nurse supervisors. The nurse supervisors would be required to evaluate their nurses' performance every six months and then conduct a performance appraisal interview with each nurse in which the previous six months' performance would be discussed. An action plan would then be developed with specific goals for improvement.

Many of the supervisors seldom conducted performance appraisal interviews and some had never done one. They complained that there was no time to meet with every nurse and that it was a difficult and unpleasant process that was a waste of time. Some were uncomfortable with the process and found it to be very stressful for everybody concerned. They said that it caused a lot of anxiety for them and the nurses.

Nonetheless, the training program was mandatory and all nurse supervisors had to attend. Many of them reluctantly did so complaining that it would be a waste of time and that it would not make any difference in how things were done in the hospital.

The training program began with a lecture about how to conduct performance appraisal interviews. The consultant first explained that the purpose of a performance appraisal interview is to give feedback to employees on how well they are performing their jobs and then plan for future growth and development. He then discussed different types of performance appraisal interviews such as the "tell-and-sell interview," the "tell-and-listen interview," and the "problem-solving interview." This was followed by a list of guidelines on how to conduct effective interviews such as asking the employee to do a self-assessment, focus on behaviour not the person, minimize criticism, focus on problem-solving, and be supportive. The trainees were then instructed on how to set goals and develop an action plan for improvement.

After the lecture the trainees were asked to conduct role plays in which they take turns playing the part of a supervisor and employee. They were provided with information about a nurse's job performance and had to discuss it in the role play and then develop an action plan. However, some of the trainees left the session at this time refusing to participate. Others did not take it seriously and made a joke out it. There was a lot of laughing and joking throughout this part of the program.

After the role play there was a group discussion about the role-play experience and this was followed by a review of the key points to remember when conducting performance appraisal interviews.

Although the supervisors were supposed to begin conducting performance appraisal interviews shortly after the training program, very few actually did. Some said they tried to do them but could not find time to interview all of their nurses. Others said that they followed the consultant's guidelines but they did not see any improvement in how they conducted interviews or in how nurses reacted to them. Some said it continued to be a stressful experience that was uncomfortable for them and their nurses and decided to stop doing them.

Performance appraisal interviews were still a rare occurrence at the hospital one year later. Furthermore, many of the nurses were not practising the new nursing model and as a result, nursing care was inconsistent throughout the hospital and often unsatisfactory.

Questions

1. Consider the relevance of Gagne's learning outcomes for the performance appraisal interview training program. What were some of the expected learning outcomes of the training program and what did trainees learn?

2. Explain the success of the training program using conditioning theory and social learning theory. How do these theories explain why the training program was not more effective, and how could the program be improved using some of the concepts from each theory?

3. Discuss the extent to which adult learning principles were incorporated into the training program. What principles were included and which ones were absent? What could the consultant have done differently to make better use of adult learning theory principles?

4. Evaluate the training program in terms of Kolb's learning styles and learning cycle. What aspects of the program relate to each of the modes of learning? What learning style or styles are most likely to benefit from the program and which ones are not? How could the program be changed to make better use of Kolb's learning cycle?

5. Comment on the supervisor's motivation to learn. What effect might their motivation to learn have had on the success of the training program? Using the different theories of motivation, explain how the hospital administration and the consultant might have increased the supervisor's motivation to learn.

References

[1]Schettler, J. (2002, August). Welcome to ACME Inc. *Training, 39* (8), pp. 36–43.

[2]Hinrichs, J.R. (1976). Personnel training. In Dunnette, M.D. (Ed.), *Handbook of industrial and organizational psychology* (pp. 829–60). Skokie, IL: Rand McNally.

[3]Hinrichs, J.R. (1976).

[4]Gagne, R.M. (1984). Learning outcomes and their effects: Useful categories of human performance. *American Psychologist 39*, 377–85.

[5]Zemke, R. (1999). Toward a science of training. *Training 36* (7), 32–36.

[6]Kanfer, R., & Ackerman, P. L. (1989). Motivation and cognitive abilities: An integrative/aptitude-treatment interaction approach to skill acquisition. *Journal of Applied Psychology, 74*, 657–90.

[7]Kanfer, R., & Ackerman, P. L. (1989).

[8]Skinner, B.F. (1953). *Science and human behaviour*. New York: McMillan.

[9]Delahoussaye, M. (2001, March). Training top 50: Capital One. *Training, 38*(3), 70–71.

[10]Pearce, J.M. (1987). A model of stimulus generalization in Pavlovian conditioning. *Psychological Review, 94*, 61–73.

[11]Bandura, A. (1986). *Social foundations of thought and action: A social cognitive theory*. Englewood Cliffs, NJ: Prentice-Hall.

[12]Luthans, F., & Davis, T. (1983). Beyond modelling: Managing social learning processes in human resource training and development. In Baird, C., Schneier, E., & Laird, D (Eds.), *The training and development sourcebook*. Amherst, MA: Human Resource Development Press.

[13]McLaughlin, K. (2001, March). Training top 50: Edward Jones. *Training, 38*(3), 78–79.

[14]Bandura, A. (1997). *Self-efficacy: The exercise of control*. New York: W.H. Freeman & Co.

[15]Bandura, A. (1997).

[16]Haccoun, R.R., & Saks, A.M. (1998). Training in the twenty-first century: Some lessons from the last one. *Canadian Psychology, 39*, 33–51.

[17]Bandura, A. (1986).

[18]Frayne, C.A., & Latham, G.P. (1987). Application of social learning theory to employee self-management of attendance. *Journal of Applied Psychology, 72,* 387–92. Latham, G.P., & Frayne, C.A. (1989). Self-management training for increasing job attendance: A follow-up and a replication. *Journal of Applied Psychology, 74,* 411–16.

[19]Gist, M.E., Stevens, C.K., & Bavetta, A.G. (1991). Effects of self-efficacy and post-training intervention on the acquisition and maintenance of complex interpersonal skills. *Personnel Psychology, 44,* 837–61.

[20]Knowles, M. (1990). *The adult learner.* Gulf Publishing: Houston, TX.

[21]Kolb, D. A. (1984). *Experiential learning.* Englewood Cliffs, NJ: Prentice-Hall.

[22]Kolb, D. A. (1984).

[23]Kolb, D. A. (1984).

[24]Whetten, D. A., & Cameron, K. S. (2002). *Developing management skills* (Fifth Edition). Upper Saddle River, NJ: Prentice Hall.

[25]Delahoussaye, M. (2001, March).

[26]Adams, C. (2001, November). Learning in the fast lane. *The Training Report,* 1–3.

[27]Adams, C. (2001, November).

[28]Maslow. A. H. (1970). *Motivation and personality* (2nd edition). New York: Harper & Row.

[29]Maslow. A. H. (1970).

[30]Alderfer, C. P. (1969). An empirical test of a new theory of human needs. *Organizational Behavior and Human Performance, 4,* 142–75.

[31]Vroom. V. H. (1964). *Work and motivation.* New York: Wiley.

[32]Locke, E.A., & Latham, G.P. (1990). *A theory of goal setting and task performance.* Englewood Cliffs, NJ: Prentice-Hall.

[33]Locke, E.A., & Latham, G.P. (1990).

[34]Cannon-Bowers, J. A., Rhodenizer, L., Salas, E., & Bowers, C. A. (1998). A framework for understanding pre-practice conditions and their impact on learning. *Personnel Psychology, 51,* 291–320.

[35]VandeWalle, D., Cron, W. L., & Slocum, J.W. Jr. (2001). The role of goal orientation following performance feedback. *Journal of Applied Psychology, 86,* 629–40.

[36]VandeWalle, D., Brown, S. P., Cron, W. L., & Slocum, J. W. Jr. (1999). The influence of goal orientation and self-regulation tactics on sales performance: A longitudinal field test. *Journal of Applied Psychology, 84,* 249–259. VandeWalle, D., Cron, W. L., & Slocum, J.W. Jr. (2001). The role of goal orientation following performance feedback. *Journal of Applied Psychology, 86,* 629–40.

[37]Colquitt, J. A., Lepine, A., & Noe, R. A. (2000). Toward an integrative theory of training motivation: A meta-analytic path analysis of 20 years of research. *Journal of Applied Psychology, 85,* 678–707.

[38]Barbian, J. (2002, March). Training top 100: AmeriCredit. *Training, 39*(3), 46–47.

[39]Colquitt, J. A., Lepine, A., & Noe, R. A. (2000).

[40]Colquitt, J. A., Lepine, A., & Noe, R. A. (2000).

[41]Burke, L. A. (2001). Training transfer: Ensuring training gets used on the job. In L. A. Burke (Ed.), *High-Impact Training Solutions: Top Issues Troubling Trainers.* Quorum Books: Westport, CT. Colquitt, J. A., Lepine, A., & Noe, R. A. (2000).

Chapter 4

The Needs Analysis Process

www.cfbsuffield
mfrc.org

CFB SUFFIELD

On a base once known as a secretive centre for biological and chemical warfare research, located on a section of windswept and barren prairie the size of Prince Edward Island in southeast Alberta, municipal emergency response teams are practising for bioterrorist attacks as part of a counterterrorism training program.

CFB Suffield is the only place within NATO where troops can train outside with live chemical agents, one reason it recently attracted a Toronto emergency response team and a group of U.S. Marines now on duty in Afghanistan.

Toronto dispatched a group of police, firefighters, and paramedics to Suffield, where they handled the liquid form of sarin and mustard gas in a series of simulated terrorist attacks designed to replicate a chemical assault on a major Canadian city. Ottawa-Carleton and Calgary have also done so.

Wearing sealed protective suits and respirators under the searing sun, they practised detecting and decontaminating the blistering agent, and treating mass casualties after a mock terrorist attack.

In another exercise, they handled liquid sarin at a simulated terrorist lab after a mock leak. The nerve agent was made famous when terrorists used it in a gas form during a 1995 attack on the Tokyo subway system.

In addition to a mock terrorist lab, the base has a plane, bus, and post office as well as a mock subway station to replicate possible terrorist targets for training purposes. Several federal government reports have cautioned in recent years that cities were ill prepared to respond to a commercial chemical accident, while almost none were prepared for a chemical or biological attack.

After the terrorist attacks on the U.S. on September 11, 2001, cities such as Toronto responded with improved equipment and co-ordination among police, fire, and medical staff and training at Suffield where a new counterterrorism centre is under construction.[1]

This vignette highlights an important aspect of the training and development process. Events and concerns inside and outside of an organization can lead to the need for new knowledge, skills, and abilities and training programs. Prior to September 11, 2001, the type of training taking place at CFB Suffield would not have been considered by Canadian cities. However, the terrorist attacks of September 11 have created a strong need for this type of training. This is clearly a very good example of the link between the environment and the need for training as described in Chapter 1. It also demonstrates the important role of a needs analysis in the training and development process. In this chapter, you will learn about the needs analysis process and how to determine if training is the best solution to performance problems.

What is a Needs Analysis?

Needs analysis is the cornerstone and foundation of training and development. In fact, it is often referred to as the most important step in the training and development process.[2] **Needs analysis** (also known as needs assessment) is a process designed to identify gaps or deficiencies in employee and organizational performance. Needs analysis is concerned with the gaps between actual performance and desired performance. It is a "formal process of identifying needs as gaps between current and desired results, placing those needs in priority order based on the cost to meet each need versus the cost for ignoring it, and selecting the most important needs (problems or opportunities) for reduction or elimination."[3]

Needs analysis

A process to identify gaps or deficiencies in employee and organizational performance

Needs analysis helps to identify gaps or deficiencies in individual, group, or organizational performance. The way to identify performance gaps is to solicit information from those who are affected by the performance problem. A needs analyst gathers information from key people in an organization about the organization, jobs, and employees to determine the nature of performance problems. This information identifies the problem, which is simply the difference between the way the work is being done and the most cost-effective way of doing it. In the simplest terms, needs = required results – current results.[4]

The goal of needs analysis is to identify the differences between what is and what is desired or required in terms of results, and to compare the magnitude of gaps against the cost of reducing them or ignoring them. Obviously, performance gaps could be the result of many factors, and the solutions might include training as well as other interventions. A thorough needs analysis can help an organization prioritize its needs and make informed decisions as to what problems need to be resolved. Thus, needs analysis identifies, prioritizes, and selects needs that will have an impact on internal and external stakeholders.[5] A needs analysis helps to identify the causes and solutions to performance problems.

The Needs Analysis Process

Needs analysis is a process that consists of a series of interrelated steps. Figure 4.1 outlines the needs analysis process that we will be discussing in this chapter. As described in Chapter 1, the process starts with an *itch* or a problem. If the performance problem is important, stakeholders are consulted and a needs analysis is conducted. There are three levels of needs analysis: an organizational analysis, a task analysis, and a person analysis. The collection of information and the needs analysis process concludes with a number of important outcomes.

FIGURE 4.1

The Needs Analysis Process

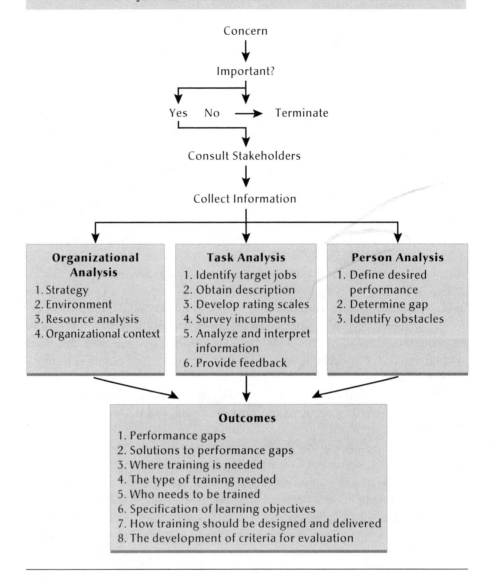

Concern

↓

Important?

Yes   No ⟶ Terminate

↓

Consult Stakeholders

↓

Collect Information

Organizational Analysis
1. Strategy
2. Environment
3. Resource analysis
4. Organizational context

Task Analysis
1. Identify target jobs
2. Obtain description
3. Develop rating scales
4. Survey incumbents
5. Analyze and interpret information
6. Provide feedback

Person Analysis
1. Define desired performance
2. Determine gap
3. Identify obstacles

Outcomes
1. Performance gaps
2. Solutions to performance gaps
3. Where training is needed
4. The type of training needed
5. Who needs to be trained
6. Specification of learning objectives
7. How training should be designed and delivered
8. The development of criteria for evaluation

Step One: A Concern

The process of identifying training needs originates slowly and informally with a concern. This concern is sometimes referred to as an *itch* or a *pressure point*, something that causes managers to notice it. This concern might be as subtle as noticing that employees are treating customers in an abrupt manner, or observing that employees are spending a lot of time asking one another for help with a new system. Other concerns might be recognizing a shift in regular activities, such as an increase in defective parts, accidents, or complaints.[6]

Sometimes the pressure comes from the external environment such as when legislation regarding employee relations is changed, or the competition

84   Managing Performance Through Training and Development   NEL

introduces a highly competitive service feature. At IBM, one needs-identification program began with the CEO's comment that about 10 percent of all complaints addressed to him involved client dissatisfaction with IBM's handling of telephone calls.[7]

Step Two: Its Importance

After a concern has been raised, the next step is to determine if the concern is central to the effectiveness of the organization. The training manager must be aware of the strategic orientation of the organization. The goals, plans, introduction of products and services, changes in technology, practices, and regulations should be clear. Human resource policies must be linked with the strategic directions of the company as discussed in Chapter 1 and the training strategy should support the organization's efforts to achieve its goals.[8]

In IBM's case, one strategic goal was customer satisfaction, and further analysis revealed that 70 percent of all customer contact was by telephone. The complaints about telephone calls had to be taken seriously because the concern was central to the effectiveness of the organization.[9]

Another important concern is saving money. Does current performance cost the company in lost productivity or dissatisfied customers? If the performance problem is important, then there must be some way to demonstrate that correcting the problem will result in increased productivity or client satisfaction. A concern is important (i.e., worthy of further exploration and analysis), if it has an impact on outcomes that are important to the organization and its effectiveness.

Step Three: Consult Stakeholders

The next step in the needs analysis process is to involve the stakeholders who have a vested interest in the process and outcomes.[10] Support from key players in the organization is necessary from the beginning of the needs analysis process.

At a minimum, top management should understand the rationale for the needs analysis. Training analysts must obtain agreement on why the needs analysis is being done and who will be involved. Managerial expectations must be clarified.[11] Likewise, other stakeholders, such as employees or their collective representatives, should be consulted. At IBM, interviews with employees revealed that they believed they treated customers courteously, and that the managers were antagonistic about learning telephone skills. The attitude was, "just train the secretaries and switchboard operators," even though managers and even financial analysts were receiving calls from customers. The trainers at IBM worked hard to obtain agreement and support from employees on the need for a full analysis. Management sent out a strongly worded message to employees that there was a problem and that together they were going to fix it. Indeed, the manager of U.S. operations made telephone effectiveness one of five key measures of effectiveness. (The others included profit and revenue measures.)[12]

All stakeholders must buy into the needs analysis process to ensure that the data collection will result in accurate information and that they have a vested interest in the success of the program. The linking of the training plans to business strategy and the involvement of key stakeholders resulted in dramatic improvements in customer satisfaction at IBM.

Step Four: Data Collection

The next stage in the needs analysis process is the most extensive and involves the documentation of the concern through the collection of information from three levels of analysis. The three levels of needs analysis are the *organizational*, the *task*, and the *person* or *employee*.

Although overlaps between the three areas of analysis occur, each plays a distinctive role. The analysis of the organization provides information about its strategies and context and answers the question, "Where is training needed in the organization?" The task analysis provides information about the tasks and the relevant knowledge, skills, and abilities needed to perform selected jobs and answers the question, "What knowledge, skills, and abilities are required to perform the job effectively?" And a person analysis provides information about an employee's level of performance and answers the question, "Who needs to be trained?" We describe each level of analysis and the procedures for conducting a needs analysis later in the chapter. Next, we describe some of the outcomes of the needs analysis process.

Needs Analysis Outcomes

At the beginning of this chapter we referred to needs analysis as the cornerstone of the training and development process and noted that it is one of the most important steps. This is due in large part to the outcomes of needs analysis as shown in Figure 4.1.

Once a needs analysis has been completed, the information has to be examined and interpreted. The focus then shifts to an understanding of the performance problem and the search for the most effective solutions.

The needs analysis results in a number of outcomes that set the stage for the rest of the training and development process. Besides clarifying the nature of performance gaps, a needs analysis helps to determine if training and development is a good solution to performance problems or if some other intervention might be more effective. If training and development is part of the solution, a needs analysis sets the stage for the training and development process by identifying where training is needed in the organization, what type of training is required, and who in the organization should receive training.

Needs analysis information is also used to write training objectives and to design training programs (e.g., what training content should be included in the training program, what training methods would be most effective, etc.). Finally, the information obtained from a needs analysis is also used in the development of measures for training evaluation.

Most of the outcomes of the needs analysis process revolve around determining the best solution to performance problems and how to proceed if training is determined to be part of the solution. Later in the chapter we dis-

The climate of an organization refers to the collective attitudes of its employees toward work, supervision, and company goals, policies, and procedures. One aspect of climate that is particularly important for training is the training transfer climate.

Training transfer climate refers to characteristics in the work environment that can either facilitate or inhibit the application of training on the job. A strong training transfer climate is one in which there exists cues that remind employees to apply training material on the job, positive consequences such as feedback and rewards for applying training on the job, and supervisor and peer support for the use of newly acquired skills and abilities. The training transfer climate has been found to be a strong predictor of training effectiveness and whether or not trainees apply newly trained skills on the job.[14]

Another important component of an organization's context is its culture. An organization's culture refers to the shared beliefs and assumptions about how things are done in an organization. Organizations can be differentiated from each other on the basis of their culture. For example, some organizations have innovative cultures while others have risk-taking cultures. One type of culture that is particularly important for training and development is a learning culture.

A **learning culture** refers to a culture in which members of an organization believe that knowledge and skill acquisition are part of their job responsibilities and that learning is an important part of work life in the organization.[15]

Information about an organization's training transfer climate and learning culture is important because it can help to determine if a training program is likely to be effective in an organization as well as whether or not some pre-training intervention is required to improve the climate and/or culture prior to the design and delivery of a training program. It might also indicate that an alternative solution to a performance problem would be more effective than a training program. This is an important part of an organizational analysis because training is not likely to be effective in organizations where the climate for training transfer and/or the culture for learning is not strong.

The influence of the training transfer climate and learning culture on training effectiveness demonstrates how important the role of the organizational context is for a training program's success and the need to conduct an organizational analysis. Whether or not employees apply what they learn in training on the job has a lot to do with an organization's transfer climate and learning culture because they can either facilitate or hinder the implementation and success of a training program.

Once the strategy, environment, resources, and context of an organization have been assessed, the information gathered can be used to determine if a training program is required to help an organization achieve its goals and objectives and if it will be successful. However, additional information is required about the tasks that employees perform, as well as employees' knowledge, skills, and abilities and current level of job performance and task mastery. This additional information can be obtained by conducting a task analysis and a person analysis.

Training transfer climate
Characteristics in the work environment that can either facilitate or inhibit the application of training on the job

Learning culture
A culture in which members of an organization believe that knowledge and skill acquisition are part of their job responsibilities and that learning is an important part of work life in the organization

Task Analysis

Before we discuss task analysis, it is useful to first review the terms used to describe jobs. A job consists of a number of related activities, duties, and tasks. A task is the smallest unit of behaviour studied by the analyst and describes the specific sequence of events necessary to complete a unit of work.

A **task analysis** consists of a description of the activities or work operations performed on a job and the conditions under which these activities are performed. A task analysis reveals the tasks required for a person to perform a job and the knowledge, skills, and abilities that are required to perform the tasks successfully.

There are six steps involved in a task analysis:

1. Identify the target jobs.
2. Obtain a job description.
3. Develop rating scales to rate the importance of each task and the frequency that it is performed.
4. Survey a sample of job incumbents.
5. Analyze and interpret the information.
6. Provide feedback on the results.

1. Identify the Target Jobs

After a problem or performance discrepancy has been identified in an organization, the focus shifts to the job level in order to determine which jobs are contributing to the performance problem and have a performance gap. More than a job title is required here. For example, the title *associate* often describes quite different types of jobs, depending upon the department or level within any organization. These target jobs may be identified by managers.

2. Obtain a Job Description

A **job description** lists the specific duties carried out through the completion of several tasks. In large organizations, most positions have a description of the tasks and minimum qualifications required to do the job. If this description has not been updated within the last year, consult with both the manager and several employees in the position (subject-matter experts) to obtain a current listing of tasks and qualifications. The job description should contain a summary of the major duties of the job, a listing of these duties, the knowledge, skills, and abilities required to perform the task, and the conditions under which they are performed. All tools and specialized knowledge should be listed.

After preparing a job description, the list of duties should be reviewed with subject-matter experts, managers, job incumbents in interviews, or focus groups. The analyst will then develop a list of tasks to be performed; the knowledge, skills, and abilities needed to perform the tasks; a list of necessary tools, software, or equipment; and an understanding of the conditions under which the tasks are performed. You can see that the result looks very much

Task analysis

The process of obtaining information about a job by determining the duties, tasks, and activities involved and the knowledge, skills, and abilities required to perform the tasks

Job description

A statement of the tasks, duties, and responsibilities of a job like a job description with job specifications. (A job specification is a statement of the knowledge, skills, and abilities required to perform a job.)

Creating job descriptions and making lists of tasks and duties does have its downside. Critics argue that jobs change too rapidly and these lists are quickly out of date. Therefore, some job analysts have begun to develop a list of job competencies. A **competency** is a cluster of related knowledge, skills, and abilities that forms a major part of a job and that enables the job holder to perform effectively.[16] Competencies are behaviours that distinguish effective performers from ineffective performers. Competencies can be knowledge, skills, behaviour, or personality traits. (Most analysts prefer not to use personality traits such as "charisma," and instead want to describe the behaviour underlying the trait.)

Examples of competencies for managers include setting goals and standards, coaching, making decisions, and organizing. As you can see, competencies are very similar to skills. But skills can be very specific, such as "negotiate a collective agreement," whereas competencies are generic and universal: "win agreement on goals, standards, expectations, and time frames." The Banff Centre for Management has developed competency profiles for senior leaders so that they can assess needs and then train.[17] An example taken from their profile is listed in Table 4.1.

The goal is to develop competencies that are teachable (i.e., we can observe them and describe them). If these competencies are then associated with effective performance, we can use them as a base to increase the effectiveness of employee's on-the-job work behaviour. Competencies can then be used instead of job descriptions.

3. Develop Rating Scales to Rate the Importance of Each Task and the Frequency that it is Performed

Rating scales must be developed in order to rate the importance of each task as well as how often a task is performed. Tasks that are more important to the

Competency

A cluster of related knowledge, skills, and abilities that enables the job holder to perform effectively

---

TABLE 4.1

A Competency Profile for Senior Leaders

Core Competency ability to obtain buy-in of key stakeholders to new directions

Level 1: communicates new directions so that everyone affected knows the new directions

Level 2: leads team through discussions and research to identify key new themes and goals that everyone can accept and use

Level 3: key stakeholders are consulted and have input to direction setting

Level 4: all stakeholders are engaged in a process to rewrite the new directions in terms that relate specifically to their roles

Source: MacNamara, D. (1998, November 16). Learning contracts, competency profiles the new wave in executive development. *Canadian HR Reporter*, pp. G8–G10. Reprinted by permission of Carswell, a division of Thomson Canada Limited.

effective performance of a job as well as those that are frequently performed need to be identified. These ratings are important for determining the content of a training program and for identifying what employees must do in order to perform a job effectively.

4. Survey a Sample of Job Incumbents

Job incumbents as well as supervisors and subject-matter experts who are familiar with the job must then provide the task importance and frequency ratings. A questionnaire, structured interview, as well as observation of employees performing their jobs can be used to rate the importance of tasks and the frequency with which they are performed. An example of a survey is shown in Table 4.2.

5. Analyze and Interpret the Information

Once the tasks have been identified and the importance and frequency ratings have been made, the information must be analyzed and interpreted. This usually involves some elementary statistical analyses to identify those tasks that are the most important and frequently performed. Statistical software packages can assist in this task and can be used for more complex analyses. Comparisons between groups may reveal additional important information. Job incumbents may rate their own performance highly, while their managers may feel that employees are not working up to standard. New employees may feel that there are no barriers to optimum performance, while those with several years of service might perceive problems.

TABLE 4.2

Sample Task Analysis Survey

For each of the following areas of skill, knowledge, and ability, please make two ratings. Looking at your own job, assess the importance of the task by circling a number from 1 (not important) to 5 (very important). Then, consider your own level of competence in that task and rate it from 1 (not at all competent) to 5 (extremely competent).

TASK	IMPORTANCE	COMPETENCE
Knowledge: ability to explain technical information to co-workers.	1 2 3 4 5	1 2 3 4 5
Control: ability to develop procedures to monitor and evaluate activities.	1 2 3 4 5	1 2 3 4 5
Planning: ability to schedule time, tasks, and activities efficiently.	1 2 3 4 5	1 2 3 4 5
Coaching: ability to provide verbal feedback to assist in the development of more effective ways of handling situations.	1 2 3 4 5	1 2 3 4 5

One study found that experienced police officers spent less time in traffic activities, and more in non-crime-related tasks than recent recruits, validating the need to collect background information on respondents.[18] Conducting a training course without understanding the participants and the environment may result in less-effective learning and transfer of skills to the workplace.

6. Provide Feedback on the Results

Because employees and managers might not be aware of the need for training, it is important to provide small groups of managers and employees with feedback about the responses to task analysis. This feedback encourages employees to talk about areas of strengths and weaknesses and to propose solutions to problems. By owning the problem and generating the solution, employees may be more willing to change their behaviours and managers will be more likely to support a training program.

The result of a task analysis should be information on the key task requirements for certain job categories and the associated job specifications (knowledge, skills, and abilities). This sets the stage for the design of training programs because it specifies the tasks that employees must be trained to perform as well as the knowledge and skills that they need to perform effectively.

A limitation of a task analysis, however, is that it emphasizes observable behaviours rather than mental processes, and it assumes that the tasks are performed by individuals rather than groups. Many jobs today, however, involve mental processes and teamwork. In the next section, we briefly describe some new approaches to task analysis that focus on mental processes and teamwork.

Cognitive Task Analysis and Team Task Analysis

The traditional approach to a task analysis focuses on behaviours rather than mental processes such as decision making. A task analysis also assumes that individuals work on their own rather than in a group. However, many jobs today involve complex mental tasks and involve group work. How then does one conduct a task analysis for jobs that involve mental tasks or that involve group work? The answer is a cognitive task analysis and a team task analysis.

A **cognitive task analysis** refers to a set of procedures that focus on understanding the mental processes and requirements for performing a job.[19] It differs from the more conventional task analysis in that the focus is on the mental and cognitive aspects of a job rather than observable behaviours like typing or driving that are the focus of a traditional task analysis.

Cognitive task analysis describes mental and cognitive activities that are not directly observable such as decision making, problem solving, pattern recognition, and situational assessment. A traditional task analysis focuses on what gets done while a cognitive task analysis focuses more on the details of how tasks get done.

Although cognitive task analysis is useful for any job that has cognitive elements, it is especially useful in jobs that are complex, dynamic, and have high-stakes outcomes. It can identify important elements of job performance

Cognitive task analysis
A set of procedures that focus on understanding the mental processes and requirements for performing a job

such as decisions, cues, judgments, and perceptions that are important for effective job performance, and are usually not identified by a traditional task analysis. As a result, important cognitive elements can then be incorporated into training and development programs. Although cognitive task analysis has begun to receive a great deal of attention in recent years, it is a relatively new technique that is still being developed.[20]

As indicated earlier, the traditional task analysis is not suited to the analysis of jobs that involve group work. Given that so many jobs today involve groups, a task analysis must be able to identify the knowledge and skills required to work in a group. Therefore, in recent years there has been an attempt to find ways to conduct a team task analysis.

A **team task analysis** is similar to a task analysis in that the tasks of the job must be identified. However, an assessment of team-based competencies (knowledge, skills, and attitudes) associated with the tasks is also required.

Teamwork competencies include things such as how to communicate, interact, and coordinate tasks effectively with team members. The main objective is to identity the key team competencies required for the tasks of the job, which will be used to write training objectives and to design a training program.[21]

There are a number of important differences between a traditional task analysis and a team task analysis. The main difference is that a team task analysis must identify the interdependencies of the job as well as the skills required for task coordination. Another difference is that a team task analysis must also identify the cognitive skills that are required for interacting in a team.

In general, a team task analysis should focus on the knowledge of task-specific goals; knowledge of task procedures, strategies, and timing; knowledge of team members' roles and responsibilities; interpositional knowledge; and knowledge of teamwork. A team task analysis can be conducted through the use of individual and group interviews, a review of existing documents, observation, questionnaires, and by examining past important events.[22]

Like a task analysis, a cognitive and team task analysis identifies the tasks that an employee must be able to perform and the knowledge, skills, and abilities required. However, this type of analysis does not indicate whether employees are able to perform the tasks or whether they have the necessary knowledge, skills, and abilities. This information is obtained from a person analysis, the topic that we now turn to.

R P C

Person Analysis

The third level of analysis focuses on the person performing a job. **Person analysis** is the process of studying employee behaviour to determine if performance meets the work standards. A standard is the desired level of performance—ideally the quantifiable output of a specific job.[23]

A person analysis examines how well an employee performs the critical tasks and their knowledge, skills, and abilities. The objective is to provide answers to these kinds of questions: How well does the employee perform the tasks? Who, within the organization, needs training? And what kind of training do they need? A three-step process should help answer these questions:

Managing Performance Through Training and Development

1. Define the desired performance.
2. Determine the gap between desired and actual performance.
3. Identify the obstacles to effective performance.

1. Define the Desired Performance

The first step is to establish standards for performance. These norms will be important in the needs analysis, during training, and in evaluating the effectiveness of training. The idea is to determine the standard or the acceptable level of task performance. This enables a comparison of each employee's performance level against the standard in order to identify discrepancies and the need for training.

2. Determine the Gap between Desired and Actual Performance

In this step, a comparison is made between the standard level of performance and each employee's performance. Employee performance data can be obtained from performance appraisals, work samples, observations, self-assessments of competencies, and formal tests. CIBC uses formal tests to determine competencies of financial advisers.[24] Results from the "Financial Advisor Skills and Capabilities Assessment" are used by employees to gain self-awareness and to prepare a developmental plan. More objective sources might be found in records of output, complaints, accidents, rejects, lost time, maintenance hours, and equipment efficiency. The employee's performance can be compared with industry norms or with that of other workers.

3. Identify the Obstacles to Effective Performance

When there exists a gap between the standard and an employee's performance, it is necessary to determine the cause or source of the gap. Performance weakness can be the result of deficiencies in execution as well as deficiencies in knowledge, skills, or abilities. Sometimes, the gap is the result of the worker not knowing the standard, not receiving adequate feedback about performance relative to the standard, and not being rewarded for meeting the standard. A lack of goals and feedback are often the reason for substandard performance. Table 4.3 lists a variety of potential barriers to effective performance.

Once the obstacles to performance have been identified, the next step in the needs analysis process is to determine solutions to performance problems and if training is a possible solution to a performance problem. In the next section, we present a framework for determining solutions to performance problems.

Determining Solutions to Performance Problems

If you consider all the barriers to performance listed in Table 4.3, only the first two (lack of knowledge and skills) suggest a training solution. Clearly, the solution to performance problems is not always going to be training. Saying "I've got a training problem" is like going to the doctor and saying you have

TABLE 4.3

Barriers to Effective Performance

HUMAN	TECHNICAL	INFORMATION	STRUCTURAL
Lack of knowledge	Poor job design	Ill-defined goals/objectives	Overlapping roles and
Lack of skills	Lack of tools/equipment	Lack of performance	responsibilities
Lack of motivation	Lack of standardized	measurements	Lack of flexibility
Counterproductive	procedures	Raw data, not normative or	Lack of control systems
reward systems	Rapid change in technology	comparative data	
Group norms		Resources suboptimized	
Informal leaders		Ineffective feedback	
Organizational political			
climate			

Source: Adapted from Chevalier, R.D. (1990). Analyzing performance discrepancies with line managers. *Performance and Instruction, 29* (10). Reprinted by permission of International Society for Performance Improvement. Copyright 1990. Performance & Instruction, Vol. 29, No. 10, www.ispi.org. Chevalier, R. "Analyzing performance discrepancies with line managers."

an aspirin problem.[25] Training, like aspirin, is a solution, not a problem. How then do we determine if training is the best solution to performance problems?

Figure 4.2 presents a decision tree developed by Mager and Pipe to assist in determining if training is the best solution to performance problems. Let's now review the branches in this decision tree.

First, when a performance deficiency is noted, the manager must decide if the problem is worth spending either time or money to correct. For example, a manager might be irritated by employees who wear their hair shoulder length, but having short hair will make absolutely no difference to productivity or other measures of effectiveness. The exception might be in a manufacturing environment, where long hair would pose a safety hazard (solved easily by wearing a head covering).

If, however, the performance deficiency is considered important, then the true analysis begins. Is it a skill deficiency? The key to getting at this issue is to ask a critical question: Could the employee perform the task if his or her life depended on it? Could your employees produce six units per hour if their lives depended on it? If the answer is "Yes," then the solution is not to teach them something they already know how to do. Rather, the solution is to provide the environment that allows or encourages them to do it.

Moving to the right side of Figure 4.2, the analyst attempts to determine the cause of poor performance by asking a number of questions. Is the person punished for performing? While this question seems odd, organizational life is full of examples of penalties for good performance. The assistant who works twice as hard as another is punished by being given more work. The manager who stays within his/her budget is punished by having it slashed the following year. In these and other cases, behaviour that should be

FIGURE 4.2

Mager and Pipe's Flow Diagram for Determining Solutions to
Performance Problems

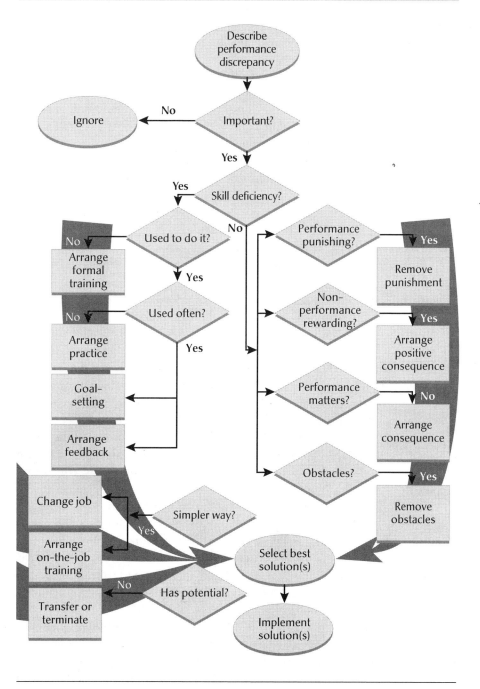

Source: Mager, R. F., & Pipe, P. (1984). *Analyzing performance problems*. Belmont, CA: Lake Publishing.

rewarded is actually punished. Such penalties and punishments for what is in effect good performance should be eliminated.

The next issue is whether or not rewards are linked to effective performance. Are there positive consequences for performing as desired? Sometimes when an employee does something good, the manager says nothing, on the assumption that the employee is being paid to do the work. However, good performance that is not reinforced tends to disappear.

Sometimes, employees assume that their performance does not matter to anyone. When managers sit in their offices and fume over sloppy work but give no feedback to employees, or arrange no consequences for poor performance, the sloppy work will continue. Working with the human resource staff, managers need to develop contingency management programs that reward employees for good performance.

Contingency management is grounded in the belief that every act has a consequence and if the consequence is perceived as a reward, then the act will be repeated. If there is no consequence or the consequence is something negative or punishing, the action will not be repeated.

Imagine the classroom where the instructor never acknowledges students whose hands are raised to ask questions. Eventually, the students will learn to keep their hands down. Ensuring that no students ask questions can be done even faster by punishing those who ask questions with sarcastic or humiliating replies. Thus, the behaviour of hand raising or asking questions is eliminated, even when the instructor insists that he or she values classroom discussion.

By analyzing rewards and punishments, managers might realize that they are asking for safe procedures but punishing those who slow down production. Quality might be the all-important word on the sign in the factory, but employees might be praised for quantity. The determination of what constitutes effective performance, and the management of reinforcement for achieving it, is a far more powerful instrument of change than a training program.

Training will not be a good solution when the environment is the cause of poor performance. Environmental obstacles to effective performance might involve a lack of authority, inadequate tools or technology, conflicting responsibilities, work overload, and so on. Removing these obstacles in the work environment and replacing them with a more supportive environment might be the best solution to a performance problem.

To restate the critical question asked earlier: Could the employee perform the task if his or her life depended on it? If the answer is "Yes," they could perform the task if their life depended on it, then say NO to training. If the employee cannot do the task if his or her life depended on it, then consider a number of other changes before training.

Following the left side of Figure 4.2, consider if the employee ever performed the task and perhaps just needs some practice. Is the employee aware of the standards, does he or she have specific and challenging goals, and is he or she receiving performance feedback? As discussed in Chapter 3, goal-setting is a very effective motivational technique that can improve performance when goals are specific and challenging. Furthermore, when employees receive performance feedback they can compare their performance to their

Contingency management

Practices based on the belief that every act has a consequence and if the consequence is perceived as a reward, then the act will be repeated goal and regulate their own behaviour and performance. Thus, before considering training as a solution, it is important to consider practice, feedback, and/or goal-setting as part of the solution to a performance problem.

Other alternatives instead of formal training might be a change in work tasks and responsibilities, a transfer to a job that better fits the employee's knowledge and skills, or in extreme circumstances termination. Alternatively, an employee might just require some on-the-job training rather than a formal training program (see Chapter 7 for a review of on-the-job training methods).

As you can see, training is just one solution for managing performance problems. There are other solutions that might be more effective and less costly than training. Furthermore, even the best-designed training programs are not always effective because the environment does not support the change in behaviour and performance.

Training is, however, often the best solution to performance problems under the following conditions:

- the task is performed frequently
- the task is difficult
- correct performance is critical
- the employee does not know how to perform as required (cannot do it)
- performance expectations and goals are clear, and employees receive feedback on their performance
- there are (or will be) positive consequences for correct work behaviour; there are not negative consequences for performing as required
- other solutions (such as coaching) are ineffective or too expensive (e.g. terminating employees and rehiring those with required skills)

If the needs analysis reveals that the tasks are not frequently performed, that they are not critical, and that perfection is not required, then performance-improvement solutions such as job aids and on-the-job training might be more appropriate. Sometimes more radical solutions might even be appropriate such as changing employees through firing and hiring, re-designing the job, changing the equipment, or changing the organizational structure.

Even if training is determined to be the best solution, the costs and benefits of training must first be estimated. Trainers must ask questions such as "What is the cost of the training?" and "What are the benefits to training?" (Chapter 11 addresses these questions.) Another consideration is the legal requirement to certify knowledge and skill levels of employees. A further point is the pressure exerted by top management to conduct the training. It is hoped that this pressure is a result of the organization's strategies and objectives.

In summary, the best way to determine if training is an appropriate solution to performance problems is to first conduct a thorough needs analysis, identify performance obstacles, and then consider various solutions to performance problems as shown in Figure 4.2. A checklist of the questions to ask to determine if training is the best solution to performance problems is provided in The Trainer's Notebook.

Methods of Needs Analysis

We have been discussing the needs analysis process and the collection of information about the organization, task, and employees. By this point, you might be wondering where the information for a needs analysis comes from and how it is collected. In this section, we review the methods and sources of needs analysis.

There are many methods and techniques for conducting a needs analysis. The methods tend to differ in terms of the quality and type of information obtained, as well as the time and cost of collecting it. This section describes some of the most common methods of needs analysis.

Steadham (1980) has developed a useful summary of nine basic needs analysis methods that are described in Table 4.4 along with their advantages and disadvantages. The nine methods are: observation, questionnaires, key consultation, print media, interviews, group discussion, tests, records and reports, and work samples.

There is some research that suggests that some methods of needs analysis are better than others in terms of response rate, quality, usefulness of the data, and cost. One study tested three techniques: closed-ended survey, open-ended survey, and focus groups. A combination of the closed-ended survey and focus-group interviews provided the most practical, useful, and cost-effective information.[26] The best method, however, will depend on the time and money available, the experience of the analyst, and the nature of the responses.

Surveys, however, are one of the most often used methods of needs analysis due to their low cost and the ability to collect information from large numbers of respondents. Some software firms have developed surveys that can be customized to include questions from broad climate issues to specific job standards. There are many firms that have designed needs analysis software, some of which can be tailored to clients' needs. This technology allows HR personnel to develop customized surveys quickly, and to analyze results by region, unit, and so on. One HR system contained 200 000 pieces of information on 500 employees. This system tapped every skill of every employee ranging from forklift and fuel-tank exchange procedures to probing abilities.[27]

There are many sources of needs analysis information. Among the most important and often used are employees and managers as well as subject-matter-experts who are familiar with a job. Some retail stores assess the competence of their sales staff through the use of professional shoppers who rate sales performance against established standards. A bank tests employee knowledge using a computer-based analysis, and then compares the results with supervisory rankings.[28]

In many cases, data on employees' performance and training needs is obtained from employees who rate their own performance and indicate their training needs. This is usually referred to as self-assessment. Self-assessment has its benefits and its limitations. Employees might be more motivated to be trained if they have some input in deciding on their needs. However, expressions of needs include feelings or desires and may have no relation to performance.[29]

Several studies have found weak relationships between employees' self-assessment of performance and managerial assessments.[30] A review of 55 studies failed to find a strong relationship between self-evaluation of ability and other measures of performance.[31] However, a study at IBM demonstrated that employees can be trained in self-assessment by learning to break down a job into its component parts and to analyze skills.[32] This method has the added benefit of the employees' accepting ownership of their development plans.

In summary, there are many methods for conducting a needs analysis as well as different sources of information. Because of the differences in information provided by the various methods and sources, the best approach is usually one that includes several methods and sources. Surveying only job incumbents about their perceptions of their own abilities might not result in the most objective information about performance gaps. Employees may have wish lists for training that do not meet the needs of their units or that do not address their own weaknesses. Managers, too, should be asked for their performance evaluations. Those who have frequent interaction with job incumbents, such as customers and employees in other departments, should also be surveyed. These different perspectives will result in more accurate and complete information. It also enables analysts to distinguish between perceived needs (what training courses employees feel they need), demand needs (what managers request), and normative needs (training needed to meet industry, unit, or job comparative standards).[33]

Obstacles to Needs Analysis

Now that you know all about the needs analysis process, you might be surprised to learn that many organizations do not conduct a thorough needs analysis, at least not to the extent that it is described in training textbooks.[34]

TABLE 4.4

Advantages and Disadvantages of Nine Basic Needs Analysis Methods

METHODS	ADVANTAGES	DISADVANTAGES
Observation • Can be as technical as time–motion studies or as functionally or behaviourally specific as observing a new board or staff member interacting during a meeting. • May be as unstructured as walking through an agency's offices on the lookout for evidence of communication barriers. • Can be used normatively to distinguish between effective and ineffective behaviours, organizational structures, and/or process.	• Minimizes interruption of routine work flow or group activity. • Generates in situ data, highly relevant to the situation where response to identified training needs/interests will impact. • (When combined with a feedback step) provides for important comparison checks between inferences of the observer and the respondent.	• Requires a highly skilled observer with both process and content knowledge (unlike an interviewer who needs, for the most part, only process skills). • Carries limitations that derive from being able to collect data only within the work setting (the other side of the first advantage listed in the preceding column). • Holds potential for respondents to perceive the observation activity as "spying."
Questionnaires • May be in the form of surveys or polls of a random or stratified sample of respondents, or an enumeration of an entire "population." • Can use a variety of question formats: open-ended, projective, forced-choice, priority-ranking. • Can take alternative forms such as Q-sorts, or slipsorts, rating scales, either predesigned or self-generated by respondent(s). • May be self-administered (by mail) under controlled or uncontrolled conditions, or may require the presence of an interpreter or assistant.	• Can reach a large number of people in a short time. • Are relatively inexpensive. • Give opportunity of expression without fear of embarrassment. • Yield data easily summarized and reported.	• Make little provision for free expression of unanticipated responses. • Require substantial time (and technical skills, especially in survey model) for development of effective instruments. • Are of limited utility in getting at causes of problems or possible solutions. • Suffer low return rates (mailed), grudging responses, or unintended and/or inappropriate respondents.
Key Consultation • Secures information from those persons who, by virtue of their formal or informal standing, are in a good position to know what the training needs of a particular group are: a. board chairman b. related service providers c. members of professional associations d. individuals from the service population	• Is relatively simple and inexpensive to conduct. • Permits input and interaction of a number of individuals, each with his or her own perspectives of the needs of the area, discipline, group, etc. • Establishes and strengthens lines of communication between participants in the process.	• Carries a built-in bias, since it is based on views of those who tend to see training needs from their own individual or organizational perspective. • May result in only a partial picture of training needs due to the typically nonrepresentative nature (in a statistical sense) of a key informant group.
Print Media • Can include professional journals, legislative news/notes, industry "rags," trade magazines, in-house publications.	• Is an excellent source of information for uncovering and clarifying normative needs. • Provides information that is current, if not forward-looking. • Is readily available and is apt to have already been reviewed by the client group.	• Can be a problem when it comes to the data analysis and synthesis into a useable form (use of clipping service or key consultants can make this type of data more useable).

Method	Advantages	Disadvantages
Interviews • Can be formal or casual, structured or unstructured, or somewhere in between. • May be used with a sample of a particular group (board, staff, committee) or conducted with everyone concerned. • Can be done in person, by phone, at the work site, or away from it.	• Are adept at revealing feelings, causes of, and possible solutions to problems that the client is facing (or anticipates); provide maximum opportunity for the client to represent himself spontaneously on his own terms (especially when conducted in an open-ended, nondirective manner).	• Are usually time-consuming. • Can be difficult to analyze and quantify results (especially from unstructured formats). • Unless the interviewer is skilled, the client(s) can easily be made to feel self-conscious.
Group Discussion • Resembles face-to-face interview technique, e.g., structured or unstructured, formal or informal, or somewhere in between. • Can be focused on job (role) analysis, group problem analysis, group goal setting or any number of group tasks or themes, e.g., "leadership training needs of the board." • Uses one or several of the familiar group facilitating techniques: brainstorming, nominal group process, force-fields, consensus rankings, organizational mirroring, simulation, and sculpting.	• Permits on-the-spot synthesis of different viewpoints. • Builds support for the particular service response that is ultimately decided on. • Decreases client's "dependence response" toward the service provided since data analysis is (or can be) a shared function. • Helps participants to become better problem analysts, better listeners, etc.	• Rely for success on a skilful interviewer who can generate data without making client(s) feel self-conscious, suspicious, etc. • Is time-consuming (therefore initially expensive) both for the consultant and the agency. • Can produce data that are difficult to synthesize and quantify (more a problem with the less structured techniques).
Tests • Are a hybridized form of questionnaire. • Can be very functionally oriented (like observations) to test a board, staff, or committee member's proficiency. • May be used to sample learned ideas and facts. • Can be administered with or without the presence of an assistant.	• Can be especially helpful in determining whether the cause of a recognized problem is a deficiency in knowledge or skill, or by elimination, attitude. • Results are easily quantifiable and comparable.	• The availability of a relatively small number of tests that are validated for a specific situation. • Do not indicate if measured knowledge and skills are actually being used in the on-the-job or "back home group" situation.
Records, Reports • Can consist of organizational charts, planning documents, policy manuals, audits, and budget reports. • Employee records (grievance, turnover, accidents, etc.) • Includes minutes of meetings, weekly, monthly program reports, memoranda, agency service records, program evaluation studies.	• Provide excellent clues to trouble spots. • Provide objective evidence of the results of problems within the agency or group. • Can be collected with a minimum of effort and interruption of work flow since it already exists at the work site.	• Causes of problems or possible solutions often do not show up. • Carries perspective that generally reflects the past situation rather than the current one (or recent changes). • Need a skilled data analyst if clear patterns and trends are to emerge from such technical and diffuse raw data.
Work Samples • Are similar to observation but in written form. • Can be products generated in the course of the organization's work, e.g., ad layouts, program proposals, market analyses, letters, training designs. • Written responses to a hypothetical but relevant case study provided by the consultant.	• Carry most of the advantage of records and reports data. • Are the organization's data (its own output).	• Case study method will take time away from actual work of the organization. • Need specialized content analysts. • Analyst's assessment of strengths/weaknesses disclosed by samples can be challenged as "too subjective."

Can always get what you want
Get what you want
What you need

Source: From Steadham, S. V. (1980). Learning to select a needs assessment strategy. *Training & Development, 30* (January), 56–61. Copyright 1997, adapted from *Training & Development* magazine, American Society for Training & Development. Reprinted with permission. All rights reserved.

Given the importance of needs analysis in the training process, you might wonder why this is the case.

As it turns out, there are a number of obstacles to conducting a formal needs analysis. Understanding what these obstacles are is important because if you are aware of them then you can also learn how to overcome them.

To begin with, trainers often claim that they are not rewarded for taking the time (and money) to conduct a needs analysis. Managers prefer action over analysis and therefore want to see training resources used to train employees. They may also feel that they can accurately identify training needs and that more analysis is a waste of time and money. Managers may even have their own agendas, such as rewarding employees by sending them to exotic locations for training and therefore resist any attempt to redefine training needs.

Sometimes time is a constraint. New equipment might be arriving on Monday and it is easier to train all employees on all procedures instead of determining who needs training on which aspects of the new equipment. In fact, time is increasingly becoming a concern as a full-blown needs analysis

Training Today

Just-in-Time Needs Analysis

Needs analysis can be a time consuming process that is hard to sell to managers who want just-in-time solutions to urgent problems. When an organization is introducing new equipment, or an employee has to learn to perform an important task, the last thing that managers want to hear is "Wait, we have to do a needs analysis."

Very few trainers have the time and resources to follow the complete needs analysis process described in a textbook. However, most trainers would use some means of detecting the underlying cause of a performance problem and training needs. Here are some ways experienced trainers conduct needs analysis in a more timely and less cumbersome manner.

- *Ask a series of questions.* When a manager demands a training course for employees, the trainer should start by asking questions related to the nature of the problem and its impact on the business. (The questions of the needs analysis decision tree could be used.) Some trainers even agree to conduct a training course, as per the manager's demand, and then renegotiate the assignment as information emerges from interviews with employees before the course. Managers may be receptive to the emerging data, recognizing the need to design solutions that solve the problem.

- *Use existing information.* Surveys, interviews, and observations are expensive data-collection methods. But most organizations keep customer complaint letters, grievance files, exit interviews, and sales data, which can be re-assessed for needs assessment purposes.
- *Speed up data collection.* Use the Intranet to survey employees. Start discussion groups around issues, concerns, and problems.
- *Link assessment and delivery.* Rather than conduct a lengthy needs analysis and then design a training program, some trainers attempt to join the two together, in small steps. For example, if there are star performers, then bring them together in a forum with nonstellar performers to discuss effective techniques. The poorer performers not only are able to compare performance, but they learn how to improve at the same time.

Source: Adapted from Zemke, R. (1998). How to do a needs assessment when you think you don't have time. *Training, 35* (3), 38–44. Training: the Human Side of Business by Zemke, R. Copyright 1998 by V N U BUS PUBNS USA. Reproduced with permission of V N U BUS PUBNS USA in the format Textbook via Copyright Clearance Center.

can take months to complete and yet employees need to be trained and back on the job in a matter of weeks or even days.

Ultimately, what everyone is most concerned about is getting people trained as soon as possible. Because needs analysis is costly and time consuming, it is often overlooked as an unnecessary constraint on resources, staff, and time. The identification of training needs can turn into a comprehensive research study that takes months to complete. The cost, time, and the rigour necessary for doing a thorough needs analysis means that many organizations will simply not do one. However, conducting some data collection and analysis, rather than having no information, will almost always result in a better training program. It is therefore important for trainers to persuade management on the importance of conducting a needs analysis, and to ensure that it is included in the training budget. Furthermore, trainers need to be creative in finding ways to conduct a needs analysis within the constraints that exist in their organizations. To learn more about how some training experts have found creative ways to overcome the obstacles to needs analysis, see Training Today, "Just-in-Time Needs Analysis."

Summary

This chapter has described the needs analysis process. Three levels of needs analysis were discussed: organizational, task, and person analysis. We also described the process of how to determine solutions to performance problems and if training and development is the best solution to performance problems. Data collection methods and sources of information were also reviewed as well as the obstacles to needs analysis. It should now be clear to you that a needs analysis is critical for determining the nature of performance problems and whether or not training and development is a good solution. The importance of a needs analysis, however, does not end here. As you will see in the next chapter, a needs analysis is also necessary for writing training objectives and deciding on the content of a training program.

Key Terms

cognitive task analysis (page 93)
competency (page 91)
contingency management (page 98)
job description (page 90)
learning culture (page 89)
needs analysis (page 83)
organizational analysis (page 87)

person analysis (page 94)
resource analysis (page 88)
strategic training (page 87)
task analysis (page 90)
team task analysis (page 94)
training transfer climate (page 89)

Weblinks

The Banff Centre for Management: www.banffmanagement.com (page 91)
Bell Canada: www.bell.ca (page 88)
CIBC: www.cibc.com (page 95)
IBM: www.ibm.com/ca (page 85)

Discussion Questions

1. Debate the following: Needs analysis is a waste of time. What is most important is getting people trained as soon as possible.
2. Organizations often have data on file that can be used for the purposes of a needs analysis. Discuss the kinds of information that might already exist in an organization and how it might be useful for the purposes of an organizational, task, or person analysis.
3. If needs analysis information has not been used as the basis for the design and delivery of a training program, what are some of the reasons why organizations decide to design and deliver training programs? Are these good reasons for investing in training and development programs?
4. Discuss the reasons why organizations do not always conduct a needs analysis and what a trainer might do to overcome some of the obstacles.

Using the Internet

1. To learn more about the different methods of needs analysis and how to decide on a method for conducting a needs analysis, go to: **http://mime1.marc.gatech.edu/mm_tools/analysis.html** Explain what the Needs Assessment Matrix is and how it works as well as the Needs Assessment Decision Aid. How can these instruments be used as part of the needs analysis process and do you think that they are useful? What are the advantages and disadvantages of using the following methods for needs analysis: questionnaires, interviews, and focus groups.

Exercises

1. Think of a problem you had or were aware of at an organization that you have worked for. Describe the problem and then using Magar and Pipe's flow diagram for determining solutions to performance problems (Figure 4.2), determine the best solution. Also consider each of the solutions in the figure and explain why it would or would not be a good solution to the problem. Finally, if you know how the organization approached the problem, describe what they did and if it was an effective solution.
2. Consider your job and performance as a student and conduct each of the following types of needs analysis: a) a task analysis, b) cognitive task analysis, c) team task analysis, and d) person analysis. Based on your results, indicate the critical tasks of a student as well as how well you perform each task, and on which tasks you need to improve your performance. What do you need to do to become a better student?
3. Find a partner in the class and take turns conducting a task analysis interview. Before beginning your interview, prepare a task analysis

interview guide with questions that will help you identify tasks; rate their importance and frequency; and determine the task specifications (knowledge, skills, and abilities). The interviewee can refer to a current or previous job when answering the interviewer's questions. Also consider the relevance of a cognitive task analysis and a team task analysis.

4. Table 4.4 describes nine different methods of needs analysis. Review each of the methods and then explain what methods you think would be most appropriate for each of the following kinds of needs analysis: a) organizational analysis, b) task analysis, c) cognitive task analysis, d) team task analysis, and e) person analysis. Be sure to explain your reasoning as to why a particular method would be best for each type of needs analysis.

5. Recall a training program that you have attended as part of a current or previous job. To what extent do you think the program was based on an organizational, task, and person analysis? Try to relate specific aspects of the training program to each level of needs analysis. What performance problem was the program designed to address, and how effective was the program as a solution to the performance problem?

6. Imagine that you are a trainer in an organization that prides itself on providing employees with frequent opportunities for training. The president of the company has asked you to design and deliver a training program on team skills so that employees will be able to work in groups. He or she wants you to start training employees as soon as possible and does not want you to spend time and money conducting a needs analysis. He or she wants you to develop an action plan for the design and delivery of the program and present it in a week. How will you handle the needs analysis issue and what will you recommend? Prepare your presentation and present it to the class.

7. To find out the extent to which organizations conduct needs analysis, contact the human resources staff of an organization and conduct an interview about needs analysis. In particular, find out if the organization conducts an organizational, task, and person analysis; what kinds of information they gather when they conduct each level of needs analysis; what methods and sources they use to gather the information; and what they do with the information and how it is used as part of the training and development process. If they do not conduct a needs analysis, find out why and how they determine training needs. Students should come to class prepared to present the results of their interviews.

Case

GENERAL MOTORS

The press operation (blanker area) of the metal fabrication plant at General Motors was undergoing major changes in technology, a new operational philosophy, and new dies. ("Blanker" is a shop term for a press that cuts the shape of a part from a coil of sheet metal, like a cookie cutter. Dies are tools for imparting a shape or finish to an object or material.) Managers were concerned that employees did not have adequate knowledge, skills, and abilities (KSAs) to deal with these changes and meet production standards. To determine if training was needed, one supervisor and two members of the United Auto Workers formed a needs analysis team.

At the first meeting of the needs analysis team with the client (the blanker area's coordinator), the performance problems were identified as being unable to meet the desired production schedules, efficiency, and cost-per-cut benchmarks. The team determined that the main focus would be on training solutions, but the client would consider any nontraining issues.

The team set out to:

1. Identify symptoms and causes
2. Plan data-gathering techniques
3. Collect the data
4. Analyze and interpret the data
5. Report results and suggest solutions

Step 1. Some of the observable *symptoms* were a decrease in efficiency; an increase in transition time (the time it takes to change a die to run a different part), downtime due to lack of steel, and downtime due to repairs on dies. The team felt that some of the *causes* (reasons that could explain what they saw) were frequent scheduling changes; inefficient communication between production, scheduling, and maintenance areas; a storage room so disorganized it was difficult to locate different types of steel rolls or blanks, which in turn caused inventory problems.

Step 2. The team interviewed production and skilled trade workers, their supervisors, scheduling personnel, and the steel expediter to discuss the data-gathering technique. They discovered that the problem snowballed outside of the blanker area and affected other operations.

Step 3. The team collected more data through a survey questionnaire and more interviews. They also held roundtable discussions and assigned subject-matter experts (SME) from each area to examine their department's trouble spots. They also contacted SMEs from other GM locations to obtain additional information.

Step 4. The team prepared a list of solutions including the use of a computer program for scheduling; develop and implement an organized floor plan and layout for the storage room; colour code the dies to the presses; provide intermediate training on a software program for ordering steel and on cutting shippers; have the service department give equal priority to the blanker area and other areas.

Step 5. These possible solutions were presented to the various departments, who then came up with a final list of nine solutions: implement a new two-week scheduling program; implement a floor plan and layout for the storage room; institute a preventative maintenance program; provide dedicated service people to the blanker area; divide the blanker area into two separate areas to make it more manageable; implement a skeleton part procedure for dies scheduled for maintenance; colour code the dies to the presses; train production operators in statistical process control; provide a training solution for the steel expediter.

The team prioritized the solutions, costed them, explained the expected results and potential value and benefits, and presented this list to the blanker area coordinator. The solution that would have the most impact was to train production operators in statistical control techniques.

This solution was implemented and the results were as follows:

- 30 percent reduction in scrap rate
- 30 percent increase in efficiency
- 10 percent lower costs
- improved inventory capability and cost
- 35 to 80 percent increase in first-time quality
- less downtime for repair
- 7 percent increase in productivity
- worker pride of ownership for these achievements

Source: Adapted from Finison, K., & Szediak, F. (1997). General Motors does a needs analysis. *Training and Development, 58* (7), 103–104. Copyright 1997, adapted from *Training & Development* magazine, American Society for Training & Development. Reprinted with permission. All rights reserved.

Questions

1. Why would the needs analysis team determine that their main focus would be on a training solutions before they did any analysis?
2. Review the symptoms and causes identified in Step 1. How many of these appear to have a training solution?
3. The team developed a list of five solutions. Which of these are training solutions?
4. Critique the needs analysis done at General Motors and comment on each level of needs analysis. If you were a consultant to this project, are there any things that you would have done differently? Explain why.

References

[1]Stevenson, M. (2002, September 2). Base helps civilians prepare for chemical attacks. *The Globe and Mail*, A6. Reprinted with permission from *The Globe and Mail*.

[2]Salas, E., & Cannon-Bowers, J. A. (2001). The science of training: A decade of progress. *Annual Review of Psychology, 52*, 471–99.

[3]Leigh, D., Watkins, R., Platt, W. A., & Kaufman, R. (2000). Alternate models of needs assessment: Selecting the right one for your organization. *Human Resource Development Quarterly, 11*, 87–93.

[4]Kaufman, R. (1991). *Strategic planning plus: An organizational guide.* Glenview, IL: Scott Foreman Professional Books.

[5]Leigh, D., Watkins, R., Platt, W. A., & Kaufman, R. (2000).

[6]Mills, G.R., Pace, W., & Peterson, B. (1989). *Analysis in human resource training and organization development.* Reading, MA: Addison-Wesley.

[7]Estabrooke, M., & Foy, N.F. (1992). Answering the call of tailored training. *Training, 29* (10), 84–88.

[8]Carr, C. (1992). The three Rs of training. *Training, 29* (6).

[9]Estabrooke, M., & Foy, N.F. (1992).

[10]Geroy, G.D., Wright, P.C. & Caffrey, P.L. (1989). Establishing a multi-craft maintenance operation. *Performance and Instruction, 28* (7).

[11]Goldstein, I.L. (1993). *Training in organizations* (3rd ed.). Pacific Grove, CA: Brooks/Cole.

[12]Estabrooke, M., & Foy, N.F. (1992).

[13]Gibb-Clark, M. (2000, February 11). Employee training can backfire on firms: survey. *The Globe and Mail*, B10.

[14]Rouiller, J. Z., & Goldstein, I. L. (1993). The relationship between organizational transfer climate and positive transfer of training. *Human Resource Development Quarterly, 4*, 377–90.

[15]Tracey, J.B, Tannenbaum, S.I, Kavanagh, M.J (1995). Applying trained skills on the job: The importance of the work environment. *Journal of Applied Psychology, 80*, 239–52.

[16]Parry, S.B. (1998). Just what is a competency? *Training, 35* (6), 58–64.

[17]MacNamara, D. (1998, November 16). Learning contracts, competency profiles the new wave in executive development. *Canadian HR Reporter*, pp. G8–G10.

[18]Landey, F.J., & Vasey, J. (1991). Job analysis: The composition of SME samples. *Personnel Psychology, 44*.

[19]Salas, E., & Cannon-Bowers, J. A. (2001).

[20]DuBois, D. A. (2002). Leveraging hidden expertise: Why, when, and how to use cognitive task analysis. In K. Kraiger's (Ed.), *Creating, implementing, and managing effective training and development: State-of-the-art lessons for practice*, (pp. 80–114). San Francisco. CA: Jossey-Bass.

[21]Salas, E., Burke, C. S., & Cannon-Bowers, J. A. (2002). What we know about designing and delivering team training: Tips and guidelines. In K. Kraiger's (Ed.), *Creating, implementing, and managing effective training and development: State-of-the-art lessons for practice*, (pp. 234–59). San Francisco. CA: Jossey-Bass.

[22]Salas, E., Burke, C. S., & Cannon-Bowers, J. A. (2002).

[23]Hobbs, D.L. (1990). A training-appropriation process. *Training and Development Journal, 44* (4).

[24]Trainor, N.L. (1998, November 16). Using measurement to predict performance. *Canadian HR Reporter*, pp. 7–8.

[25]Mager, R.F., & Pipe, P. (1970). *Analyzing performance problems or you really oughta wanna*. Belmont, CA: Lear Siegler, Inc./Fearon.

[26]Preskill, H. (1991). A comparison of data collection methods for assessing training needs. *Human Resource Development Quarterly*, (Summer).

[27]Rockburn, J. (1991, October 15). Streamlining human resources. *The Globe and Mail* B15.

[28]Tritsch, C. (1991). Assessing your training. *Human Resource Executive*, (May).

[29]Latham, G.P. (1988). Human resource training and development. *Annual Review of Psychology, 39*.

[30]McEnery, J., & McEnery, J.M. (1987). Self-rating in management training needs assessment: A neglected opportunity. *Journal of Occupational Psychology, 60*, 49–60. Staley, C.C., & Shockley-Zalaback, P. (1986). Communication proficiency and future training needs of the female professional: Self-assessment versus supervisors' evaluations. *Human Relations, 39*, 891–902.

[31]Mabe, P.A., & West, S.G. (1982). Validity of self-evaluation of ability: A review and a meta-analysis. *Journal of Applied Psychology, 67*, 280–96.

[32]Bardsely, C.A. (1987). Improving employee awareness of opportunity at IBM. *Personnel*, (April).

[33]Lee, W.W., & Roadman, K.H. (1991). Linking needs assessment to performance-based evaluation. *Performance and Instruction, 30* (7).

[34]Saari, L.M., Johnson, T.R., McLaughlin, S.D., & Zimmerle, D.M. (1988). A survey of management training and education practices in U.S. companies. *Personnel Psychology, 41*(4), 731–44.

Chapter 5

Training Design and Delivery

www.krispykreme.com

KRISPY KREME

You might think that Krispy Kreme's toughest challenge would be turning out doughnuts quickly enough to suit the customers and investors who made the company's stock rise faster than its hot glazed treats. But in 1999, Krispy Kreme decided it was going to double the number of its stores within three years including expansion into Canada—and that meant finding a better, faster way to train its managers. This also meant revamping its manager-training program

The North Carolina company, which now has more than 200 stores, including five in Canada with plans to open another 50, needed to speed up and standardize the training of new managers, while also keeping better tabs on their progress. The old manager-training program consisted of 12 weeks of on-the-job training combined with four weeks of classroom training.

The company decided to hire a consulting firm to create a blended program combining multimedia online learning with its traditional classroom and on-the-job training. With a blended approach, Krispy Kreme is able to reach different kinds of learning styles. Employees could learn by doing, reading manuals, and interacting with the Web-based training.

The program starts with six weeks of on-the-job training at a certified training store, supported by Web-based training modules, video, and hard copy materials. Trainees then take a week of classroom instruction, followed by another six weeks of on-the-job and Web-based training. Training ends with a final week in the classroom.

Krispy Kreme's Management 101 went live on April 5, 2000. In the 12 months before the online course debuted, 60 employees were trained as managers. In the following 12 months, 149 were trained under the blended program. Krispy Kreme is now expanding its online program to hourly workers.[1]

Like Krispy Kreme, many companies today find themselves in need of new training programs. In the case of Krispy Kreme, they had to revamp their manager-training program in order to meet their expansion plans. Key to the design of the program was the decision to hire a consulting firm; choosing a combination of training methods; deciding where the training will take place; scheduling the training; and obtaining the necessary materials and equipment. These are just some of the many activities that are undertaken as part of the design and delivery of training and development programs, which are the focus of this chapter.

In the previous chapter, we described the process of identifying training needs and determining solutions to performance problems. When it has been determined that training is part of the solution to performance problems, a number of decisions must be made that involve transforming the needs analysis information into training objectives and a training program. In particular, the following activities need to be undertaken in the design and delivery of a training program:

1. Write training objectives.
2. Decide to purchase or design a training program.
3. Determine the training content.
4. Decide on the training methods.
5. Incorporate active practice into a training program.
6. Decide on a trainer.
7. Select the trainees.
8. Identify training materials and equipment.
9. Choose a training site.
10. Schedule the training program.
11. Prepare a lesson plan.
12. Administer the training program.
13. Deliver the training program.

In the remainder of this chapter, each of these steps will be described. To create some realism, we will use an example of a fictional organization called Vandalais Department Stores. The company is a large retail chain with 50 stores in Canada. In response to a performance problem with the sales associates in many of the stores, the company conducted a needs analysis. The needs analysis indicated that a major source of the problem was the company's use of unstructured employment interviews to make hiring decisions. As a result, many unqualified employees were being hired and then fired. Because it is well known that structured employment interviews result in better hiring decisions, the company decided that it should use structured interviews to hire future sales associates.[2] Therefore, the human resources staff will need to be trained on how to conduct structured employment interviews. The starting point is to write training objectives, the topic of the next section.

Training Objectives

A **training objective** is a statement of what trainees are expected to be able to do after a training program. Training objectives answer the question, "What should trainees be able to do at the end of a training program?" Put another way, an objective is the expected outcome of training. The objectives also describe the knowledge and skills to be acquired.

The emphasis of training is usually learning, on-the-job behaviour, and job performance. Learning involves the process of acquiring new knowledge, skills, and attitudes, while performance involves the use of these new skills, knowledge, and attitudes on the job. Training objectives usually refer to the acquisition of knowledge and/or skills as well as behaviour on the job.

Training objective
A statement of what trainees are expected to be able to do after a training program

Training objectives are an important link between the needs analysis stage and the other stages of the training and development process. In addition to stating what employees will learn and be able to do following a training program, training objectives serve a number of other purposes, which are described in Table 5.1.

Writing Training Objectives

The writing of training objectives is a skill that can be learned. Skill in writing objectives does not mean that trainers can make lists of behaviour verbs such as "recognize" and "evaluate." The real skill is the ability to rework needs analysis information into performance outcomes. A training objective should contain five key elements of the desired outcome as follows:

TABLE 5.1

Purposes of Training Objectives

Training objectives serve a number of important purposes for trainers, trainees, and managers.

TRAINERS

1. Trainees can be assessed prior to instruction to determine if they have mastered any of the objectives. Depending on the results, trainees can either omit certain sections of a training program or undertake additional training to master the prerequisites.
2. The selection of training content and methods is simplified by objectives. The choice of content and methods will be guided by the need to achieve certain objectives.
3. Learning objectives enables evaluators to develop measures for evaluation and to determine how to calculate the benefits and outcomes of a program.

TRAINEES

4. Objectives inform trainees of the goals of a training program and what they will be expected to learn and do at the end of a training program.
5. Objectives allow trainees to focus their energies on achieving specific goals, rather than to waste energy on irrelevant tasks or trying to figure out what is required of them.
6. Objectives communicate to employees that training is important and that they will be accountable for what they learn in training.

MANAGERS

7. Objectives communicate to supervisors, professional groups, and others what the trainee is expected to have learned by the end of a training program and what the trainee should be able to do.
8. Management and supervisors know exactly what is expected of trainees and can reinforce and support newly trained knowledge and skills on the job.

1. *Who is to perform the desired behaviour?* Employees and managers are the easiest to identify. In a training situation more accurate descriptors might be "all first-level supervisors," "anyone conducting selection interviews," or "all employees with more than one month of experience." The trainer is not the "who," although it is tempting for some trainees to write, for example, that the trainer will present five hours of information on communication. The goal of the instructor is to maximize the efficiency with which all trainees achieve the specified objectives, not just present the information.[3]

2. *What is the actual behaviour to be employed to demonstrate mastery of the training content or objective?* Words like "type," "run," and "calculate" can be measured easily. Other mental activities such as comprehension and analysis can also be described in measurable ways.

3. *Where and 4. when is the behaviour to be demonstrated and evaluated (i.e., under what conditions)?* These could include "during a 60-minute typing test," "on the ski hill with icy conditions," "when presented with a diagram," or "when asked to design a training session." The tools, equipment, information, and other source materials for training should be specified. Included in this list may be things the trainee may not use, such as calculators.

5. *What is the standard by which the behaviour will be judged?* Is the trainee expected to type 60 words per minute with less than three errors? Can the trainee list five out of six purposes for training objectives?

An example of a training objective that includes the five elements is as follows: The sales representative (who) will be able to make 10 calls a day to new customers in the territory assigned (what, where, when), and will be able to generate three (30 percent) sales worth at least $500 from these calls (how, or the criterion).

Finally, when the five elements are included in a training objective, then the final written objective should contain three key components:

1. **Performance:** What the trainee will be able to do after the training. In other words, what work behaviour will the trainee be able to display.

2. **Condition:** The tools, time, and situation under which the trainee is expected to perform the behaviour. In other words, where and when the behaviour will occur.

3. **Criterion:** The level of acceptable performance or the standard or criteria against which performance will be judged.

The first attempt at writing training objectives will be difficult. However, after some experience, a generalization of these planning skills will occur. Representative workers should be involved in the development of the training objectives. A team consisting of the trainer, trainees, and their supervisors would be ideal.[4] At some point, the objectives should be reviewed with and approved by the management and the supervisors of the trainees. Nadler cites a case in which a sales training program, based on a needs analysis of sales representatives, was rejected by senior management because management were secretly planning fundamental organizational changes.[5]

At this stage, the training objectives should closely resemble the task analysis. For example, one task of the job of a receptionist could be: *The receptionist* (who) *sorts 100 pieces of incoming mail by categories of complaints, requests for information, and invoices* (what) *within 60 minutes, with less than one percent processing errors* (how). This could easily become a training objective. A training objective that reads like an actual job behaviour is more likely to be approved, learned, and used on the job.

In summary, a training objective contains an observable action with a measurable criterion outlining the conditions of performance. Returning to the Vandalais Department Stores case, what do you think would be a good training objective? Based on a needs analysis, the following training objective was written:

> Employees in human resources will be able to conduct structured employment interviews during the selection process. Ninety percent of new hires will receive above-average performance ratings after six and 12 months on the job, and less than one percent will be terminated due to poor performance after one year.

Once training objectives have been developed, the next step is to design a training program. However, at this point the question that arises is whether a training program will be designed in-house by the organization or by an external consultant. Thus, one must first decide whether or not a training program will be purchased all or in part or designed in-house by the organization.

The Purchase or Design Decision

Once it has been determined that a training program is an appropriate course of action to manage a performance problem and training objectives have been developed, the organization faces a make or buy decision. Many private training companies and consultants in Canada offer an extensive array of courses on general topics such as computer training and customer service (see the Using the Internet exercise at the end of the chapter).

In many cases, it is more economical for an organization to purchase these materials, packaged in professional formats, than to develop the materials themselves, which in many cases will be used only once or twice.

For example, most HR managers do not design training courses in basic skills; they form alliances with educational institutions, community colleges, or private organizations that specialize in developing and delivering basic skills training programs.[6] Organizations also prefer to use outside consultants for sexual harassment training.[7]

The advantages of packaged programs are high quality, immediate delivery, ancillary services (tests, videos), the potential to customize the package to the organization, benefits from others' implementation experience, extensive testing, and often less expense than internally developed programs.[8]

Training programs developed internally by an organization also have some advantages including security and confidentiality, use of the organization's language, incorporation of the organization's values, use of internal content expertise, understanding of the specific target audience and organization, and the pride and credibility of having a customized program.[9]

Given the pros and cons of both alternatives, how does a training manager decide to purchase or design a training program? Obviously, one of the most important factors to consider is the cost of each alternative. A cost-benefit analysis would be necessary to determine the best option. Some types of training programs will be much more costly to design than to purchase. However, there are other factors that should also be considered in addition to cost.

For example, does the human resource department have the time and expertise to design a training program? Designing a training program from scratch requires expertise in many areas such as training methods and principles and theories of learning. If the human resource department does not have this expertise in-house then they will need to purchase all or part of a training program. As well, developing a training program is a time-consuming endeavour. Unless a human resource department has a training function and training personnel or is otherwise well staffed, it may not have the time to design or deliver training programs.

Time is also a factor in terms of how soon the organization wants to begin training. Given the amount of time required to design a new training program, if there is a need or desire to begin training as soon as possible then the organization will need to purchase a training program. In effect, the sooner that the organization wants to begin training, the less likely there will be sufficient time to design a new training program.

Another important consideration is the number of employees who will need to be trained and the extent to which future employees will also receive training. If a relatively small number of employees require training, then it is probably not worthwhile to design an entire training program. However, if a large number of employees need to receive training now and in the future, then designing a new training program from scratch makes more sense. In other words, to the extent that the training program will be used for many employees in both the short- and long-term, a decision to design the program is more favourable.

Although we have been referring to the purchase of an entire training program, it is important to realize that purchasing can involve buying particular training materials such as a video package or buying an entire training program that is specially designed for the organization. As well, a consultant could be hired to design and deliver a training program or it can be delivered by persons within the organization once it has been designed by a consultant. Recall that Krispy Kreme hired a consulting firm to design its new manager training program. Organizations can also purchase off-the-shelf training programs that are already designed and contain all the materials required to deliver a training program.

In the Vandalais Department Stores example, the company decided to design a training program with the help of a training consultant because they plan to train all current and future human resource staff in all regions of the country. There are 15 regional offices with three to five staff in the HR department in each office, all of whom will need to receive the training.

Training Content

Once a decision has been made to design a training program, decisions must be made about the training content. This is a crucial stage, as one wants to be sure that the training content matches the training needs and objectives. The importance of this has been noted by Campbell who states, "by far the highest-priority question for designers, users, and investigators of training is, What is to be learned? That is, what (specifically) should a training program try to accomplish, and what should the training content be?" (p. 188).[10]

To understand the importance of this issue, consider an organization that sells dental equipment and supplies. Although the company regularly offers new products, they do not sell very well. The reason appears to be because the sales force concentrates on repeat sales of more common supplies and materials. There are a number of reasons why this might be the case. For example, the sales force might not be sufficiently informed about the new products or they might not have the skills required to sell them. Other reasons could be a lack of motivation or an attitude problem. The point is that the content of a training program can be directed toward any one or more of these areas. Obviously, designing a training program to inform the sales force about the new products will not be very effective if what they are lacking are sales skills. Getting the content right is one of the most important stages in training design.

A trainer will have a good idea of the nature of the training content from the needs analysis and the training objectives. This is another reason why it is so important to conduct a thorough needs analysis prior to designing a training program. As well, employees' current levels of knowledge and skills can be compared to the organization's desired levels as indicated by the performance goals or objectives. The gap between the two represents the organization's training needs and determines the precise content of the training course.

According to Donald Kirkpatrick, trainers should ask themselves, "What topics should be presented to meet the needs and accomplish the objectives?" (p. 11).[11] The answers to this question should help in identifying the content to include in a training program.

However, even if one knows, for example, that employees have insufficient knowledge of how to conduct structured employment interviews, it still remains to be determined what content will be used in the training program. That is, we still need to translate training objectives into training content and to also determine the sequence in which the content will be learned.[12] It is not sufficient to simply say that the training content should focus on structured interviewing.

Being more precise about training content can occur in a number of ways. One of the most common and effective ways to identify training content is to consult with subject-matter experts who are knowledgeable in a particular area and know the topic well enough that they can specify the training content.[13] For example, to determine the content of a training program on structured employment interviews, one can consult with human resource professionals, consultants, or professors. It is also possible that some members of the organization's human resource department will have some knowledge about structured employment interviews. On the basis of the subject-matter experts' judgments one can identify the content required to achieve the training objectives.

A second source of training content is the research and theory that can be found in the academic and practitioner literature. In the case of structured employment interviews, there are dozens of articles and research papers on how to design and conduct structured interviews.

A third possibility would be to purchase an off-the-shelf training program on structured employment interviews. This would likely include a lesson plan, an instructor's guide, training materials and exercises, and perhaps a videotape. Whichever of these sources are used, it is important to realize that ultimately a judgment will have to be made about what content will best fulfil the training needs and objectives. This decision will not always be easy. For example, in the case of employment interviews, there are many different ways to conduct a structured interview.

Returning to the training program on structured employment interviews, a good place to start would be the substantial literature on interviewing. For example, a review of structured interviews identified 15 ways that employment interviews can be structured to enhance the content and evaluation process of the interview (e.g., base questions on a job analysis).[14] This information can be used in part as the content for the training program.

Based on this information, the company decided that they would train the HR staff to conduct a behaviour description interview. Behaviour description interviews ask questions about past job and life experiences that are job-relevant. For example, applicants are typically asked how they handled situations in the past that are similar to those they will face on the job.

The company hired a training consultant to design a behaviour description interview to hire sales associates. The content of the training program was based on a number of the points identified in the article on structured interviews. In particular, trainees will be trained to conduct structured employment interviews as follows:

1. Ask exactly the same questions of each candidate.
2. Limit prompting, follow-up questioning, and elaboration on questions.
3. Use behaviour description interview questions.
4. Do not allow questions from candidates until after the interview.
5. Rate each interview answer using the scales for each question.
6. Take detailed notes.
7. Use statistical rather than clinical prediction.

Now that the content of the training program has been determined, a *lesson* objective can be written, keeping in mind that the *training* objective is the overall objective of the training program. A more specific lesson objective is as follows:

> Employees in human resources will be able to conduct a structured behavioural description interview for the sales associate position and correctly perform the seven key behaviours.

Chapter 5: Training Design and Delivery

Training Methods

Once the training content has been determined, the next step is to decide what training methods will be used.[15] The topic of training methods is extensive and as a result, the next three chapters are devoted to it. For now we will present a brief introduction to this important part of training design.

Training methods can be arranged into a number of different categories such as active versus passive methods or one-way versus two-way communication. For our purposes, we will distinguish training methods in terms of where they take place since this is a fairly tangible distinction. That is, some training methods occur on the job, such as coaching and performance aids, while others take place off the job and usually in a classroom, such as lectures or games and simulations.

A variety of off-the-job and on-the-job training methods are described in Chapters 6 and 7. These methods differ in terms of their effectiveness for teaching different types of training content and for various learning outcomes. The fact is that there are many training methods from which to choose. The choice will be constrained by time, money, or tradition.

Research shows that learning and retention are best achieved through the use of training methods that promote productive responses from trainees.[16] Productive responses are those in which the trainee actively uses the training content rather than passively watches, listens, or imitates the trainer. In addition, it is also believed that training methods that encourage active participation during training also enhances learning.[17] In the next section, we discuss the importance of active practice in the design of a training program.

Ultimately, the objectives of a training program and the training content should help to determine the most appropriate training methods. The best approach, however, is usually a "blended" approach that consists of a combination of classroom training, on-the-job training, and self-paced instruction using computer technology such as CD-Roms or the Internet. A good example of a blended approach is Krispy Kreme's manager-training program, which includes classroom instruction, on-the-job training, and Web-based training.

For the structured employment interview training program, a combination of three training methods will be used. First, a lecture and discussion method is used to impart knowledge about structured interviews and behaviour description interview questions. Second, an audio-visual method with behaviour modelling will be used to demonstrate to trainees how to conduct a structured employment interview. And third, a role-play method is used so trainees have some practice and experience in learning how to actually conduct a behaviour description interview.

Active Practice

An important consideration in the design of a training program is how to facilitate and maximize trainees' learning and retention of the training content. One of the most important ways that people learn and acquire new skills is through practice.[18] It is therefore important to incorporate practice into the design of a training program. But what exactly is practice?

Practice refers to physical or mental rehearsal of a task, skill, or knowledge in order to achieve some level of proficiency in performing the task or skill or demonstrating the knowledge.[19] There is a certain degree of truth to the adage "practice makes perfect." A student who practices answering exam questions learns more than someone who just reads the text book. A manager will probably learn more about interviewing by actually conducting a mock interview than by listening to a lecture on interviewing. In general, both adults and children learn through active practice.

In the context of training, we often refer to **active practice**, which means that trainees are provided with opportunities to practice the task or use the knowledge being learned during training. Therefore, training programs should include opportunities for active practice. The effectiveness of active practice, however, depends on a number of conditions that occur before and during a training program. In the following sections, we describe different practice conditions that take place before (prepractice) and during a training program that influence the effectiveness of practice.

Prepractice Conditions

A number of conditions that occur prior to practice can improve learning and retention. These are strategies or interventions that can be implemented prior to a training program to prepare trainees for practice and include: 1. Attentional advice, 2. Metacognitive strategies, 3. Advance organizers, 4. Goal orientation, 5. Preparatory information, and 6. Prepractice briefs.[20]

Attentional advice involves providing trainees with information about the task process and general task strategies that can help them learn and perform a task. This helps to focus trainees' attention on task strategies that can aid them in learning and performing a task and to generalize what is learned in practice to other situations in which the general strategies can be applied.

Trainees can also benefit more from practice if they know how to regulate their learning through a process known as metacognition. **Metacognition** refers to a self-regulatory process that helps people guide their learning and performance (recall the discussion of self-management in Chapter 3). In this way, people can assess and adjust their progress and strategies while learning to perform a task. Trainees can learn how to do this by using metacognitive strategies. **Metacognitive strategies** (e.g., thinking out loud, self-diagnose weaknesses, pose questions to yourself during practice, answer the question "why am I doing this") refer to ways in which trainees can be instructed to self-regulate their learning of a task. Metacognitive strategies can be taught to trainees prior to training so they can self-regulate and guide their own learning and performance during practice sessions.

Advance organizers refer to activities that provide trainees with a structure or framework to help them assimilate and integrate information acquired during practice. In other words, they help trainees structure and organize information. Examples of advance organizers include outlines, text, diagrams, and graphic organizers. Advance organizers have been found to be particularly useful for learning highly complex and factual material and for low ability trainees.

Practice
Physical or mental rehearsal of a task, skill, or knowledge in order to achieve some level of proficiency in performing the task or skill or demonstrating the knowledge

Active practice
Providing trainees with opportunities to practise performing a training task or using knowledge during training

Attentional advice
Providing trainees with information about the task process and general task strategies that can help them learn and perform a task

Metacognition
A self-regulatory process that helps people guide their learning and performance

Metacognitive strategies
Refers to ways in which trainees can be instructed to self-regulate their learning of a task

Advance organizers
Activities that provide trainees with a structure or framework to help them assimilate and integrate information acquired during practice

Goal orientation

The type of goal that is set during training (mastery versus performance)

Preparatory information

Providing trainees with information about what they can expect to occur during practice sessions

Prepractice briefs

Sessions in which team members establish their roles and responsibilities and performance expectations prior to a team practice session

Massed versus distributed practice

Refers to how the segments of a training program are divided and whether the training is conducted in a single session (massed) or is divided into several sessions with breaks or rest periods between them (distributed)

Goal orientation refers to the type of goal that is set during training. You might recall the discussion from Chapter 3 that there are two types of goal orientations. Learning or mastery goals focus trainees' attention on the learning process while performance goals focus attention on the achievement of specific performance outcomes. Because mastery goals focus trainees' attention on the process of learning and skill acquisition they tend to be more effective. In fact, mastery goals have been found to result in faster skill acquisition. Thus, mastery goals appear to be most effective for practice because they focus trainees' attention on learning the task rather than on their performance during training, and they also improve motivation and self-efficacy.

Preparatory information involves providing trainees with information about what they can expect to occur during practice sessions (e.g., events and consequences). Thus, preparatory information informs trainees about what to expect during a practice session so that they can develop strategies to overcome performance obstacles. As a result, trainees who are provided with preparatory information prior to practice are better prepared to learn and perform a task. They know what to expect and how to overcome performance obstacles. Preparatory information is particularly useful for learning to perform stressful tasks where the ability to cope and overcome obstacles is critical for task performance.

A final example of a prepractice condition is specific to team training. **Prepractice briefs** involve sessions in which team members establish their roles and responsibilities and performance expectations prior to a team practice session. Prepractice briefs can improve team practice sessions especially for tasks that are fast-paced and stressful.

Conditions of Practice during Training

In addition to prepractice conditions, there are also a number of practice conditions that occur during training. They include 1. Massed or distributed practice, 2. Whole or part learning, 3. Overlearning, 4. Task sequencing, and 5. Feedback and knowledge of results.

Massed versus distributed practice has to do with how the segments of a training program are divided. Massed practice, or cramming, is practice with virtually no rest periods, such as when the training is conducted in one single session instead of being divided into several sessions with breaks or rest periods between them. Distributed or spaced practice conditions include rest intervals during the practice session.

Students might argue that they can succeed on an exam for which they have crammed, but research shows that memory loss after cramming is greater than if a student had studied over several weeks. Furthermore, organizations would prefer that trainees retain material over many months, rather than just knowing it for the course test or simulation.

Research has shown that material that was learned under distributed practice is retained longer.[21] Furthermore, a recent review of research on practice conditions found that distributed practice sessions resulted in higher performance than massed practice conditions.[22] Thus, practice is more effective when practice periods are spread over time, rather than massed together. Trainers teaching a new skill, such as negotiations, could increase learning by spacing the training and practices over a week of two-hour sessions, rather than cramming it into an eight-hour day. Distributed practice is most effective for trainees with little or no experience, when the rest periods are shorter early on but longer later in training, and for learning motor skills.[23]

Whole versus part learning has to do with whether all of the training material is learned and practised at one time or one part at a time.[24] For example, piano students often learn complex pieces one hand at a time. Research has found that the best strategy depends on the trainee and the nature of the task. Whole learning is more effective when the trainee has high intelligence, practice is distributed, the task organization of the training material is high, and task complexity is low. Generally speaking, when the task itself is composed of relatively clear and different parts or subtasks, it is best for trainees to learn and practise each part at a time and then perform all parts in one whole sequence. However, if the task itself is relatively simple and consists of a number of closely interrelated tasks, then a strategy of whole learning makes more sense.[25]

Overlearning is another condition of practice that refers to learning something until the behaviour becomes automatic. In other words, trainees are provided with continued opportunities for practice even after they have mastered the task.[26] It is an effective way to train people for emergency responses or for complex skills in which there is little time to think in a job situation. It is also important for skills that employees might not need to use very often on the job. Overlearning will help to ensure that performance of the task will be habitual or automatic. Automaticity refers to the performance of a skill to the point at which little attention from the brain is required to respond correctly.[27] Typing is the most common example of automaticity.

Overlearning is an effective method for both cognitive and physical tasks. The greater the degree of overlearning, the longer the resulting retention of the training material.[28]

Task sequencing has to do with the manner in which the learning tasks are organized and arranged. The basic idea is that learning can be improved by dividing the training material into an organized sequence of subtasks. The idea behind task sequencing was first proposed by Gagne who argued that practice is not enough for learning to occur.[29] What is most important is that the distinct subtasks be identified and arranged in a logical sequence. In this manner, a trainee will learn each successive subtask before the total task is performed. The trainee learns to perform each step or task in the proper order or sequence. According to Gagne, what is most important in the design of training is the identification of the component tasks or subtasks and the arrangement of them into a meaningful and suitable sequence.[30]

Feedback or knowledge of results involves providing trainees with information and knowledge about their performance on a training task. Research indicates that feedback is critical for learning for at least three reasons.[31] First, it allows trainees to correct mistakes and improve their performance. Second, positive feedback can help build confidence and

Whole versus part learning
Refers to whether the training material is learned and practised at one time or one part at a time

Overlearning
Continued practice even after trainees have mastered a task, so that the behaviour becomes automatic

Task sequencing
Dividing training material into an organized and logical sequence of subtasks

Feedback or knowledge of results
Providing trainees with information and knowledge about their performance on a training task

strengthen trainees' self-efficacy. Third, positive feedback can be reinforcing and stimulate continued efforts and learning.

During training, feedback can be provided to guide trainees as they attempt new behaviours. This feedback should be designed to correct performance. When incorrect responses are given, the feedback should include the correct response. Negative feedback ("you failed to acknowledge the client's problem") will not be perceived as punishing if the source is knowledgeable, friendly, trustworthy, and powerful enough to affect outcomes like promotions.[32] However, to be most effective, feedback should be accurate, specific, credible, timely, and positive.[33]

In a study of the effect of feedback on the performance of hourly workers, Miller concluded that the relevance, specificity, timing, and accuracy of the feedback are the critical factors in mastery of learning.[34] Trainees receiving this type of feedback are more likely to adjust their responses toward the correct behaviour, more likely to be motivated to change, and more likely to set goals for improving or maintaining performance.[35] Training methods such as computer-assisted instruction and structured behaviour modelling have feedback as an integral and imbedded component. See The Trainer's Notebook 1 on the key elements for providing effective feedback.

In summary, training programs can be designed to facilitate and maximize trainees' learning and retention by providing trainees with opportunities for active practice. In addition, a number of conditions of practice before and during training can be used to improve the benefits of active practice for learning and retention. Table 5.2 summarizes the conditions of practice.

The Trainer

Once a training program has been designed, attention shifts to deciding who will deliver the training. At first, this might seem like a trivial question. After all, isn't this the job of the human resources department or the training director? In some cases the answer is yes, but in many training situations the answer to this question depends on a number of important factors.

The Trainer's Notebook 1

How to Give Feedback

Feedback can be very effective in changing behaviour, if the feedback is seen as being constructive, not critical. Here are some tips on how to do it right.

- *Timing:* Try to provide the feedback immediately after the behaviour or performance is observed.
- *Be specific:* Feedback works when it is specific. Don't say, "You moved the arm wrong," but "You have the arm tilted at 30 degrees."

- *Guide:* After discussing what was poorly done, provide guidance on the correct performance. ("You had the arm tilted at a 30 degree angle; you will find it easier or quicker to tilt it 90 degrees.")
- *Reward correct performance:* "Good, you have the right 90-degree angle," not just "good."

TABLE 5.2

The Conditions of Practice

Prepractice Conditions

1. *Attentional advice*: Providing trainees with information about the task process and general task strategies that can help them learn and perform a task.
2. *Metacognitive strategies*: Refers to ways in which trainees can be instructed to self-regulate their learning of a task.
3. *Advance organizers*: Activities that provide trainees with a structure or framework to help them assimilate and integrate information acquired during practice.
4. *Goal orientation*: The type of goal that is set during training (mastery versus performance).
5. *Preparatory information*: Providing trainees with information about what they can expect to occur during practice sessions.
6. *Prepractice briefs*: Sessions in which team members establish their roles and responsibilities and establish performance expectations prior to a team practice session.

Conditions During Training

1. *Massed or distributed practice*: Refers to how the segments of a training program are divided and whether the training is conducted in a single session or is divided into several sessions with breaks or rest periods between them.
2. *Whole or part learning*: Refers to whether the training material is learned and practised at one time or one part at a time.
3. *Overlearning*: Continued practice even after trainees have mastered a task so that the behaviour becomes automatic.
4. *Task sequencing*: Refers to dividing training material into an organized and logical sequence of subtasks.
5. *Feedback and knowledge of results*: Providing trainees with information and knowledge about their performance on a training task.

First, it is important to realize the importance of a good trainer. Regardless of how well a training program is designed, the success of a program rests in large part on the trainer. In other words, no matter how good the training program is, if the trainer is ineffective, the program will suffer.

What then are the qualities of a good trainer? This question should be easy for students to answer if they consider the courses they have enjoyed and those that they found less memorable. One of the first things that comes to mind is probably the extent to which the instructor was knowledgeable about the course material. This is usually referred to as subject-matter expertise. A trainer should be well versed if not an expert on the topic or content area being taught. Not only will trainees learn more, but also the trainer will be perceived as more credible. Very often those persons who conduct training in an organization do so because they have expertise in a particular area.

Students also know, perhaps all too well, that no matter how well informed or knowledgeable the instructor, a course can still be inadequate to the extent that the instructor is not very good at delivering the material. In addition to subject-matter expertise, good trainers must also have good verbal and communication skills, interpersonal skills, and organizing and planning skills. In other words, a trainer must be able to deliver the training material and content in a manner that is understandable to trainees. Trainees are more likely to learn and be better able to recall training content when the trainer is well organized and easy to follow.[36]

A third category of trainer characteristics is the ability to make the material interesting rather than dull and boring. Students probably have had instructors who knew the material and were able to deliver it, but all the same, they did not make it very interesting. A good trainer should also be enthusiastic and excited about the training material and capable of motivating and arousing the interest of trainees.

One way for trainers to generate interest and increase trainee motivation is by being expressive during the delivery of a training program. Expressive trainers are more physically animated (e.g., posture, gesturing, eye contact) and use linguistic devices such as an enthusiastic voice as opposed to a monotone voice, and vocal fluency rather than speaking with hesitancies (e.g., "ums"). Research has shown that trainees recall a greater amount of the training content when a trainer was more expressive. There is also evidence that a trainer's expressiveness enhances trainees' motivation to learn and self-efficacy.[37]

One of the difficulties in choosing a trainer is that, on the one hand, very often those individuals who have the subject-matter expertise required to deliver a training program do not have the other skills and characteristics of a good trainer. On the other hand, those who are skilled trainers such as members of human resource departments, often do not have the subject-matter expertise to conduct many training programs in their organizations.

One solution to this problem has been to teach subject-matter experts how to become effective trainers. These programs are known as *train the trainer* and focus on the skills that are required to be an effective trainer. As described in the Training Today feature, with the increasing use of technology in the workplace, more subject-matter experts are being asked to become trainers.

In the case of the Vandalais Department Stores' structured interview training program, the consultant who designed the behaviour description employment interview was chosen to be the trainer. This is because he has the subject-matter expertise and is an experienced trainer.

The Trainees

Who should attend a training program? This is an important question as money and time can be wasted if the wrong people attend and, of course, problems are likely to continue if those who really need the training do not attend. As a starting point, one must carefully select trainees based on their

Training Subject-Matter Experts to be Trainers

Because of their technical expertise, an increasing number of employees are being drafted into the role of trainer. Organizations, especially smaller ones without training departments, have long relied on their resident experts to teach others to program their voice mail, send faxes, and log on to their computers. But as technology has transformed office equipment into souped-up vehicles on multi-lane electronic autobahns, it's not always possible to navigate just by reading the manual and relying on intuition.

Just because a person has crafted countless Microsoft™ PowerPoint™ presentations or designed award-winning Web pages doesn't mean he or she will be able to teach others to do the same. Often, organizations assume that teaching should come naturally to employees who know their stuff and have spent countless hours sitting in classes themselves. "Unfortunately, many companies have said all one needs to be a good technical instructor is subject-matter expertise," says Michael Nolan, president of Friesen, Kaye and Associates, an Ottawa firm that works with nontrainers or subject-matter experts (SMEs) who find themselves having to teach what they know to others. "It goes much farther than that. They have to have other skills that they haven't developed in the environment in which they've worked." They have to understand, for example, how adults learn, what to do when participants behave like mules, and how not to feel as though they've been caught in a klieg light when someone asks them a question they can't answer.

Nolan predicts SMEs won't replace professional trainers—even in the IT field. But when these experts are called on to share their knowledge, they need support. That's where the training department comes in. "Instructors in the training department can provide a fabulous experience by coaching and mentoring," he says.

abilities, aptitudes, and motivation. The employees must be assessed or tested to determine current knowledge and skill levels. Performance tests or interviews could be conducted to develop a base line of competencies. These tests can also act as motivators in the sense that they indicate the need for change and can also indicate if some employees already know some of the material. These knowledgeable employees can either bypass a training program or can act as coaches during the training process.

According to Kirkpatrick, the following four decisions need to be made when selecting participants for a training program[38]

1. Who can benefit from the training?
2. What programs are required by law or by government edict?
3. Should the training be voluntary or compulsory?
4. Should the participants be segregated by level in the organization, or should two or more levels be included in the same class?

The information on employees' competencies should help to answer the first question. The answer to the second question can be obtained by contacting government agencies or labour boards. With respect to the third question, Kirkpatrick argues that some programs be compulsory. If a program is voluntary then there will be some employees who need the training but will not attend. When the training material is required for a group of employees, the program should be compulsory.[39] The answer to the last question depends on the climate in an organization and the rapport that exists between different levels in the organization. The main issue is whether employees will feel comfortable enough to speak and participate if their supervisors are present. If this is the case then it is often a good idea for different levels to attend a training program together.

Training plan

Indicates who in an organization needs training, the type of training that is needed, and how the training will be delivered

Information on who requires training can be incorporated into a training plan. A **training plan** indicates who in an organization needs training (e.g., human resource staff), the type of training needed (e.g., structured employment interviewing), and how the training will be delivered (in a formal classroom).[40]

Training Materials and Equipment

All training programs require the use of training materials, supplies, and equipment. The content of a training program as well as the methods and exercises determine the materials, supplies, and equipment that will be required.

With the determination of the supplies necessary for training, such as manuals or equipment, the training budget is more easily developed, the program more accurately costed, and the actual training session more likely to run smoothly. Common supplies include computer equipment, a projector, VCRs and tapes, and workbooks or manuals. Handouts such as course outlines that indicate the course objectives, the material to be covered, and a schedule of training activities, as well as articles and copies of the trainers' slides, are often required and will have to be prepared.

For the purposes of the structured employment interview program, the following materials for trainees will be required: course booklet that includes a course outline, an article on structured interviewing and one on behaviour description interviews, copies of the instructor's slides, the role-play exercise, the behaviour description interview questions and guide for the sales associate position, and a pen and pad of paper. Materials required for the trainer include: a flipchart and markers as well as a purchased videotape showing an unstructured and structured employment interview. The equipment required will be a computer, projector, TV monitor, and a VCR.

The Training Site

The training site is the actual location or room where the training will take place. Off-the-job training can take place in rooms located within an organization's offices, a learning or training centre owned by the organization, or at a rented facility such as a hotel. Many organizations such as the Bank of Montreal and CIBC have their own training centres. However, for organizations that do not have training facilities, space must be found and rented. In this case, an important concern will be the amount of travel time required for trainees to get to the training site and ensuring that trainees have transportation.

Whether the training takes place in an organization's facilities or one that needs to be rented, a number of factors need to be considered to ensure that the training program runs smoothly.

First, the training site should be conducive to learning. This means that the training environment should be comfortable in terms of things like space, lighting, and temperature. This might seem like a trivial point, but have you ever attended a class and the room temperature was a bit on the cold side? Or how about one that was too crowded and you had to stand or sit on the floor because there was not enough space? Chances are it caused you some discomfort and interfered with your learning.

Second, the training site should be free of any noise or distractions that might interfere with or disrupt trainee learning. How often have you been in class where you had to strain to hear the instructor over the chatter coming from outside the classroom? Obviously, noise can interfere with learning. Distractions can also be a problem. This is one reason why it is sometimes preferable to conduct a training program away from the organization. Otherwise, trainees might be tempted to step out of the training session to take care of business. This, of course, is not likely if they are far from their desk and the workplace.

Third, the training site should be set up in a manner that is appropriate for a particular training course. For example, if trainees will be viewing a video, will they be able to see the screen and hear the video? If trainees will be required to work in groups, will there be sufficient room for them to move around the room and interact with group members? Are the seats arranged in a way that will allow trainees to interact and see each other, and will the trainer be able to interact with the trainees? Are the chairs movable or fixed? Again, these may be trivial issues but have you ever been in a classroom where you could not see the chalkboard or the screen at the front of the room? These types of problems can interfere with learning and negatively affect the effectiveness of a training program. An important part of training design and delivery is making sure that the training site is comfortable, free of distractions, and suitable for the training program.

Scheduling the Training Program

The scheduling of a training program must take into consideration a number of important factors. In effect, one has to arrange the training schedule so that it can accommodate all of the participants. For example, when is the best time for employees to attend a training program in terms of the day of the week, the time of day, and time of year? When will they be available to attend training? This will probably depend on the organization and the business it is in. Most businesses have periods or seasons when they are especially busy and scheduling a training program during these times is likely to result in some resistance and perhaps low attendance. One should also be sensitive to the needs and desires of employees and their supervisors. Would it be preferable to hold the training during office hours or after hours, such as in the evenings or on the weekend? Employees and their supervisors should be consulted to

Chapter 5: Training Design and Delivery

determine the best time and schedule for them to attend a training program.[41]

A second consideration is the availability of the trainer. Whether the trainers are from the human resource department or elsewhere in the organization, they will likely have many other responsibilities that will restrict their availability. Trainers from within the organization will have to receive release time from their other duties to prepare and deliver the training program. If the trainers are from outside of the organization, then they will also have some restrictions regarding their availability and will have to be contracted for a particular date.

A third consideration in scheduling the training program is the availability of the training site, equipment, materials, and so on. To the extent that the training site and equipment are regularly used, one will have to schedule them in advance. In addition, if materials need to be designed or purchased, they will need to be available in time for the training program.

Finally, when scheduling a training program, one also has to consider whether it would be best to offer it all at once, such as one day versus four two-hour sessions in the case of an eight-hour program, or all in one week versus one day each week for five weeks (or once a month for five months) in the case of a five-day program. As indicated earlier when we discussed massed versus distributed practice, this depends in part on the complexity of the training material and the experience level of the trainees. There are also issues of resources and logistics. Sometimes it is just not feasible to conduct a training program over a longer period of time. Whenever possible, however, Kirkpatrick recommends that it is best to spread the training out as an ongoing program, such as a three-hour session once a month.[42]

The Lesson Plan

The **lesson plan** is the blueprint that outlines the training program in terms of the sequence of activities and events that will take place. As such, it is a guide for the trainer that provides a step-by-step breakdown for conducting the training program. A lesson plan is important for a number of reasons.

First, a competently prepared lesson plan will make the task of competing for funding easier. Second, a good plan will enable training activity to be directed toward real training problems, not symptoms of problems. Third, the planning document will ensure that the problems under consideration can be solved by training and not some other intervention or method. Fourth, good planning leads to enhanced credibility with line managers. All of these factors combined will help the training department implement and deliver sound training programs.

A good lesson plan should be prepared in advance of a training program and should be detailed enough that any trainer could use it to guide him or her through the training program. Much of what has been determined in the previous phases will be indicated in the lesson plan. Some of the things that should be listed on the first page or cover of a lesson plan are the training objectives, classroom requirements, training aids and equipment, and trainee supplies and handouts.[43]

Table 5.3 presents the cover page of the lesson plan for the structured employment interview training program at Vandalais Department Stores. Table 5.4 presents the detailed lesson plan for the training program.

The development of a lesson plan is a critical phase in the design of a training program. It allows for both the approval and the smooth operation of training activities. It also enables expenditures to be budgeted for and monitored. The development of a lesson plan sets the stage for the administration of the training program and it is a signal to other members of the organization that training is to be conducted in a professional manner.

TABLE 5.3

Lesson Plan Cover Page

Organization:	Vandalais Department Stores
Department:	Human Resources
Program Title:	Structured Employment Interviews
Instructor(s):	Training Consultant
Time Allocation:	1 Day
Trainees:	All employees in the Human Resource Department
Where:	Vandalais Learning Centre

Training Objectives

Employees will be able to conduct a structured behaviour description interview for the sales associate position and correctly perform the seven key behaviours.

Classroom Requirements

Seating for 50 people and areas for trainees to break out into groups.

Training Aids and Equipment

VCR and TV monitor; videotape: "How to Conduct a Structured Employment Interview"; Computer and projector with screen; flipchart, paper, and markers.

Trainee Supplies

Pen and paper.

Trainee Handouts

1. Course objectives and outline.
2. Article on structured employment interviews.
3. Article on behaviour description interviews.
4. List of the seven key behaviours for conducting a structured employment interview.
5. Copy of the behaviour description interview for the sales associate position with interview questions and scoring guide and instructions.
6. Role-play exercise.

TABLE 5.4

Structured Employment Interview Lesson Plan

OBJECTIVE

Employees will be able to conduct structured behaviour description employment interview for the sales associate position and correctly perform the seven key behaviours.

Trainees: Members of the Human Resource Department.

Time: 9 a.m.– 5 p.m.

COURSE OUTLINE

9:00 – 10:00	Introduction lecture on the problem of poor employee performance of sales associates and the use of structured and unstructured employment interviews for selection.
10:00 – 10:30	Show video of an unstructured employment interview followed by a discussion.
10:30 – 10:45	Break
10:45 – 11:15	Show video of a structured employment interview followed by a discussion.
11:15 – 12:00	Review the seven key behaviours of conducting a structured employment interview.
12:00 – 1:00	Lunch
1:00 – 2:00	Lecture on behaviour description interview questions and review of the interview questions and guide developed for sales associates.
2:00 – 2:30	Review of the seven key behaviours in conducting a structured employment interview.
2:30 – 2:45	Break
2:45 – 3:30	Role-play practice exercise: In groups of three, assign participants the roles of interviewer, interviewee, and observer. Review script for roles and instruct trainees to demonstrate the seven key behaviours of a structured interview using the sales associate behaviour description interview questions. Have observer provide feedback using feedback guidelines contained in the role-play exercise booklet and evaluate the interviewer's performance on the seven key behaviours using the evaluation form provided. Switch roles until each group member plays the role of the interviewer.
3:30 – 4:30	Regroup for discussion of role-play exercise. Discuss how it felt to be the interviewer and the interviewee and the observer's perspective.
4:30 – 4:45	Review the seven key behaviours of the structured employment interview and the importance of using structured interviews and the behaviour description interview for hiring sales associates.
4:45 – 5:00	Closing. Review objectives and give pep talk about conducting structured employment interviews and using the behaviour description interview. Thank participants and hand out training certificates.

Training Administration

Once the lesson plan has been completed, there are a number of important activities that must be undertaken in order to effectively manage and administer training programs. **Training administration** involves the coordination of all of the people and materials involved in a training program. The maintenance of trainee records, training histories, customized learning opportunities, schedules, and course and material inventories is a routine, but necessary, activity. In addition to tracking registrations for programs, it is also useful to track individual career development and learning plans. Software is available that can do all these things.

In terms of particular training programs, employees and their supervisors have to be informed of each program with respect to its purpose and content, as well as where and when it will take place. In addition, those who are planning to attend need to be enrolled in the program. Trainers must also be informed of this information, as they will need to know how many trainees will be attending and the scheduling of the program. If trainees are to receive training materials or information prior to attending the program, then this will have to be prepared and sent to them in advance.

In addition, all of the materials and equipment must be ordered and prepared in time for the training program. The training site must be booked and any equipment required must be made available. In some cases, this might involve renting equipment. As well, supplies such as pens and paper must be ordered.

Finally, the training administrator will need to prepare a budget that includes the costs of all of the expenses incurred in the design and delivery of the training program. The calculation of the costs and benefits of training programs is discussed in Chapter 11.

Training administration
The coordination of all the people and materials involved in the training program

Delivery of the Training Program

Once the lesson plan has been prepared and the administrative activities have been completed, the program is ready to be implemented and delivered. For many trainers and especially novices, this is actually the most difficult part of the training process. There are, however, a number of fairly basic steps to follow when delivering a training program. According to Gagne, a training program should have the following nine events of instruction:[44]

1. *Gain attention.* Draw trainees into the learning by presenting a thought-provoking problem.
2. *Describe the goal.* Inform trainees of what they will learn and what they will be able to accomplish.
3. *Stimulate recall of prior knowledge.* Discuss what trainees already know and how it is relevant and connected to the training material.
4. *Present the material to be learned.* Present the material in a logical sequence one subtask at a time (i.e., task sequencing).
5. *Provide guidance for learning.* In addition to presenting the training content, provide trainees with guidance and tips on how best to learn the material.

6. *Elicit performance practice.* Give trainees an opportunity to practise and apply the training knowledge and skills.
7. *Provide informative feedback.* Let trainees know if their responses and behaviours are correct, and why they are correct or incorrect.
8. *Assess performance.* Test trainees on their learning of the training material and mastery of the task.
9. *Enhance retention and transfer.* Discuss with trainees how the training material can be applied to their job and actual work situations they have encountered.

While these activities are fairly straightforward, there are many potential problems that trainers must deal with when delivering a training program. To learn more about these problems and to identify some solutions, Richard Swanson and Sandra Falkman conducted a study in which they asked novice trainers about the problems they have had when delivering a training program. After content analyzing the responses, the authors identified the following 12 common training delivery problems:[45]

1. *Fear.* Fear that is due to a lack of confidence and feeling anxious while delivering the training program.
2. *Credibility.* The perception that they lack credibility in the eyes of the trainees as subject-matter experts.
3. *Personal experiences.* A lack of stories about personal experiences that can be used to relate to the training content.
4. *Difficult learners.* Don't know how to handle problem trainees who may be angry, passive, or dominating.
5. *Participation.* Difficulty getting trainees to participate.
6. *Timing.* Trouble with timing and pacing of the training material and worries about having too much or too little material.
7. *Adjusting instruction.* Difficulty adjusting the training material to the needs of trainees or being able to redesign the presentation of material during delivery.
8. *Questions.* Difficulty using questions effectively and responding to difficult questions.
9. *Feedback.* Unable to read trainees and to use feedback and evaluations effectively.
10. *Media, materials, facilities.* Concerns about how to use media and training materials.
11. *Opening, closing techniques.* The need for techniques to use as icebreakers, introductions, and effective summaries and closings.
12. *Dependence on notes.* Feeling too dependent on notes and trouble presenting the material without them.

These 12 common delivery problems of novice trainers have three basic themes: (1) problems pertaining to the trainer, (2) problems pertaining to how the trainer relates to the trainees, and (3) problems pertaining to presentation techniques. Fortunately, the authors of this study also asked expert trainers for strategies and solutions for dealing with each of the 12 delivery problems. For example, to deal with the problem of fear, a trainer should be well prepared, use icebreakers, begin with an activity that relaxes trainees and gets them talking and involved, and acknowledge one's fear and understand that it is normal.[46] See The Trainer's Notebook 2 for solutions to the 12 delivery problems.

The Trainer's Notebook 2

Solutions to the Most Common Training Delivery Problems

1. Fear.

A. Be well prepared and have a detailed lesson plan.
B. Use icebreakers and begin with an activity that relaxes trainees.
C. Acknowledge the fear and use self-talk and relaxation exercises prior to the training.

2. Credibility.

A. Don't apologize. Be honest about your knowledge of the subject.
B. Have the attitude of an expert and be well prepared and organized.
C. Share personal background and talk about your area of expertise and experiences.

3. Personal experiences.

A. Relate personal experiences.
B. Report experiences of others and have trainees share their experiences.
C. Use analogies, refer to movies or famous people who relate to the subject.

4. Difficult learners.

A. Confront the problem learner and talk to them to determine the problem.
B. Circumvent dominating behaviour by using nonverbal behaviour such as breaking eye contact or standing with your back to the person.
C. Use small groups to overcome timid behaviour and structure exercises where a wide range of participation is encouraged.

5. Participation.

A. Ask open-ended questions and provide positive feedback when trainees participate.
B. Plan small group activities such as dyads, case studies, and role plays to increase participation.

C. Invite participation by structuring activities to allow trainees to share early in the program.

6. Timing.

A. Plan for too much material and prioritize activities so that some can be omitted if necessary.
B. Practise presenting the material many times so that you know where you should be at 15-minute intervals.

7. Adjusting instruction.

A. Determine the needs of the group early in the training and structure activities based on them.
B. Request feedback by asking trainees how they feel about the training during breaks or periodically during the training.
C. Redesign the program during breaks and have a contingency plan in place.

8. Questions.

Answering questions

A. Anticipate questions by writing out key questions that trainees might have.
B. Paraphrase and repeat a question so everyone hears the question and understands it.
C. Redirect questions you can't answer back to the trainees' and try to find answers during the break.

Asking questions

A. Ask concise and simple questions and provide enough time for trainees to answer.

9. Feedback.

A. Solicit informal feedback during training or breaks on whether the training is meeting their needs and expectations and watch for nonverbal cues.

continued

Continued from previous page

B. Do summative evaluations at the conclusion of the training to determine if the objectives and needs of trainees have been met.

10. Media, materials, facilities.

Media

A. Know how to operate every piece of equipment you will use.
B. Have backups such as extra bulbs, extension cords, markers, tape, and so on, as well as bringing the material in another medium in case one has problems.
C. Enlist assistance from trainees if you have a problem and need help.

Materials

A. Be prepared and have all the material placed at trainees' workplace or ready for distribution.

Facilities

A. Visit facility beforehand to see the layout of the room and where things are located and how to set up.
B. Arrive at least one hour early to set up and handle any problems.

11. Opening, closing techniques.

Openings

A. Develop a file of ideas based on experimentation and observation.
B. Develop and memorize a great opening.
C. Relax trainees by greeting them when they enter, taking time for introductions and creating a relaxed atmosphere.

Closings

A. Provide a simple and concise summary of the course contents using objectives or the initial model.
B. Thank participants for their time and contribution to the course.

12. Dependence on notes.

A. Notes are necessary.
B. Use cards with an outline or key words as prompts.
C. Use visuals such as notes on the frames of transparencies or your copy of the handouts.
D. Practise and learn the script so you can deliver it from the key words on your note cards.

Source: Swanson, R.A., & Falkman, S.K. (1997). Training delivery problems and solutions: Identification of novice trainer problems and expert trainer solutions. *Human Resource Development Quarterly, 8,* 305–14. © 1997 by Jossey-Bass Inc. This material is used by permission of John Wiley & Sons, Inc.

Model of Training Effectiveness—Training Design

Before concluding this chapter, let's return to the model of training effectiveness that was presented in Chapter 3. Recall that the model showed that, in addition to training, 1. trainees' cognitive ability, training motivation, self-efficacy, personality, and attitudes have a direct effect on trainee learning and retention; 2. learning and retention have a direct effect on individual behaviour and performance; and 3. individual behaviour and performance have a direct effect on organizational effectiveness.

Based on what you have learned in this chapter, we can add training design factors to the model. Recall that active practice and practice conditions before training (prepractice) and during training influence learning and retention. Figure 5.1 shows a revised model of training effectiveness in which training, trainee characteristics, and training design influence learning and retention.

FIGURE 5.1

Model of Training Effectiveness

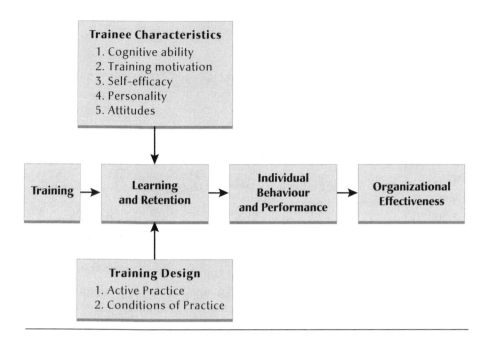

Summary

This chapter described the main steps in the design and delivery of a training program. First, we described the elements and components of training objectives. Next we discussed the decision to purchase or design a training program and the advantages and disadvantages of each. We then described the main activities involved in designing a training program including the content, methods, active practice, conditions of practice, the trainer, trainees, training equipment and material, the training site, scheduling, the lesson plan, and training administration. Finally, we discussed how a training program can be effectively delivered following the nine events of instruction and we presented solutions to 12 common delivery problems.

One of the most important factors discussed in this chapter was deciding on the use of training methods. As we will see in the next three chapters, there are many possible off- and on-the-job methods of training as well as new forms of technology-based training methods.

Key Terms

active practice (page 121)
advance organizers (page 121)
attentional advice (page 121)
feedback or knowledge of results (page 123)

goal orientation (page 122)
lesson plan (page 130)
massed vs. distributed practice (page 122)
metacognition (page 121)

Weblinks

Discussion Questions

1. Discuss the following: Practice makes perfect and enough practice will lead to learning and retention.
2. What factors should an organization consider when deciding to purchase or design a training program, and what are the advantages and disadvantages of a purchase or design decision?
3. What are the characteristics of a good trainer and what effect do these characteristics have on trainee learning, retention, and on-the-job behaviour? Do you think that a trainer can learn to be a good trainer or is it something you are born with?
4. Discuss the conditions of practice before and during training and how they can improve learning and retention.

Using the Internet

1. To find out about the kinds of training programs that can be purchased, go to: **www.trainingreport.ca** and click on the Directory of Training Suppliers and Consultants.

   First, review the category listings and try to find an area that you are familiar with, perhaps something relevant to a current or prevous job or an area that interests you. Second, go to the listings within your chosen category and find out about the kinds of training programs that can be purchased. Describe the content of the programs, the methods, and any other design characteristics that are indicated. Prepare a short report about the category and the kind of training programs available for purchase.

Exercises

1. Think of the best and worst training experience that you have ever had. For each one, indicate the purpose of the training, the objectives, and the content. Then make a list of all the reasons why you feel that it was the best and worst training experience you have ever had using the

material presented in this chapter. Based on your lists, what are some of the things that make a training program effective?

2. How expressive are you as a trainer? To find out and improve your expressiveness, prepare a short (5 – 10 minute) lecture on a topic of interest to you or perhaps something on training from the text. Then give your lecture to the class. The class can then evaluate your verbal and nonverbal expressiveness. Make a list of the things that you can do to improve your expressiveness.

3. If you have a driver's licence, then you probably remember what it was like to learn how to drive. Chances are you stepped into a car with a friend or family member who told you what to do. And if you have ever taught someone how to drive, you probably did the same thing. Did you remember to tell them everything they needed to know? What are the things you told them to do first? Could you have done a better job teaching them to drive? Probably. Refer to the section of this chapter on task sequencing. Recall that task sequencing involves dividing a task into its component parts or subtasks, and then ordering them into a meaningful or logical sequence. Now try to design a driver training program based on task sequencing. In other words, make a list of all of the subtasks involved in driving a car and then organize them into a logical sequence for the purpose of teaching somebody how to drive.

4. Contact the human resources department of an organization and request a meeting with somebody in the department whom you can interview about the organization's training programs. Develop a series of questions so that you can learn about each of the following design issues in terms of a particular training program that the organization has implemented:

- Was the training program designed by the organization or purchased? What were the reasons for designing or purchasing the program?
- What is the content of the training program and how was it developed?
- Who is the trainer of the program and how was he or she chosen?
- Who were the trainees and how and why were they chosen to attend the program?
- What training methods were used and why?
- What training materials and equipment were used?
- Was a lesson plan prepared for the program? If not, why? If so, what things were included on it?
- Describe the training facility and why it was chosen.
- Describe the schedule of the training program and how it was determined.
- Who administered and coordinated the training program and what did this involve?

- How was the delivery of the training program conducted? What are some problems that have occurred in the delivery of the training program and what strategies are used to deal with them?

  Based on the information you have acquired, conduct an evaluation with respect to how effectively you think each of the stages were performed, and list some recommendations to improve each stage.

5. Have you ever wondered what your instructor does to prepare for a class? To find out, choose one of your classes and try to describe each of the following:
   - the objectives of the class
   - the content of the class
   - the trainer (experience, job title, etc.)
   - who the trainees (students) are (e.g., major, work experience, etc.)
   - the training methods used
   - the training materials and equipment
   - the training site
   - the class schedule
   - the lesson plan
   - the administration of the class (what was involved?)
   - the delivery of the material (events of instruction) and any delivery problems and strategies used to deal with them

   Based on your description, how effective was the class? How can it be improved?

6. Recall a training program that you attended in a previous or current job. Describe the objectives and content of the program and any opportunities for active practice. What did you practice and how helpful was it for your learning and retention? Describe the extent to which any of the conditions of practice were used either before or during the training program and how they affected your learning and retention. What changes would you recommend to improve trainees' learning and retention?

7. Identify a skill that you would like to acquire. Some examples might be to use a particular software package or perhaps to improve your written or oral presentation skills. Now develop training objectives for a training program on the skill that you have chosen using the five elements and three components of training objectives described in the chapter. Exchange your objectives with another student and assess each other's objectives in terms of the criteria outlined in the chapter for writing training objectives.

8. Read the following training objectives and identify what is wrong with them. Then re-write them so that they conform to the elements and components of training objectives described in the chapter.
   - The trainer will spend 30 minutes discussing time-management tips.
   - The trainees will be able to manage their time more effectively.
   - The purpose of the seminar is to teach time-management techniques.

- After attending the course, employees will be able to make lists and put letters beside the items on the list, enabling them to manage time more effectively.

Training the Sales Force

Sales at a large telecommunications company were down for the third quarter. Management reviewed several strategies to improve sales and concluded that one solution would be to improve training for the large, dispersed sales force.

For the sake of expediency, the training department began using a needs analysis they conducted several years before as a basis to develop enhanced training. Their plan was first to update the original needs analysis, and then to develop new training strategies on the basis of what they found. They also began investigating new training technologies as a possible means to reduce training delivery costs. However, management was so intent on doing something quickly that the training department was ultimately pressured into purchasing a generic, off-the-shelf training package by a local vendor.

One of the features of the package that appealed to management was that the course could be delivered over the Web, saving the time and expense of having the sales force travel to the main office to receive the training. Hence, even though the package was costly to purchase, the company believed that it was a bargain compared to the expense of developing a new package in-house and delivering it in person to the sales force.

Six months after the training had been delivered, sales were still declining. Management turned to the training department for answers. Because no measures of training performance had been collected, the training department had little information upon which to base its diagnosis. For lack of a better idea, members of the training department began questioning the sales force to see if they could determine why the training was not working.

Among other things, the sales people reported that the training was slow and boring, and that it did not teach them any new sales techniques. They also complained that, without an instructor, it was impossible to get clarification on things they did not understand. Moreover, they reported that they believed that sales were off not because they needed training in basic sales techniques, but because so many new products were being introduced that they could not keep up. In fact, several of the sales people requested meetings with design engineers just so they could get updated product information.

The training department took these findings back to management and requested that they be allowed to design a new training package, beginning with an updated needs analysis to determine the real training deficiencies.

Source: Excerpt taken from Salas, E., & Cannon-Bowers, J. A. (2000). Design training systematically. In E. A. Locke's (Ed.), *Handbook of principles of organizational behavior*. Oxford, UK. Blackwell Publishers Ltd. Case questions prepared by Alan Saks.

Questions

1. Comment on the company's decision to purchase a generic, off-the-shelf training package by a local vendor. What were the advantages and disadvantages of this and do you think that it was a good idea for the company to purchase the training rather than to have it designed in-house? Explain your answer.

2. What effect did the original needs analysis have on the content of the training program and the decision to have it delivered over the Web? What effect would a new needs analysis have had on the training program? What does this case say about the linkages between a needs analysis, training objectives, training content, and the effectiveness of a training program?

3. Comment on the use of the Web as the main method of training. What are the advantages and disadvantages of this method of training, and what other methods might have been more effective?

4. Discuss the role that practice played in the training program and its effectiveness? What does the case say about the role of active practice in training?

5. If you were to design the training program in light of some of the issues raised in the case, describe what you would do in terms of training objectives, training content, training methods, active practice and the conditions of practice, and the delivery of the training program. How would your training program be different from the one described in the case and would it be more effective?

Running Case Part 1

VANDALAIS DEPARTMENT STORES

Refer to the Vandalais Department Stores case described in the chapter. Discuss how you would incorporate active practice and the following practice conditions into the structured employment interview training program:

1. Pre-practice conditions: a. Attentional advice, b. Metacognitive strategies, c. Advance organizers, d. Goal orientation, e. Preparatory information, and f. Pre-practice briefs.

2. Practice conditions during training: a. Massed or distributed practice, b. Whole or part learning, c. Overlearning, d. Task sequencing, and e. Feedback and knowledge of results.

References

[1]Frankola, K. (April, 2002). When choosing training, the medium depends on the message. Workforce Online, www.workforce.com/section/11/article/23/18/52.html. Bertin, O. (2003, May 16). Krispy Kreme on a roll in Canada. *The Globe & Mail*, B4..

[2]Campion, M.A., Palmer, D.K., & Campion, J.E. (1997). A review of structure in the selection interview. *Personnel Psychology, 50,* 655–702. Pulakos, E.D., & Schmitt, N. (1995). Experience-based and situational interview questions: Studies of validity. *Personnel Psychology, 48,* 289–308.

[3]Kibler, R.J., Barker, L.L. & Miles, D.T. (1970). *Behavioral objectives and instruction.* Boston: Allyn and Bacon, Inc.

[4]Laird, D. (1985). *Approaches to training and development* (2nd ed.). Reading, MA: Addison-Wesley.

[5]Nadler, L. (1990). *Designing training programs: The critical events model.* Reading, MA: Addison-Wesley.

[6]Hays, S. (1999, April). Basic skills training 101. *Workforce, 78* (4), 76–78.

[7]Ganzel, R. (1998, October). What sexual harassment training really prevents. *Training, 35* (10), 86–94.

[8]Nadler, L., & Nadler, Z. (1990). *The handbook of human resource development* (2nd ed.). New York: John Wiley and Sons.

[9]Nadler, L., & Nadler, Z. (1990).

[10]Campbell, J.P. (1988). Training design for performance improvement. In Campbell, J.P. & Campbell, R.J. (Eds.), *Productivity in organizations: Frontiers of industrial and organizational psychology* (pp.177–216). San Francisco, CA: Jossey-Bass.

[11]Kirkpatrick, D.L. (1994). *Evaluating training programs: The four levels.* San Francisco, CA: Berrett-Koehler Publishers.

[12]Campbell, J.P. (1988).

[13]Campbell, J.P. (1988).

[14]Campion, M.A., Palmer, D.K., & Campion, J.E. (1997).

[15]Campbell, J.P. (1988).

[16]Campbell, J.P. (1988).

[17]Thoms, P., & Klein, H.J. (1994). Participation and evaluative outcomes in management training. *Human Resource Development Quarterly, 5,* 27–39.

[18]Hinrichs, J.R. (1976). Personnel training. In Dunnette, M.D. (Ed.), *Handbook of industrial and organizational psychology* (pp. 829–60). Skokie, IL: Rand McNally.

[19]Cannon-Bowers, J. A., Rhodenizer, L., Salas, E., & Bowers, C. A., (1998). A framework for understanding pre-practice conditions and their impact on learning. *Personnel Psychology, 51,* 291–320.

[20]Cannon-Bowers, J. A., Rhodenizer, L., Salas, E., & Bowers, C. A., (1998).

[21]Baldwin, T.T., & Ford, J.K. (1988). Transfer of training: A review and directions for future research. *Personnel Psychology, 41,* 63–105.

[22]Donovan, J. J., & Radosevich, D. J. (1999). A meta-analytic review of the distribution of practice effect: Now you see it, now you don't. *Journal of Applied Psychology, 84,* 795–805.

[23]Bass, B.M., & Vaughn, J.A. (1969). *Training in industry: The management of learning.* Belmont, CA: Wadsworth. Donovan, J. J., & Radosevich, D. J. (1999).

[24]Baldwin, T.T., & Ford, J.K. (1988).

[25]Baldwin, T.T., & Ford, J.K. (1988).

[26]Baldwin, T.T., & Ford, J.K. (1988).

[27]Yelon, S., & Z. Berge. (1992, September). Practice-centred training. *Performance and instruction*, 8–12.

[28]Driskell, J.E., Willis, R.P., & Copper, C. (1992). Effects of overlearning on retention. *Journal of Applied Psychology, 77,* 615–22.

[29]Gagne, R.M. (1962). Military training and principles of learning. *American Psychologist, 17,* 83–91.

[30]Gagne, R.M. (1962).

[31]Baldwin, T.T., & Ford, J.K. (1988).

[32]Ilgen, D.R., Fisher, C.D., & Taylor, M.S. (1979). Consequences of individual feedback on behaviour in organizations. *Journal of Applied Psychology, 64,* 349–71.

[33]Campbell, J.P. (1988).

[34]Miller, L. (1965). *The use of knowledge of results in improving the performance of hourly operators.* General Electric Company, Behavioral Research Service: Detroit.

[35]Locke, E.A., & Latham, G.P. (1990). *A theory of goal setting and task performance.* Englewood Cliffs, NJ: Prentice-Hall.

[36]Towler, A. J., & Dipboye, R. L. (2001). Effects of trainer expressiveness, organization, and trainee goal orientation on training outcomes. *Journal of Applied Psychology, 86,* 664–73.

[37]Towler, A. J., & Dipboye, R. L. (2001).

[38]Kirkpatrick, D.L. (1994).

[39]Kirkpatrick, D.L. (1994).

[40]Ford, J.K., Major, D.A., Seaton, F.W., & Felber, H.K. (1993). Effects of organizational, training system, and individual characteristics on training director scanning practices. *Human Resource Development Quarterly, 4,* 333–51.

[41]Kirkpatrick, D.L. (1994).

[42]Kirkpatrick, D.L. (1994).

[43]Donaldson, L., & Scannell, E.E. (1986). *Human resource development: The new trainer's guide* (2nd ed.). Reading, MA: Addison-Wesley.

[44]Zemke, R. (1999). Toward a science of training. *Training, 36* (7), 32–36.

[45]Swanson, R.A., & Falkman, S.K. (1997). Training delivery problems and solutions: Identification of novice trainer problems and expert trainer solutions. *Human Resource Development Quarterly, 8,* 305–14.

[46]Swanson, R.A., & Falkman, S.K. (1997).

Chapter 6

Off-the-Job Training Methods

www.whirlpool
corp.com

WHIRLPOOL CORP.

Two or three times a year, Whirlpool Corp., one of the world's largest makers of household appliances, selects a group of seven young people from around the country to live together for eight weeks in a leased, seven-bedroom house not far from its corporate headquarters in Benton Harbor, Michigan. The recruits will eventually be dispatched to train sales staffs at retailers such as Sears Roebuck and Co. and Lowe's Cos. Inc. to sell the company's appliances.

The recruits spend their days mastering the company's household appliances, which are periodically swapped for different models, even that of a competitor, for comparison testing. During the course of their stay, they prepare more than 900 plates of food, wash no fewer than 120 bags of laundry, and perform countless hours of loading and reloading of the company's refrigerators, dish washers, and dryers.

They smear white bags with mustard, relish and other stain-generating condiments, just to see if they can bleach them out; they prepare three times as much pasta as they need, simply to see how microwave and convection oven cooking differs from that of a traditional oven. There are written tests, oral presentations, and almost daily quizzes on attributes and idiosyncrasies of washers, dryers, and microwave ovens.

Company executives insist the reality-based training program is not a gimmick. Rather, they say, it is a more pragmatic and effective way of preparing its youthful marketing representatives than the lectures and slide shows that make up so many corporate initiations. Forcing the recruits, a diverse group of men and women, to use the full range of Whirlpool products night and day will produce a better informed and more consumer-friendly sales staff, the company says.

According to the company's national training manager, Whirlpool's live-in training program is an ideal way to train new hires that are right out of college. After their two months of experience of cooking and cleaning as well as building relationships, the new recruits are ready to take their "Real Whirled" experience to the real world.[1]

Whirlpool Corp. uses a unique method of training its new employees. Although it takes place off the job, new hires learn about the company's products and acquire important interpersonal and team skills that will be useful on the job. In this chapter, we introduce you to training methods that take place away from the job site and are usually referred to as off-the-job training. This chapter discusses the most common off-the-job training methods.

The chapter presents training methods in order of degree of trainee involvement, from passive to active. We start with lectures, because there is relatively little trainee input, and end with action learning where trainees manage the learning process. Table 6.1 lists the 10 off-the-job training methods described in this chapter.

Many of the instructional methods presented in this chapter take place in a classroom setting although some methods such as games and simulations also take place outside a classroom. In Canada, classroom delivery is the primary method of providing training. In a survey conducted by The Conference Board of Canada, participating organizations indicated that 80.3 percent of all training time is delivered via the classroom.[2]

Lecture Method

There are few people who have not experienced a lecture. A **lecture** transmits information orally with little trainee involvement. The trainer organizes the content to be learned and then presents it to trainees.

There are a number of advantages of a lecture. Large amounts of information can be transferred to groups of trainees in a relatively short period of

RPC

Lecture
A training method in which the trainer organizes the content to be learned and presents it orally with little trainee involvement

TABLE 6.1

Off-the-Job Training Methods

1. Lecture—A training method in which the trainer organizes the content to be learned and presents it orally with little trainee involvement.
2. Discussion—Two-way communication between the trainer and trainees as well as among trainees.
3. Audio-visual methods—Various forms of media that are used to illustrate key points or demonstrate certain actions or behaviours.
4. Case study—A training method in which trainees discuss, analyze, and solve problems based on a real situation.
5. Case incident—A training method in which one problem or issue is presented for analysis.
6. Behaviour modelling—A training method in which trainees observe a model performing a task and then attempt to imitate the observed behaviour.
7. Role play—A training method in which trainees practice newly learned skills in a safe environment.
8. Games—Activities characterized by structured competition that allow employees to learn specific skills.
9. Simulations—Operating models of physical or social events designed to represent reality.
10. Action learning—A training method in which trainees accept the challenge of studying and solving real-world problems and accept responsibility for the solution.

time, at a minimal expense. Key points can be emphasized and repeated. Trainers can be assured that trainees are all hearing the same message, which is useful when the message is extremely important, such as instructions or changes in procedures. A lecture is also useful as a method to explain to trainees what is to follow in the rest of a training session. For example, a lecture could be used to highlight the key learning points of a video or role play. Many employees are comfortable with the lecture method because they are familiar with it and it requires little participation.

However, a lecture, as some of us have experienced, does have its drawbacks as a training method. While useful for the acquisition of declarative knowledge, it is not as effective for the development of skills or for changing attitudes. The lecture does not accommodate any differences in trainee ability, and all trainees are forced to absorb information at the same rate. Trainees are also forced to be passive learners with little opportunity to connect the content to their own work environment, or to receive feedback on their understanding of the material. To overcome these disadvantages, trainers often build in time for discussion, questions and answers, and other opportunities for trainee involvement.

Tips for Trainers

Trainers can use the lecture method effectively by following a number of guidelines. For example, "Where do I begin?" is a question asked by most first-time trainers. The answer is: "First you have to know what you want to do (the objective) and how much information you need to impart." Training objectives were described in Chapter 5, but on a pragmatic level the trainer should be able to write a concise statement describing what the trainees will be able to do or accomplish by attending a lecture.

Either through previously gained knowledge or the ability to research a topic, the trainer will gather and arrange information in a logical manner. Logic could dictate a progression from the general to the specific, or from the specific to the general, depending upon the subject matter. This information can be transcribed onto cards or sheets of paper. An effective technique is to rule off a wide (5 cm to 8 cm) margin down the right-hand side of each page. Then detailed information can be placed in the body of the page, while headings are written in the margins.

It has been suggested that no more than six major points should be illustrated during each half hour of a lecture.[3] It takes practice to get the timing of a lecture right. Only through experience can one judge the amount of material needed for any given amount of time. It is helpful to break the lecture into 10 to 15 minute segments with a short stretch time in between and to summarize the material at both the beginning and the end, and stop occasionally to allow trainees to catch up and to write their own summaries. Finally, time should be scheduled for questions and answers.

A trainer who drones on for an entire hour is rarely effective. Depending on audience needs and motivation level, the delivery should be punctuated with a variety of supplementary material or exercises. Stories, case incidents, graphics, humour, trainee presentations, videos, and question and answer sessions are some of the techniques a trainer can use to maintain interest and, perhaps even more important, to instill in the trainee the love of, or at the least, respect for the subject matter. Trainers not only represent themselves but also function as ambassadors for their institution or firm and their discipline. A poor lecture not only shows the trainer in a bad light but also can lead to negative trainee attitudes toward the training.

To ensure that trainees are listening, Bata Limited requires employees attending conferences, which are largely lecture based, to return to work prepared to give a session to their peers on what they have learned, and what is applicable to their company.[4]

Discussion Method

The **discussion method** is one of the primary ways to increase trainee involvement in the learning process by allowing two-way communication between the trainer and trainees as well as among trainees. It has been known for some time that group discussion serves at least five purposes:

Discussion method
Allows two-way communication between the trainer and trainees as well as among trainees

1. It helps trainees recognize what they do not know but should know.
2. It is an opportunity for trainees to get answers to questions.
3. It allows trainees to get advice on matters that are of concern to them.
4. It allows trainees to share ideas and derive a common wisdom.
5. It is a way for trainees to learn about one another as people.[5]

Group discussions facilitate the exchange of ideas and are good ways to develop critical thinking skills. Social and interpersonal skills are also enhanced. However, group discussions are not effective with large numbers of participants because many remain silent or unable to participate. Some group members will dominate while the contributions of others will not be useful. Still others may become dogmatic in their positions on issues. Group discussions take a lot of training time and must be carefully facilitated to manage the outcomes.

Tips for Trainers

The discussion method is most effective when the trainer can convince group members that a collective approach has some advantage over individual approaches to a problem.[6] Thus, the trainer should create a participative culture at the beginning of a training program. The trainer's task, then, is to get trainees to buy into the process as an activity that is both interesting and useful.

The major difficulty with the discussion method is that comments tend to be addressed to the trainer. When faced with this situation, the best technique is to reflect the questions or comments back to the trainees. Not surprisingly, positive reinforcement is critical. Reluctant participants are drawn out, while the trainer utilizes the energy of more assertive individuals. When the group strays off topic, the trainer gently refocuses the discussion, supporting the participation while changing the substance.[7]

The key to successful discussions is to ensure that one trainee does not dominate the discussion. The trainer does not have to be obvious (e.g., putting all the dominant personalities together). More subtle techniques can be used. For example, trainees can be given roles that change with each discussion—scribe, presenter, and discussion leader. If groups are kept small—four to six seems to work best—then most trainees have something to do, increasing participation and decreasing chances for some individuals to dominate the process. It is harder to be aggressive when taking notes or trying to summarize the thoughts of others.

Trainers dealing with groups of mixed educational backgrounds must also be aware of reading speed and literacy problems. Often group discussions require trainees to read a passage, case incident, or problem. Reluctance or hostility to do so might point to illiteracy. Be gentle, work the informal group process by finding a place in a hallway for someone to quietly read the material, or if this process is too obvious, summarize the main points before you assign the work. People who don't read well often have excellent memories; with care, they'll get by.[8]

Of note, too, is that groups should be assigned a well-defined, easily understood task, one that is doable within the allotted time frame. Trainees should be given every opportunity to look good in front of their peers, especially if they have to report back to the group. Since many training facilities are less than ideal, seating arrangements will vary. Any configuration that puts trainees in close proximity to one another will do, but a circle arrangement with no obvious leader's position or place is probably best. Size of the group is also important. More than 10 would be hard to handle if everyone is to participate.

RPC

Audio-visual methods

Various forms of media that are used to illustrate key points or demonstrate certain actions or behaviours

Audio-Visual Methods

Audio-visual methods refer to various forms of media that trainers can use to illustrate key points or demonstrate certain actions or behaviours. Videos and slides are often used by trainers to supplement lectures and discussions. A video is often used to illustrate a way to behave in a certain situation or to demonstrate effective and ineffective behaviours. Many managers have learned correct interviewing techniques through videos. Slides highlight the important parts of a lecture or discussion allowing trainees to remember key points.

One advantage of audio-visual methods is the ability to control the pace of the training. A slide or a video clip can be used to clarify a concept. Trainees receive consistent information from these methods no matter where or how often the training is given. Most important, a video can show a situation that is difficult for a trainer to describe, such as a hostile customer or a dangerous malfunction in equipment. Video allows a trainer to show complex and dynamic situations in a realistic manner. Not surprisingly, videos remain one of the most popular methods of training.

Tips for Trainers

Before a video is shown, the trainer should discuss the learning objectives, the key points, and instruct trainees to pay particular attention to certain key parts.

Trainees should understand how the video fits into the rest of the training program and should be given sufficient guidance so that they know what to look for and focus on. Slides should not overwhelm trainees with information and they should be easy to read and follow. Too much information or print that is too small and difficult to read can undermine their usefulness.

Case Study Method

A **case study** is a training method in which trainees discuss, analyze, and solve problems usually based on a real situation. The primary use of the case study method is to encourage open discussion and analysis of problems and events. Trainees apply business-management concepts to relevant real-life situations.

The case study method teaches trainees to think for themselves and develop problem-solving skills while the trainer functions as a catalyst for learning. Case studies develop analytical ability, sharpen problem-solving skills, encourage creativity, and improve the organization of thoughts and ideas.[9]

The objectives of a case study are (1) to introduce realism into trainees' learning, (2) to deal with a variety of problems, goals, facts, conditions, and conflicts that often occur in the real world, (3) to teach trainees how to make decisions, and (4) to teach trainees to be creative and think independently.[10] Therefore, most cases present situations in which the problems are correctable.

The case study method is often used in business schools to teach students how to analyze and solve realistic organizational problems. In fact, more than 70 percent of business schools use the case study method. Several studies have found that using cases improves communication skills, problem solving, and enables students to better understand management situations.[11]

For the case method to be effective, however, certain requirements must be met. For example, the qualifications of both the trainees and the trainer affect the ability to analyze cases and to draw conclusions. As well, space and time dimensions are important. Trainees need time to analyze cases properly. Finally, case studies and discussions work best in an open and informal atmosphere.[12]

Cases may be written in various styles, presenting either single problems or a number of complex interdependent situations. They may be concerned with corporate strategy, organizational change, management, or any problem relating to a company's financial situation, marketing, human resources, or a combination of these activities. Some case reports describe the organization's difficulties in vague terms, while others may state the major problems explicitly.

In addition to the various styles of case writing, methods of presentation also differ. Cases do not always have to be in written form. Sometimes it is more effective to present cases using audio-visual techniques. This approach has advantages for both the trainees and the trainers in that trainers do not have to do as much research and writing, and trainees are able to identify better with the characters.[13] A second alternative to a written case presentation is the live case method. Businesses may contact schools to report certain

Case study
A training method in which trainees discuss, analyze, and solve problems based on a real situation

problems. Students then analyze the situation and report back to the company. This approach has been called operational consulting.[14]

Tips for Trainers

Certain requirements should be met when writing a case study. The case should be a product of a real organizational situation. A fictitious case could be regarded with boredom and distrust as the setting might seem too unrealistic.[15] Ideally, cases should be written by more than one person. Collaboration on the presentation of facts ensures a more realistic situation and helps to reduce biases. Although it is difficult, the case writer must not make assumptions and only facts should be included. The author of a case, then, must relate core issues to the reader, not personal bias.

Case studies often concentrate on the corporate strategy of a company within an industry setting. The complexity of business situations makes decisions and analyses challenging. In addition, despite their length, most cases do not contain complete information on the organization or all the relevant inputs. This incompleteness is part of the benefit of using the case method, as trainees must learn to deal with incomplete data.[16]

As a case study is a description of a typical management situation, it is often difficult to know what to include and what to omit. Most cases give an overall description of the company and the industry situation although the length of a case report varies. A typical case, however, will be up to 20 typewritten pages. The key issues and the relevant details should be included to give the reader enough information to make a qualified decision.

Cases vary depending on the intended purpose of the writer and according to the issue being examined. Some case studies disclose what management decisions were made when attempting to solve an organization's problems while others require one to develop solutions and recommend courses of action.

A teaching note provides communication between the case writer and those who teach the case. In its strictest sense, a teaching note would include information on approaches to teaching a specific case. Some teaching notes, however, are more detailed, containing samples of analyses and computations. In addition, teaching notes may state the objectives of the case and contain additional company information not available to trainees.[17]

As most of these cases are excessively long and extremely complex, they have not generally found favour with trainers in business, particularly those training front-line supervisors. There is an offshoot of this technique, however, called the case incident method that can be used to great advantage with a wide variety of trainees at many levels.

Case Incident Method

Case incident

A training method in which one problem or issue is presented for analysis

Unlike the typical case study, a **case incident** is usually no more than one page in length and is designed to illustrate or to probe one specific problem, concept, or issue. Most management textbooks include a case incident at the end of each chapter. The case incident has become one of the most accessible ways of injecting an experiential or real-world component into a lecture.

Case incidents are useful when the trainer wants to focus on one topic or concept. Because they are short, trainees can read them during a training session and valuable time will not be taken up by differences in trainees' reading speeds. When larger, more traditional cases are used, advance preparation is necessary to read and review the case material. The brevity of a case incident reduces the need for preparation and reading skills so all trainees can participate without a lot of advance reading and preparation.

Another advantage of a case incident is that trainees are able to use their own experiences. If the material is written well, the problem presented in each incident will encourage the application of current knowledge, leading to increased confidence, and trainee input and participation.

The main disadvantage of case incidents is that some trainees are bothered by the lack of background material. Indeed, at times it is necessary for trainees to make assumptions and trainers may be asked by some trainees to sketch in the background. They can be especially problematic for trainees who have limited knowledge and work experience. A lack of work or life experiences tends to elicit shallow answers based on speculation and ill-informed opinion.

Case incidents have been used successfully in both high-tech and in more traditional organizations. Supervisors seem to like the hands-on aspects of solving a specific management problem. Similarly, students have found the case incident method to be a welcome relief from the traditional lecture method. Case incidents have been found to be valuable in class sizes of up to 70.

Tips for Trainers

Case incidents can be used in several ways. Trainees can be divided into groups with one member assigned the task of making notes while another can be designated the group spokesperson. The groups discuss the case incident and answer questions. The trainer then has each group spokesperson present their answers. This process can then lead into a general group discussion.

Another approach is to have the trainees read the case incident and then discuss it as one group. This method is especially useful when an example is needed to illustrate a specific point. The technique here would be to stop the training, ask the trainees to read the incident, and then lead the group in a short discussion. As soon as the point has been made, the trainer should continue quickly, so as not to lose the trainees' interest. Alternatively, a case incident can be used to illustrate a point at the start of a training program or used as an exercise at the end of a training program.

Behaviour Modelling

People learn by observing the behaviour of others and so it should not surprise you that observation is a popular and effective method of training. **Behaviour modelling** is a training method in which trainees observe a model performing a task and then attempt to imitate the observed behaviour.

Behaviour modelling

A training method in which trainees observe a model performing a task and then attempt to imitate the observed behaviour

Behaviour modelling is based on social learning theory and observation learning that was described in Chapter 3. It is an extremely effective method for learning skills and behaviours. Behaviour modelling has been used to teach interpersonal skills such as supervision, negotiation, communication, and sales as well as motor skills.

Trainers have to carefully plan behaviour modelling training and ensure that trainees are provided with opportunities to practice the observed behaviour, receive feedback on their performance of the task, and are motivated to use the new behaviour on the job. Trainees will resist behaviour modelling if the behaviours are incongruent with common work practices.

Tips for Trainers

Behaviour modelling is based on four general principles of learning: 1. Observation (modelling); 2. Rehearsal (practice); 3. Reinforcement (reward); and 4. Transfer.[18] The process is fairly straightforward. Trainees observe a model performing a specific task such as handling a customer complaint or operating a machine.

The performance of a task can be observed on video or it can be performed live. The model should be someone with whom the trainee can identify with and is perceived as credible. Under these conditions, the trainee is more likely to want to imitate the model's behaviour.

In addition, the trainees must have sufficient trust in the trainer to experiment (i.e., to try new behaviour in front of a group). Sometimes, a traditional and ineffective scenario is demonstrated first to increase motivation to try the new positive behaviour. John Cleese of Monty Python fame used this technique very effectively in his humorous video series on interviewing.

The training task should be broken down into key learning points or behaviours to be learned as a series of critical steps that can be modelled independently. After viewing the model, the participants practice the behaviour, one step at a time. When one step is mastered and reinforced, the trainer moves to the next critical skill. Specific feedback must follow the performance of each step. This step-by-step process results in the development of skills and the confidence (self-efficacy) needed to use them.[19]

Transfer of the new skill and behaviours to the workplace is always the weak link in the process. Old patterns are comfortable and familiar, especially when there is some resistance in the work environment to new ways of doing things. However, by overlearning the skill as discussed in Chapter 5, its use can become automatic. In addition, the reinforcement of newly acquired skills on the job ensures their repetition and continued application. When these reinforcers are in place, behaviour modelling can have long-lasting and positive outcomes.[20]

Role play

A training method in which trainees practise newly learned skills in a safe environment

Role Play

A **role play** is a method of training in which employees are given the opportunity to practice new behaviours in a safe environment. The emphasis is on doing and experiencing. This training method is most useful for acquiring interpersonal and human relations skills and for changing attitudes.

A role play consists of three phases: 1. Development, 2. Enactment, and 3. Debriefing. First, a role play must be carefully designed to achieve its objectives. Development involves the design of a role play that usually consists of a scenario in which there are two actors. For example, if sales clerks are learning how to interact with customers, a role play might involve a customer returning an item and asking for a refund. The scenario provides information on the time, place, roles, encounter, and instructions on what each role player should do.

During the enactment phase, trainees are provided with the role play information and scenarios and are assigned roles. Usually there are two role players and sometimes a third trainee who is an observer. Trainees are given some time to become familiar with the scenario and their roles, and then act out the role play. Usually the trainees will rotate so that each one spends some time in each role.

By playing a role, trainees can develop empathy for others and learn what it feels like to be in a particular role. For example, when a customer service representative is given instructions to play the part of a disgruntled customer with a major problem, he or she can experience the frustrations of responses like "That's not my department," and "Just fill in that form over there, no, not that one."

After the enactment phase is the debriefing phase, which is considered to be the most important stage of a role play, and should last two to three times longer than the enactment phase. In this phase, participants discuss their experiences and the outcomes of their role play. Correct behaviours are reinforced and connections with key learning points and trainees' jobs are made. This is done by establishing the facts (what happened, what was experienced), analyzing the causes and effects of behaviours, and planning for skill or attitude changes on the job.

Tips for Trainers

While role playing allows trainees to practice and learn new skills, trainees sometimes resist it. As a result, the role of the trainer is crucial. Trust has to be established and an open and participative climate is necessary. Trainees should be warmed up by involving them in minor role situations. The trainer can reinforce risk taking and use mistakes as learning opportunities. Trainers could ask people to show all the incorrect ways to handle an angry customer. When a critical mistake is made, the trainer can start again or rewind the case. In one role play, a police officer was testing methods of talking to a potential suicide victim on a bridge. The officer made the fatal mistake of saying, "Go ahead, I dare you," and the role play partner jumped. The trainer immediately stated, "Well, that approach didn't work, would you like to try another?" He rewound the case and demonstrated the true value of role playing—the opportunity to practice behaviours in a safe environment.

One of the limitations of a role play is that unlike behaviour modelling, trainees are not shown exactly what to do and how to behave prior to participating in a role play. As a result, some trainees might not be successful in a role play and might even display incorrect behaviours. Furthermore, much of what happens during a role play is left in the hands of the role players. This means that it is extremely important for the trainer to draw out the incorrect and correct behaviours during the debriefing phase. Otherwise, trainees might not learn the appropriate behaviours following a role play.

Games

Activities characterized by structured competition that allow trainees to learn specific skills

Games

Games involve activities characterized by structured competition that allow trainees to learn specific skills. Games tend to have rules, principles, and a system for scoring. For example, an employment law game called *Winning through Prevention* teaches human resource managers about lawful termination, discrimination, and workplace safety. Players who answer correctly get promoted and those who answer incorrectly are faced with a lawsuit.[21]

Business games often require teams of players to compete against each other to gain a strategic advantage, market share, or to maximize profits. They can involve all areas of management practice and often require the players to gather and analyze information, and to make business management decisions. As a result, business games tend to focus on the development of problem-solving, interpersonal skills, and decision-making skills.

Some business games are relatively simple and focus on a particular functional area such as marketing, human resources, or finance. Other games are much more complex and try to model an entire organization. Participants might have to operate a company and make all kinds of decisions and solve business problems. They would then receive feedback and have the opportunity to practice particular skills.

Games incorporate many sound principles of learning such as learning from experience, active practice, and direct application to real problems. They are used to enhance the learning process by injecting fun, competition, generating energy, and providing opportunities for people to work together.

A disadvantage of the use of games is the possibility of learning the wrong things, a weak relation to training objectives, and an emphasis on winning.[22] In addition, trainees sometimes get so caught up in the game that they lose sight of the importance of learning. Although trainees seem to enjoy games and respond enthusiastically to them, there is not very much evidence on how effective games are for improving skills and on-the-job performance.

To find out more about the kinds of games being used today, see Training Today, "The Games Trainees Play."

Tips for Trainers

The design of a game begins with a critical question: "What is the key task to be learned?" At the beginning of the exercise, the trainer should state the learning objective so that trainees don't just focus on winning the game but understand what they will learn. In addition, the roles of the players must be clearly defined.

Games should be as realistic as possible and be a meaningful representation of the kind of work that participants do. If they are not realistic, participants might not take them seriously. This will obviously undermine learning and the application of new skills on the job. To be most effective, games should be well planned and prepared, linked to training objectives, and include a debriefing session so that trainees understand the purpose of the game and the critical skills and behaviours to be learned.[23] As well, because there are many kinds of games available, trainers need to be familiar with them and to carefully choose one that best meets an organization's needs and objectives.

Simulations

Simulations are a form of training that involves the use of operating models of physical or social events that are designed to represent reality. They attempt to recreate situations by simplifying them to a manageable size and structure. They are models or active representations of work situations that

R P C

Simulations
Operating models of physical or social events designed to represent reality

---

Training Today

The Games Trainees Play

A number of companies today specialize in corporate training programs that are anything but traditional. Games such as "human slingshot" and "Sumo wrestling" and one in which trainees fly in a two-seater plane and engage in an aerial dogfight with lasers are fun, unusual, and not for the faint of heart. They stretch trainees' limits but can offer valuable insights.

Some of the most intense courses in Canada are offered by a company called Survival in the Bush, Inc. Located in rural eastern Ontario, they offer programs from Thunder Bay to Labrador.

Interested companies must first determine the goals they want to achieve and how gung-ho they are about bushwhacking. The training can take place on the grounds of the company or at one of many secluded outdoor locales. The courses run all year round, which means that trainees might have to trudge through ice and snow.

Companies that decide to rough it in the bush can expect to find themselves building shelters and fires, foraging for edible items such as nonpoisonous wild plants, learning how to navigate in the woods and preparing wild game for meals. Trainees develop leadership skills, an appreciation for team work, and learn how to make decisions under very stressful situations.

In the United States, a company called Total Rebound regularly hosts programs in Toronto, Vancouver, Montreal, and Calgary in which they provide over-the-top interactive games that are designed to be fun and educational.

Among the games are "human slingshot," which involves bungee cords, "soft bouncy racing lanes" and "Sumo Wrestling" in which participants wear giant, flesh-coloured, vinyl, foam-filled suits. In a game called "Hornet Adventure," trainees are taken to a United States' aircraft carrier called The Hornet where they are shown how to build and launch rockets at a target floating 3,000 feet off in San Francisco Bay. The company also custom designs games according to a company's needs.

These games are designed to teach trainees how to communicate and collaborate, to break down barriers between people, and to help team members recognize qualities and skills that they did not know they or others in their group had. One of the most important aspects of such cutting-edge training programs is that they allow trainees to develop individual skills and leadership abilities.

Source: Excerpt from Hendley, N. (2002, October). Games without frontiers: extreme corporate training. *The Training Report*, pp. 1–2. Reprinted by permission of The Training Report, Crownhill Publishing Inc.

are designed to increase trainee motivation, involvement, and learning. They are also used when training in the real world might involve danger or extreme costs.

Simulations are a popular method of training that are widely used in business, education, and the military. For example, simulations are typically used in medicine, maintenance, law enforcement, and emergency management settings. The military and the commercial aviation industry are purported to be the biggest users of simulation-based training.[24]

Some simulations, known as equipment simulators, use equipment that mimics the equipment and machinery in the workplace. **Equipment simulators** are mechanical devices that are similar to those that employees use on the job. They are designed to simulate the kinds of procedures, movements, and/or decisions required in the work environment.

A good example of an equipment simulator is a flight simulator that is used to train pilots to fly. Flight simulators mimic flights exactly but pose no risk to humans or equipment. Equipment simulators are also used to train astronauts, air traffic controllers, and maintenance workers.

Simulations can also be designed to simulate social situations and interactions. Royal Bank Financial Group of Canada trained 58,000 employees in coaching skills using a five-hour CD-ROM simulation.[25] Canadian telecommunications company TELUS had its entire sales force attend a three-day realistic selling simulation. Sales teams compete against each other to win an account and this required them to understand the client's needs and to develop solutions.[26]

Simulations can also be used to develop managerial and interpersonal skills. For example, organizational simulations require participants to solve problems, make decisions, and interact with various stakeholders. Trainees can learn how organizations operate and acquire important managerial and business skills.

Simulations are commonly used to train employees involved in emergency response work such as firefighters and police officers. You might recall the chapter-opening vignette in Chapter 4 that described how police, firefighters, and paramedics are being trained to handle biological weapons in a series of simulated terrorist attacks designed to replicate a chemical assault on a major Canadian city. Trainees practised detecting and decontaminating chemical agents, and treating mass casualties after a mock terrorist attack. In another exercise, they handled liquid sarin at a simulated terrorist lab after a mock leak.[27]

These kinds of simulations are becoming more common since the terrorist attacks in the United States. For example, in May 2003 a week-long staged disaster was conducted to test Canadian and U.S. preparedness for a terrorist attack. Simulated attacks in Seattle were designed to test the local, state, and federal government response to a possible terrorist attack. The simulation involved 8,500 people from 100 local, state, and federal agencies in the United States as well as the Canadian government at a cost of US$16 million.[28]

A major disadvantage of equipment simulators and simulations is that they are usually very expensive to develop and in the case of emergency

Equipment simulators

Mechanical devices that are similar to those that employees use on-the-job response simulations, very expensive to stage. On the positive side, simulations are an excellent method for adding some realism into a training program. They are especially useful in situations where it would be too costly or dangerous to train employees on the actual equipment used on the job.

Tips for Trainers

In order to be most effective, simulations should have physical and psychological fidelity. **Physical fidelity** has to do with the similarity of the physical aspects of a simulation (e.g., equipment, tasks, and surroundings) to the actual job. Simulators should be designed to physically replicate and resemble the work environment. That is, the simulation should have the appearance of the actual work site. For example, a flight simulator should look like the cockpit of an actual airplane with respect to the various controls, lights, and instruments.

Psychological fidelity has to do with the similarity of the psychological conditions of the simulation to the actual work environment. Simulations should be designed so that the experience is as similar as possible to what trainees experience on the job. In other words, the simulation should include on-the-job psychological conditions such as time pressures, problems, conflicts, and so on.

Simulations allow a great deal of flexibility as complicating factors or unexpected events can be built into the program. For example, in a pilot-training simulation, a blizzard can be introduced. However, trainers should ensure that simulations have both physical and psychological fidelity.

To learn more about how to make experiential training methods such as role plays, games, and simulations more effective, see The Trainer's Notebook, "Getting the Most Out of Experiential Training Methods."

Action Learning

In Chapter 5, active practice was described as an important component of a training program for trainee learning and retention. A good example of a training method that provides active practice is action learning.

Action learning provides trainees with opportunities to test theories in the real world. Reginald Revans, the originator of action-learning principles, emphasizes that the learner develops skills through responsible involvement in some real, complex, and stressful problem.[29] The action-learning method compels trainees to identify problems, develop possible solutions, test these solutions in a real-world, real-time situation, and evaluate the consequences. The aim is to solve a business problem.

The goals of action learning are to involve and to challenge the trainee and move employees from passive observation to identification with the people and the vision of the organization. This method moves trainees from information receivers to problem solvers. Action learning incorporates more of the adult learning principles than any other method of training.

The majority of the time spent in action learning is dedicated to the diagnosis of problems in the field. The problems and the inherent value systems

Physical fidelity

The similarity of the physical aspects of a simulation (e.g., equipment, tasks, and surroundings) to the actual job

Psychological fidelity

The similarity of the psychological conditions of the simulation to the actual work environment

Action learning

A training method in which trainees accept the challenge of studying and solving real-world problems and accept responsibility for the solution

Getting the Most Out of Experiential Training Methods

Experiential training methods such as role playing, games, and simulations encourage trainee participation. Learning theory teaches us that by increasing trainee participation, active involvement, learning and retention will be enhanced. But not always.

Many training methods put trainees on the spot—literally in the spotlight, forced to act in situations in which they feel very uncomfortable. One executive was encouraged to describe a time at work when he had faced a difficult situation in order to illustrate how corrective counselling worked. The person playing the role of counsellor criticized him extensively, with no intervention from the trainer. The outcome can be worse than losing face and not learning. Trainees may not want to return to any training program or they may actively sabotage subsequent sessions.

Here are some tips for trainers to make effective use of experiential training methods:

- Don't use games and role plays just to play and have fun. There must be a purpose, a learning outcome that you should share with the trainees.
- Try the exercise you have designed or chosen. If you are uncomfortable doing it, don't use it.

- Don't think that unlearning previous habits means going through extremely difficult events, like boot camp. People don't learn to swim by being thrown into the deep end of the swimming pool.
- Not every one has to participate in a participative workshop. Some people can play different roles (such as observing or note taking) rather than the high profile "let us show them how they are doing it wrong" simulations.
- Warm-up exercises and limiting the size of the group might also create a supportive environment in which to risk behaviour by role playing or asking questions.
- If an individual does lose face, trainers can make favourable comments by focusing on the correct actions, inviting observers to empathize with the person facing the difficulties of the task in the exercise, and asking the others to appreciate the risks taken by those who did play the game.

Source: Becker, R. (1998). Taking the misery out of experiential training. *Training, 35* (2), 79–88. Training: The Human Side of Business by Becker, R. Copyright 1998 by V N U BUS PUBNS USA. Reproduced with permission of V N U BUS PUBNS USA in the format Textbook via Copyright Clearance Center.

supporting the problems are assessed and challenged. This work is always done in groups and learning by-products include group and interpersonal skills, risk taking, responsibility, and accountability.[30]

Professions use action learning to train and socialize their students. For example, students in social work are often sent to work with the homeless or welfare recipients. These students are encouraged to apply their theoretical knowledge in the field. Industry is using the precepts of action learning when employees take responsibility for quality-improvement projects.

Action learning requires a commitment of energy and time from participants and their managers. Solving real organizational problems can be stressful for trainees. The difficulties of working in teams on real problems can lead to conflict and increased anxiety and stress.

Tips for Trainers

Action learning projects must be challenging and deal with real organizational concerns. Trainees should buy into the importance of the project and the organizational problem and receive some release time to work on the project. In addition, some training in group skills to enable collaboration might also be necessary. The group working on the project should be small (four to seven members) enough to develop trust but contain a diverse set of skills to enable creative solutions. The learning process should be monitored and the trainees held accountable for their proposed solutions.

Which Training Method Is Best?

In this chapter, we have described some of the most common off-the-job training methods. In Chapter 7, you will learn about on-the-job training methods, and in Chapter 8 you will find out about technology-based training methods. With so many training methods available, it is natural to ask, "Which training method is best?" and "How does a trainer choose a training method?" There is of course no easy or straightforward answer to this question. However, we will try to provide some guidelines for choosing training methods.

In terms of the effectiveness of the various methods, one survey conducted by one of the authors of this text that was completed by 150 experienced professional trainers (members of the Canadian Society of Training and Development), revealed a hierarchy of effectiveness. As a general principle, the more highly involved the trainee in the learning process and the more the training situation resembles the job, the more likely it is that transfer to the job will occur. These methods include on-the-job and one-on-one training, simulations, role plays, behaviour modelling, self-study, case studies, and multimedia. A combination of these methods results in even greater transfer. Other methods, such as lectures, discussions, video conferencing, and lunch and learn programs, were not suitable for transfer to the job, perhaps because these techniques allow (and indeed require) that trainees be passive absorbers of information.[31]

Two large surveys of training directors found that nine different training methods were effective in achieving different types of training goals.[32] For example, the case study method was rated as most effective for problem-solving skills and computer-based instruction was rated best for knowledge retention. The role-play method was evaluated as the best for changing attitudes and developing interpersonal skills. However, these are only individual perceptions and do not provide information on actual trainee achievements.

It is important to realize that ultimately the effectiveness of a training method depends on its achievement of training objectives. Thus, the choice of what training method to use for a particular training program should start with the program's objectives. For example, if the objective is declarative knowledge, you might choose the lecture method. However, if the objective is the acquisition of interpersonal skills, then you might want to use the role-play method. In general, the lecture method will be most effective when you want to impart large amounts of information quickly and at low cost to large groups of trainees. To teach skills such as interviewing or negotiations, the most effective methods are behaviour modelling and role playing.

In addition to a training program's objectives, a number of other factors need to be considered when choosing a training method. For example, a method might be extremely effective for achieving a program's objectives, but too expensive to develop and implement. Thus, trainers must also consider the cost and benefits of training methods. Another important factor to consider is whether or not trainees will be expected to apply what they learn in training on the job. Trainers will choose one method over another if a trainee is more likely to apply the newly acquired skills on the job.

Table 6.2 summarizes these three decision factors and rates 10 on- and off-the-job training methods against them. The table does not, however, list other factors that are also important such as the skill and preferences of the trainer. A trainer might be more skilled at using some methods than others and might also have a personal preference for using some methods. For example, if a trainer does not understand technology, then that option might be eliminated.

Another critical factor is the characteristics and preferences of trainees. Trainees are likely to vary in terms of what training methods will motivate them and maximize their learning. For example, not all trainees are going to be motivated enough for action learning and some will not have the literacy skills necessary to understand a lengthy case study. Also important is the support from management in terms of time and resources. Employees might not

TABLE 6.2

Choosing a Training Method

Method is Effective for the…

| Method | Training objective[1] | | | Costs[2] | | Use on the job[3] |
	knowledge	skills	attitudes	Dev$	Admin$	Transfer
Lecture	yes	no	no	low	low	low
Video	yes	no	yes	high	low	med
Discussion	no	no	yes	low	low	low
Behaviour modelling	no	yes	no	high	high	high
Role play	no	yes	yes	mod	mod	high
Case study	yes	med	yes	mod	low	med
Case incident	med	med	med	med	med	med
Games	no	med	no	med	med	low
Simulations	yes	yes	no	high	high	high
Tech-based training	yes	yes	no	high	low	high

[1] Determine the training objective and match the training methods to that objective
[2] Consider the costs of the method (development and administration) and its potential benefits
[3] Determine suitability for transfer to the job

be allowed the time necessary to participate in action learning but given just enough time off work to attend a lecture. One also has to consider the availability of equipment that might be required for a simulation.

Finally, although we have discussed training methods one by one, in reality trainers mix and combine them (e.g., case studies with lecturing). In fact, you might recall that in Chapter 5 we discussed Krispy Kreme's manager-training program that combines traditional classroom training, on-the-job training, and online learning. This is known as a blended approach to training delivery. A **blended delivery approach** refers to the use of "various instructional media ranging from classes and workbooks to Web-based courses and self-study CD-ROM modules."[33]

A blended delivery approach has a number of benefits. It allows participants to learn in ways that work for them, allows multiple learning outcomes to be achieved, and increases the possibility that the training will be applied on the job. Trainers must therefore be skilled in a variety of approaches to learning. According to a recent survey in the United States, 24 percent of training courses use a blended delivery approach with smaller companies (100 to 499 employees) using a blended approach the most.[34]

In conclusion, when it comes to training methods, each method has its place. There are many factors to consider when deciding on training methods. The choice depends on the following factors: 1. The training objectives; 2. The cost of development and implementation; 3. The potential for trainees to transfer to the job; 4. The trainer's skill and preferences; 5. Trainee characteristics and preferences; and 6. Organizational support and resources. Ultimately, mixing, adapting, and blending methods is likely to be the best approach for maximizing trainee learning and a training program's effectiveness.

Blended delivery approach

The use of various instructional media ranging from classes and workbooks to Web-based courses and self-study CD-ROM modules

Summary

This chapter focused on off-the-job training methods and described 10 of the most frequently used methods. The advantages and disadvantages of each method were described as well as suggestions for their use. The chapter concluded with a discussion of how to choose training methods and identified six factors to consider. The importance of combining methods and using a blended delivery approach was also discussed.

Key Terms

action learning (page 159)
audio-visual methods (page 150)
behaviour modelling (page 153)
blended delivery approach (page 163)
case incident (page 152)
case study (page 151)
discussion method (page 149)

equipment simulators (page 158)
games (page 156)
lecture (page 147)
physical fidelity (page 159)
psychological fidelity (page 159)
role play (page 154)
simulations (page 157)

Weblinks

Bata Limited: www.bata.ca (page 149)
Royal Bank Financial Group of Canada: www.royalbank.com (page 158)
TELUS: www.telus.ca (page 158)

Discussion Questions

1. Whirlpool Corp. executives believe that their reality-based training program is a more pragmatic and effective way of preparing its youthful marketing representatives than the lectures and slide shows that make up so many corporate training programs. Do you agree or disagree? Compare and contrast Whirlpool's reality-based training program to the off-the-job training methods described in this chapter. How does it compare and what are the advantages and disadvantages?

2. With the rising concerns about airport security in Canada and the United States, there has been an urgent need to change the way that security personnel are hired and trained. In the United States, the U.S. Department of Transportation was given one year to recruit, screen, hire, and train more than 28,000 airport passenger and baggage screeners for every airport in the United States. In terms of training, what training methods do you think should be used? Review the training methods listed in Table 6.1, and discuss the advantages and disadvantages of using each method to train the airport passenger and baggage screeners. What methods do you think will be most effective and why?

3. What are the advantages and disadvantages of each of the training methods listed in Table 6.1, and when would it be best to use each method? What method do you prefer when you are being trained and why?

Using the Internet

1. To find out about the kinds of games that are used in training, visit the following websites:

   www.survivalinthebushinc.com

   www.totalrebound.com

   www.fightercombat.com

   Indicate the kinds of games that each company offers for corporate training. What are the objectives of these games and what do employees actually do? What knowledge and skills do employees learn from these games and how effective do you think they are? Using the criteria described in the chapter for choosing a training method, evaluate the use and effectiveness of these games for training.

Exercises

1. Prepare a five-minute lecture on a topic of your choice following the information on lectures outlined in the text. Find a partner in your class and review each other's lecture. If time permits, give your lecture to the class or a small group and discuss its effectiveness. What would make your lecture more effective?

2. Choose a training program you have taken that you really liked and one that you did not like. For each one, indicate the training methods that were used (see Table 6.1) and how they were used. What effect did the methods have on your satisfaction of the program and your learning? What methods might have improved your satisfaction and learning?

3. Think of a work situation you have either experienced or observed that would lend itself to a role play (e.g., a customer complaining to an employee). Design a role play in which you describe a situation and the role of two role players. Be clear about the purpose of the role play in terms of its objectives and what the role players are expected to learn from it. Be sure to include instructions to participants about the situation and the relationship between the characters. The instructor can now either have you describe your role play to the class and/or have class members enact it. If role plays are enacted, be sure to also include a debriefing session afterwards.

4. Describe the major tasks involved in performing a previous or current job and how employees are trained. Then review each of the training methods in Table 6.1 and describe how they might be used to train employees for the job. What training methods do you think would be most effective? Which ones would you recommend and why?

5. For this exercise, your task is to design a short game that can be played in class to learn a skill such as communication, team skills, leadership, negotiations, etc. In groups of two or three, choose a skill to focus on, and then design a game to learn the skill. Your game must be designed so that other members of the class can play it during class time. Write a brief description of your game indicating the objectives, the players, the rules, and what team members have to do to get points or win. The instructor can now either have you describe your game to the class and/or have class members actually play it. After playing the game, be sure to discuss how effective it was for learning the skill and the players' reaction to it.

6. You have been asked to develop a course to teach senior executives how to use e-mail. Which training method would you use and why (see Table 6.1)?

7. Consider the potential of action learning as an instructional method for your course on training and development. Do you think that action learning would be an effective method? Design an action learning project for your training and development course. Be specific in terms of the objectives, the skills to be developed, and the problems to be worked on and solved.

8. Contact the human resources department of an organization to learn about the training methods they use to train employees. In particular, you should inquire about:

- What training methods they use, what they use them for, and why they use them?
- Do they use a blended approach to training, why or why not?
- Do they use certain training methods for particular training programs?
- Do they prefer to use certain training methods more than others?
- What training methods do they believe to be the most effective for training employees in their organization?

Case

MAKING CUSTOMERS HAPPY

Intense competition among retailers today has made customer service a top priority. At stores such as the Gap and Wal-Mart, employees welcome customers into the store with cheery greetings. Sales staff now have to do much more than simply operate the cash register. They need to have good communication and interpersonal skills in order to provide customers with excellent service. They need to be courteous, polite, and helpful.

Providing good customer service requires training programs that teach employees how to interact with customers. Many retail companies provide customer service training programs that teach employees how to be friendly, courteous, and helpful. For example, several years ago Safeway, North America's second-largest supermarket chain, made the headlines when some employees complained about the company's "superior service" program that required them to smile at customers, engage in eye contact with them, and respond cheerfully to customers' wants.

Consider a large retail clothing store that decided it too needed to improve customer service. To be competitive, the store wanted employees to be more active and involved with customers. A training program was designed so that in addition to learning how to use the company's sales register system, which had always been the focus of the training program, the employees would learn how to greet customers, offer assistance, help them find what they are looking for, solve customer complaints and problems, and provide courteous, helpful, and friendly service.

The training program began with a lecture in which the trainer described the importance of customer service and the objectives of the training program. Trainees were also instructed on how to provide good service and how they should behave when they are interacting with customers.

Following the lecture, a video tape was shown that consisted of different scenarios in which employees were shown interacting with customers. In one scenario, a customer could not find what he was looking for and asked the employee for assistance. The employee was not friendly and told the customer to try looking down another aisle. In another incident, a customer complained to an employee about something she had purchased that was less expensive at another store. She demanded a price reduction or her money back. The customer began raising her voice and the employee yelled at the customer and told her to leave the store. Similar incidents of poor customer service were also shown in the video.

After the video, the trainer asked trainees what was wrong with each scenario and how the employee should have behaved to provide better customer service. At the end of the discussion, the trainer provided a brief lecture outlining the key points shown in the video. This was followed by another video that showed scenarios of employees providing good customer service. A brief discussion and lecture followed in which the trainees were asked to describe what the employee did to provide good service. The trainer then concluded the session by highlighting the key customer service behaviours.

Trainees then had to take a test on their knowledge of customer service. The test consisted of multiple choice questions that asked trainees to choose the most appropriate behaviour in different situations with customers. Most of the trainees did very well on the test and upon completing the training program, they all received a customer service qualification certificate.

Back on the job, however, some employees had difficulty dealing with customers. For example, in one incident a customer demanded his money back for a pair of pants that had shrunk after cleaning. He started blaming the employee for the store's poor quality and called the employee an idiot. The employee didn't know what to do and just walked away. In another incident, a customer came into the store to pick up a shirt that he had asked an employee to hold for him. The item had been sold and it was the last one in the store. The employee apologized saying that it was sold to somebody else by accident. However, the customer insisted that the employee call the customer who bought the shirt and have them return it. The employee said she could not do that and told the customer how sorry she was. The customer refused to leave the store unless the employee called the customer who bought the shirt. The employee threatened to call security if the customer did not leave the store. He finally left but not before causing a big scene in the store in front of many other customers.

Questions

1. Describe the training methods used in the customer service training program. Do you think these were appropriate methods to use and were they used appropriately?
2. How effective was the training program? What are its strengths and weaknesses?
3. What other training methods could have been used to make the training program more effective? Review the methods in Table 6.1 and indicate how effective each one would be using the criteria in the chapter to select training methods.

4. If you were to redesign the customer service training program, what training methods would you use and why?
5. What does this case say about training methods and the effectiveness of a training program?

Running Case Part 2

VANDALAIS DEPARTMENT STORES

Refer to the Vandalais Department Stores case described in Chapter 5. First, consider the training methods currently being used. What are the training methods that are being used in the structured employment interview training program, and what are the advantages and disadvantages of using each of them? If you were designing this training program, would you choose to use the same training methods? Explain your reasoning.

Second, consider each of the training methods in Table 6.1. For each one, answer the following questions:

1. Describe how each training method might be used for the structured employment interview training program.
2. What are the advantages and disadvantages of using each training method for the structured employment interview training program?
3. How effective do you think each training method would be for the structured employment interview training program?
4. If you were designing the structured employment interview training program, what training methods would you use and why?

References

[1] Excerpt from Barboza, D. (September 15, 2000). New recruits get a taste of "Real Whirl." *The Globe and Mail*, M2 (New York Times Service).

[2] Harris-Lalonde, S. (2001). Training and development outlook. *The Conference Board of Canada*. Ottawa.

[3] Renner, P. (1988). *The quick instructional planner.* Vancouver: Training Associates Ltd.

[4] Kulig, P. (1998, November 2). Conferences: personnel development or personal perk. *Canadian HR Reporter*, p. 20.

[5] Zander, A. (1982). *Making groups effective.* San Francisco: Jossey-Bass Publishers.

[6] Gabris, G. 1989. Educating elected officials in strategic goal setting. *Public Productivity and Management Review, 13* (2), 161–75.

[7] Conlin, J. (1989). Conflict at meetings: Come out fighting. *Successful Meetings, 38* (6), 30–36. Renner, P. (1988). Wein, G. (1990). Experts as trainers. *Training and Development Journal, 44* (7), 29–30.

[8] Keller, S., & Chuvala, J. (1992). Training: Tricks of the trade. *Security Management, 36* (7).

[9] Pearce, J.A., Robinson, R.B., Jr., & Zahra Shaker, A. (1989). *An industry approach to cases in strategic management.* Boston: Irwin Publishing.

[10] Yin, R.K. (1985). *Case study research: Design and methods.* Beverly Hills: Sage Publications.

[11] Wright, P. (1992). The CEO and the business school: Is there potential for increased cooperation? *Association of Management Proceedings: Education, 10* (1), 41–45.

[12]Craig, R.L. (1987). *Training and development handbook: A guide to human resource development* (pp. 414–29). New York: McGraw-Hill Inc.

[13]Craig, R.L. (1987).

[14]Schnelle, K. (1967). *Case analysis and business problem solving.* New York: McGraw-Hill.

[15]Craig, R.L. (1987).

[16]Kenny, B., Lea, E., & Luffman, G. (1992). *Cases in business policy* (2nd ed.). Oxford: Blackwell Publishers.

[17]Leenders, M.R., & Erskine, J.A. (1973). *Case research: The case writing process.* London: University of Western Ontario Press.

[18]Robinson, J.C. (1982). *Developing managers through behaviour modelling.* Austin: Texas.

[19]Georges, J.C. (1988). Why soft-skills training doesn't take. *Training, 25* (4), 44–45.

[20]Buller, M., & McEvoy, G. (1990). Exploring the long-term effects of behaviour modelling training. *Journal of Organizational Change Management, 3* (1).

[21]Atkins, E. (1999, March) Winning through prevention. *Workplace News,* p 9.

[22]Greenlaw, B., Herron, M., & Ramdon, L. (1962). *Business simulation in industrial and university education.* Englewood Cliffs, NJ: Prentice-Hall.

[23]Tannenbaum, S. I., & Yukl, G. (1992). Training and development in work organizations. *Annual Review of Psychology, 43,* 399–441.

[24]Salas, E., & Cannon-Bowers, J. A. (2001). The science of training: A decade of progress. *Annual Review of Psychology, 52,* 471–99.

[25]Salopek, J. (1998). Workstation meets Playstation. *Training and Development, 52* (8), 26–35.

[26]Connal, D. Baskin, C. (2002, November). Transforming a sales organization through simulation-based learning: a TELUS Communications case study. *Training Report,* 4–5.

[27]Stevenson, M. (2002, September 2). Base helps civilians prepare for chemical attacks. *The Globe and Mail,* A6.

[28]Patrick, K. (2003, May 13). Staged disaster a test for assault readiness. *The Globe and Mail,* A13.

[29]Revans, R.W. (1982). *The origins and growth of action learning.* Gock, Sweden: Bratt-Institute for Neues Lernen.

[30]Revans, R.W. (1984). Action learning: Are we getting there? *Management Decision Journal, 22* (1), 45–52.

[31]Belcourt, M., & Saks, A.M. (1998, February). Training methods and the transfer of training. *Canadian Learning Journal,* 3.

[32]Newstrom, J.W. (1980). Evaluating the effectiveness of training methods. *Personnel Administrator, 25* (1), 55–60. Carrol, S.J., Paine, F.T., & Ivancevich, J.J. (1972). The relative effectiveness of training methods—expert opinion and research. *Personnel Psychology, 25,* 495–510.

[33]Galvin, T. (2002, October). 2002 Industry report. *Training, 39*(10), 24–73.

[34]Galvin, T. (2002, October).

Chapter 7

On-the-Job Training Methods

www.ssloral.com

SPACE SYSTEMS/LORAL

In 1990, Space Systems/Loral acquired Ford Aerospace and its 30-year tradition of satellite innovation. Since them, the Palo Alto, California-based company has been designing, manufacturing, and integrating satellites and satellite systems that provide the foundation for the burgeoning wireless age. For prospective employees of the aerospace industry, Space Systems/Loral's history of playing among the stars continues to lure the next generation of scientific intelligentsia.

With breakthrough technology continually reshaping its industry, Space Systems/Loral's workforce is constantly evolving. Scientific experts act as coaches and mentors so that each fresh generation of engineers and physicists is guided through the application of the complicated technology involved in satellite design and development.

The process begins with the Space Systems/Loral College Hire and Leadership Development Program, which targets about 12 U.S. colleges and universities to attract and recruit the specialized talent it needs. Graduates are welcomed at New Hire Orientation and immediately begin the industry assimilation program or "Satellite 101" class.

Within their first month, they are matched with a mentor and participate in a workshop to learn how to make the most of the mentoring opportunity. During the early weeks of the new hires' careers at Space Systems/Loral, management creates individualized learning tracks made up of three, 6-month rotational assignments. To broaden their skill sets even further, the new recruits are also offered a concurrent program of leadership development courses.

To train its nearly 2,700 employees, the company employs seven senior trainers who make up the company's professional training team. The team is responsible for delivering more than 145 courses to employees each year. To compliment the training staff, the company maintains a cadre of 40 or so "adjunct" trainers recruited and trained to support the professional training team. This ensures that employees have high-quality training opportunities on a just-in-time basis.

In 2000, Space Systems/Loral hired 47 engineers, business majors, and information technology graduates of which 41 are still with the company. According to the manager of learning and development, people are drawn to the company because of the nature of the work as well as the extensive technical training, leadership development, team training, mentoring, and the integration with the more experienced workforce. Perhaps not surprisingly, all 61 graduates recruited for the class of 2001 are still with the company.[1]

Training at Space Systems/Loral is a good example of an organization that uses a number of on-the-job training methods to train and develop new hires. In this chapter, we will focus on some of the most common methods of on-the-job training such as coaching, mentoring, and job rotation that are all part of Space Systems/Loral training program.

Table 7.1 lists the six types of on-the-job training methods described in this chapter. We begin with the most basic form of on-the-job training—when one person trains another person on how to do something—and conclude with some of the more expensive and time-consuming methods.

On-the-Job Training (OJT) Methods

The most common method of training is **on-the-job training** in which a trainee receives instruction and training at his/her workstation from a supervisor or an experienced coworker. Most of us can probably remember a time when someone was assigned the job of training us to perform a task such as operating a cash register or learning how to make a request for supplies. Although on-the-job training has been practised since at least the Middle Ages, the United States army formalized the concept during World War II.

There are a number of approaches of on-the-job training. Table 7.2 provides a description of the many ways in which on-the-job training can be accomplished such as training a group of employees on the spot, observing performance and providing feedback, and so on.

On-the-job training is an important part of training at McDonald's Canada. As one of Canada's largest employers of youth, the company needs to train thousands of new crew members every year. Although the company

On-the-job training
A training method in which a trainee receives instruction and training at his or her workstation from a supervisor or an experienced coworker

TABLE 7.1

On-the-Job Training Methods

1. Job instruction training—A formalized, structured, and systematic approach to on-the job training.
2. Performance aid—A device that helps an employee perform his or her job.
3. Job rotation—A training method in which trainees are exposed to many functions and areas within an organization.
4. Apprenticeship programs—Training that combines on-the-job training with classroom instruction.
5. Coaching—A training method in which a seasoned employee works closely with another employee to develop insight, motivate, build skills, and to provide support through feedback and reinforcement.
6. Mentoring—A method in which a senior member of an organization takes a personal interest in the career of a junior employee.

once used videos and classroom training, it now uses a buddy system combined with hands-on training and visual aids. A more experienced employee or "buddy" works with a new member individually on the job. In addition, laminated visual aids are used to show the steps in a task at each station and as a form of visual reinforcement. New crew members can refer to it during training and on the job. The combination of hands-on training and visual reinforcement is believed to result in higher levels of trainee confidence (self-efficacy) and performance.[2]

OJT is especially useful for small businesses where most new employment is being created. Small businesses rarely offer courses and workshops for employees. Thus, OJT is ideal for them because of the limited investment needed to conduct the training. In fact, a recent survey found that 43 percent of small and medium-sized enterprises use informal training methods such as on-the-job training, tutoring, and mentoring, while only 2 percent use only formal training such as the classroom, seminars, and workshops. Forty-three percent said that they use both informal (on-the-job) and formal training methods.[3]

Although on-the-job training is the most common approach to training, it has also been described as the most misused.[4] This is due to a number of problems that limit its effectiveness. One of the biggest problems is that on-the-job training is often not well planned or structured.

A related problem is that most people assigned the task of training others on the job have not received training on how to be a trainer. As a result, managers and employees do not have the knowledge and skills required to be effective trainers and are not familiar with important learning principles such as practice, feedback, and reinforcement.

Another problem is that inept employees will transfer undesirable work habits and attitudes to new employees. Furthermore, the traditional ways of

TABLE 7.2

Approaches to On-the-Job Training

On-the-spot lecture	Gather trainees into groups and tell them how to do the job.
Viewed performance/ Feedback	Watch the person at work and give constructive feedback, such as when the sales manager makes a call with a new salesperson.
Following Nellie	The supervisor trains a senior employee, who in turn trains new employees (showing the ropes).
Job-aid approach	A job aid (step-by-step instructions or video) is followed while the trainer monitors performance.
The training step Sequence	The trainer systematically introduces the task. Following a planned sequence. On-the-spot lecture, gather trainees into groups, and tell them how to do the job.

doing things will be passed on to new employees, which means that existing problems as well as poor attitudes and behaviours will persist.

Other problems occur when those doing the training are worried that newly trained employees will one day take over their jobs. Further, some trainers might abuse their position by making the trainee do all the dirty work and the trainee might not learn important skills. In addition, OJT can be time consuming and some employees feel penalized when they can't earn as much money or meet their goals because of the time they have had to spend training others. It is for all these reasons that OJT is not always effective and has been referred to as the most used and misused training method.[5]

The main problem with the traditional unstructured approach to on-the-job training is that it results in training that is inconsistent, inefficient, and ineffective. However, when the process is carefully planned and structured, it can be a highly effective method of training that is also consistent and efficent.[6]

In fact, in one of the few studies to test the effectiveness of on-the-job training, structure was shown to be very important. In the study, a group of newly hired workers received training on how to operate a manufacturing process. One group received traditional on-the-job training in which one worker was trained by the supervisor, and then each person trained another one (similar to the Following Nellie approach described in Table 7.2). A second group was trained by a supervisor who used a structured approach to on-the-job training.

The results showed that the structured approach was considerably more effective. Trainees who received structured on-the-job training reached a predetermined level of skill and productivity in one-quarter the time it took to train the other group. They also produced 76 percent fewer rejects, and their troubleshooting ability increased by 130 percent. This study highlights the importance of building structure into on-the-job training and how it can have a positive effect on the performance of trainees and the organization.[7]

In the next section, we describe a method for carefully planning and structuring on-the-job training that is known as job instruction training.

Job Instruction Training

While the traditional unstructured approach to on-the-job training is ineffective, more structured approaches can be highly effective. The best known structured approach to on-the-job training is job instruction training. **Job instruction training** is a formalized, structured, and systematic approach to on-the-job training.

Job instruction training consists of four steps: 1. Preparation, 2. Instruction, 3. Performance, and 4. Follow up. During the preparation phase, the trainer breaks down the job into small tasks, prepares all the equipment and supplies necessary to do the task, and allocates a time frame in which to learn each task. The instruction phase involves telling, showing, explaining, and demonstrating the task to the trainee. During the performance stage, the trainee performs the task under guidance from the instructor who provides feedback and reinforcement. Each task is learned in a similar way until the whole job can be completed without error. In the follow-up

Job instruction training
A formalized, structured, and systematic approach to on-the-job training

stage, the trainer monitors the trainee's performance and provides feedback. Each of these steps is described in more detail below.

1. Preparation

The key activity during the preparation phase is to develop a communications strategy that fits the trainee and to find out what the trainee already knows. The instructor needs to understand the background, capabilities, and attitudes of his or her trainees as well as the nature of the tasks to be performed before choosing a technique or combination of techniques. If the training is too easy or difficult for a trainee, the instructor can make adjustments to suit his or her needs. Note that trial and error has *not* been included here. Very few circumstances justify throwing an employee into a new position without proper training. Learning from one's mistakes is not only inefficient, but can be humiliating, dangerous, or lead to poor customer relations.

The second part of the preparation phase concerns the trainee. There are three stages: putting the trainee at ease, guaranteeing the learning, and building interest and showing personal advantage.[8]

1. The trainer must remember that the trainee might be apprehensive. It is unwise to begin too abruptly. Some small talk might be appropriate to relax the trainee and to set the tone for the training sessions. Most individuals learn more readily when relaxed. A short conversation concerning any matter of interest—the weather, sports, a work-related item—should be effective. Obviously, the topic chosen must be suitable for the situation.

2. When the conversation does turn to the training session, the trainer needs to guarantee to the employee that learning is possible. Again, use a simple statement, "Don't worry about this machine, Sally; in about three hours you'll be operating it almost as well as everyone else. I've trained at least 10 people in this procedure." The trainee now knows that it is possible to learn (i.e., learning will take place) and that the instructor has the ability to teach the process, adding to her confidence and self-efficacy.

3. Although the instructor might be interested, the trainee might be apprehensive or might not understand the effect that training will have on the quality of his or her worklife. Developing trainee enthusiasm sometimes is difficult, but pointing out some personal gain helps to create interest. The idea that the training activity will lead to something positive creates the opportunity to design rewards: more self-esteem, easier work, higher-level work, less routine, more control over work, greater opportunity or security. Once the appropriate reward is found (provided it can be obtained), most employees will respond positively.

Some people will resist, however, as training is change and individuals accept change at different rates. The trainee preparation phase will identify those who are not responding. As the trainer is responsible for meeting measurable objectives, it is important to evaluate the likelihood of cooperation among trainees so that individual remedial action can be taken.

One way to defuse resistance is to train employees in order of their perceived enthusiasm. When the resisters see others reaping the rewards of training, they usually agree to be trained, albeit grudgingly.

2. Instruction

If the trainee is to perform a task or an operation, he or she should be positioned slightly behind or beside the instructor so that the job is viewed from a realistic angle. The trainer can then proceed as follows:

1. Show the trainee how to perform the job.
   - Be sure to break the job into manageable tasks and present only as much as can be absorbed at one time. Remember, too, that individuals learn at different speeds, so some trainees, for example, might be able to learn six or seven sequences at once, while others can absorb only four or five.
   - Repeat Step 1 as necessary and be patient.
   - Don't forget to tell why as well as how.
   - Point out possible difficulties as well as safety procedures.
   - Encourage questions.
2. Repeat and explain key points in more detail.
   - Safety is especially important.
   - Take the time to show how the job fits into any larger systems.
   - Show why the job is important.
   - Show why key points are more important than others.
   - Repeat Step 2 as necessary and be patient.
   - Encourage questions.
3. Allow the trainee to see the whole job again.
   - Ask questions to determine the level of comprehension.
   - Repeat Step 3 as necessary and be patient.
   - Encourage questions.

3. Performance

Following the instruction phase, the trainee should be given an opportunity to perform the task. This can be done in the following manner:

1. Ask the trainee to perform less difficult parts of the job.
   - Try to ensure initial success.
   - Don't tell how. If possible, ask questions, but try to keep trainee's frustration level low.
   - Ask the trainee to explain the steps.
2. Allow the trainee to perform the entire job.
   - Gently suggest improvements where necessary.
   - Provide feedback on performance.
   - Reinforce correct behaviour.

4. Follow-up

Once the performance stage is complete, the trainee will be left on his/her own to perform the task. This does, not, however mean that the training is over. It is important that the trainer keep track of the trainee's performance and provide support and feedback. The trainer should leave the trainee to work alone; indicate when and where to find help if necessary; supervise closely and check performance periodically; and then gradually taper off instruction as the employee gains confidence and skill.

While the steps of job instruction training might seem elaborate, they must be applied with the complexity and possible safety hazards of the job in mind. Very simple tasks might require only one demonstration. As well, employees bring different skills and backgrounds to the workplace. Competent preparation will eliminate overtraining and the resultant boredom and inattention.

Tips for Trainers

Sloman studied three British National Training Award winners that paid particular attention to the OJT delivery. From their programs he developed a set of rules governing good on-the-job training.[9]

First, job instruction training should not be managed differently from other types of training. Second, it should be integrated with other training methods. Third, ownership must be maintained even when consultants are used. And fourth, trainers must be chosen with care and trained properly. In addition to being experts in the skill area, they must want to be trainers and have good communication skills. Patience and respect for differences in the ability to learn are also important as the trainer sets the initial mood or climate of the learning experience.[10]

Once suitable individuals are found they should be trained (train-the-trainer) and then recognized and rewarded for training others. It is of little use to give training responsibilities to an already busy employee without restructuring his or her job to include a training element. Nor is increased pay always the most sought after reward (although it doesn't hurt). Recognition, the chance to add variety to the workday, respect from new employees, training certificates, and the prospect of either promotion or cross-training all help to make the experience worthwhile for the individual.

See The Trainer's Notebook 1 on the characteristics of effective on-the-job instructors.

Performance aid

A device that helps an employee perform his/her job

Performance Aids

A **performance aid** is any device that helps an employee perform his/her job. Performance aids can be signs or prompts ("Have you turned off the computer?"); trouble-shooting aids ("If the red light goes on, the machine needs oil"); instructions in sequence ("To empty the machine, follow the next five steps"); a special tool or gauge (a long stick to measure how much gas is in an inaccessible tank); flash cards to help counsel clients; pictures (of a perfectly set table, for example); or posters and checklists.[11]

Effective On-the-Job Instructors

OJT instructors should be selected and trained and even certified before they begin instructing others in job tasks. The experience they must obtain and skills that they must learn include:

- at least one year's experience working in the job task area, including possessing hands-on experience performing all tasks that will be taught
- ability to conduct task analysis, write measurable and observable performance objectives, and prepare effective training aids

- skills in coaching techniques
- ability to evaluate performance, give feedback, and reinforcement
- organizational and time management skills
- flexibility in adapting to trainees with different levels of skills experience, and abilities.

Source: Adapted from Walter, D. (1998). Training and certifying on-the-job trainers. *Technical Training* (March/April), pp. 32–34.

For example, employees learning about hazardous-waste management could be provided with a checklist that summarizes the major steps for handling radioactive material. This checklist, if prepared as a colourful poster, will increase the chances of employee application. As indicated earlier, McDonald's uses laminated visual aids to remind trainees of the steps in a task and as a form of visual reinforcement that trainees refer to during training and once they are on the job.

The reasoning behind the use of performance aids is that requiring the memorization of sequences and tasks sometimes takes too much training time, especially if the task is not repeated daily. They are also useful when performance is difficult, is executed infrequently, can be done slowly, and when the consequences of poor performance are serious.[12] As well, new employees can be on the job more quickly if armed with a series of temporary performance aids. Finally, routine (and not so routine) trouble-shooting and repair responses can be performed much more quickly and with less frustration.

Employees who are placed in positions where they must react very quickly might not be able to rely on memory. A panel operator in a nuclear power plant, for example, may have 15 seconds (or less) to perform a series of safety sequences. In the less hectic world of insurance sales, one manager found that a potentially sound sales trainee constantly neglected to complete the entire sales sequence and paperwork. Both these employees, despite their vastly different work environments, were helped by performance aids.

In the first instance, an indexed manual containing various operating sequences was developed and placed on a wheeled trolley within easy reach of all the operators' positions. The sales problem was solved by creating a checklist containing all the steps or tasks to be completed each time the salesperson visited a prospective client. The employee completed and checked off each step and the sheet was signed and dated. The manager then reviewed each call with the trainee. In this case, the checklist was discarded after about three weeks as the sales trainee was performing to the standards set by management.[13]

Tips for Trainers

When designing visual performance aids that help employees remember key information, all the skills of the graphic artist's craft should be utilized. Ease in reading, space between letters, colour, boldness, symbols, and graphic language ("Pull Here!") are all used to communicate more effectively.[14] Audio aids also must clearly communicate intent. A taped warning ("Connect your safety harness!") may be useless, but a buzzer alarm is hard to ignore.

When designing a training program, it is important to consider how performance aids might save time and money. With ingenuity, the trainee's worklife not only can be made easier, but significant improvements in performance, downtime, and safety records can result. Performance aids work even better with the use of technology. Performance aids that use technology are called electronic performance-support systems and they are described in Chapter 8.

Job rotation

A training method in which trainees are exposed to many functions and areas within an organization

Job Rotation

Job rotation is a training method in which trainees are exposed to many functions and areas within an organization. Job rotation is often used as part of an ongoing career-development program, especially for employees who are destined to management positions. The objective is for an employee to learn a variety of skills from both doing a variety of tasks and by observing the performance of others. Typically the individual will be supervised by a supervisor who is responsible for the individual's training. Through this process a trainee can acquire a number of skills required to perform different tasks and also learn about the organization.

Job rotation broadens an individual's knowledge and skills by providing him/her with multiple perspectives and areas of expertise. This is precisely why Space Systems/Loral creates individual learning tracks for new hires that consist of three 6-month rotational assignments. The purpose is to broaden new hires' skill sets.

Indeed, the practice of line managers temporarily taking staff jobs has met with some success.[15] A variety of cross-job and project-based experiences can be devised to create a pool of leadership talent capable of responding to emergencies and to rapidly changing business environments while making the constant incremental changes necessary for corporate survival.[16]

Some organizations benefit from job rotation more than others. In highly technical environments, for example, it may be difficult for some employees to be productive in areas for which they are untrained. Short-term assignments and planned observations may prove more useful so that nontechnical managers gain familiarity with technical processes without actually managing the unit or division.[17]

Job rotation is an effective method of training employees who need to learn a variety of skills. By providing employees with a series of on-the-job experiences in which they work on a variety of tasks, jobs, and assignments, they will acquire the skills required to perform their current job as well as future job responsibilities.

Research on job rotation has generally been supportive. It not only results in an improvement in knowledge and skills but it also has a number of career benefits such as higher job satisfaction, more opportunities for career advancement, and a higher salary.[18]

Tips for Trainers

A disadvantage of job rotation is that if an employee does not spend enough time in a department or working on an assignment, he or she might not have sufficient time to get up to speed and complete an assignment. Thus, a trainee might acquire only a superficial understanding of a job or department and this might result in some frustration. Therefore, it is important that job rotation be carefully planned and structured so that trainees receive sufficient exposure and experience on each assignment to make it a worthwhile learning experience. In addition, the assignments should be tailored to each individual's training needs as is the case at Space Systems/Loral where management creates individualized learning tracks for each new hire's rotational assignments.

It is also important that job rotation be part of a larger training program and integrated with other training methods. That is, job rotation should be only one component of a training program and learning process and supplemented with classroom instruction and coaching or mentoring. For example, at Space Systems/Loral new hires receive classroom instruction, coaching, and mentoring in addition to job rotation. Thus, the rotational assignments are just one component of the training of new hires. Coaching and mentoring are important because trainees need some guidance and supervision throughout the job rotation process.

Apprenticeship Programs

Apprenticeship programs are methods of training that combine on-the-job training with classroom instruction. The on-the-job component is used to teach the requisite skills of a particular trade or occupation. Classroom instruction, which comprises a relatively minor portion of the program (usually about 10 percent), teaches related theory and design concepts.

For example, the four-year plumber program includes only three 8-week in-school sessions. In the classroom, plumber apprentices learn such things as the physical properties of piping and other plumbing materials, industry codes, safety rules and operating procedures, trade tools and equipment, soldering techniques, and the characteristics of various fittings and piping systems. On the job, the trainees become familiar with relevant codes, regulations, and specifications, and learn to install, service, and test systems and equipment.

In Canada, the apprenticeship system covers more than 65 regulated occupations in four occupational sectors: construction (e.g., stone mason, electrician, carpenter, plumber), motive power (motor-vehicle mechanic, machinist), industrial (industrial mechanic, millwright), and service (baker, cook, hairstylist). In some of these regulated occupations, apprentices must

Apprenticeship programs
Training that combines on-the-job training with classroom instruction

earn a certificate of qualification by passing a provincial government examination. Apprentices who pass an interprovincial examination with a minimum grade of 70 percent are awarded a red seal, indicating their qualifications are acceptable across Canada.

Apprenticeship training differs from other training methods in that it is regulated through a partnership between government, labour, and industry. In Canada, the federal government pays for in-school training and income support. Provincial governments administer the programs and pay for classroom facilities and instructors. Employers absorb the costs of workplace training and apprentices initiate the process by finding employers willing to sponsor them.

Unlike corporate-sponsored training programs that address the specific needs of an organization, apprenticeships are focused on the collective training needs of specific occupations within broad industrial categories.[19] Consequently, the skills learned through apprenticeship training are transferable within an occupation, across a province, and across Canada.

In the construction industry, carpenters, electricians, plumbers, and masons are trained to meet standards recognized throughout the trade. This flexibility provides advantages to the worker and the industry when regional fluctuations occur in the supply and demand of skilled labour. However, the system is highly dependent on employers, for they must accept the responsibility for establishing and maintaining adequate standards of job performance.

Tips for Trainers

Despite the recent infusion of government funding, much of Canada's apprenticeship system remains antiquated. Outmoded legislation, outdated curricula, poor pay for teachers, archaic entry and completion regulations, and low-prestige entry modes still combine to discourage many young people from considering careers in the skilled trades. Program expansion and enhancement would be key elements in creating apprenticeships that meet the needs of current and future industries, while developing attractive and challenging career alternatives for a greater segment of our labour force.

In determining acceptable qualifications and performance standards for the future, industry and government must address the special needs of new labour groups like women and minorities, eliminating standards or test criteria that might unjustly limit opportunities. For example, criteria pertaining to physical strength might be relaxed or eliminated by making simple changes in job design. Employers that intend to utilize apprenticeships also will need to become more sensitive to the special needs of working mothers and to the various religious or cultural backgrounds of employees. As well, more flexible work schedules may be required to better accommodate those with family or other commitments.

Given the skills shortage crises faced by many industrial sectors, it is likely that increased emphasis will be placed on apprenticeship programs, as this method is one of the most effective and practical ways of teaching skills occupations. It has been predicted that the shortage of skilled workers in Canada could reach one million by the year 2020 unless there is a change in the country's approach to education and training. Not surprisingly, the Minister of Human Resources recently launched a series of round table meetings with government, business, and labour to find ways to address the skills shortage problem including apprenticeship programs.[20]

Coaching

Coaching is a training method in which a seasoned employee, usually a manager, works closely with an employee to develop insight, motivate, build skills, and to provide support through feedback and reinforcement. The coach also guides the employee in learning by helping to find experts and resources for learning and development.

Coaching has become very popular in many organizations today. Coaching programs have been effective in enhancing skills and improving performance in a wide range of areas including interpersonal skills, communication skills, leadership skills, cognitive skills, and self-management skills. It is especially effective for helping people apply what they have learned in the classroom on the job.[21]

Research has found coaching to be highly effective for both individuals and organizations. In general, the results of a number of studies indicate that individuals who participated in coaching showed dramatic improvements in specific skills and overall performance. Coaching has also been found to improve working relationships and job attitudes, and to increase the rate of advancement and salary increases.

Benefits to organizations have been found in productivity, quality, customer service, reduced customer complaints, retention, cost reductions, and bottom-line productivity. Thus, coaching is not only popular but it is also effective.[22]

Although coaching has evolved into a motivational technique that is seen as a prelude to progressive discipline and as a method for dealing with performance problems, it will be discussed here as a vehicle for self-development in a more positive and proactive sense. In fact, this approach represents the current paradigm for coaching.[23]

The coaching process involves the planned use of opportunities in the work environment to improve or to enhance employee strengths and potential. Weaknesses are considered only if they prevent the employee from functioning, or if they are below the manager's tolerance level.[24]

The key elements in the coaching process are "planned," "opportunities in the work environment," and "strengths." First, the process revolves around an agreed-upon plan or set of objectives developed mutually by employee and coach. Development does not occur haphazardly or by chance. The process proceeds in a logical agreed-upon fashion. Second, the work environment is the training laboratory (sometimes expanded to include the community). Transfers, special assignments, vacation replacements, and conference speaking engagements are all potential coaching opportunities. The necessary formal infrastructure, perhaps attached to the firm's appraisal or evaluation system, must be in place for the system to work.[25]

Coaching

A training method in which a seasoned employee works closely with another employee to develop insight, motivate, build skills, and to provide support through feedback and reinforcement

The coaching process begins with a dialogue between coach and employee, during which a set of objectives is defined. Then, coaching opportunities are identified by a mutual examination of the environment. A long-term plan is struck, along with an evaluation or measurement procedure. As well, the process is fitted into the employee's career-development goals and made part of the organization's long-term strategies.

The employee performs the agreed-upon task and then reports to the coach both informally and formally during the annual or semi-annual evaluation. They discuss the results of the current program and then plan the next round of activity.[26] With practice, this approach develops into a continual transfer of skills and an ongoing process.[27]

Several devices can be used as coaching tools. For example, a special-project assignment that will enhance a specific skill is a useful approach, as there is no need to reorganize other work or to hire additional staff. Conversely, job rotation often requires extensive preparation for employees to exchange entire jobs on a long-term basis.

Another useful coaching technique is to design a method or schedule of representation, either at meetings or as committee members. Depending upon the skill or knowledge to be developed, the benefits can be significant, as this long-term exposure to more senior colleagues benefits the employee, while freeing the coach for other tasks. In large retail organizations, for example, a management trainee may be rotated through several departments before choosing one in which to specialize.

Where assignments outside the regular work area are impractical, job redesign or restructuring might be considered. Here, some portion of the job is changed so that new skills must be used. The restructuring of one job may, of course, affect the work of others. Job redesign should be part of an overall work strategy that embraces an entire work unit.

There may be situations in which even job restructuring is impossible. The coach might then have no choice but to suggest job enlargement—the employee taking on more work. Although often not a popular alternative, it may be necessary that an employee perform certain new tasks to grow professionally. A larger job may be the only answer. This approach will work best with individuals who have been on the job for some time and have mastered the tasks. A less-experienced person might panic when faced with more work.

As the last three coaching activities to be mentioned here—conference attendance, professional memberships, and teaching/publishing—take place outside the firm, the coach must be concerned with control over the process. Conferences, in particular, can be treated as social events rather than as serious opportunities to learn. Although there may be spinoff benefits (e.g., exposure to leading experts or networking), conferences must be chosen where attendance will meet a clearly defined purpose.

Similarly, professional societies can be used for a number of purposes—networking, publicity, leadership development, training, updating, and group-participation enhancement. Again, these functions need to serve a planned purpose. If, for example, an employee's job provides little opportunity to manage others, the coach might suggest a term as chairperson of the annual conference committee. Likewise, an employee who shows promise as a speaker might be coaxed into volunteering as master of ceremonies for a fundraiser, thus gaining more experience in public speaking.

Undoubtedly, many more ideas for coaching could be found. For example, some senior executives hire professional coaches to improve their skills. The key is to constantly remind oneself that coaching is the *planned* acquisition of skills and knowledge through the use of existing, or carefully modified, opportunities in the work or professional environments. This focus will prevent both the squandering of developmental opportunities on those who won't benefit and the loss of many potential training activities.

Tips for Trainers

To make coaching work, the employee and the coach must trust each other. Otherwise the employee will see development as extra work. Indeed, perhaps the most important aspect of the coaching process is ongoing dialogue and feedback. It is only under these conditions that employees participate willingly in a two-way process that often requires extra effort and risk taking.[28]

Therefore, it is important that the coach build trust and understanding so that employees will want to work with him/her. It is also important that a coach is able to relate to the person he/she is coaching. And to be most effective, coaching should be used as part of a broader process of learning rather than a stand alone program.[29]

Finally, like any training program, the effectiveness of coaching should be evaluated. Coaching programs are expensive and time-consuming so it is important to determine if they are accomplishing what they are supposed to.

To learn more about how to design an effective coaching program, see The Trainer's Notebook 2, "A Well-Designed Coaching Process."

Mentoring

A key part of Space Systems/Loral's training of new hires is a mentoring program that matches each new hire with a mentor within their first month in the organization. Further, new hires participate in a workshop to learn how to make the most of their mentoring experience. But what is mentoring and what is its purpose?

Mentoring is a method in which a senior member of an organization takes a personal interest in the career of a junior employee. A mentor is an experienced individual, usually a senior manager, who provides coaching and counselling to a junior employee.

Mentors play two major roles: career support and psychosocial support. **Career support** activities include coaching, sponsorship, exposure, visibility, protection, and the provision of challenging assignments. **Psychosocial support** includes being a friend who listens and counsels, who accepts and provides feedback, and who offers a role model for success.[30]

The mentor–protégé relationship used to be an informal one with a senior person recognizing the talent of a junior employee and wishing to help.

Career support

Mentoring activities that include coaching, sponsorship, exposure, visibility, protection, and the provision of challenging assignments

Psychosocial support

Mentoring activities that include being a friend who listens and counsels, who accepts and provides feedback, and a role model for success

A Well-Designed Coaching Process

A well-designed coaching process should address the following issues:

1. **Contracting**: The process should begin by identifying the key stakeholders (the coach, the person being coached, the person's boss or designated sponsor, and human resource contact). The coach should discuss expectations, roles, and responsibilities with each of them. Specific learning goals and clear expectations for how and when performance will improve should also be discussed.

2. **Coaching Sessions**: There are three parts to the coaching session: 1. The Opening—Expectations should be clarified and a working agenda should be established. The two parties should get to know each other, build trust, and establish rapport. 2. Practice—This is the heart of the coaching process. The coach facilitates learning through hands-on-practice of real-world situations, instructions, modelling, feedback, and discussion. 3. Action Planning—This involves coming up with a specific plan to put new behaviours into action by specifying things such as what to do, when to do it, how to do it, how to evaluate the outcome, how they will get feedback from others, and how they will modify or build on what they did.

3. **On-the-Job Activities Between Sessions**: Participants need to be encouraged to practice and apply what they have learned on a daily basis.

4. **Evaluation of Progress**: Progress should be discussed periodically with each of the stakeholders and participants should be encouraged to regularly seek feedback, encouragement, and support from their organizational sponsors.

Source: Based on Peterson, D. B. (2002). Management Development: Coaching and Mentoring Programs. In *Creating, Implementing, and Managing Effective Training and Development: State-of-the-Art Lessons for Practice* by Kraiger © 2002 and Jossey-Bass. This material is used by permission of John Wiley & Sons, Inc.

However, organizations now recognize mentoring as a valuable employee development tool and have moved to formalize the relationships.

Like coaching, mentoring is also popular in organizations today and is also an expensive investment [31] However, mentoring has a more narrow focus than coaching in that its focus is on the career development of junior employees.

According to David Peterson, mentoring can serve a number of purposes for organizations. It can help to accelerate the career progress of underrepresented groups; transmit the culture and values to newer managers; and pass on the accumulated wisdom of seasoned leaders.[32] Mentoring involves exposure to senior management activities that are valuable and beneficial for one's growth and development.

Research has found that mentoring is highly effective for those who are mentored and their organizations. Both professional and academic research consistently has indicated that intensively mentored professionals have greater career prospects and higher incomes than others. Research has found a positive relationship between mentoring, promotion, and income, as well as enhanced satisfaction with wages and benefits.[33]

To learn about the latest approach to mentoring, see Training Today, "Mentoring On-Line."

Mentoring On-Line

When we think of mentoring, we usually think of a senior employee sitting in an office with a junior employee having a face-to-face discussion. However, thanks to technology, mentoring can now take place on-line. Mentors and protégés no longer have to work in the same office or even in the same company. As a result, mentors and protégés can communicate with each other and rarely meet face-to-face.

The very nature of mentoring is being transformed by the use of the Internet. The convenience of e-mail and its ability to bridge geographic distances has made e-mentoring an increasingly popular form of mentoring. It permits time-effective, controlled interaction between the protégé and mentor.

Besides the advantage of being able to bridge geographic distances, e-mentoring also makes it easier for a mentor to establish mentoring relationships with more people because the process is more time-effective than traditional mentoring methods. It also allows the mentor and protégé to keep a record of their e-mail discussions, which is useful when assessing a protégé's progress.

E-mentoring is attractive to many organizations. For example, organizations that foster relationships between working professionals and students looking for career help are turning to e-mentoring in growing numbers.

WWW IBM Canada Ltd. has decided to pilot an e-mentoring program designed to help girls in Grades 7 and 8 develop an awareness of career opportunities in IT. The students are matched with female IBM employees for the balance of the school year. The mentors include computer programmers and Web designers as well as sales people and administrators. Each protégé is in touch with her mentor for about half an hour each week.

SmartForce Publishing Ltd., a provider of Internet-based training services, offers a 24-hour on-line mentoring service to help e-students who are stuck on an assignment or who just need to know if what they are doing is correct.

Many companies providing e-learning programs also want to include mentors as part of the learning process. The growing number of on-line students means that on-line mentoring will become increasingly popular.

Sources: Based on Sommers, J. (2000, November 10). Mentoring goes on-line with help of e-mail. *The Globe and Mail*, E17. Finn, M. (2000, February 25). Mentors keep e-students on course. *The Globe and Mail*, T2.

Tips for Trainers

Mentoring can be an effective method of learning that benefits both the mentor and the person being mentored. However, to be effective it is important that the roles and expectations of the mentor and protégés are clear and well understood. It is also important that they agree on how often they will meet, what types of topics they will discuss, and what career activities will be part of the protégé's development.

Both the mentor and protégé should have some guidelines on how the process will work. Researchers have highlighted several areas of concern to managers wishing to implement formal mentoring programs:[34]

- *Choice of mentors.* Mentors must be motivated to participate in the program and to make sufficient time available to their protégé. They also need to be knowledgeable about how the organization really works. Participation should be voluntary. Inevitably, some assigned relationships will not work out. A procedure needs to be in place to allow either party to cancel the arrangement without too much loss of face, and employees should feel free to end the relationship without fear of retaliation.

- *Matching mentors and protégé(s).* Matching is an important process that needs to be handled with care. Should males be matched with males; females with females? There may not be enough senior women to mentor all the junior women. Hostility from men when women network with one another make some women reluctant to take on the mentoring role.[35] Those mentors close to retirement perform better in both the vocational and psychosocial functions.[36] It is important that the relationship remain confidential and for the protégé to know that it will be confidential. The right mentor must be chosen. The protégé is unlikely to feel comfortable, for example, if the mentor is his or her boss.

- *Training.* Mentors and protégés both need training. This process should entail more than giving mentors a book to read about mentoring. It should, for example, involve the opportunity to share experiences about mentoring. The training of protégés, usually as part of the induction process, is partly concerned with demonstrating the organization's commitment to mentoring, but also involves setting appropriate expectations for the mentoring relationship. Mentors could be chosen for this training, based on their previous track record in developing employees.

- *Structuring the mentoring relationship.* Some programs set out time limits on the relationship and specify minimum levels of contact. Goals, projects, activities, and resources are spelled out. The program is evaluated and those areas in which either mentors or protégés report dissatisfaction are redesigned. While commitment must be made at all levels, it is at the individual level that the process can most easily break down. Signals sent by derailed mentoring schemes include delay between assignment and first meeting with protégé, poor meeting locations (e.g., the cafeteria), and infrequent contacts.

Finally, to be effective, mentoring programs must receive continued supported from management. And because most mentors are volunteers, there should be some benefits and incentives to those who participate as mentors in mentoring programs. The workshop at Space Systems/Loral is a good example of how to make the most out of mentoring by preparing mentors and protégés.

Off-the-Job versus On-the-Job Training Methods

You have now learned a great deal about on- and off-the-job training methods. In Chapter 6, we discussed some of the factors to consider when choosing a training method. In the final section of this chapter, we will review some of the advantages and disadvantages of on- and off-the-job training methods.

Off-the-Job Training Methods

Off-the-job training methods have a number of advantages. First, a trainer can use a wide variety of training methods when training is done off the job. For example, a trainer can use a lecture method with discussion along with audio-visual methods such as a video and slides, a case study or case incident, as well as games and simulations. Thus, a trainer has many possibilities when training is provided off the job and will therefore be better able to tailor a training program to the needs and preferences of trainees. The trainer is also able to choose a combination of methods that will be most effective given the objectives and content of a training program.

Another advantage of off-the-job training is that the trainer is able to control the training environment. In other words, the trainer can choose a training site that is comfortable, free of distractions, and conducive to learning. A trainer does not have as much control over the learning environment when training is conducted on the job.

A third advantage is that a large number of trainees can be trained at one time. This is particularly the case when the lecture method is used. Thus, off-the-job training is generally more efficient given that so many more trainees can be trained at one time.

There are of course a number of disadvantages of off-the-job training methods. First, off-the-job training can be much more costly than on-the-job training. This is due to the costs associated with the use of training facilities, travel, accommodation, food, and so on. However, as you will see in the next chapter, such costs can be almost completely eliminated with the use of technology.

A second disadvantage of off-the-job training is that because the training takes place in an environment that is different from the environment in which trainees will be required to apply what they learn in training, trainees might have some difficulty making the transition from the training environment to the work environment. For example, while a trainee might be able to perform a training task in a role play during training, he or she might have some difficulty performing the task on the job. Thus, the application of training material on the job or what is known as the transfer of training (see Chapter 9) can be more difficult with off-the-job training.

On-the-Job Training Methods

There are also a number of advantages and disadvantages of on-the-job training. A major advantage of on-the-job training is that the cost is much lower given that the need for training facilities, travel, accommodation, and so on is eliminated. Thus, on-the-job training tends to be much less costly than off-the-job training.

A second advantage is the greater likelihood of the application of training material on the job. That is, because training takes place in trainees' actual work area, the application is much more direct and in some cases immediate. Thus, there is less difficulty in the transfer of training since the training site and work site are the same.

There are, however, a number of disadvantages. First, the work environment is full of distractions that can interfere with learning and interrupt training. Noise might make it difficult for trainees to hear and understand the trainer, and at times the trainer might be interrupted to solve a problem or work on something else.

Second, when trainees are being trained on an actual machine or equipment in the work place, there is always the potential for damage to expensive equipment. This could also shut down production for a period of time adding to the cost of damaged equipment that needs to be repaired or replaced.

A third problem is the disruption of service or slow down in production that occurs during training. You have probably had the experience of being served by an employee who is being trained. The result is usually slower service and the potential for errors. Thus, on-the-job training can result in a reduction in productivity, quality, and service.

Finally, when there are safety issues associated with the use of equipment or dangerous chemicals, on-the-job training can compromise safety. A trainee learning on the job can make a mistake and harm him or herself, other employees, or customers. Therefore, extra precaution and care needs to be taken whenever on-the-job training involves working with equipment or dangerous chemicals.

As you can see, there are both advantages and disadvantages associated with on- and off-the-job training methods. Being aware of and understanding them can be helpful when choosing a training method. For example, when there is a need to train a large number of employees, off-the-job training would be more practical. When the cost of training is an issue, on-the-job training might be more feasible. Thus, issues of practicality and feasibility are important considerations when choosing a training method.

Finally, it should be apparent to you that the choice of a training method is not really about whether it is used on or off the job. In fact, effective training programs often combine on- and off-the-job training methods. Recall that Space Systems/Loral combines both on- and off-the-job training methods to orient and train new hires.

Ultimately, what is most important is mixing and combining methods to best suit a particular training need. This is not only the case with respect to on- and off-the-job training methods, but also for technology-based training methods, which are discussed in Chapter 8.

Summary

This chapter has described some of the most common forms of on-the-job training methods and serves as a compliment to the off-the-job training methods described in Chapter 6. It was noted that on-the-job training is the most common method of training as well as the most misused. However, when on-the-job training is carefully planned and structured, it can have a positive effect on employee learning and performance. Although each of the methods of training described in this chapter takes place on the job, they differ in terms of what they are best suited for and when they should be used.

Therefore, it is important to match each method with the objectives of a training program and the needs of trainees. Finally, we noted that there are advantages and disadvantages of on- and off-the-job training methods, and that effective training programs mix and combine both kinds of training methods along with technology-based methods, which are described in the next chapter.

Key Terms

apprenticeship programs (page 181)
career support (page 185)
coaching (page 183)
job instruction training (page 175)

job rotation (page 180)
on-the-job training (page 173)
performance aid (page 178)
psychosocial support (page 185)

Weblinks

IBM Canada Ltd.: www.ibm.com/ca (page 187)
McDonald's Canada: www.mcdonalds.ca (page 173)

Discussion Questions

1. Describe the similarities and differences between coaching and mentoring? When would you use coaching and when would you use mentoring?
2. How should an organization decide if they should use on-the-job training? What are the advantages and disadvantages?
3. Why do you think on-the-job training is the most common method of training? Why is on-the-job training also called the most misused method of training? What can organizations do to avoid the problems of on-the-job training?
4. Describe the objectives of apprenticeship programs and how they are used in Canada. Why do you think the apprenticeship program in Canada has not been more successful, and what can be done to improve it? What are the consequences of not improving it?

Using the Internet

1. For information on thousands of courses, go to the Human Resources Development Canada interactive website training inventory at **www.trainingiti.com**. Identify the methods used to teach various topics. Choose three courses that you would like to take, and identify the training method used. Discuss the advantages and disadvantages of each of the methods.

Exercises

1. Recall the most recent job you had and how you were trained. Were you trained on the job? If you were trained on the job, describe the experience. What exactly did the trainer do and how did it impact your learning? Was your on-the-job training experience effective, why or why not? What could have been done differently to make it more effective? If you have not been trained on the job, describe how on-the-job training might be used to train employees doing your job.

2. As a student, you have probably experienced some problems studying, writing assignments, or perhaps writing exams. If you were to act as a tutor to train another student with some of these problems, what method of training would you use and why? Consider each of the on-the-job training methods in Table 7.1 and indicate how you would use them and how effective they would be for training a student to become a "better" student.

3. Ask your friends if they would accept a paid training experience that consisted of the following benefits:

   • they would be given structured classroom training and on-the-job assignments
   • they would be coached and supervised throughout the learning experience
   • they would be paid to learn
   • they would be certified at the end of learning the job
   • they would be guaranteed employment at high wages

   If they answer "Yes!" then tell them about becoming an apprentice electrician or carpenter. What is their reaction? Do students resist the certification programs in the traditional vocations and embrace certification in human resources or technology? Why?

4. Assume that you have just been hired as a trainer in an organization that hires many recent college and university graduates every year. The company does not have a formal mentoring program and your job is to try to get one started. Prepare a proposal to convince management of the importance and need for a formal mentoring program. You should also describe how the program will work and what will be required to get it started. You can then either have another member of the class review your proposal and provide feedback or you can present your proposal to the class.

5. Using the job instruction training method, design a training program to perform a task you are familiar with. It could be a task you have had to perform in a current or previous job, or it could be something that is not work-related such as how to fix a flat tire, how to drive a car, how to ride a bike, etc. Design your training program following the steps outlined in the chapter. Then have another member of the class review your training program and provide feedback. Alternatively, you can

provide a demonstration in front of the class and have the class critique your training program and provide feedback.

6. Very often, experienced employees are called upon to train a new employee on the job. In most cases, the employee has not received any training on how to train others. Chances are that some day you will be asked to train a new employee or perhaps you have already had to. To prepare yourself for this task, consider how well prepared and qualified you are. Review the material in The Trainer's Notebook 1, "Effective On-the-Job Instructors." Using this information, assess your qualifications to train somebody on the job. What are your strengths and weaknesses? Prepare an action plan to develop areas that need improvement. If you have already had to train somebody on the job, how effective were you and what do you need to work on to improve?

7. Contact the human resource department of an organization to find out about their use of on-the-job training. In particular, you should inquire about:

- Do they use on-the-job training, and if so what do they use it for (what employees, what kinds of job), why do they use it, and how effective is it?

- How formal and systematic is their on-the-job training? Is it carefully planned, do trainers receive training and instruction, are the trainers carefully selected, are they rewarded for their efforts, and are they evaluated?

- Do they follow the steps of the job instruction training method? How well is each of the steps performed?

- Based on what you have learned in this chapter, is the organization doing a good job in providing on-the-job training? What are they doing right and wrong?

- What advice would you give the organization to improve their on-the-job training?

Case

TPK Appliances

When TPK, a manufacturer of small appliances—electric kettles, toasters, and irons—automated its warehouse, the warehouse crew was reduced from 14 to 4. Every one of the displaced stockmen was assigned to another department, as TPK had a history of providing stable employment.

Jacob Peters, a stockman with more than 15 years of service, was transferred to the toaster assembly line to be retrained as a small-parts assembler. When he arrived to begin his new job, the foreman said, "This may be only temporary, Jacob. I have a full staff right now, so I have nothing for you to do, but come on, I'll find you a locker." As there really was no job for him, Jacob did nothing for the first week except odd jobs such as filling bins. At the beginning of week two, Jacob was informed that a vacancy would be occurring the next day, so he reported for work eager to learn his new job.

The operation was depressingly simple. All Jacob had to do was pick up two pieces of metal, one in each hand, place them into a jig so that they were held together in a cross position, and press a button. The riveting machine then put a rivet through both pieces and an air jet automatically ejected the joined pieces into a bin.

"This job is so simple a monkey could do it," the foreman told Jacob. "Let me show you how it's done," and he quickly demonstrated the three steps involved. "Now you do it," the foreman said. Of course, Jacob did it right the first time. After watching him rivet two or three, the foreman left Jacob to his work.

About three hours later, the riveter started to put the rivets in a little crooked, but Jacob kept on working. Finally, a fellow worker stopped by and said, "You're new here, aren't you?" Jacob nodded. "Listen, I'll give you a word of advice. If the foreman sees you letting the rivets go in crooked like that; he'll give you hell. So hide these in the scrap over there." The co-worker then showed Jacob how to adjust the machine.

Jacob's next problem began when the air ejection system started jamming. Four times he managed to clear it, but on the fifth try, he slipped and his elbow hit the rivet button. The machine put a rivet through the fleshy part of his hand, just below the thumb.

It was in the first aid station that the foreman finally had the opportunity to see Jacob once again.

Questions

1. Comment on the strengths and weaknesses of Jacob's on-the-job training.
2. What does this case tell you about the traditional approach to on-the-job training?
3. If you were the trainer, how would you have trained Jacob?
4. If the job instruction training method was used, how would the training of Jacob be conducted? Explain how each step would proceed.
5. Describe any other methods of on- or off-the-job training that might be used to train Jacob. What do you think would be the most effective, practical, and feasible methods?

Running Case Part 3

VANDALAIS DEPARTMENT STORES

Refer to the Vandalais Department Stores case described in Chapter 5 and answer the following questions:

1. Should on-the-job training methods be used as part of the training program? What would be the benefit of including on-the-job training methods as part of the structured employment interview training program?
2. Consider using some of the on-the-job training methods listed in Table 7.1 for the structured employment interview training program. Describe how each training method might be used, the advantages and disadvantages of using it, and how effective you think each method would be for the training program.
3. If you were designing the structured employment interview training program, what training methods would you include and why?

References

[1] Excerpt from Barbian, J. (March 2002). Training top 100: Space Systems/Loral. *Training*, 66.

[2] (1999, May/June). McDonald's stresses hands-on training. *The Training Report*, p.10.

[3] Dulipovici, A. (2003, May). Skilled in Training: Results of CFIB surveys on training.

[4] Sisson, G. R. (2001). *Hands-on training*. Berrett-Koehler Publishers, Inc. San Francisco: CA.

[5] Sisson, G. R. (2001).

[6] Sisson, G. R. (2001).

[7] Sisson, G. R. (2001).

[8] Broadwell, M. (1969). *The supervisor and on-the-job training*. Reading, MA: Addison-Wesley.

[9] Sloman, M. (1989). On-the-job training: A costly poor relation. *Personnel Management 21* (2), 38–42.

[10] Renner, P.F. (1989). *The instructor's survival kit*. Vancouver: Training Associates Ltd. Tench, A. (1992). Following Joe around: Should this be our approach to on-the-job training? *Plant Engineering, 46* (17), 88–92.

[11] Meyers, D. (1991). Restaurant service: Making memorable presentations. *Cornell Hotel and Restaurant Administration Quarterly, 32* (1), 69–73. Ukens, C. (1993). Cards help pharmacists counsel patients in a flash. *Drug Topics, 137* (1), 24–27.

[12] Ruyle, K. (1991, February/March). Developing intelligent job aids. *Technical and Skills Training*, 9–14.

[13] Arajis, B. (1991). Getting your sales staff in shape. *Graphic Arts Monthly, 63* (5), 125–127.

[14] Arajis, B. (1991). Cowen, W. (1992). Visual control boards are a key management tool. *Office Systems, 9* (10), 70–72. King, W. (1994). Training by design. *Training and Development, 48* (1), 52–54.

[15] Zemke, R. (1998). In search of self-directed learners. *Training, 35* (5), 61–68.

[16] McCall, M. (1992). Executive development as a business strategy. *Journal of Business Strategy, 13* (1), 25–31. Miller, F. (1993). Management development. *Training and Development, 11* (8), 16.

[17] Rothwell, W. (1992). Issues and practices in management job notation programs as perceived by HRD professionals. *Performance Improvement Quarterly, 5* (1), 49–69.

[18] Campion, M. A., Cheraskin, L., & Stevens, M. J. (1994). Career-related antecedents and outcomes of job rotation. *Academy of Management Journal, 37*, 1518–542.

[19] Moskal, B. (1991). Apprenticeship: Old cure for new labor shortage? *Industry Week, 240* (9), 30–35.

[20] McCarthy, S. (2001, February 27). Skilled-worker shortage could reach one million. *The Globe and Mail*, A1.

[21] Peterson, D. B. (2002). Management development: Coaching and mentoring programs. In K.Kraiger's (Ed.), *Creating, implementing, and managing effective training and development: State-of-the-art lessons for practice*, (pp.160-191). San Francisco. CA: Jossey-Bass.

[22] Peterson, D. B. (2002).

[23] Peterson, D. B. (2002).

[24] Lovin, B., & Casstevens, E. (1971). *Coaching, learning, and action*. New York: American Management Association. Frankel, L., & Otazo, K. (1992). Employee coaching: The way to gain commitment. *Employment Relations Today, 19* (3), 311–20.

[25] Blakesley, S. (1992). Your agency … leave it better than you found it. *Managers Magazine, 67* (4), pp. 20–22.

[26] Kroeger, L. (1991). Your team can't win the game without solid coaching. *Corporate Controller, 3* (5), 62–64.

[27] Azar, B. (1993). Striking a balance. *Sales and Marketing Management, 145* (2), 34–35. Whittaker, B. (1993). Shaping the competitive organization. *CMA Magazine, 67* (3), p. 5.

[28] Kruse, A. (1993). Getting top value for your payroll dollar. *Low Practice Management, 19* (3), 52–57.

[29] Peterson, D. B. (2002).

[30] Noe, R. A. (1999). *Employee training and development*. Boston: Irwin McGraw-Hill.

[31]Peterson, D. B. (2002).

[32]Peterson, D. B. (2002).

[33]Dreher, G., & Ash, R. (1990). A comparative study of mentoring among men and women in managerial, professional, and technical positions. *Journal of Applied Psychology, 75* (5), 539–46. Scandura, T. (1992). Mentorship and career mobility: An empirical investigation. *Journal of Organizational Behaviour, 13* (2), 169–74.

[34]Jackson, C. (1993). Mentoring: Choices for individuals and organizations. *The International Journal of Career Management, 5* (1), 10–16. Noe, R. A. (1999).

[35]Gallege, L. (1993). Do women make poor mentors? *Across the Board, 30* (6), 23–26.

[36]Mullen, E.J. (1998). Vocational and psychosocial mentoring functions: Identifying mentors who serve both. *Human Resource Development Quarterly, 9* (4), 319–31.

Chapter 8

Technology-Based Training Methods

Chapter Learning Objectives

After reading this chapter you should be able to:

- compare and contrast technology-based training and traditional training methods
- define the different methods of technology-based training
- compare and contrast instructor-led and self-directed learning
- define and give examples of asynchronous and synchronous training
- define and discuss computer-based training, e-learning, distance learning, electronic performance support systems, and video conferencing
- discuss the advantages and disadvantages of technology-based training
- discuss the effectiveness of technology-based training programs and how to design them to maximize trainee learning
- discuss the future of technology-based training

www.hbc.com

HUDSON'S BAY COMPANY

If you walk into a restaurant in any of the Hudson's Bay Company stores, you might come across the best cinnamon buns the restaurant has ever made. That's because HBC has launched a new e-learning program that includes courses on everything from health and safety, merchandise loss prevention, employee development for managers, and even cinnamon bun making.

Computer-based training is not new at HBC. Canada's oldest retailer decided to meld computers and training back in 1991 when they offered mainframe computer-based courses to their employees. That mainframe system carried the company's training load—a total of 146 courses and 60,000 course-units being taken every year on average until 1997. By then many people had PCs in their homes. The system dropped off in popularity and the company stopped developing courses for it. The company needed something new and current because it planned to do more training than ever.

With 70,000 employees in roughly 550 locations, e-learning made sense. It would allow the company to cut down on its travel and class-room training expenses, and could even help administer quick training modules to the 10,000 employees hired over the Christmas holiday season.

The company turned to the Bell e-Learning Centre, which works with companies to create a complete training environment for employees including self-serve and live online courses. The vision is to have hundreds of compelling online courses for employees, available anytime, anywhere.

The new system can handle all of the extras that typically make courses attractive to employees, including video and sound capabilities, synchronous learning and the ability to track their performance and forward it to their supervisors for consideration in promotions.

The cost of developing online courses is roughly $10,000—because of all the added bells and whistles—compared to the $3,000 to $5,000 HBC used to spend to develop material for its mainframe system. And the system itself came at a significant price tag. But David Crisp, senior vice-president of human resources at HBC, says the benefits are clear: Once all of the course development is completed, getting an employee to take an online course probably costs about $10, compared to the $200 a company can easily spend, per person, on travel expenses and classroom costs. "And if we want to roll out a course to 30,000 people, this is a pretty inexpensive way to do it," adds Crisp.

The new system also includes what HBC terms "product knowledge" courses, meaning an employee hired to staff the jewellery counter will be able to sit down and take a one-hour course on the difference between gold plated and 18k gold and other relevant information. That product knowledge, Crisp says, will ultimately enhance customer satisfaction and boost sales.[1]

Like many companies today, the Hudson's Bay Company has begun to invest in technology-based training. Besides being able to offer a wide assortment of training programs, computer-based training can be provided to large numbers of employees at any time.

In Chapters 6 and 7, we described traditional methods of off- and on-the-job training. In this chapter, we describe technology-based training methods. We begin by defining technology-based training and then describe some of the different types of technology-based training methods.

What is Technology-Based Training?

ⓇⓅⒸ

Organizations are increasingly using technology-based training to deliver training.[2] In the United States, technology-based training comprises 25 percent of workplace training today, and by the year 2004 it is expected that organizations will spend $14.5 billion on technology-based training. Thus, by all measures technology-based training has arrived and is on the rise.[3]

The importance of technology-based training became especially apparent following the September 11, 2001 terrorist attacks in the United States. Many organizations found themselves with no choice but to turn to technology-based training. This was seen immediately following the attacks as thousands of workers required instant training. Various forms of technology-based training proved to be an essential means of getting thousands of people trained in a short period of time.[4]

In addition, because of the cancellation of many training programs following the terrorist attacks, due in large part to people's reluctance to fly, many organizations turned to technology-based methods that allowed employees to take training without having to travel. For example, the large pharmaceutical company, Pfizer cancelled many international training programs following the attacks. To replace the cancelled classroom training programs, they accelerated the use of its Interactive Distance Learning program, which involves a virtual studio at its learning centre where training courses are digitally broadcast via satellite and broadband to the homes of more than 1,000 managers and sales representatives.[5]

In their Annual Industry Report of formal training in the United States, *Training* magazine defines **technology-based training** as "Anything that involves using technology to deliver lessons. Examples include: Web-based training (Internet, intranet, extranet); computerized self-study, including CD-ROM/DVD/diskette; satellite/broadcast TV; and video conferencing, audio-conferencing and teleconferencing." (p. 25) Any technology that delivers education or training, or supports the delivery of these subjects, would be included in the definition.[6] Thus, although it might appear as if this kind of

Technology-based training
Anything that involves using technology to deliver lessons

training is something new and different, in reality it is really about the use of technology to facilitate learning and training.[7]

Traditional training

Anything that does not involve using technology to deliver lessons

The magazine defines **traditional training** as "Anything that does not involve using technology to deliver lessons. Examples include: classroom training with a live instructor in front of a room or a computer lab full of learners (regardless of the instructor's use of technology during class, i.e., videotapes, audiocassettes, etc.); noncomputerized self-study (textbooks/ workbooks); noncomputerized games; seminars/lectures; and outdoor programs." (p. 25)[8]

While most people understand that computers are being used for training, one of the most confusing things about technology-based training is the many different terms and labels that are used to refer to the various forms of technology-based training. Although there are technical distinctions between some of the methods, the distinctions are generally not apparent to trainees and often have to do with where the programs and data are located and the ease with which they can be updated.[9]

Nonetheless, it is important to be aware of the terms used to describe the different types of technology-based training. Table 8.1 provides a list and definitions of the different types of technology-based training.

By all measures, the use of technology-based training methods has been steadily increasing. According to the results from *Training* magazine's 2002 Industry Report, 24 percent of organizations have a separate training budget for technology-based training. In terms of the use of various forms of technology, 40 percent of companies indicated they always use CD-ROM/DVD/ diskettes; 49 percent said they always use Internet/intranet/extranet; 10 percent always use satellite/broadcast TV; 19 percent said they always use teleconferencing; and 16 percent said they always use video conferencing. The frequency of use of these methods, however, was found to vary by industry. The report also found that 48 percent of all training delivered by computer and not instructor-led involved self-paced Web courses, and 41 percent involved the use of CD-ROM/DVD/diskette. Self-paced Web courses were more likely to be used by larger companies while CD-ROM/DVD/diskette were used more by smaller companies. It is also worth noting that they found that 24 percent of training courses used a blended approach to training delivery.[10]

The use of training technologies in Canada has also increased dramatically over the last decade. According to the Conference Board of Canada, 13 percent of all training in Canada is being delivered using learning technologies and some companies have made major advances.[11] For example, at Cisco Systems Canada Co., 80 percent of sales staff training is now done on-line compared to just a few years ago when 90 percent was done in the classroom. Employees access the company's website to find out about new Cisco networking products and how to install products. Because the courses are up and running much faster than traditional classroom programs, employees can learn about new products in one week compared to three months.[12]

In terms of the actual percentages, The Conference Board of Canada found that in the year 2000, 14.6 percent of organizations reported using tel-

TABLE 8.1

Types of Technology-Based Training

Internet: a loose confederation of computer networks around the world that is connected through several primary networks

Intranet: a general term describing any network contained within an organization; refers primarily to networks that use Internet technology

Extranet: a collaborative network that uses Internet technology to link organizations with their suppliers, customers, or other organizations that share common goals or information

CD–ROM: a format and system for recording, storing, and retrieving electronic information on a compact disc that is read using an optical drive

Electronic performance support system (EPSS): an integrated computer application that uses any combination of expert systems, hypertext, embedded animation, and/or hypermedia to help a user perform a task in real time, quickly and with a minimum of support from other people

Electronic simulation: a device or system that replicates or imitates a read device or system

Multimedia: a computer application that uses any combination of text, graphics, audio, animation, and/or full-motion video

Teleconference: the instantaneous exchange of audio, video or text between two or more individuals or groups at two or more locations

Television cable, satellite: the transmission of television signals via cable or satellite technology

Source: Harris-Lalonde, S. (2001). Training and development outlook. Reprinted by permission of *The Conference Board of Canada*. Ottawa.

evision signals (cable, satellite); 61 percent used CD-ROMs; 38.4 percent used internal Internet technology (intranet, extranet); and 37.2 percent used external Internet technology (Internet, World Wide Web).[13]

Table 8.2 presents the percentage of courses using technology-based methods to deliver training in Canadian organizations. One of the ways that these methods differ is in terms of whether the training is instructor-led or self-directed, the focus of the next section.

Instructor-Led and Self-Directed Learning

Technology-based training can take many forms. Like more traditional approaches to training, some forms of technology-based training involve an instructor or facilitator who might lead, facilitate, or teach on-line. Technology-based training that is instructor-led is known as **instructor-led training** or **ILT**. Some examples of ILT are on-line discussions and video conferencing.

Instructor-led training (ILT)

Training methods that involve an instructor or facilitator who in the case of technology-based training, might lead, facilitate, or teach on-line

TABLE 8.2

Percentage of Courses Using Technology-Based Training Methods to Deliver Training in Canada in the Year 2000

METHODS	PERCENT
Internet	10.1
Intranet	9.7
CD-ROM	9.0
Electronic Performance Support System (EPSS)	12.0
Multimedia	18.3
Teleconferencing	6.0
TV (cable, satellite)	6.2

Source: Harris-Lalonde, S. (2001). Training and development outlook. Reprinted by permission of *The Conference Board of Canada*. Ottawa.

Self-directed learning (SDL)

A process in which the individual identifies the resources necessary to learn and then manages the learning experience

In some cases, the instructor is highly involved in the training and leads the process. In other cases, a course or program involves self-study and the instructor is available for answering questions and assistance.[14]

However, one of the main advantages of technology-based training is that it does not always have to be instructor-led but rather, can be self-paced and controlled by the trainee. This is known as self-directed learning.

Self-directed learning (SDL) is a process that occurs when individuals or groups seek out the necessary resources to engage in learning that enhances their careers and personal growth. Employees assess their own needs, use a variety of organizational resources to meet those needs, and are helped with evaluating the effectiveness of meeting their needs. SDL can be as simple as a booklet that describes a new procedure or a multimedia program that teaches project management skills.

Self-directed learning has become increasingly popular because traditional methods of training lack the flexibility to respond quickly to dramatic and constant organizational change and trainees' needs. Technology-based self-directed learning allows trainees to access training materials and programs when they want to, at their own pace, and sometimes in the sequence they prefer. This usually involves computer-based or Web-based training materials.

Motorola Inc. implemented a SDL approach to its training program. Forty percent of their employees undertook self-study courses. The research showed that the average cost for the SDL was $7.76 per hour, compared to $13.34 hourly for classroom instruction. The results demonstrated that SDL was as effective or better than the traditional training approach.

Web-based education tools is making Motorola Inc. more efficient. At Motorola U, about 30 percent of employee training now involves self-directed learning and the goal is to reach 50 percent in the next year. The major benefit for Motorola has been the time savings. With technology-based self-directed learning, employees can complete a course in five hours rather than eight hours in a traditional classroom. This also means that the company can triple the amount of training that employees receive since they require a minimum of 40 hours a year per employee.[15]

Closely related to self-directed learning is self-development. SDL provides knowledge and skills for the immediate job, while the focus of self-development is to develop skills for the long term for one's career. Although employers are increasingly moving toward developing their human resources through self-development learning, employees need a process by which to increase their capabilities and skills.

Despite the rhetoric, there appears to be one issue constantly overlooked: employees need help with self-development. Employee-initiated career development does involve *self-responsibility*, although the irony is that most of us need help with it. There are elements of *partnership* not only between the individual and the organization, but also with fellow employees through peer mentoring. There is *integration* at the individual level in addition to the individual–organization interface.[16]

Self-development, therefore, is a function that must be carefully planned, monitored, and nurtured, otherwise, self-responsibility can become a synonym for neglect. This is especially important for technology-based training because if left on their own, employees might not complete courses or take the courses that they need to improve their skills.

Table 8.3 lists some of the benefits and limitations of self-directed learning.

Computer-Based Training and E-Learning

Over the last decade, the use of a computer to deliver training has been referred to as computer-based training and e-learning. Although these terms are often use synonymously, there are differences. **Computer-based training** refers to training that is delivered via the computer for the purpose of teaching job-relevant skills. It can include text, graphics, and/or animation and be delivered via CD-ROMs, intranets, or the Internet.[17] Among the various forms of computer-based training, Web-delivered and CD-ROM formats have received the most attention.

A related and increasingly popular term for technology-based training is e-learning. **E-learning** refers to the use of computer network technology such as the intranet or Internet to deliver training for the purpose of job-relevant knowledge and skill.[18] Thus, e-learning is a specific type of computer-based learning and is limited to the use of computer network technology. It would not include the use of CD-ROMs. In this chapter, we will use the broader term, computer-based training, which includes e-learning.

It has been estimated that Canadian companies spent $1.7 billion on computer-based training in the year 2000.[19] Although computer-based training represents a small proportion of the total spending on training, more and more organizations are moving in this direction. To find out about one Canadian company that is using computer-based training, see Training Today 1, "Internet Training at Taco Time Canada."

Computer-based training

Training that is delivered via the computer for the purpose of teaching job-relevant knowledge and skills

E-learning

The use of computer network technology such as the intranet or Internet to deliver training for the purpose of job-relevant knowledge and skill

TABLE 8.3

The Benefits and Limitations of Self-Directed Learning

BENEFITS

- trainees can learn at their own pace and determine their desired level of expertise
- trainees build on their knowledge bases and training time may be reduced; trainees learn what is relevant to their needs
- trainees become independent and acquire skills enabling them to learn more efficiently and effectively, reducing dependence on formal training
- people can learn according to their own styles of learning

LIMITATIONS

- trainees may learn the wrong things or may not learn all there is to know; one suggestion to remedy this problem is to negotiate a learning contract with specific learning objectives and performance measures
- trainees may waste time accessing resources and finding helpful material; the trainer could become a facilitator, directing employees toward useful resources
- SDL takes time—the employee has to learn active knowledge-seeking skills, has to acquire knowledge-gathering skills, must learn to tolerate inefficiencies and mistakes; the trainer, too, must learn to give up a power base and move from expert to helper

Asynchronous and Synchronous Training

An important characteristic of computer-based training has to do with when it is available. In this regard, computer-based training can be asynchronous or synchronous.

When training is **asynchronous**, it is pre-recorded and available to employees at any time and from any location. When training is **synchronous**, it is real-time and trainees must be at their computer at a specific time. Currently, asynchronous learning is much more common than synchronous learning.

Asynchronous and synchronous training programs vary in their sophistication. For example, at the most basic level, an asynchronous program might simply involve the posting of text, information or instructions on a website. More sophisticated programs can include graphics, animation, audio and video thereby providing a multimedia program. This combined with simulations, interactive exercises, tests, and feedback can result in a much more engaging and active learning experience. While the use of multimedia involves greater involvement on the part of the trainee, it is much more expensive to design and develop.

Asynchronous training

Training that is pre-recorded and available to employees at any time and from any location

Synchronous training

Training that is real-time and requires trainees to be at their computer at a specific time

Internet Training at Taco Time Canada

Taco Time Canada recently introduced an Internet course on customer service that was previously delivered in the classroom. Employees access the course by signing onto a website and then viewing video segments that feature the company's customer-service trainer doing what he used to do in the classroom.

Trainees take a pre-test to establish their baseline skills, receive a workbook, and complete quizzes that are e-mailed to them at the end of each segment. They also receive a checklist that reminds them to review the information and a follow-up action plan.

Why would a company like Taco Time Canada move away from classroom training to computer-based training? For starters, the company can now provide consistent and effective training to all of its employees, something that is very difficult to do with traditional training methods especially when you have 2,000 employees located in 120 stores across Canada, many in small towns.

The cost for the company is also estimated to be much less. The average fee per employee for customer-service training in the classroom is $395 compared to $100 for the Internet version, which is split between headquarters and each franchisee. The company also saves thousands of dollars in travel and accommodation expenses that it would cost to send trainees to a training site.

Other advantages for the company are the availability and convenience for employees who can take the course at any time; the appeal of a contemporary medium that appeals to young people who make up the majority of fast-food workers; and the ability of employees to take the course at their own pace and to review segments of it as they desire. The company plans to develop additional Internet courses on various topics.

Source: Christie McLaren, E-training cooks up customer service tips. *The Globe and Mail*, May 31, 2002, T4. Reprinted by permission of Christie McLaren.

A basic synchronous program might simply involve "chat" sessions in which trainees log on at the same time and participate in a discussion of some topic. More sophisticated programs might have trainees from various locations log into the training at a set time and receive instruction from a trainer who also facilitates a discussion, shows slides, and answers trainees' questions and provides feedback.[20]

In the following sections, we present two common forms of asynchronous training, distance learning and electronic performance support systems. We then discuss a popular form of synchronous learning, video conferencing and satellite technology.

Distance Learning

Computer-based training is increasingly being used for distance learning. **Distance learning** and distance education are general terms that refer to learning methods in which information is communicated from a central source to individuals or groups at locations separate from the source, usually through the use of technology. The most common methods of distance learning include correspondence courses, which can include audio- and videocassettes, supplemented by workbooks and even supervised off-site exams.

Distance learning

Learning methods in which information is communicated from a central source to individuals or groups at locations separate from the source, usually through the use of technology

Distance learning is considered valuable for students or employees who live in remote areas, when there is an insufficient number of students enrolled in a course to justify hiring an instructor, for trainees who are less mobile than others because of parenting or work responsibilities, and for trainees who have disabilities.

A major advantage for students is the ability to control the pace and place of learning. However, motivation seems to be a big problem in learning. Students report feeling isolated and missing the collegial nature of classroom learning.[21] Another problem is the high cost of course development, particularly when advanced technology is used. However, the advantage of nearly universal access overrides concerns about motivation and cost.

An increasing number of universities are now providing Internet courses. Students log on to a website where they can access course materials. There is, however, a great deal of variation in terms of how these courses are designed and what they deliver. Some simply provide text information such as the instructor's notes and slides. Others show videotaped lectures and some include audio-recorded lectures that are accompanied by slides.

Some universities now provide degree programs taken entirely over the Internet. For example, Athabasca University in Alberta now offers an online MBA program. The number of students taking distance education courses at the university has doubled in three years and the university now has 25 percent of the Canadian e-learning MBA market.

Given the increasing enrolment in Canadian colleges and universities expected over the next decade, Internet courses and degree programs are likely to become even more popular.[22]

Electronic Performance Support Systems

Electronic performance-support system (EPSS)

A computer-based system that provides information, advice, and learning experiences on the job to improve performance

An **electronic performance support system (EPSS)** is a computer-based system that improves employee productivity by providing on-the-job access to integrated information, advice, and learning experiences.[23] They are computer programs that help solve work-related problems. These systems provide several types of support including assisting, warning, advising, teaching, and evaluating. Thus, in some ways they are a modern version of a performance aid.

The goal of an EPSS is to provide whatever is necessary to generate performance and learning at the time it is needed. When the accounting firm KPMG needed to train all its employees on a new tax planning service, it chose EPSS over classroom training. The EPSS saved in delivery time (consultants did not need to spend three weeks in classrooms) and reduced costs in updates.[24]

Alberta Pacific Forest Industries at their Sarnia plant extol the advantages of EPSS for their safety, maintenance, and laboratory training: learning occurs when workers need it most, on site; it allows for continual upgrading; it allows for individual differences in the pace of learning; and it allows links to suppliers' training and tracks learning accomplishments.[25]

EPSS offers even more advantages than computer-based training programs. With EPSS, information is accessed only when it is needed. Only the information that is needed is given; there is no information overload. It is unrealistic to expect that enough information can be crammed into everyone's memory during training, then banked for access later.

EPSS is particularly useful for training in high-turnover jobs, like hotel staff and tasks that are difficult, are performed infrequently, and must be performed perfectly.[26]

As increasing numbers of employees use personal computers, EPSS will become more common for training employees such as cashiers, bank tellers, insurance agents, and so on. If you want to experience using an EPSS, then just ask for help the next time you are preparing a Microsoft® Powerpoint® presentation or even trying to figure out how do a task when writing a letter in Microsoft® Word.

Video Conferencing

Video conferencing consists of linking a subject-matter expert to employees by means of two-way television. This can involve the transmission of television signals via cable or through satellite technology. Whatever the actual means of transmission, the basic idea is that people at two or more locations are able to see, hear, and speak with one another thus permitting simultaneous meetings in different locations.

Video conferencing is used to bring in an expert from another location, to hold meetings with staff working in various locations, and to communicate corporate information that needs to be rapidly disseminated and accepted.

Political conditions and incidents like the Gulf War and the September 11, 2001 terrorist attacks in the United States (which made some executives wary of travel terrorism) as well as decreases in the costs of technology, have made video conferencing more acceptable and affordable than ever. In addition, employees in remote locations and those with limited flexibility (e.g., with child-care arrangements), stand to benefit from this technology, which allows them to be trained at their own workplace.

Companies like Stentor claim that training by live TV reduces the travel and labour costs of training, gets consistent or uniform training quickly to a large number of people, brings the subject-matter expert to all trainers, enhances company revenues by implementing training faster (down from three months to two weeks), and distributes complex information over shorter periods of time. BCTel uses simulations and video conferencing to teach financial skills to employees in a deregulated environment.[27]

The disadvantage of video conferencing is that less personal attention is given to trainees. However, this problem can be remedied by having a facilitator on-site or by allowing for interactive questioning while training takes place. For a good example of this, see Training Today 2, "Satellite Television at the Bank of Nova Scotia."

Video conferencing
Linking an expert to employees via two-way television and satellite technology

Satellite Television at the Bank of Nova Scotia

The Bank of Nova Scotia has begun to use interactive training sessions that are broadcast to employees across the country by satellite television.

Scotiabank uses satellite television technology to train employees in branches across Canada. For example, they trained 2,000 employees at 25 locations across the country on RRSPs. Trainees had to first use the Internet to review course materials on-line prior to attending the training. To keep employees engaged, they completed quizzes and participated in opinion polls throughout the session by pushing buttons on their phone sets. During breaks, there were group discussions and case study analyses that were led by previously trained managers at each meeting site. During the broadcast, trainees asked questions by telephone.

For Scotiabank and its employees, this method of training has many advantages. With some 28,000 employees spread all over the country, the bank is able to train thousands of employees at one time without having to bring them together in one location or to send trainers all over the country. It also ensures that a consistent message is sent to all employees and everyone hits the ground running at the same time. In fact, employees return to their branches the day after training and begin to apply their new product knowledge.

An added benefit to employees is the opportunity to learn about what their fellow employees around the country are doing and to share ideas and best practices. This also helps to create a sense of cohesion, which is difficult in such a large and geographically diverse organization.

Source: Galt, V. (2003, January 22). Bank tunes in to TV training. *The Globe and Mail*, C1, C5. Reprinted with permission from *The Globe and Mail*.

Technology-Based Training: Advantages and Disadvantages

Now that you are familiar with technology-based training, you might be wondering how it compares to traditional methods of training. Like on- and off-the-job training methods, there are advantages and disadvantages of technology-based training.

For trainees, the ability for self-directed learning has a number of advantages such as not having to coordinate and arrange one's schedule and workload to accommodate training schedules. Trainees do not have to take courses when they are offered or wait until a group of trainees are ready to take a course. They can learn when they want to or "just in time." Trainees also do not have to leave work to attend training, and can even learn while they are at home or away from work. They can also progress at their own pace.

Perhaps most beneficial for trainees is the flexibility and convenience of being able to learn when they want to or need to, and to do so from any location where they have access to a computer. This, of course, is the ultimate example of "just-in-time" training. Employees do not have to sign up and wait for a course to be available; it is available whenever they need it. In terms of flexibility, employees can pause during training and continue at a later time without missing a beat. And because of the ability to learn at work or at home, employees do not have to spend time travelling to distant training locations. Geographic flexibility is a major advantage.

From the organization's perspective, there are a number of advantages of computer-based training. One advantage is that they can ensure that all trainees receive the same training. The main reason that the Hudson's Bay Company uses computer-based training is that it can standardize training for all of its employees.[28] Thus, organizations can deliver standardized and consistent training to large numbers of employees across the organization and even worldwide. This is especially important for training programs in which all employees need to be trained across many locations. Leaving the training to each location could result in differences in terms of content, delivery, and effectiveness.

Another advantage is that large numbers of employees can be trained within a short period of time as was the case following the terrorist attacks in the United States. With technology-based training, there is no limit to the number of employees who can be trained, as one is not constrained by the number of instructors available or the need for classroom space.

Technology-based training also makes it possible to track employees' performance on learning exercises and tests. This kind of tracking is especially important for training programs that are mandatory and completion, certification, or attaining a certain level of performance is legally mandated such as for health and safety training. The technology can generate tests that can provide legal documentation for proof of competency levels. When an accident or safety incident results in a lawsuit, the employer can prove that a training program was completed and that a desired level of competence was reached. These training statistics could reduce corporate liability. Technology also allows trainees to track their own progress and test themselves.

Perhaps the greatest advantage from the organization's perspective is the cost savings. Computer-based training can result in increased efficiencies and a reduction in the cost of training.[29] Although the costs of development can be very high, in the long-term the cost of training is lower due to the elimination of the costs associated with travel, training facilities, hotel rooms, meals, trainers, and employee time off from work while travelling and attending training. In addition, the high overhead costs of traditional training make technology-based training especially advantageous to companies with national or international employees.

The savings reported by some companies are quite significant. For example, Dow Chemical estimates that the implementation of a Web-based training system saved the company $30 million in one year. They saved $20 million as a result of a reduction in the time employees spend in training, and $10 million due to a reduction in administrative time, classroom facilities, trainers, and the cost of printed material.[30]

There are of course some disadvantages of technology-based training. For trainees, there is less interpersonal contact. Furthermore, individuals have learning preferences and styles and if a trainee prefers to receive training in a classroom with a trainer and other trainees, then the use of technology would disadvantage that employee.

For organizations, there is the disadvantage that some employees will be uncomfortable with computers and might resist training. This is particularly likely for older workers who are more likely to be inexperienced using computers. There is also the potential for problems to arise if employees do not have computers that can run the programs.

Trainers who are not computer literate might also resist and fear the change to technology. A low-threat opportunity to allow trainers to test the multimedia approach is to place the learning stations in the classroom.[31] Most industry analysts perceive these two barriers as temporary problems. Technology-based training will become a standard way of supplying information, particularly for the current generation that is comfortable with computers and technology.

The major disadvantage for organizations is the cost of development, especially for sophisticated multimedia programs. Estimates are that it takes 200 to 300 hours of design and development time to produce one hour of instruction.[32] A full-motion colour-and-sound courseware would likely cost $200,000 for 30 hours of instruction. This requires a considerable upfront investment in information technology and staff. At Motorola where about 30 percent of employee training is computer-based, it was estimated that $20 million to $27 million will be spent in one year on e-learning.[33]

Although the cost to design and develop technology-based training is considerably higher than traditional classroom training, once a program has been developed there is the potential for considerable cost savings thus making technology-based training less costly than classroom training in the long-term. This is most likely to be the case when large numbers of employees require training, they are geographically dispersed, and the training will be frequently repeated.[34]

How Effective is Technology-Based Training?

While technology-based training provides many advantages for trainees and organizations, ultimately what really matters is how effective it is for learning. Unfortunately, few studies have actually studied the effectiveness of technology-based training, especially compared to more traditional methods of classroom training. Nonetheless, there is some research that does bear directly on this issue.

Some of the earliest reports on the effectiveness of technology-based training were very optimistic and often touted the huge gains such as increased task mastery, higher motivation and retention, improvements in job performance, and reductions in learning time compared to traditional classroom training. Unfortunately, such claims do not have their basis in empirical research. In fact, at this time, the most we can say is that technology-based training is effective for trainee learning, especially for training that emphasizes cognitive learning and for less complex material. On the other hand, it might not be as effective for learning complex material, soft skills, psychomotor skills, or team skills.[35]

Although there is some research that indicates technology-based training is on average more effective than traditional classroom training, given the limited amount of research in this area and the fact that some studies found no differences between technology-based training and classroom training, one needs to be cautious about concluding that technology-based training is more effective. Furthermore, the effectiveness of technology-based training is likely to depend on a number of factors such as the design of the program, the content of the program, the trainees, and the type of technology.[36]

Some research has also studied the time it takes to complete training. There is some evidence that technology-based training can result in a reduction in the time to completion. However, this appears to be most likely only when trainees have some prior experience using technology. In some cases, such as when trainees do not have IT experience or when trainees experience technology problems and interruptions, the time to completion might actually be greater for technology-based training compared to classroom training.[37]

A final issue regarding the effectiveness of technology-based training is trainees' motivation to take technology-based training programs, if they complete them, and their attitudes towards technology-based training. There is some research that indicates that employees are not likely to take or complete courses that are optional. That is, unless a course is required or when there is a strong reason for employees to take a course, they are not likely to do so. Employees have been found to be more likely to complete an e-learning training program when there is an incentive for doing so, some form of accountability, or when the program content is job-relevant.

Finally, unless trainees experience technical problems, they tend to respond positively to technology-based training programs. A number of studies have reported that after taking a technology-based training program, trainees report satisfaction with their learning experience, more positive attitudes towards technology-based training, and a willingness to try it again.[38]

In summary, while the research does not indicate that technology-based training is superior to more traditional methods of training, there is sufficient evidence to indicate that technology-based training is effective for trainee learning. Furthermore, technology-based training can reduce the time it takes to complete training although this is by no means guaranteed.

The Design of Technology-Based Training

The advent of technology for the use of learning and training has created somewhat of a craze and many organizations have been quick to jump on the e-learning bandwagon. Unfortunately, because technology is the focus, many of the important design principles described in Chapter 5 are forgotten or ignored.

It is important to keep in mind that the technology simply provides a new means or medium for providing and delivering training and learning experiences. Whether or not a training program is effective depends more on how it is designed rather than the sophistication of the technology that is used to deliver it. Therefore, in this section, we will review some of the important issues and concerns with regard to the design and delivery of technology-based training programs.

As described in Chapter 5, to maximize learning and retention, training programs should incorporate adult learning principles, active practice, and the conditions of practice. These principles and conditions should also be incorporated into technology-based training programs. Trainees need to have opportunities for active practice even if they are sitting at a computer terminal.

Fortunately, there are many ways to actively engage and involve trainees using technology. This is because interactive features can be designed into computer-based training programs such as providing trainees with choices that link them to various parts or segments of a program and to related sites for additional information. Some programs enable trainees to choose the sequence in which they want to complete training modules as well as exercises and activities they want to complete. This not only actively engages trainees, but it also gives them control over their learning in terms of how they structure their learning experience.

Learning principles such as practice and feedback should also be designed into computer-based training programs. The use of simulations such as interacting with an angry customer have been incorporated into programs and are good examples of how active practice and psychological fidelity are designed into computer-based training.

It is also important that feedback be provided to employees. Fortunately, this is something that can be done very effectively using computer-based training because tests and exercises can be incorporated into a program that provides trainees with immediate feedback on test performance. The feedback can range from a simple prompt indicating that the answer is right or wrong to the execution of another program segment in which trainees are routed through a complex maze of reviews and reinforcements based on their responses and answers.

Feedback can also be used to accompany simulations like the one discussed above in which the trainee interacts with an angry customer. The trainee would be required to choose from a number of options how he/she would respond to the customer throughout the simulation. The trainee receives immediate feedback when the customer responds to his/her actions. In addition, a coach can be designed into the simulation to provide trainees with feedback about the correctness of their choices and hints on how to proceed. Trainees can then take the simulation again until their performance improves.

Finally, it is important to realize that in order for trainees to benefit from technology and in particular, computer-based training, they must have the motivation and ability to use the technology and computers. Trainees must have computer literacy and self-efficacy. This means that some individuals will be more willing and able to learn through technology-based training while others will be better suited for more traditional methods of training. It also means that some trainees will require computer training to improve their computer literacy and self-efficacy prior to taking a computer-based training program.

Clearly, there are many things to consider when designing technology-based training programs. See The Trainer's Notebook for a checklist of the main steps involved in getting started.

The Future of Technology-Based Training

The field of training technology is changing rapidly and the use of computers to deliver training has increased dramatically over the last several years. It has been predicted that organizations will reduce classroom training by nearly 20 percent and replace it with computer-based training. The increase in storage capacity of personal computers, the growth of expert and authoring systems, and the development of generic courses support this change.[39]

Thus, there is little doubt that the use of computers and technology for training has taken off and is here to stay. The advantages and benefits far

---

The Trainer's Notebook

Technology-Based Training Checklist

1. **Determine a Strategy**: An important first step is to create a strategy for learning technology in your organization. Some factors to consider include key technologies; the amount of money you have; resource requirements such as people and tools; a rollout plan for the technologies including IT standards in your organization and database of choice for applications; and specifications for learning technologies in your organization, such as specific quality or design requirements for new applications. Your strategy is a blueprint for solutions and a roadmap for all future activities and purchasing.

2. **Functional Requirements Specification (FRS)**: Write a detailed FRS to assess your needs and help select a supplier with the appropriate capabilities. The FRS is the specific technology-enabled solution you want to implement and includes functionality (what should the application do and how should it operate?); IT specifications; user-interface specs; legacy system interface; user characteristics; hardware and software; manuals; and explicit restrictions.

3. **Write a Request for Proposal (RFP)**: A RFP is a document that describes in detail the type, nature, and details of what you are seeking. Distribute your RFP to several potential suppliers and create a criteria scorecard so you can check off suppliers' capabilities.

4. **Statement of Work**: Once you have chosen a supplier, start working on a statement of work. It will ensure that the work you are contracting out is completed in a timely manner. Make sure it contains clearly written objectives that describe attainable deliverables.

5. **Pilot-Test the Application**: Once the project is close to completion, form a pilot group to try out the application. The group should be part of the target audience for the application.

6. **Get the Application into a Production Environment**: A production environment is made up of the server centres run by the IT department. If your application goes down while it is on a production server, there's a backup and recovery plan to get it up and running and to restore any lost data.

Source: Hartley, D. (2000, July). All aboard the e-learning train. *Training & Development*, 54(7), 37–42.

---

outweigh the disadvantages. At this point, the main issues have to do with how to best design technology-based training programs, how best to blend them with more traditional methods, and how to make them more effective for trainee learning, retention, and transfer to the job.

While many have predicted the demise of more traditional classroom methods of training, the reality is that they will continue to be used and combined with technology-based methods. Many organizations realize the value of a blended approach to training that combines traditional classroom methods with technology-based methods. A blended approach is likely to be most effective especially for delivering certain types of training and for appealing to trainees with different learning styles and preferences.

The real question is not whether one should use a traditional method of training versus technology-based training, but rather, what combination of the two will be most effective. In general, computer-based training programs are most effective for providing trainees with knowledge and information at a pace dictated by the trainee, while traditional methods of training are best suited for more interactive learning experiences.[40]

For trainers, the important issues revolve around when to use technology-based training and when is it most likely to be effective. This means that trainers need to consider training objectives, the content of training, design factors, and trainee characteristics. For some types of skills such as soft skills, psychomotor skills, and team skills, more traditional forms of training will still be necessary and perhaps more effective than technology-based training. Thus, not surprisingly, most experts agree that technology-based training will never completely replace traditional classroom or face-to-face training methods.[41]

Finally, given the high cost involved in the design and development of technology-based training, the costs and benefits will be a major factor in whether or not an organization chooses to use technology or more traditional methods of training. The costs are most likely to lead to benefits when there are many trainees, numerous locations where training is required, considerable distance to the training site, and when the training is frequently repeated.[42]

Summary

This chapter described technology-based training methods and serves as a complement to the on- and off-the-job training methods that were described in Chapters 6 and 7. The different types of technology-based training methods were described including computer-based training, e-learning, distance learning, electronic performance-support systems, and video conferencing. We also described how technology-based training can differ in terms of whether it is instructor-led or self-directed, and whether it is asynchronous or synchronous. The advantages, disadvantages, and effectiveness of technology-based training were also discussed as well as the design and future of technology-based training.

Key Terms

asynchronous training (page 204)

computer-based training (page 203)

distance learning (page 205)

e-learning (page 203)

electronic performance-support system (EPSS) (page 206)

instructor-led training (page 201)

self-directed learning (SDL) (page 202)

synchronous training (page 204)

technology-based training (page 199)

traditional training (page 200)

video conferencing (page 207)

Weblinks

Athabasca University: www.athabascau.ca (page 206)

Bank of Nova Scotia: www.scotiabank.com (page 208)

Cisco Systems Canada Co.: www.cisco.com (page 200)

Dow Chemical: www.dow.com (page 209)

Motorola Inc.: www.motorola.com (page 202)

Taco Time Canada: www.tacotimecanada.com (page 205)

Discussion Questions

1. In both Canada and the United States, the actual use of training technologies has fallen below projections and, in fact, the adoption of training technologies has been relatively slow. What are some of the reasons for this and what are the potential barriers to the adoption of training technologies?

2. Compare and contrast technology-based training methods to traditional methods of training. Why would an organization choose to use some forms of technology-based training rather than traditional methods? For example, why not send training videos to employees rather than investing in computer-based training? Are there some types of industries, organizations, or jobs in which technology-based training or traditional training would be more appropriate and more effective?

3. What are the advantages and disadvantages of technology-based training for trainees, trainers, and organizations?

4. If you had the choice, would you choose to take a distance education course that involved on-line learning or a traditional classroom course? Which would you prefer and why? Do you think your study habits, course satisfaction, learning, and grades would differ in an on-line course versus a traditional classroom course? Explain your reasoning.

Using the Internet

1. To learn more about e-learning in Canada, visit The Conference Board of Canada at **www.conferenceboard.ca/education/reports/default.htm** and find the link to the e-learning in Canada survey findings. Review

the survey findings and then prepare a brief report in which you summarize the main findings and outline the main issues and concerns facing Canadian organizations. Some of the things to consider include the challenges to implementing e-learning, the benefits, the evaluation of e-learning programs, and the future use of e-learning by Canadian organizations.

2. Athabasca University in Alberta is one of Canada's leading universities in distance education and on-line learning. To find out more about how distance education works at AU, visit their website at **www.athabascau.ca**. What is the most common method of course delivery and how does it work? How do e-Classes work at AU? As a student yourself, how would you like to be involved in distance education and e-Classes? What are the advantages and disadvantages of these approaches for learning?

3. A good example of a company that has converted many of its training programs to technology-based training is Cisco Systems. To learn more about e-learning at Cisco Systems go to **www.cisco.com**. Find out about Cisco's three-part framework to optimize learning and performance and how they are using e-learning. What is the company's e-learning strategy, and how effective is the company's E-Learning Connection? What can other organizations learn from Cisco Systems about e-learning?

Exercises

1. Describe the most recent traditional training program you have attended in terms of its objectives, content, design, and methods. Now think about how the program might be translated into a computer-based training program. Describe what the program would be like and how you would design it. Do you think it would be more or less effective than the traditional training program?

2. Contact the human resource department of an organization and ask them if you can conduct a brief interview with the training staff about their use of technology-based training methods. Some of the things you might consider include:
   a. Do they use technology for training, and if so, what forms of technology-based training are they using and what are they using them for?
   b. Why did they decide to use technology for training?
   c. How effective has the use of technology been for training? How have they evaluated its effectiveness and what has the impact been on employees and the organization?
   d. Do they plan to use technology-based training in the future, and if so, in what way, for what purposes, and for what reasons?

3. Contact the human resource department of an organization to find out if they have e-learning training programs. Once you have found an organization that has developed an e-learning program, find out how they designed the program and how it works. Some of the things to consider include:

    a. What are the training objectives?

    b. What is the training content?

    c. Who are the trainees?

    d. How has the program been designed and does it include interactive elements?

    e. Does the program incorporate learning principles and if so, how have they been incorporated into the program.

4. Choose a class from a course you are currently taking, and describe it in terms of the following design factors from Chapter 5:

    - what are the objectives of the class
    - what is the content of the class
    - who is the trainer (experience, job title, etc.)
    - who are the trainees (students) are (e.g., major, work experience, etc.)
    - what training methods were used
    - what training materials and equipment were used
    - the training site
    - the lesson plan
    - the administration of the class (what was involved?)
    - the delivery of the material (events of instruction) and any delivery problems and strategies used to deal with them

    Now consider how the class might be designed and delivered as a computer-based course. Review your answers to each of the above design factors, and then translate them into a computer-based program. In other words, what would be the objectives, content, methods, materials and equipment, lesson plan, etc.

    How effective do you think the class will be as a computer-based course? Compare and contrast it to the classroom version. What are the advantages and disadvantages of each for students, instructors, and the university or college? Which one would you prefer and why?

5. One of the concerns about technology-based training is the tendency to focus too much on the technology and not enough on the principles of learning and conditions of practice. Refer back to Chapter 5 and the conditions of practice in Table 5.2. Describe how each of the conditions of practice might be designed into a computer-based training program.

6. As described in Chapter 5, the delivery of a training program should follow Gagne's nine events of instruction. But does this also apply to technology-based training? Describe how each of the nine events of instruction might be designed into computer-based training programs.

E-LEARNING AT FLOTATION LTD.

Jenny Stoppard was excited about her new position as vice president of human resources at Flotation Ltd., a manufacturer of life jackets and other flotation devices. However, she knew she had her work cut out for her.

The president of the company had clearly stated that one of her first tasks was to take a close look at the training function. Although Flotation Ltd. had a reputation as a company with a well-trained workforce, the president now wanted to see some hard evidence to back up the company's training investment. The president wanted to increase productivity per person by 50 percent over the next three years, and Jenny was expected to spearhead the effort.

"Yes, we cycle people through a lot of courses. But I'm not satisfied with the bottom line. I know that while Dad was president he swore by old Sam — said he was the greatest. I don't know anymore. Maybe a whole new approach is needed. Anyway, I want you to take a close look at Sam's operation," said the president.

Sam was the company's veteran trainer who was liked by everybody in the organization. For 20 years he had been training employees at Flotation Ltd. He was only three years away from retirement and was not likely to respond favourably to Jenny and her new mandate.

The president introduced Jenny to Sam as his new boss and the key player in the drive to increase the company's competitiveness. He also told Sam to do everything in his power to cooperate with her.

Jenny knew she had her work cut out for her. She not only had to revamp the training function, but she also had to deal with Sam who was pretty much set in his ways. How was she going to achieve the president's goals and at the same time get Sam on board?

After thinking about her situation for several days, Jenny came across an article on e-learning and how it has saved some companies millions of dollars a year in training. Suddenly, she had found the solution.

"Why not convert some of Sam's courses to e-learning programs on the company's website?" she thought to herself. "This would certainly be a whole new approach and I could save the company money and get Sam involved since he would be responsible for preparing his course material for the program. Surely Sam would be excited to know that his training courses would continue even after he has retired."

Both the president and Sam were very excited about the potential of e-learning at Flotation Ltd. Jenny was given the go ahead to begin designing the first course. Jenny and Sam decided that the first course should be Sam's sales training program, which was one of his best. It would also be useful for the company's sales staff who would be able to take the program while they were on the road selling.

The first thing that Jenny did was to arrange for Sam to be videotaped delivering the course. Then she had Sam prepare some text material and additional information about some of the key learning points. With the help of the IT people, the video and text were placed on the company's website. The program was designed so that when an employee logged onto the site they could watch the video of Sam and at certain points during the video they could click on an icon for more information. The video would then stop and the additional information would appear on the screen. After reading the material they could then return to the video.

When the program was set up and ready to go, the sales staff received a memo telling them about the company's first e-learning program and how to access it on the company's website. The memo was titled "Learn how to improve your sales skills on-the-road" and "Attend Sam's best training program anytime and anywhere." Everybody was very excited about this new approach to training, and Sam was thrilled to know that he was the main attraction.

However, although the program was launched with much fanfare, the results were less than glowing. In fact, after the first six months very few of the sales staff had taken the course. Many said that they did not have time to take it. And of those who did, less than half actually completed it.

When asked about it, some of the sales staff said that it was not very interesting. Some said they would rather attend a live version of the course and others said they didn't see what the advantage was of taking an e-learning course. Some thought it was just a big waste of the company's time and money.

The president asked to see Jenny to find out how things were going and if they were on track for achieving the company's productivity goals. Jenny did not know what she would tell him. Sam tried to console her by telling her that it had only been six months and the sales staff just needed time to get used to learning on-line. Jenny wasn't so sure. She wondered if e-learning wasn't just a fad that she foolishly jumped into.

Questions

1. Do you think that e-learning was a good idea for Flotation Ltd.? Could e-learning help the company realize the president's productivity goals?
2. Comment on the e-learning program that Jenny and Sam designed. What are the indicators that suggest that it has not been a success? Is it possible that there are other indicators that might suggest that it is more effective than it appears?
3. Comment on how the program was designed and the use of learning principles and the conditions of practice. Do you think the program could be redesigned to make it more effective, and if so how would you proceed?
4. If you were Jenny, what would you tell the president and what would you do about e-learning at Flotation Ltd.? Should Jenny give up on e-learning or wait another six months before making a decision?

VANDALAIS DEPARTMENT STORES

Refer to the Vandalais Department Stores case described in Chapter 5 and answer the following questions.

1. Do you think that technology-based training methods can be used for the structured employment interview training program? Explain your reasoning.
2. Should technology-based training methods be used? What would be the advantages and disadvantages of using technology-based training for the structured employment interview training program?
3. What form of technology-based training would you recommend for the structured employment interview training program and why? How effective would it be compared to the traditional methods being used for the training program?

References

[1](2002, December). Canada's oldest store embraces e-learning. *The Training Report*, p. 4. Reprinted by permission of *The Training Report*.

[2]Tomlinson, A. (2002, March 25). T & D spending up in U.S. as Canada lags behind. *Canadian HR Reporter*, p.1.

[3]Eure, R. (2001, March 21). Companies embrace e-training. *The Globe and Mail*, B16. (2001, June 18). Businesses find a new class of e-learning. *The Globe and Mail*, R12.

[4]Caudron, S. (2002, February). Training in the post-terrorism era. *Training and Development*, 24–30.

[5]Galvin, T. (2002, October). 2002 Industry Report. *Training*, 24–73.

[6]Galvin, T. (2002, October).

[7]Wanberg, C. R., Brown, K. G., Welsh, L. T., & Simmering, M. J. (2002). E-Learning: Emerging uses, best practices, and future directions. Paper presented at the 17th Annual Conference of the Society for Industrial and Organizational Psychology, Toronto.

[8]Galvin, T. (2002, October).

[9]Brown, K. G., & Ford, J. K. (2002). Using computer technology in training: Building an infrastructure for active learning. In K. Kraiger's (Ed.), *Creating, implementing, and managing effective training and development: State-of-the-art lessons for practice*, (pp. 160–91). San Francisco. CA: Jossey-Bass.

[10]Galvin, T. (2002, October).

[11]Harris-Lalonde, S. (2001). Training and development outlook. *The Conference Board of Canada*. Ottawa.

[12]Ray, R. (2001, May 25). Employers, employees embrace e-learning. *The Globe and Mail*, E2.

[13]Harris-Lalonde, S. (2001).

[14]Wanberg, C. R., Brown, K. G., Welsh, L. T., & Simmering, M. J. (2002).

[15]Eure, R. (2001, March 21).

[16]German, C., & Heath, C. (1994). Career development 2000. *Training and Development, 12* (5), 12–14.

[17]Brown, K. G., & Ford, J. K. (2002).

[18]Wanberg, C. R., Brown, K. G., Welsh, L. T., & Simmering, M. J. (2002).

[19]McLaren, C. (2002, May 31). E-training cooks up customer service tips. *The Globe and Mail*, T4.

[20]Wanberg, C. R., Brown, K. G., Welsh, L. T., & Simmering, M. J. (2002).

[21]Robinson, J.C. (1982). *Developing managers through behaviour modelling*. Austin: Texas.

[22]Johnston, A.D. (2002, November 18). The university crunch. *Maclean's*, 115 (46), 20–28.

[23]Raybould, B. (1990, November–December). Solving human performance problems with computers—A case study: Building an electronic performance support system. *Performance and Instruction*, 4–14.

[24]Smith, K. (1996, April). EPSS helps accounting firm reduce training time, improve productivity during transition to new service emphasis. *Lakewood Report on Technology for Learning*, p. 8.

[25]Kulig, P. (1998, March 23). When training meets performance support. *Canadian HR Reporter, 11* (6), 17–18.

[26]Gebber, B. (1991). Help! The rise of performance support systems. *Training, 28* (12), 23–29. Ruyle, K. (1991, February/March). Developing intelligent job aids. *Technical and Skills Training*, 9–14.

[27]Filipczak, B. (1994). Distance teamwork. *Training, 31* (4), 71.

[28]Allan, K. (1993, June). Computer courses ensure uniform training. *Personnel Journal*, 65–71.

[29]Brown, K. G., & Ford, J. K. (2002).

[30]Wanberg, C. R., Brown, K. G., Welsh, L. T., & Simmering, M. J. (2002).

[31]O'Keefe, B. (1991, September/October). Adopting multimedia on a global scale. *Instruction Delivery Systems*, 6–11.

[32]Miles, K.W., & Griffith, E.R. (1993, April/May). Developing an hour of CBT: The quick and dirty method. *CBT Directions*, 28–33.

[33]Eure, R. (2001, March 21).

[34]Wanberg, C. R., Brown, K. G., Welsh, L. T., & Simmering, M. J. (2002).

[35]Wanberg, C. R., Brown, K. G., Welsh, L. T., & Simmering, M. J. (2002).

[36]Wanberg, C. R., Brown, K. G., Welsh, L. T., & Simmering, M. J. (2002).

[37]Wanberg, C. R., Brown, K. G., Welsh, L. T., & Simmering, M. J. (2002).

[38]Wanberg, C. R., Brown, K. G., Welsh, L. T., & Simmering, M. J. (2002).

[39]Brown, K. G., & Ford, J. K. (2002).

[40]Wanberg, C. R., Brown, K. G., Welsh, L. T., & Simmering, M. J. (2002).

[41]Eure, R. (2001, March 21).

[42]Wanberg, C. R., Brown, K. G., Welsh, L. T., & Simmering, M. J. (2002).

Transfer
of Training

Chapter Learning Objectives

After reading this chapter, you should be able to:

- define transfer of training as well as positive, negative, zero, horizontal, and vertical transfer
- describe the major barriers to the transfer of training
- describe Baldwin and Ford's model of the transfer of training process
- describe the activities that managers can do before, during, and after training to improve the transfer of training
- describe the activities that trainers can do before, during, and after training to improve the transfer of training
- describe the activities that trainees can do before, during, and after training to improve the transfer of training
- define identical elements, general principles, and stimulus variability and explain how they can improve the transfer of training
- explain what a transfer enhancement procedure is and describe relapse prevention, self-management, and goal setting interventions

HEALTH PARTNERS

Health Partners is a nonprofit organization that administers Medicard and Medicare coverage for 130,000 patients in Philadelphia. The company spent two and half years and $3 million building and installing a major upgrade to its data-processing system. For the organization, the new system was seen as a godsend—a software tool sophisticated enough to cope with the mountains of data on doctor visits, wheelchair authorizations, and other services of which Health Partners had to make sense. To the company's 360 employees, however, the new system was an unfamiliar program with complicated commands and multiple windows—a monster waiting on their desktops to devour them.

Although the company had spent tens of thousands of dollars to outside training consultants, because of delays in the installation of the system, the training was a distant memory in most employees' minds. As a result, a new round of training was needed as well as follow-up support not to mention a motivational campaign to boost slumping corporate morale.

The task was handed over to the company's new Organizational Learning Centre (OLC). Rather than outsource the training, the OLC identified a handful of employees who were the top performers in the initial training course and persuaded them to become part-time instructors and support resources for the rest of the staff. In addition, rather than conducting gruelling daylong crash courses, OLC broke the training into a longer series of 45-minute sessions that employees could fit into their work schedules, and offered plenty of chances for employees to retake the training and reinforce their skills. And rather than organize the curriculum by tasks, OLC organized it by department and invited staffers from other departments to attend so they could get a better understanding of how the entire company utilized the system. The OLC also devoted a portion of the training time to talking with employees about the inevitable stress of going through changes in the workplace and the benefits that might be gained from successfully weathering it.

Within weeks managers reported that their employees, who had been stuck pondering screen menus for 10 minutes at a time on day one, were able to click through in a third of the time after taking the courses. The initial wave of complaints from client hospitals and administrators about logjams just as quickly dropped to virtually nil. And the palpable sense of dread among the workforce had been replaced by an eagerness to sign up for refresher courses.[1]

Health Partners invested a great deal of time and money in a new data-processing system. However, in order for it to be a success, employees had to learn the new system and then actually use it on the job. This is not an easy task. Research has shown that many trainees do not actually apply what they learn in training on the job. In fact, at Health Partners employees dreaded the change to the new system. Nonetheless, the company was successful in getting employees to learn the new system and to use it on the job. This process is known as the transfer of training. This chapter describes the transfer of training process and outlines the major role players and practices for facilitating and improving the transfer of training.

What is Transfer of Training?

Organizations concerned about their training investment are interested in knowing how much of what is learned in training translates into changes on the job. A training program is just the acquisition phase for knowledge, skills, and/or attitudes. Trainers can often demonstrate that trainees leave training with new knowledge and skills. But if trainees do not apply their newly acquired knowledge and skills on the job, then most of the resources spent on training are wasted.

Organizations are increasingly concerned about the value-added of human resource programs. When it comes to training, they are concerned about the *transfer* of training. **Transfer of training** refers to the application of the knowledge and skills acquired in a training program on the job and the maintenance of acquired knowledge and skills over time.[2] Thus, there are two conditions of transfer of training. *Generalization* refers to the use or application of learned material to the job. *Maintenance* refers to the use or application of learned material on the job over a period of time. Transfer of training occurs when learned material is generalized to the job context and maintained over a period of time on the job.

The extent to which a training program transfers to the job can be described as zero, positive, or negative transfer. When transfer is positive, trainees effectively apply their new knowledge, skills, and attitudes acquired in training on the job. If transfer is zero, then trainees are not using new knowledge and skills on the job. When transfer is negative, training has had a negative effect and trainees are performing worse as a result of a training program. The purpose of this chapter is to find out why transfer is sometimes zero or negative and what can be done to make it positive.

A final distinction to note about the transfer of training is the difference between horizontal and vertical transfer. **Horizontal transfer** involves the transfer of knowledge and skills across different settings or contexts at the same level. This is in fact the focus of this chapter and is consistent with how we have defined transfer of training. That is, we are concerned about the extent to which trainees' transfer what they learn in training from the training setting to the job setting.

Vertical transfer refers to transfer from the individual or trainee level to the organizational level. In other words, it is concerned with the extent to

Transfer of training

The generalization of knowledge and skills learned in training on the job and the maintenance of acquired knowledge and skills over time

Horizontal transfer

The transfer of knowledge and skills across different settings or contexts at the same level

Vertical transfer

Transfer from the individual or trainee level to the organizational level or the extent to which changes in trainee behaviour or performance transfer to organizational level outcomes which changes in trainee behaviour or performance transfer to organizational level outcomes. For example, if trainees' improve their job performance will this result in an increase in the organization's overall performance? Vertical transfer represents the link between employee behaviour and organizational effectiveness.

This is an important distinction to understand because transfer to the job (i.e., horizontal transfer) might not lead to changes in organizational outcomes (i.e., vertical transfer). Furthermore, there are differences in terms of how to improve each type of transfer. The focus of this chapter is on horizontal transfer, which is a necessary condition for vertical transfer.[3]

The Transfer Problem

Transfer of training is a major problem for trainers and organizations. For decades it has been reported that there exists a transfer of training problem in organizations. Although the estimates of transfer have varied over the years, they have for the most part been quite low with studies reporting that between 60 and 90 percent of what is learned in training is not applied on the job.[4]

In the only Canadian study, it was found that although trainees apply 62 percent of what they learn in training on the job immediately after attending a training program, this drops to 44 percent after six months, and to 34 percent one year after attending training. The respondents, who were experienced training professionals, also indicated that an average of 51 percent of training investments result in a positive change or improvement in employees' performance, and an average of 47 percent results in an improvement in organizational performance.[5]

There are many reasons why training does not transfer. Table 9.1 provides a list of some of the major barriers to the transfer of training. In the next section, we will describe the transfer of training process, which sets the stage for understanding how to improve and facilitate the transfer of training.

The Transfer of Training Process

One way to understand how to improve the transfer of training is to first examine the factors that contribute to positive transfer of training. A good place to start is with a well-known model of the transfer of training process by Tim Baldwin and Kevin Ford.[6]

As shown in Figure 9.1, Baldwin and Ford's model of the transfer of training process can be understood in terms of three main factors: training inputs, training outputs, and the conditions of transfer. The training inputs include trainee characteristics, training design, and the work environment. The training outputs include learning and retention. The conditions of transfer refer to transfer generalization and maintenance as described earlier.

According to the model, trainee characteristics, training design, and the work environment have a direct effect on learning and retention. Trainee characteristics, the work environment, and learning and retention have a direct effect on transfer generalization and maintenance.

TABLE 9.1

Barriers to the Transfer of Training

- Immediate manager does not support the training.
- The culture in the work group does not support the training.
- No opportunity exists to use the skills.
- No time is provided to use the skills.
- Skills could not be applied to the job.
- The systems and processes did not support the skills.
- The resources are not available to use the skills.
- Skills no longer apply because of changed job responsibilities.
- Skills are not appropriate in our work unit.
- Did not see a need to apply what was learned.
- Old habits could not be changed.
- Reward systems don't support new skills.

Source: Phillips, J.J., & Phillips, P.P. (2002). 11 reasons why training and development fail ... and what you can do about it. *Training, 39* (9), 78–85. Training: The Human Side of Business by Phillips, P.P. Copyright 2002 by V N U BUS PUBNS USA. Reproduced with permission of V N U BUS PUBNS USA in the format Textbook via Copyright Clearance Center.

An important implication of the model is that learning and retention are a necessary but not sufficient condition for transfer. This is because trainee characteristics and the work environment also play a critical role in whether or not trainees apply what they learn in training on the job. To better understand the role of the training inputs, we will now describe them in more detail.

Training Inputs

Training inputs include trainee characteristics, training design, and the work environment.

Trainee Characteristics

As was described in Chapter 3, trainee characteristics are an important determinant of trainee learning and retention. Thus, it should not surprise you that trainee characteristics are also important for the transfer of training. In fact, the same trainee characteristics that influence learning are also important for transfer. Trainee differences in these characteristics can help us understand why some trainees are more likely to transfer than others.

In Chapter 3, the importance of cognitive ability, training motivation, self-efficacy, and personality characteristics were discussed in relation to learning and retention. Recall that these factors were included in the training effectiveness model and that they have a direct effect on learning and retention. They also have a direct effect on the conditions of transfer. In other words, trainees with higher cognitive ability, motivation to learn, and self-efficacy are more likely to transfer. In addition, trainees with an internal locus

FIGURE 9.1

Baldwin and Ford's Model of the Transfer of Training Process

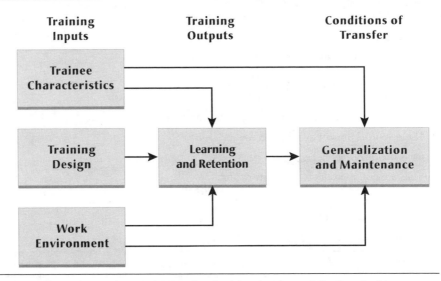

Training Inputs — Training Outputs — Conditions of Transfer

Trainee Characteristics

Training Design → Learning and Retention → Generalization and Maintenance

Work Environment

Source: Baldwin, T.T, & Ford, J.K. (1988). Transfer of training: A review and directions for future research. *Personnel Psychology, 41,* 63–105. *Personnel Psychology* by Baldwin, T.T. & Ford, J.K. Copyright 1988 by Personnel Psychology Inc. Reproduced with permission of Personnel Psychology Inc. in the format Textbook via Copyright Clearance Center.

of control and a high need for achievement are also more likely to apply what they learn in training on the job.

Recall from Chapter 3 that another factor that influences learning and transfer is trainee attitudes. Employees with higher job involvement, job satisfaction, and organizational commitment are more likely to learn and transfer.[7]

Training Design

Another important training input is the design of a training program. Sometimes training programs do not result in positive transfer because of the failure to incorporate design factors that enable trainees to understand how to apply what they learn on the job. Recall the discussion in Chapter 5 on active practice and the conditions of practice for learning and retention. Trainee learning is likely to suffer if these conditions are not included in a training program.

There is also a number of learning principles that can be incorporated into the design of a training program to improve the transfer of training. These learning principles include identical elements, stimulus variability, and general principles.

First, trainers should ensure that the training situation reflects the work environment or what is known as identical elements. **Identical elements** involve providing trainees with training experiences and conditions that closely resemble those in the actual work environment. Identical elements theory states that transfer will occur only if identical elements are present in

Identical elements

Providing trainees with training experiences and conditions that closely resemble those in the actual work environment both the old (training course) and new situations.[8] Identical elements have been shown to increase trainees' retention of motor and verbal behaviours.[9]

But what exactly is identical? We discussed this issue in Chapter 6 with respect to simulations. At that time it was noted that in order to be most effective, simulations should have physical and psychological fidelity. Physical fidelity involves making the conditions of a training program such as the surroundings, tasks, and equipment similar to the work environment. Psychological fidelity has to do with the extent that trainees attach similar meanings to the training experience and the job context.

A second principle is known as general principles. **General principles** involve teaching trainees the general rules and theoretical principles that underlie the use and application of trained knowledge and skills. In other words, the training program provides trainees with an explanation of the theory and principles behind a skill or task that they are learning how to perform. On-the-job application is more likely when trainees are taught the general rules and theoretical principles that underlie training content.[10]

Finally, **stimulus variability** involves providing trainees with a variety of training stimuli and experiences such as multiple examples of a concept or practice experience in a variety of situations. The idea is that trainees' understanding of training material can be strengthened by providing numerous examples of a concept because they will see how the concept can be applied in a variety of situations. This will enable greater generalization of the new skills and prevents the potential problem that learning will be limited to a narrow range of situations.[11]

Stimulus variability can be incorporated into a training program in a number of ways, such as by using different models that vary in terms of their characteristics (e.g., gender or age), modelling different situations (e.g., different types of negotiation scenarios for a training program on negotiation skills), and by using models with different levels of competence in performing the training task (successful and unsuccessful). As well, trainers can increase stimulus variability simply by describing a variety of examples and experiences related to the training content, and by asking trainees to discuss their own work experiences in relation to the training material. Using several examples during the course of a training program has been found to be more effective than simply repeating the same example.

The Environment

The third input factor in Baldwin and Ford's model is the work environment. Characteristics of the work environment can influence transfer before training (the *pretraining* environment) as well as after training (the *posttraining* environment). Let's first consider the pretraining environment.

Management actions prior to training sends signals and messages to employees about the importance of training and the extent to which the organization supports training. These messages can influence employees' training motivation. For example, if management's actions convey messages that training is not important, employees will not be motivated to attend training and less likely to learn. In addition, if employees face constraints in

General principles

Teaching trainees the general rules and theoretical principles that underlie the use and application of particular skills

Stimulus variability

Providing trainees with a variety of training stimuli and experiences, such as multiple examples of a concept, or practice experiences in a variety of situations their job such as a lack of time, equipment, and/or resources, they will not be highly motivated to learn given that the work environment would prevent them from using new skills.[13]

Events that occur after a training program in the posttraining environment can also influence the transfer of training. Factors in the posttraining environment can encourage, discourage, or prevent employees from applying new knowledge and skills on the job. One of the most important characteristics of the posttraining environment is the amount of support provided by trainees' supervisors. Supervisor involvement, influence, and support for training is a key factor that affects the transfer process. Trainees who have supervisors who are more supportive of training are more likely to be motivated to attend training, to learn and retain training content, and to transfer what they learn in training on the job. There are a number of important activities that supportive supervisors can do before and after training that are described later in this chapter.[14]

At this point, it would be helpful to recall the discussion of an organizational analysis and the organizational context in Chapter 4. At that time, two important aspects of the work environment were described: the transfer climate and a learning culture. As described in Chapter 4, a **transfer climate** refers to characteristics in the work environment that can either facilitate or inhibit the application of training on the job. A strong transfer climate is one in which there exists cues that remind employees to apply training material on the job, positive consequences such as feedback and rewards for applying training on the job, and supervisor and peer support for the use of newly acquired skills and abilities. A positive and supportive transfer climate has been shown to result in greater learning, retention, and the transfer of training.[15]

A **learning culture** refers to a culture in which members of an organization believe that knowledge and skill acquisition are part of their job responsibilities and that learning is an important part of work life in the organization. Research has shown that the transfer of training is greater in organizations that have a learning culture.[16] Review The Trainer's Notebook 1, "A Learning Culture Diagnosis" to determine if you work for an organization that has a learning culture.

In summary, Baldwin and Ford's model of the transfer of training process indicates that transfer generalization and maintenance is a function of trainee characteristics, the work environment, and learning and retention. Learning and retention are a function of trainee characteristics, training design, and the work environment. The model suggests a number of practical implications for facilitating and improving the transfer of training that is the focus of the remainder of this chapter.

Transfer climate

Characteristics in the work environment that can either facilitate or inhibit the application of training on the job

Learning culture

A culture in which members of an organization believe that knowledge and skill acquisition are part of their job responsibilities and that learning is an important part of work life in the organization

Facilitating and Improving the Transfer of Training

In the previous section, we noted that the transfer of training is influenced by factors that occur before a training program (i.e., the pretraining environment), during training (training design), and after training (the posttraining environment). In this section, we will describe practices and activities that take place before, during, and after training to improve the transfer of training. Further, we will also show that positive transfer of training requires the involvement of three key role players: management, trainers, and trainees. We will describe the activities that each role player can do at each of the three time periods.

Table 9.2 presents a transfer of training framework that guides this section of the chapter. It shows the activities that can be performed by each of the role players before, during, and after training to facilitate and improve the transfer of training.

Transfer of Training Activities Before Training

Effective training and the probability of positive transfer should begin before a training program is designed and delivered. There are many pretraining activities that are relatively easy to include as part of the training process that can facilitate the transfer of training. This is in part due to the fact that the pre-training work environment has a direct effect on trainees' motivation to learn, learning, and the application of what is learned in training on the job. The work environment can send messages to employees about the importance of training and learning and should therefore be carefully constructed and managed. This means that management has an especially important role to play before training.

TABLE 9.2

Transfer Of Training Framework

TRANSFER OF TRAINING ACTIVITIES BEFORE TRAINING

Management:
- Decide who should attend training.
- Meet with employees prior to training to discuss training programs (e.g., WIIFM).
- Get employee input and involvement in the training process.
- Provide employees with support for learning and training (e.g., release time to prepare for training).

Trainer:
- Ensure application of the ISD model.
- Make sure that trainees and supervisors meet and discuss the training.
- Find out supervisor and trainee needs and expectations.
- Make sure that trainees are prepared for the training.

Trainees:
- Find out about training programs prior to attendance.
- Meet with supervisor to discuss the training program and develop an action plan.
- Prepare for the training program.

TRANSFER OF TRAINING ACTIVITIES DURING TRAINING

Management:
- Participate in training programs.
- Attend training programs before trainees.
- Reassign employees' work while they are attending training.

Trainer:
- Incorporate conditions of practice, adult learning principles, and other learning principles (e.g., identical elements) in the design of training programs.
- Include content and examples that are relevant and meaningful to trainees.

Trainees:
- Enter a training program with a positive attitude and the motivation to learn.
- Engage yourself in the training program by getting involved and actively participating.
- Develop an action plan for the application of training on the job.

TRANSFER OF TRAINING ACTIVITIES AFTER TRAINING

Management:
- Ensure that trainees have immediate and frequent opportunities to practice and apply what they learned in training on the job.
- Encourage and reinforce trainees' application of new skills on the job.
- Develop an action plan with trainees for transfer and show support by reducing job pressures and workload, arrange practice sessions, publicize transfer successes, give promotional preference to employees who have received training and transfer, and evaluate employees' use of trained skills on the job.

Trainer:

- Provide transfer enhancement procedures (TEPs) or post-training transfer intervention at the end of the content portion of a training program that is designed for the purpose of improving the transfer of training.
- Have trainees prepare and commit to a performance contract for the transfer of trained skills on the job.
- Conduct follow-up or booster sessions following a training program.
- Stay involved in the training and transfer process by conducting field visits to observe trainees use of trained skills, provide and solicit feedback, and provide continued support and assistance to trainees.

Trainees:

- Begin using new knowledge and skills on the job and as often as possible.
- Meet with supervisor to discuss opportunities for transfer.
- Form a "buddy system" or a network of peers who also attended the training program.
- Consider high-risk situations that might cause a relapse and develop strategies for overcoming them and avoiding a relapse.
- Set goals for transfer and use self-management.

Management

One of the first things that a manager or supervisor should do prior to training is to carefully decide who should attend training. This involves more than just the identification of employees' needs for training. Recall from our earlier discussion that trainee characteristics are an important determinant of learning and retention as well as transfer. Therefore, it is important that trainees who are selected to attend training programs will learn to perform training tasks and transfer what they learn on the job.

The extent to which a trainee is likely to learn and benefit from a training program is known as readiness to learn or trainability. **Readiness to learn/trainability** refers to the extent to which an individual has the knowledge, skills, and abilities and the motivation to learn the training content. An equation for readiness to learn/trainability combines ability, motivation, as well as perceptions of the work environment as follows:[17]

$$\text{Readiness to learn/Trainability} = (\text{Ability} \times \text{Motivation} \times \text{Perceptions of the Work Environment})$$

According to this equation, trainees are more likely to learn or are more trainable when they have the ability to learn the training content; when they are motivated to learn; and when they perceive the work environment as supportive of their learning and use of new knowledge and skills on the job. All three of these components are important and they are not additive. In other words, being high on one factor will not make up for a low rating on another factor. For example, a trainee might have the ability to learn and be motivated to learn, but if he/she does not believe that the work environment will support learning, then he/she will score low on readiness to learn and trainability.

Readiness to Learn/Trainability

The extent to which an individual has the knowledge, skills, and abilities and the motivation to learn the training content

Therefore, it is important that all three components be high before sending trainees to a training program.

Readiness to learn/trainability has a number of implications for choosing and preparing trainees for training. First, it suggests that trainees must have the ability to learn the training material and to perform the training task. This means that managers should only send trainees to training programs if they have the required abilities. One way to do this is to have employees complete a trainability test that tests them on their ability to learn the training content.

Trainability test

A test that measures an individual's ability to learn and perform training tasks

A **trainability test** is a test that measures an individual's ability to learn and perform training tasks in order to predict whether an individual will successfully complete a training program.[18] This is typically done by having individuals take a minicourse or learn a sample of the training that is representative of the training content of a training program. They then take a test that measures their learning and performance of the tasks. Trainability tests have been shown to be effective in predicting training success and job performance in many jobs such as carpentry, welding, dentistry, and forklift operating. Although they have most often been used for psychomotor skills, they are just as applicable for other types of skills and knowledge tests. These kinds of training pre-tests can also be used to determine what kind of remedial training an individual might require in order to prepare them for a training program or to tailor a training program to their needs. Thus, managers can maximize the acquisition and transfer of new knowledge and skills by assessing employees' readiness to learn and trainability prior to training.[19]

If trainees are lacking in some knowledge or experience that is a necessary prerequisite for a training program, then precourse work or assignments might be given to prepare trainees for a training program. In some cases trainees might have to attend some form of basic skills training prior to attending a training program. This is often the case when trainees require literacy training before attending technical training programs. This helps to ensure that trainees have the necessary knowledge and ability required to benefit from a training program.

Training motivation is also important, as trainees who are motivated to learn will in fact be more likely to learn and transfer. Therefore, managers must also consider employees' motivation to attend a training program. Sending employees who are not motivated is a waste of time and resources. In this regard, a manager might only send employees to training if they are motivated to learn. Alternatively, a manager might also attempt to increase employees' motivation to learn.

There are several ways to increase motivation to learn. First, supervisors can meet with employees to discuss their training needs and decide on a training plan to meet those needs. Prior to actually attending a training program, supervisors can discuss the content and the benefits of a training program with their employees and set goals for learning and how they will apply what they learn on the job. They should also discuss the objectives of a training program so that employees know what is expected of them and what they will be accountable for in terms of learning and the use of new knowledge and skills on the job. Trainees who know that they will be required to participate in follow-up activities or an assessment have stronger intentions to transfer what they learn in training.[20]

Employees also need to know why they are attending a training program and what benefits they can expect from it. It is up to management to inform trainees about the importance and relevance of attending a training program and the potential benefits of learning and transfer. Trainees need to know what's in it for them or what is sometimes referred to as "WIIFM" (what's in it for me). This relates back to our discussion of motivation in Chapter 3. In this regard, the linkages of expectancy theory are especially useful for motivating trainees and dealing with the WIIFM question.

Trainees who have had discussions regarding their careers and who have established career goals and plans are more likely to benefit from training than others.[21] Where possible, trainees should be told of the benefits of learning new skills. These benefits could range from fewer client problems and increased speed in processing orders to more personal incentives such as promotion or increases in pay.

There is some evidence that trainees will be more motivated and will achieve greater learning when they have some choice in attending a training program than when attendance is mandatory. In one study, managers who could choose whether to attend a performance-appraisal workshop achieved more from attending the workshop than those who were forced to attend. Providing detailed information about the workshop, which was designed to facilitate the managers' attendance decision, rather than just providing the typical positive overview, also resulted in greater achievement.[22]

Some, however, argue that it is better to make attendance mandatory. The idea behind this argument is that by making attendance mandatory, managers communicate the importance of training and ensure that all employees are using the same skills.[23] One study did find that a mandatory course resulted in higher intentions to transfer training to the workplace.[24] However, this appears to be the case when training is highly valued in an organization. When training is not so highly valued, it appears that providing employees with some choice is beneficial. The main point, however, is that trainee involvement and input in the training process, whether it is discussing training needs, allowing trainees to decide what training programs to attend, and/or providing input regarding training content and methods, can enhance motivation to learn, learning, and transfer.

Finally, supervisors also need to show their support for training before an employee is sent to a training program. One way of doing this is to have them complete a questionnaire and respond to questions about the need for and potential application of training material. CIBC requires managers who have requested training to answer questions such as: What is the training need? What are the employees doing now and what should they be doing? Why do you feel that training will solve the problem? What would you want employees to be able to do after the training? Having managers complete a contract can also commit them to a training program and ensure their support for it. Such a contract is presented in Table 9.3. Supervisors can also demon-

TABLE 9.3

Training Support Contract—Supervisor

I, _____ , agree to

- provide time for the employee to complete precourse assignments.
- provide release time for attendance, and ensure that the employee's workload is undertaken by others to eliminate interruptions.
- review the course outline with the employee, and discuss situations in which the newly acquired knowledge and skills can be used.
- provide timely opportunities to implement the skills, and reinforce new behaviours upon the return of the trainee.

Signature _____

Title _____

strate their support for training by providing employees release time to prepare for training and by providing encouragement.[25]

Implementing these activities before training begins will focus attention on learning and demonstrate to trainees the importance of training, learning, and transfer.

Trainer

There are a number of things that trainers can do before training to facilitate the transfer of training. First, trainers should ensure that the training system is operating according to the instructional systems design model presented in Chapter 1. That is, a trainer should ensure that a needs analysis has been conducted, appropriate training objectives have been developed, and that important learning and design principles have been incorporated into the design of the training program.

Second, the trainer should ensure that both trainees' supervisor and trainees are prepared for the training program. For example, the trainer should ensure that supervisors have taken appropriate actions with respect to the trainability of trainees. The trainer should also make sure that supervisors and trainees meet to discuss the objectives, content, and benefits of the training program and that trainees know what is expected of them in terms of learning and changes in their on-the-job behaviour.

Third, the trainer should know what supervisors and trainees expect from the trainer and the training program. Thus, to some extent a trainer might have to tailor a training program to the particular needs and expectations of supervisors and trainees. The trainer should also be aware of the needs of trainees in terms of relevant content, examples, and methods. Thus, the trainer must ensure that the training program is relevant and meaningful for trainees. In this way a trainer can adjust a training program to trainees' needs and thereby improve the probability of learning and transfer.

Finally, the trainer should ensure that trainees are prepared for the training program and have taken any required prerequisite courses and have the necessary readings, assignments, and/or pre-training exercises. Preparation might also include asking trainees to think about any work-related problems and issues that they are currently dealing with and how the training program might help to solve them. These efforts on the part of the trainer should ensure that trainees show up for a training program ready and motivated to learn.

Trainees

Trainees often show up for training programs with little knowledge of what they are going to learn or what is expected of them. This is obviously not going to lead to a high level of motivation to learn, learning, or transfer. Trainees need to be much more involved in their training and the training process. There are a number of things that trainees can do before training to increase their involvement and the likelihood that they will learn and transfer.

First, trainees should find out why they are being asked to attend a training program, what the training objectives are, and what is expected of them in terms of learning and on-the-job behaviour. Second, trainees should meet with their supervisors to discuss the training program and develop a plan of action for learning and transfer. Trainees should also ask their supervisor about the support they can expect while they are away from work and attending a training program, and the support they will receive when they return to their job.

Finally, trainees should prepare for the training program to ensure that they are ready to learn and that they will benefit from the training. This might involve doing some preparatory reading, pre-training exercises or assignments, or simply thinking about any work-related problems they are experiencing that they can bring with them to the training program. These activities will help ensure that trainees are knowledgeable about the training program and its objectives and are prepared and motivated to learn.

Transfer of Training Activities During Training

Although it is the responsibility of the trainer to actually implement and deliver a training program, there are also important activities that trainees and managers can perform during training to improve learning and transfer.

Management

Managers can facilitate the transfer of training during training by showing their support for training. One way of doing this is to actually attend a training program. If managers cannot attend a training program, then they should consider speaking about the importance and relevance of the training at the start of a program or participating as a trainer if possible. At the very least, they should visit the session at some time to show their support.[26]

It also helps if managers have already taken a training program. Managers are more likely to support training if they have been trained or have participated as trainers in a training program. In this way, managers can both model the behaviour and observe its occurrence. Senior executives at Vancouver-based Finning Ltd., the world's largest Caterpillar dealer, are the first to attend training and help deliver the training.[27] This cascading effect tells employees that management is serious about learning and the application of new skills on the job. In addition, when managers are required to teach the new skills, they learn them very well. They are also aware that their employees are watching them to see if they practise what they preach.

There are also a number of things that management can do to assist employees while they are away from work and attending a training program. For example, they can reassign some of their workload so that they don't have to worry about falling behind while they are being trained. They can also ensure that trainees will not be interrupted during training. This not only puts trainees at ease while they are being trained, but it also signals to employees that management supports training and considers it a high priority.

Trainer

As described earlier, there are several ways to design training programs to improve and facilitate the transfer of training. In particular, training programs should include active practice and the conditions of practice (e.g., task sequencing, feedback and knowledge of results), adult learning principles (e.g., problem centred focus, use of work-related experience), as well as principles of learning such as identical elements, general principles, and stimulus variability.

Trainers can also increase trainee's motivation to learn during training. This can be done by explaining the future value of a skill and by using training content and examples that are familiar and meaningful to trainees.[28] Trainees learn and remember meaningful material more easily than material unrelated to their work.[29] Trainers can use information, problems, and anecdotes collected from the needs analysis to provide the link between training material and work situations. New material should be introduced using terms and examples familiar to trainees.

Trainees

There a number of things that trainees can do during training to maximize their learning. First, trainees should begin a training program with a positive attitude and a willingness and motivation to learn. During the actual training program, trainees should actively engage themselves by taking notes, participating in discussions and exercises, asking and answering questions, and interacting with the trainer and the other trainees.

Before leaving a training program, trainees should develop an action plan for the application of training on the job and be prepared to discuss their learning and plan of action with their supervisor and co-workers. These activities should help to maximize trainee learning and facilitate the transfer of training.

Transfer of Training Activities After Training

After a training program, trainees are often motivated to try to use their new skills on the job. However, only some are able to do so successfully. Some will stop trying after a few attempts because they receive no support or reinforcement for the use of their new knowledge and skills on the job. Others will give up because they encounter barriers and obstacles that make it difficult if not impossible for them to apply their new knowledge and skills on the job. Still others will give up just because the old ways of doing things are easier and faster. Therefore, it is extremely important that managers, trainers, and trainees participate in post-training activities that facilitate the transfer of training.

Management

Transfer of training can be inhibited by the "bubble" syndrome, in which the trainee is expected to use the new skills without support from the environment.[30] Management can burst the bubble by ensuring that the time between training and on-the-job application is minimal, and by providing trainees with support and reinforcement for the use and application of their new knowledge and skills on the job.

One of the most important things that managers can do following a training program is ensure that employees have immediate and frequent opportunities to practice and apply what they learned in training on the job. Assignments and opportunities to try new skills should be given as soon as trainees return from a training program. Managers can also help by allowing trainees time to try or even experiment with new behaviours without adverse consequences.

In addition to providing employees with opportunities to transfer, managers must also encourage and reinforce the application of new skills on the job. In fact, one of the major reasons for a lack of transfer is that reinforcement is usually infrequent or nonexistent. Behaviour that is not reinforced is not repeated. If the sales representative dutifully submits the reports as learned in training but no one even notices they are filed, then the representative will waste no further energy doing this task.

A Xerox study showed that only 13 percent of trainees were using their new skills six months after training when management did not coach and support their use.[31] Therefore, managers must reward and reinforce employees for using new skills and behaviours acquired in training on the job. Trainees who use new skills on the job should be provided with praise, recognition, positive feedback, more challenging assignments, additional opportunities for training, and other extrinsic rewards. This not only directly reinforces employees for their transfer behaviour, but it also sends a signal to other employees that training is important and learning and transfer will be rewarded. In effect, it helps to create a positive transfer climate.

There are many other things that managers can do to facilitate transfer such as the development of an action plan for transfer, reducing job pressures and workload, arranging for co-workers to be briefed by trainees about a training program, arranging practice sessions, publicizing successes, giving promotional preference to employees who have received training, and evaluating employees' use of trained skills on the job.[32] Calgary-based Western Gas Marketing, Ltd., a subsidiary of TransCanada PipeLines Ltd., rates their managers on the application of new skills on their performance-appraisal form.[33]

Trainer

There are a number of things that a trainer can do after a training program to improve the transfer of training. One of the most important things a trainer can do is provide an intervention at the end of the content portion of a training program that is designed specially for the purpose of improving the transfer of training. These interventions are known as transfer enhancement procedures (TEPs) or posttraining transfer interventions. Three transfer enhancement procedures are relapse prevention, self-management, and goal-setting.

Relapse Prevention

Relapse prevention

A post-training transfer intervention that teaches trainees to anticipate transfer obstacles in the work environment that might make transfer difficult and to develop coping skills and strategies to overcome them

Relapse prevention (RP) interventions teach trainees to anticipate transfer obstacles and high risk situations in the work environment that might make transfer difficult and to develop coping skills and strategies to overcome them. A relapse occurs when trainees revert back to using the old skills or pre-training behaviour. Relapse prevention sensitizes trainees to the possibilities of a relapse and "immunizes" them against obstacles in the environment that might cause one.[34] It sensitizes trainees to barriers in the workplace that might inhibit or prevent them from successful transfer. The technique was adapted from programs for treating addictive behaviours such as smoking, drugs, and alcohol.

Relapse prevention interventions make trainees aware that relapse can occur and that temporary slips are normal. Trainees are asked to identify obstacles and barriers to transfer and high-risk situations in which a relapse is likely to occur. Some high-risk situations that might lead to a relapse are time pressure and deadlines, work overload, lack of necessary tools, equipment, and resources, and the lack of opportunities to apply trained skills on the job.[35] For each barrier or high-risk situation, trainees develop a coping strategy. For example, if workers think they will abandon their new skills when there is too much work, time-management techniques could be discussed and used to prevent a relapse. In this way, trainees are prepared to anticipate and prevent relapses and recover from temporary lapses.

Relapse prevention programs do make a difference. Trainees who receive training in relapse prevention have higher levels of course knowledge and use the knowledge on the job more than trainees who do not receive it. Relapse prevention has also been found to improve trainees' ability and desire to transfer. There is also some evidence that relapse prevention interventions are especially effective when the transfer climate is not very supportive of training.[36]

To find out how one company prepared trainees for transfer obstacles, see Training Today, "Improving Transfer at Delta Hotels and Resorts."

Self-Management

In Chapter 3 we discussed self-management as one of the components of social learning theory. We also noted that employees can be trained to learn how to manage their behaviour. **Self-management** interventions focus on behavioral change and usually involve teaching trainees to perform a series of steps to manage their transfer behaviour. The steps of self-management include anticipating performance obstacles, planning to overcome obstacles, setting goals to overcome obstacles, monitoring one's progress and rewarding oneself for goal attainment. A number of studies have shown that self-management results in greater skill generalization and higher performance on a transfer task.[37]

See The Trainer's Notebook 2 for a guide to implementing a self-management intervention.

Self-management

A post-training transfer intervention that teaches trainees to manage their transfer behaviour

Goal-Setting

In Chapter 3, we described goal-setting theory and its relevance for the design and effectiveness of training programs. Many studies have shown that individuals who set specific, difficult, and challenging goals achieve higher levels of performance.[38]

The importance of goal-setting for training has been the focus of many studies in recent years. From these studies, we know that learning and

Training Today

Improving Transfer at Delta Hotels and Resorts

At Delta Hotel and Resorts where employees are guaranteed ongoing training, the company expanded a one-day training program into a two-day program by adding practice sessions to each module and a final session for identifying roadblocks to on-the-job application. Trainees developed an action plan for those problems they could control and another plan for those they had only indirect control over. They also made a list of problems beyond their control that they presented to management.

In a group of 17 trainees of whom 10 were identified by trainers and managers as skeptics, an action plan was presented to Delta's general manager. A few weeks after the training ended, the trainees not only met their own objectives, but they challenged management to make the changes they suggested.

Examining roadblocks was a key part of the program. When trainees are asked to come up with reasons why they might not use the training, they are also likely to come up with solutions to overcome the roadblocks and use the training.

Source: Gardner, P. (1998, November). Cynics, snorters, doodlers and skeptics—whatcha gonna do? www.trainingreport.ca/articles/story.cfm?StoryID=88.

The Trainer's Notebook 2

A Guide for Implementing Self-management

A five-step self-management program, which has proven to be effective in increasing the transfer of training, consists of the following:

- *Identify performance obstacles.* Ask trainees to identify situations that make it difficult to apply the material in their work situations.
- *Plan to overcome obstacles.* After a group discussion of the obstacles, give trainees time to develop strategies to deal with the obstacles. As a group, prepare a list of do's and don'ts.

- *Set goals.* Ask trainees to set goals.
- *Self-monitor progress.* Based on their goals, require trainees to develop means of determining whether they met those goals.
- *Self-administer rewards.* Ask trainees to design a system for rewarding themselves if the goals are achieved.

Goal-setting intervention

An intervention that instructs trainees about the goal-setting process and how to set specific goals for the use of trained skills on the job

Performance contract

An agreement outlining how the newly learned skills will be applied on the job

Booster sessions

Extensions of training programs that involve periodic face-to-face contact between the trainer and trainees

transfer is more likely when trainees set specific and challenging goals. Therefore, it makes sense to introduce goal-setting into training as a post-training transfer intervention to improve transfer.

Goal-setting interventions teach trainees about the goal-setting process and to set specific goals for the use of trained skills on the job. Several studies have found that goal-setting interventions improve learning and the transfer of training.[39]

Something else trainers can do to facilitate transfer is to have trainees prepare a performance contract. A **performance contract** is a statement, mutually drafted by the trainee and the trainer near the end of a training program, that outlines which of the newly acquired skills are seen as beneficial and how they will be applied to the job. A copy can then be given to the trainer, a peer, or the supervisor, who will monitor progress toward these goals. Trainees could then submit progress reports to human resources and their supervisor. A variation on the timing (i.e., signing the contract jointly before a training program) alerts the trainee to the critical elements of the program and commits the supervisor to monitoring progress.[40] Trainees should also receive a follow-up report to training from the training department. They should know what will be expected and that these results will be discussed with their supervisors.

Trainers can also facilitate the transfer of training by scheduling follow-up or booster sessions. **Booster sessions** are extensions of training programs that involve periodic face-to-face contact between the trainer and trainees. They can involve a review of the training material and/or a discussion of some of the problems that trainees have had using their trained skills on the job as well their successes.

Ultimately, what is most important is that trainers continue to be involved in the transfer process after training. Besides follow-up and booster sessions, trainers should maintain their involvement in the training and transfer process by conducting field visits to observe trainees' use of trained skills, provide and solicit feedback, and provide continued support and assistance to trainees.[41]

Trainees

Following a training program, one of the first things that trainees should do is begin to use their new knowledge and skills on the job. Failure to use the training material when one returns to work is likely to result in a low likelihood of transfer. To ensure adequate opportunities for skill application and support, trainees should meet with their supervisor and discuss opportunities for transfer. Trainees might also benefit by establishing a "buddy system" or a network of peers who also attended a training program and can provide assistance and support as well as reinforce each other for using their trained skills on the job.[42] This can also help ensure that trainees persist in the application of trained skills on the job and avoid a relapse.

Finally, whether or not trainees receive a post-training transfer intervention, they should still try to incorporate each of the transfer enhancement procedures as part of their transfer strategy. That is, they should consider high-risk situations that might cause a relapse and develop strategies for overcoming them. They should also set goals for transfer and use self-management to manage their transfer behaviour. In other words, trainees should practise using their new skills on the job, monitor their transfer performance, and reward themselves for attaining their transfer goals.

Model of Training Effectiveness—Transfer of Training

Before concluding this chapter, let's return to the model of training effectiveness that was presented in Chapters 3 and 5. Recall that the model shows that: 1. trainee characteristics (i.e., cognitive ability, training motivation, personality, self-efficacy, and attitudes) and the conditions of practice have a direct effect on trainee learning and retention; 2. learning and retention have a direct effect on behaviour and performance; and 3. behaviour and performance have a direct effect on organizational effectiveness. We can now add a number of other links to the model based on the material presented in this chapter.

First, we can add a direct link from trainee characteristics and the work environment to individual behaviour and performance. This follows from Baldwin and Ford's model. We can also add a direct link from training design, which now includes learning principles (i.e., identical elements, stimulus variability, and general principles) in addition to active practice and the conditions of practice, to learning and retention. Thus, the model now shows that behaviour and performance (i.e., transfer) is influenced by learning and retention, trainee characteristics, and the work environment.

The final linkage in the model is from transfer behaviour and performance to organizational effectiveness. Recall that this linkage is known as vertical transfer. Vertical transfer refers to the link between individual-level

FIGURE 9.2

A Model of Training Effectiveness

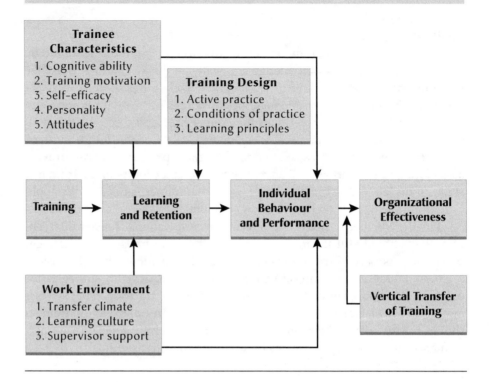

training outcomes and organizational outcomes. While a change and improvement in employees' behaviour and performance (i.e., horizontal transfer) is necessary for vertical transfer, it is important to realize that the relationship is not one-to-one. In other words, positive horizontal transfer does not guarantee vertical transfer.

Summary

This chapter described the transfer of training process with particular emphasis on the factors that influence the transfer of training. Baldwin and Ford's model of the transfer of training process was presented as a framework for understanding how to facilitate and improve the transfer of training. In addition, activities for improving the transfer of training at different time periods (before, during, and after training) and on the part of three main role players (management, trainer, and trainees) were described. It should be clear to you that the transfer of training is something that must be addressed throughout the training process—before, during, and after training. Furthermore, positive transfer of training is the responsibility of all of the major stakeholders and requires the involvement of management, trainers, and trainees. This means that improving the transfer of training requires a systematic program of activities and practices that involve all of the key players throughout the training process.

Key Terms

booster sessions (page 242)

general principles (page 229)

goal-setting intervention (page 242)

horizontal transfer (page 225)

identical elements (page 228)

learning culture (page 230)

performance contract (page 242)

readiness to learn/trainability (page 233)

relapse prevention (page 240)

self-management (page 241)

stimulus variability (page 229)

trainability test (page 234)

transfer climate (page 230)

transfer of training (page 225)

vertical transfer (page 225)

Weblinks

CIBC: www.cibc.com (page 235)

Delta Hotels and Resorts: www.deltahotels.com (page 241)

Finning Ltd.: www.finning.com (page 238)

Western Gas Marketing, Ltd.: www.transcanada.com (page 240)

Xerox: www.xerox.com (page 239)

Discussion Questions

1. Refer to Table 9.1, "Barriers to the Transfer of Training." For each of the barriers, describe what can be done in order to remove the barrier and facilitate the transfer of training. Be sure to indicate at what stage during the training process you would do something to remove the barrier (i.e., before, during, and/or after), and who would be involved (i.e., manager, trainer, and/or trainee).
2. Refer to the Health Partners chapter-opening vignette and describe the activities that might have facilitated the transfer of training. At what point during the training process were these activities implemented and who were the role players involved?
3. What is the difference between horizontal and vertical transfer and how are they related?

Using the Internet

1. To find out how to assess the transfer of training in an organization, go to **www.t2ed.com** and review the free stuff selection. Then select the Transfer of Training Evaluation Model (TOTEM) and review the sample page. Describe what TOTEM is and how it works. What do the scales measure and how can they help an organization evaluate and improve the transfer of training?

2. Psychologists can use personality and interest tests to determine whether employees have the interests and traits to benefit from training. These tests have to be validated for the training courses in your organizations, and in most cases, must be administered by a psychologist. However, you can see what tests look like and complete some online by going to **www.2h.com**. Scan the list of inventories, tests, and surveys and identify those that might be useful for predicting success in a training program. What tests do you think would be useful for testing an employee's trainability and why?

Exercises

1. After the final exam, do students forget 90 percent of what they learn in their courses? How could you design an educational experience for students so that they would remember and use 90 percent of the material learned in the classroom?
2. Think about the most recent training experience you had in a current or previous job. What did you learn and to what extent did you apply what you learned on the job? Did you transfer immediately after training? Six months after training? One year after training? What factors do you think explain why you did or did not transfer what you learned in training on the job? Is there anything that the trainer or your supervisor could have done to increase your chances of transfer? Is there anything you could have done yourself to improve your transfer? (Note: This exercise can also be done by interviewing somebody about their training experiences, e.g., another member of the class, a friend or family member.)
3. Students acquire a great deal of knowledge and information from their courses but does this learning transfer to their work experiences? Describe any courses you have taken that did actually result in transfer from school to work. What factors do you think contributed to your transfer and could they be used in the design of other courses?
4. Describe how you would use the principles of identical elements, general principles, and stimulus variability to improve the learning and transfer of your courses. In other words, what should an instructor do to incorporate these learning principles into his/her classes?
5. Assume the role of a training consultant who has been hired by an organization with a transfer of training problem. Your task is to conduct a diagnosis of the transfer system to find out why there is a transfer problem. Therefore, you need to develop a diagnostic tool to find out where the barriers exist. Using the material in this chapter, develop a series of questions that take into account the different time periods of the training process (i.e., before, during, and after), and the main role players (management, trainer, and trainees). What questions will you ask and who will you interview and/or survey?
6. Review the transfer enhancement procedures described in the chapter and then consider how they might be used to help students learn their

course material and apply it on the job. You could consider your course on training and development or perhaps a course on managerial skills. Your task is to design one of the following interventions: relapse prevention, self-management, or goal-setting. You can then either have another member of the class review your intervention and provide feedback or if time permits, deliver your intervention to the class.

7. To find out about transfer of training in an organization, contact the human resource department of an organization and ask the following questions:

    - To what extent do trainees apply what they learn in training on the job immediately after training, six months after training, and one year after training?

    - What are the main barriers or obstacles to transfer of training in your organization?

    - What kinds of things do you do to try to improve the transfer of training?

    - Are there things you do before, during, and after training to improve transfer?

    - What are the responsibilities of managers, trainers, and trainees for the transfer of training?

    - What have you found to be most effective for ensuring that trainees apply what they learn in training on the job?

Case

THE SCHOOL BOARD

Carlos daSilva was sitting at his desk in the training office, thinking about his meeting scheduled for 2 p.m. He was looking forward to the meeting with the superintendent of the school board, knowing that he would be praised for the multimedia interactive communications program he had designed.

For years, parents, students, and teachers had been complaining that nobody listened, that decisions were made without participation, and that good ideas went unacknowledged. A needs analysis (using a survey of teachers and students) had confirmed that these problems were widespread.

As a recently appointed trainer with a strong background in teaching, Carlos tackled the communications problem as his first assignment. He designed what he considered to be the finest three-day communications program in any school board. He had spent months on the design: finding videos, CD-ROMS, exercises, and games that taught active listening, upward communication, brainstorming, and other areas identified in the survey.

However, the meeting with the superintendent went poorly. Although some teachers loved playing with the latest teaching technology in the communications course, most did not change their behaviour at work. A second

Chapter 9: Transfer of Training

analysis showed that the old problems persisted. Carlos did not know what to say or what he would do.

Questions

1. What are some of the reasons why Carlos's training program did not transfer?
2. Discuss some of the barriers to transfer that might be operating at the school board.
3. Describe some of the things that Carlos might have done to improve the transfer of training before, during, and after the training.
4. What are some of the activities that Carlos might have the trainees and management do to improve the transfer of training?
5. Discuss the importance of horizontal and vertical transfer in the case. What type of transfer should Carlos be most concerned about and what should he do?

Running Case Part 5

VANDALAIS DEPARTMENT STORES

Refer to the Vandalais Department Stores case described in Chapter 5 and answer the following questions.

1. Discuss some of the barriers that might inhibit the transfer of the structured employment interview training program.
2. Design a transfer-of-training program by describing some of the activities before, during, and after training to improve the transfer of the structured employment interview training program. Be sure to indicate the role players involved.
3. Describe how you might use each of the following transfer enhancement procedures:
   - self-management
   - relapse prevention
   - goal-setting

   If you only had time to use one of these procedures, which one would you use and why?

References

[1]Kiger, P. J. (2002, November). Health partners delivers training that works. *Workforce, 81* (12), pp. 60–64.

[2]Baldwin, T.T., & Ford, J.K. (1988). Transfer of training: A review and directions for future research. *Personnel Psychology 41*, 63–105.

[3]Kozlowski, S. W. J., Brown, K. G., Weissbein, D. A., Cannon-Bowers, J. A., & Salas, E. (2000). A multilevel approach to training effectiveness: Enhancing horizontal and vertical transfer. In K. J. Klein & S.W.J. Kozlowski (Eds.), *Multilevel theory, research, and methods in organizations* (pp. 157–210). San Francisco: Jossey-Bass.

[4]Phillips. J. J., & Phillips, P. P. (2002, September). 11 reasons why training and development fails…and what you can do about it. *Training, 39* (9), 78–85.

[5]Saks, A.M., & Belcourt, M. (1997, September). Transfer of training in Canadian organizations. *Update,* 9–10.

[6]Baldwin, T.T., & Ford, J.K. (1988).

[7]Colquitt, J. A., Lepine, A., & Noe, R. A. (2000). Toward an integrative theory of training motivation: A meta-analytic path analysis of 20 years of research. *Journal of Applied Psychology, 85,* 678–707.

[8]Bass, B.M., & Vaughn, J.A. (1969). *Training in industry: The management of learning.* Belmont, CA: Wadsworth.

[9]Baldwin, T.T., & Ford, J.K. (1988).

[10]Baldwin, T.T., & Ford, J.K. (1988).

[11]Baldwin, T.T., & Ford, J.K. (1988).

[12]Baldwin, T.T., & Ford, J.K. (1988).

[13]Tannenbaum, S. I., & Yukl, G. (1992). Training and development in work organizations. *Annual Review of Psychology, 43,* 399–441.

[14]Baldwin, T.T., & Ford, J.K. (1988). Tannenbaum, S. I., & Yukl, G. (1992).

[15]Rouiller, J. Z., & Goldstein, I. L. (1993). The relationship between organizational transfer climate and positive transfer of training. *Human Resource Development Quarterly, 4,* 377–90.

[16]Tracey, J.B, Scott, I.T., & Kavanagh, M.J. (1995). Applying training on the job: The importance of the work environment. *Journal of Applied Psychology 80* (2), 239–52.

[17]DeSimone, R. L., Werner, J. M., & Harris, D. M. (2002). *Human Resource Development.* Harcourt, Inc.: Orlando, FL.

[18]Tannenbaum, S. I., & Yukl, G. (1992).

[19]Goldstein, I. L., & Ford, J. K. (2002). *Training in Organizations.* Wadsworth: Belmont, CA.

[20]Baldwin, T.T., & Magjuka, R.J. (1991). Organizational training and signals of importance: Linking pretraining perceptions to intentions to transfer. *Human Resource Development Quarterly, 2,* 25–36.

[21]William, T.C., Thayer, P.W., & Pond, S.B. (1991). Test of a model of motivational influences on reactions to training and learning. *Paper presented at the meeting of the Society for Industrial and Organizational Psychology,* St. Louis, MI.

[22]Hicks, W.D., & Klimoski, R.J. (1987). Entry into training programs and its effects on training outcomes: A field experiment. *Academy of Management Journal, 30,* 542–52.

[23]Broad, M.L., & Newstrom, J.W. (1992). *Transfer of training.* Reading, MA: Addison-Wesley.

[24]Baldwin, T.T., & Magjuka, R.J. (1991).

[25]Tannenbaum, S. I., & Yukl, G. (1992).

[26]Burke, L. A. (2001). Training transfer: Ensuring training gets used on the job. In L. A. Burke (Ed.), *High-Impact Training Solutions: Top Issues Troubling Trainers.* Quorum Books: Westport, CT.

[27]Clemmer, J. (1992, September 15). Why most training fails. *The Globe and Mail,* B26.

[28]Bass, B.M., & Vaughn, J.A. (1969).

[29]McGehee, W., & Thayer, P.W. (1961). *Training in business and industry.* New York: Wiley.

[30]Hatcher, T., & Schriver, R. (1991, November-December). Bursting the bubble that blocks training transfer. *Technical and Skills,* 12–15.

[31]Zucker, L. (1987). Institutional theories of organization. *Annual Review of Sociology 13,* 443–464.

[32]Broad, M.L., & Newstrom, J.W. (1992).

[33]Clemmer, J. (1992, September 15).

[34]Tziner, A., & Haccoun, R.R. (1991). Personal and situational characteristics influencing the effectiveness of transfer of training improvement strategies. *Journal of Occupational Psychology 64* (2), 167–77.

[35]Burke, L. A. (2001).

[36]Burke, L. A. (2001).

[37]Gist, M., Bavetta, A., & Stevens, C. (1990). Transfer training method: Its influence on skill generalization, skill repetition, and performance level. *Personnel Psychology, 43,* 501–23. Gist, M., Stevens, C., & Bavetta, A. (1991). Effects of self-efficacy and post-training intervention on the acquisition and maintenance of complex interpersonal skills. *Personnel Psychology, 44,* 837–61.

[38]Locke, E.A., & Latham, G.P. (1990). *A theory of goal setting and task performance.* Englewood Cliffs, NJ: Prentice-Hall.

[39]Richman-Hirsch, W. L. (2001). Posttraining interventions to enhance transfer: The moderating effects of work environments. *Human Resource Development Quarterly, 12,* 105–20. Wexley, K.N., & Nemeroff, W.F. (1975). Effectiveness of positive reinforcement and goal setting as methods of management development. *Journal of Applied Psychology 60,* 446–50.

[40]Leifer, M.S., & Newstrom, J.W. (1980, August). Solving the transfer of training problems. *Training and Development Journal,* 34–46.

[41]Burke, L. A. (2001).

[42]Baldwin, T.T., & Ford, J.K. (1988). Burke, L. A. (2001).

Chapter 10

Training Evaluation

Chapter Learning Objectives

After reading this chapter, you should be able to:

- define training evaluation and the main reasons for conducting evaluations
- discuss the barriers to evaluation and the factors that affect whether or not an evaluation is conducted
- describe the different types of evaluations
- describe the models of training evaluation and the relationship between them
- describe the main variables to measure in a training evaluation and how they are measured
- discuss the different types of designs for training evaluation as well as their requirements, limits, and when they should be used

www.bell.ca

BELL CANADA

Years ago, when Bell Canada installed a new telephone system for its business clients, it also sent out service advisors whose task it was to train the employees to use the new system. These training sessions consisted of "show and tell" activities where the instructors demonstrated the use of the telephone. Simple as the training was it was expensive, costing millions of dollars annually. With the introduction of electronic equipment, the functionality of the telephone systems—and complexity for the users increased exponentially.

Initially the company attempted to use the traditional training approach with purchasers of the electronic systems. However, a training evaluation was conducted and it showed that the training was not effective. At the end of the training, customer knowledge of the operation of the electronic telephones was quite low.

A number of attempts were then made to improve the situation. Different types of training, presented by either Bell Canada or user personnel did not make any significant difference in terms of training effectiveness.

However, these training evaluation studies did detect an important fact. No matter how training was conducted, the user's knowledge of a limited number of functions—those they used a lot—increased after training, indicating that practice seemed to have a significant effect on learning.

This suggested that providing end users with an instructional aid might help them gain greater benefit from the electronic system. To that end, a special instruction booklet was prepared and trainees were provided with a brief instructional session teaching the users how to use the instruction booklet.

The results of the evaluation showed that the use of the instruction booklet resulted in greater user mastery than the formal training course. Thus, the training evaluation was very useful in a) demonstrating that the traditional training method was ineffective b) that changing the instructors had no effect but c) that the use of a well-developed instruction booklet had greater effect.

As a result of the evaluation, the traditional training program was discontinued and replaced with the much shorter instruction on the use of the booklet, thereby saving large amounts of money. Thus, the training evaluation paid off because it directly led to modifications to the instructional strategy and showed that a less expensive alternative (the booklet) was superior to the more expensive traditional approach (formal training).

Training programs are designed to have an effect on employee learning and behaviour, however, as the case at Bell Canada demonstrates, this is not always the case. Fortunately, an evaluation was conducted which indicated that the program was not effective. As a result, it was possible to make changes to improve the effectiveness of the training program.

In this chapter, you will learn about the evaluation of training and development programs. In particular, you will learn about the different variables to measure and how to measure them, as well as the different designs for conducting a training evaluation.

What is Training Evaluation?

Training programs may be launched for a number of reasons: they may be used to improve competencies (e.g., learning the use of a new software), to modify attitudes (e.g., preparing a manager posted to an international assignment), and/or to modify behaviours (e.g., leadership training). Organizations invest in improving employee competencies, attitudes, and behaviours because such improvements are expected to lead to positive results for organizations (e.g., improved productivity).

Training evaluation is concerned with whether or not these expected outcomes materialize as a result of training. They are designed to assist decision-making about training programs: Should the organization cancel or continue a training program? Should an existing training program be modified? How should it be modified?

Training evaluation is a process designed to assess the value—the worthiness—of training programs to employees and to organizations. Training evaluation assesses this value by analyzing data collected from trainees, supervisors or others familiar with the trainees and with the job context. Using a variety of techniques, objective and subjective information is gathered before, during, and after training to provide the data required to estimate the value of a training program.

Training evaluation is not a single procedure. Rather, it is a continuum of techniques, methods, and measures that inform management about the value of training programs. At one end of the continuum lie simple procedures that are easy to implement and that can provide some potentially useful information about the value of a training program. Asking participants how much they enjoyed a training program is one example of a simple evaluation procedure. However, the information that such a procedure provides and the conclusions that can be reached are limited.

At the other end of the training evaluation continuum lie more elaborate procedures. These procedures provide managers with more information of a richer quality regarding the value of a training program. A more involved training evaluation might assess how much of the trained skills trainees apply on the job (i.e., transfer of training) and how much performance improvement has resulted from the training effort. More extensive training evaluations might be used to diagnose the training program's success in

Training evaluation
A process to assess the value–the worthiness–of training programs to employees and to organizations

enhancing key psychological factors, such as trainee motivation and self-efficacy. Some evaluation designs can even estimate the specific contribution of training to any changes observed in the organization, sometimes in dollar terms. The more sophisticated the design, the more complete the information, the better the conclusions and the greater the confidence with which they can be stated.

However, more sophisticated evaluation procedures are more costly and more complex to implement. Hence, the quality and completeness of the information gathered involves a trade-off with the costs and complexity of the techniques chosen. In some cases, less sophisticated evaluation procedures may be quite suitable while in other cases the same procedures will not yield useful information.[1] Conversely, very sophisticated procedures required in one situation might be overkill in another. The key is that the specific training evaluation procedures required depends on the specifics of the training situation and on the decisions that need to be made as a result of that evaluation.

Why Conduct Training Evaluations?

The evaluation of training programs and systems is done for many reasons. In the contemporary business environment, understaffing is chronically prevalent. With little time available for training, it is critical that employees and organizations waste little of it on unprofitable training programs. Guided by evaluation results, it is a managerial responsibility to improve training. Training evaluation is therefore of value to:

- Assist managers in identifying the training program most applicable to employees and to assist management in the determination of who should be trained.
- Determine the cost-benefits of a program and to help ascertain which program or training technique is most cost-effective (see Chapter 11).
- Determine if the training program has achieved the expected results or solved the problem for which training was the anticipated solution.
- Diagnose the strengths and weaknesses of a program and pinpoint needed improvements.
- Use the evaluation information to justify and reinforce the value and credibility of the training function to the organization.

Although in practice, training evaluation in most organizations has not changed much in the last thirty years, there are signs that things are beginning to change.[2] A recent survey by the American Society for Training and Development—the major professional association in the field—has begun to formally monitor evaluation activities of organizations. This signals a growing interest in evaluation as a mechanism for improving training and development.

Barriers to Training Evaluation

Because of the usefulness of training evaluation, many organizations conduct some form of evaluation for most of their training programs. A recent survey conducted by the American Society for Training and Development (ASTD) showed that 75 percent of the organizations evaluate their training programs.[3] The overwhelming majority of training evaluations are simple, limited to trainee reactions. Less than 20 percent of organizations evaluate changes in job performance. A survey of Canadian training evaluation practices found a similar pattern of results.[4]

Studies of training professionals showed that many employers do not conduct training evaluations because they are perceived to be too complicated to implement, too time consuming, and/or too expensive.[5] Some training managers do not conduct evaluations because top management does not demand them and because it is difficult to isolate the effects of training among many other variables that might also be having an effect on employees and the organization. Thus, barriers to training evaluation fall into two categories: pragmatic and political.

Pragmatic Barriers to Training Evaluation

Evaluating training programs requires knowledge about research design, measurement, and data analysis. Understandably, some training managers feel insecure about taking on such a task. However, the training evaluation process has been unduly mystified. The principles, techniques, and procedures involved in training evaluation are logical and straightforward, and most can be easily implemented. Moreover, training evaluations require that information (objective and/or perceptual measures) about trainees be gathered from the trainees, their supervisors, and/or co-workers, and in some cases even by subordinates. These measures are sometimes collected before and after training as well as after trainees return to the job. Valuable training and job time needs to be diverted to these data collection tasks, and many managers hesitate or are unable to tax the organizational resources for the purpose of evaluation. However, with the advent of modern information technologies (e.g., Web-based questionnaires and computerized work performance data) the disruptive impact of data collection can now be seriously eased.

Political Barriers to Training Evaluation

Evaluations are conducted when there is pressure from management to do so (see Training Today). In the absence of such pressures, many training managers would rather forego the exercise. One risk associated with training evaluation is that they might demonstrate that part of or an entire training program is not effective. Whereas this should be considered a valuable finding, it remains that some trainers fear that negative evaluation results might reflect poorly on them, the training function, and the training choices they make. Moreover, some trainers do not conduct evaluations themselves because this might be perceived as a conflict of interest (how can the person doing the training also be the one responsible for evaluating its effectiveness?). As a result, many feel that evaluations should be conducted by an external professional thus siphoning funds from the training budget. Diverting training money to cover evaluation costs is a choice that, understandably, many training managers find difficult. However, as long as training managers make use of the established methods of evaluation and document them, there is little ground for concern about conflict of interest.

⓭⓮⓯

Types of Training Evaluation

Most training evaluations focus on the impact of a training program on trainees' perceptions and behaviours. Perceptions are assessed through questionnaire measures while behavioural data may require a combination of techniques including self-reports, observation, and performance data. Evaluations may be distinguished from each other with respect to: 1) the data gathered and analyzed, and 2) the fundamental purpose for which the evaluation is being conducted.

Training Today

Upper Management's Role in Training Evaluation

A few years ago there was a rash of serious accidents among employees of a large transportation company. Some of these accidents were the direct or indirect result of operator errors due to the consumption of drugs and alcohol. As a result, the firm declared a zero tolerance policy towards the use of such substances. The policy required that no employee may use substances that may impair effective and safe job performance whether or not these substances are legal. The key element of the policy was that all supervisors were directly and personally responsible for enforcing the policy. Supervisors who failed to enforce the policy would themselves be subject to sanctions that could include dismissal.

The training department was directed to develop and administer a training program to all supervisory and managerial personnel in the company. However, the CEO of the company also insisted that the training program be evaluated to ensure that it was effective. As a result,

the training department, which normally only administered "smile sheets" to evaluate their training programs, launched a much more sophisticated training evaluation program that included three measurement times and the collection of information on dozens of variables. Clearly, this effort was launched because the training program had attained high visibility and because top management demanded it. The training evaluation did uncover some problems with the training program and suggested a number of changes. However, none of these changes were ever implemented. This occurred because top management showed no interest in the results of the evaluation study, as these became available several months after the training program was administered.

The moral of the story is that high level visibility can stimulate evaluation actions. But maintaining that visibility is important to ensure that the evaluation results will prove of practical use.

1. **The data gathered and analyzed:** Evaluations differ with respect to the type of information that is gathered and how that is accomplished.

   a. The most common training evaluations rely *on trainee perceptions at the conclusion of training* (did the participants like it?) while more sophisticated evaluations go further to analyze the extent of trainee learning and the posttraining behaviour of trainees.

   b. More recently there has been a growing emphasis on evaluation studies that also assess the *psychological forces* that operate during training programs and that impact outcome measures such as learning and behaviour change. Research in this area has helped to identify psychological states (affective, cognitive, and skills based) that are important training outcomes because of the influence they have on learning as well as to improvements in job behaviours.[6]

   c. Finally, information about the *work environment* to which the trainee returns can be useful in evaluation.[7] For example, measures of training transfer climate and a learning culture have been developed.[8] Training programs provided by organizations that rank higher on these dimensions tend to be more effective. Specific organizational events and policies—such as the on-the-job opportunities to practice new skills or trainee expectations about the type of support they will receive on the job have been found to influence training success.[9] One study showed that (self-reported) transfer of training was higher for trainees who perceived a strong alignment between training and the firm's strategic vision.[10]

2. **The purpose of the evaluation:** Evaluations also differ with respect to their purposes. Worthen and Sanders distinguished between *formative evaluation* and *summative evaluation*.[11]

   a. **Formative training evaluations** are designed to help evaluators assess the value of the training materials and processes (e.g., the clarity, complexity, and relevance of the training contents, how they are presented, and the training context). Hence, formative evaluation provides data that is useful to training designers and instructors because its key goal is program improvement.

   b. **Summative evaluations** are designed to provide data about a training program's worthiness or effectiveness. Cost-benefit analyses (see Chapter 11) are usually summative. Economic indices are often an integral and important part of these types of evaluations. Consequently, training managers show great interest in these results.

   A further distinction can be made between *descriptive* and *causal evaluations*. **Descriptive evaluations** provide information describing the trainee once they have completed the program. What has the trainee learned in training? Is the trainee more confident about using the skill? Is it used on the job? Most evaluation designs have descriptive components. **Causal evaluations** are used to determine if the training caused the posttraining behaviours. Causal evaluations require more sophisticated experimental and statistical procedures.

Formative evaluations
Provide data about various aspects of a training program

Summative evaluations
Provide data about the worthiness or effectiveness of a training program

Descriptive evaluations
Provide information that describes the trainee once they have completed a training program

Causal evaluations
Provide information to determine if training *caused* the posttraining behaviours

Models of Training Evaluation

Models of training evaluation specify the information (the variables) that needs to be measured in training evaluation and their interrelationships. The dominant training evaluation model is Donald Kirkpatrick's hierarchical model.[12] It proposes that training evaluation involves four levels or key outcomes: trainee reactions (level 1), learning (level 2), behaviours (level 3), and results (level 4). Levels 1 to 3 focus on the effects of training on trainees while level 4 focuses on the effects of training on the organization.

However, research and practical experience has indicated that Kirkpatrick's model can be improved. The Decision-Based Evaluation model and the COMA model are two recent models that we will also describe.[13]

®℗©

Kirkpatrick's Hierarchical Model: The Four Levels of Training Evaluation

Donald Kirkpatrick's hierarchical model is the best known and most frequently used training evaluation model. It identifies four "levels" of training evaluation criteria. A program is "effective" when:

1. Trainees report positive "reactions" to a training program (reactions).
2. Trainees learn the training material (learning).
3. Trainees apply what they learn in training on the job (behaviour).
4. Training has a positive effect on organizational outcomes (results).

The model states that the four levels are arranged in a "hierarchy" such that each succeeding level provides more important information than the previous level. The model also assumes that all levels are positively related to one another and that each level has a causal effect on the next level. Hence, positive trainee reactions (level I) cause trainees to learn more (level II), which in turn increases on the job behaviour of the new skill (level III), and behavioural change, in turn, impacts organizational effectiveness (level IV)—the ultimate reason for conducting training in organizations. Thus, a complete training evaluation would assess all four levels.

Critique of Kirkpatrick's Model

Kirkpatrick's contribution to training evaluation cannot be underestimated. It has contributed to the greater use of evaluation in organizations. The model provides a systematic framework for assessing training that has guided countless evaluation projects. Its apparent simplicity, clarity, and good sense has helped demystify training evaluation.

However, a number of recent research studies, especially those conducted by Elwood Holton and by George Alliger and his colleagues have thrown doubt about the validity of the hierarchical model.[14] For example, one can like a training program and learn little or one may learn a great deal during training and not necessarily translate this knowledge into on-the-job behaviour changes.

The model has also been criticized for its lack of precision: what exactly is meant by "reactions" or knowledge? (See section "Training Evaluation Variables.") Those who have studied the model's practicality have pointed out that the model may not be sufficiently diagnostic. For example, knowing that training leads to little behaviour change does not tell us why or what can be done about it. But perhaps the most important critique has been that Kirkpatrick requires *all* training evaluations to rely on the same variables and outcome measures. The current view is that the type of evaluation, as well as the measures and procedures, should be selected as a function of the organizational situation and the purposes of the evaluation. One model does not fit all training evaluation situations.

COMA Model

Haccoun, Jeanrie, and Saks proposed the **COMA** model as a mechanism for enhancing the usefulness of training evaluation questionnaires by identifying and measuring those variables that research has shown to be important for transfer of training.[15] Instead of relying exclusively on reaction and declarative learning measures, COMA suggests the measurement of variables that fall into four categories: Cognitive, organizational environment, motivational, and attitudinal variables.

COMA

A training evaluation model that involves the measurement of **C**ognitive, **O**rganizational, **M**otivational, and **A**ttitudinal variables

Cognitive Variables

Cognitive variables refer to the level of learning that the trainee has gained from a training program. Both declarative and procedural learning might be measured but the latter is more important because it is more strongly related to transfer than the former.

Organizational Environment

Organizational environment refers to a cluster of variables that are generated by the work environment and that impact transfer of training. This includes the opportunity to practice and the degree of support that is provided to trainees to help make more extensive and better use of trained skills on the job.

Motivation to Transfer

Motivation to transfer refers to the desire to transfer on the job what was learned in training. As indicated in Chapter 9, motivation has been shown to be a powerful and persistent influence on the transfer of training. A distinction can be made between motivation to learn, which was described in Chapter 3, and the motivation to transfer.

Attitudes

Attitudes refer to individuals' feelings and thinking processes. Chief among these beliefs are self-efficacy, perceptions of control, and expectations about self and the environment.

Therefore, according to the COMA model, training evaluation should assess the degree to which, immediately after training, a) trainees have mastered the skills ("**C**"); b) trainees perceive that the "organizational environment" (including peers and supervisors) will support and help them apply the skills ("**O**"); c) trainees are motivated to apply the skills on the job ("**M**"); and d) trainees share attitudes and beliefs that allow them to feel capable of applying their newly acquired skills on the job ("**A**").

Decision-Based Evaluation Model

Decision-Based Evaluation (DBE) is a model recently proposed by Kurt Kraiger. As with the Kirkpatrick and COMA model, Decision-Based Evaluation specifies the variables to be measured. However, it goes further than either of the two preceding models in that, a) DBE identifies the *target* of the evaluation (what do we wish to find out from the evaluation); b) its *focus* (what are the variables we will measure); and c) it suggests the *methods* that may be appropriate for conducting the evaluation.

For example, the model specifies three potential "targets" for the evaluation: Trainee change, organizational pay-off, and program improvement. If trainee change is of consequence, the evaluator is directed to specify the "focus" of the change: Are we interested in assessing the level of trainee changes with respect to learning, behaviours, or to the psychological states (such as motivation and self-efficacy). Each evaluation study may include one or more foci. Once the focus or foci are selected, the model suggests the appropriate data collection method (e.g., surveys, job sample information, objective data etc).

Decision-Based Evaluation is a marked improvement, for different reasons, over both Kirkpatrick's model and the COMA model. Unlike Kirkpatrick's model, it identifies and ties the specific variables that should be measured in the evaluation (focus) depending on the chosen target. Unlike COMA, DBE is general to any evaluation goals (targets), not just transfer of training. Further, it is the only model that also specifies the types of methods that can be used for an evaluation. And most importantly, DBE is a more flexible model. It does not advocate a *one best way* for training evaluation nor does it compel the measurement of a single set of variables (as do Kirkpatrick and COMA) for all evaluations. DBE is the only training evaluation model that clearly specifies that evaluations should and must always be guided by a key question: What is the target of the evaluation?

Training Evaluation Variables

Training evaluation requires that data be collected on important aspects of training. These variables have been identified in the training evaluation models. Table 10.1 lists the main variables that are measured in training evaluation and how they are measured.

Training evaluation variables are relatively easy to construct. In this section, we will review some of the basic techniques and formats that may be used to construct them. Table 10.2 shows sample questions and formats for measuring each type of variable.

TABLE 10.1

The Main Variables Measured in Training Evaluation

VARIABLE	DEFINITION	HOW MEASURED
Reactions	Trainee perceptions of the program and/or specific aspects of the course.	Questionnaires, focus groups, interviews.
Learning	Trainee acquisition of the program material. Declarative learning is knowing the information. Procedural knowledge is being able to translate that knowledge into a behavioural sequence.	Multiple choice or True-False tests (declarative); situational and mastery tests (procedural).
Behaviour	On-the-job behaviour display, objective performance measures.	Self-reports, supervisory reports, direct and indirect observations, production records.
Motivation	Trainee desire to learn and/or transfer skills.	Questionnaires.
Self-efficacy	Trainee confidence in learning and/or behaviour display on the job.	Questionnaires.
Perceived and/or anticipated support	The assistance trainees obtain and/or the assistance trainees expect.	Questionnaires.
Organizational perceptions	How trainees perceive the organization's culture and climate for learning and transfer.	Standardized questionnaires.
Organizational results	The impact of training on organizational outcomes.	Organizational records.

Reactions

Trainee opinions and attitudes about a training program are usually measured immediately following training. Typically, they are survey type questions in which trainees indicate their answers on a rating scale. Reaction measures are easy to administer, collect, and analyze, and the questions may focus on the trainees overall reactions to a training program (e.g., Overall, how satisfied were you with the training program?) and/or on specific elements of a program (e.g., To what degree were you satisfied with the instructor?).

In a major study involving thousands of responses to reaction questionnaires, Morgan and Casper identified six dimensions that underlie reaction measures: satisfaction with the instructor, the training process, the materials, the course structure, the assessment process, and the perceived usefulness (utility) of the training.[16]

TABLE 10.2

Measuring Training Evaluation Variables

VARIABLE	EXAMPLE OF QUESTION	EXAMPLE OF ANSWER FORMAT
Reactions	"How much of the course content can be applied in your job?" (utility reaction measure) "How satisfied were you with the content of the program?" (affective reaction measure)	1 = None; 2 = Little; 3 = Some; 4 = Much; 5 = All. 1 = Not at all satisfied, 2 = Not satisfied, 3 = Somewhat satisfied, 4 = Satisfied, 5 = Very satisfied
Learning	Declarative: True or False: The earth is square. Multiple choice: What statement best describes the earth? Procedural Mastery: You need to write a letter using a computer. From the list below pick the four steps required to do so and list them in the order with which they should be performed.	Declarative True ___ False ___ Multiple choice: round, square, triangular, flat. Procedural Step Required Order Turn computer on Yes 1 Set the margins Yes 4 Select "new document" Yes 3 Open the word processor Yes 2 Test the hard drive No —
Behaviour	Self-report: How many "cold calls" have you made in the last week? Observation: By others including the supervisor and the analyst. May also include subordinates or customers.	Open-ended frequency scale (number of times) or rating scale: Always, Sometimes, Rarely, Never.

TABLE 10.2 *(Continued)*

VARIABLE	EXAMPLE OF QUESTION	EXAMPLE OF ANSWER FORMAT
Motivation	How important is it to reduce accidents at work?	1 = Very important; 2 = important 3 = neither important nor unimportant 4 = somewhat unimportant 5 = very unimportant
	The consequences to you of applying the behaviour at work?	Will make my job 1 = much harder, 2 = somewhat harder, 3 = no effect, 4 = somewhat easier, 5 = much easier
	How likely is it that if you do apply the trained behaviours there will be fewer accidents?	1 = extremely likely, 2 = somewhat likely, 3 = neither likely nor unlikely, 4 = unlikely, 5 = extremely unlikely.
	The product of the three sets of questions produces the motivation scores.	
Self-efficacy	How confident are you that you can explain the new policy to your subordinates?	1, not at all confident 2, 3, 4, to 5 very confident.
Perceived and/or anticipated support	I expect that my supervisor will help and support me in my attempts to apply my new skills on the job.	1 = completely disagree, 2, 3, 4, to 5 = completely agree.
Organizational perceptions	Supervisors give recognition and credit to those who apply new knowledge and skills to their work.	Standardized questionnaires
Organizational results	How much has quality improved as a result of the training program?	Number of units rejected per day; Number of items returned per month; Number of customer complaints per week.

Reaction measures can be quite different, but two types have received the most attention: affective and utility reaction measures. **Affective reactions** assess trainees' *likes and dislikes* of a training program. **Utility reactions** refer to the perceived *usefulness* of a training program.

Whereas trainers are interested in the likes and dislikes of trainees (affective reactions), research has shown that affective reaction measures bear little relationship to other important training outcomes including learning and behaviour. On the other hand, *utility* reaction measures are related to learning and behaviour.[17] Hence, collecting utility reactions is important because they tell us more about whether or not the trainee will transfer newly acquired skills to the job than do affective reactions.

Irrespective of the type of reaction measure used, they can be collected in a number of ways. The most common method is a questionnaire that is administered at the end of a training program. The questions are listed on one

Affective reactions

Reaction measures that assess trainees' *likes and dislikes* of a training program

Utility reactions

Reaction measures that assess the perceived *usefulness* of a training program side of the page and a rating scale is placed next to each question (see Table 10.3 for an example). However, reactions can also be measured by open-ended discussions with trainees using focus groups or interviews though such an approach might prove to be more expensive and time consuming and more subject to the biases of the interviewer.

The questions and the answers may be formatted in any number of different ways: a) in the form of a statement (e.g., "The course materials captured my interest") for which the trainee indicates his/her degree of agreement (strongly agree, agree, neither agree nor disagree, disagree, strongly disagree) or b) in the form of direct questions (e.g., "How effective was the instructor?") to which the trainee chooses a response from a linear rating scale (very effective, effective, moderately effective, somewhat ineffective, very ineffective). Most rating scales have between four and seven response choices though more or fewer points can be used.

Reaction measures are useful for a number of reasons. First, because they are obtained at the completion of a training program, they provide trainers with immediate feedback and allow them to make quick adjustments. As well, positive feedback can signal to management and employees that the program is worthwhile and effective. A second benefit of reaction measures is that trainees who have had a chance to comment on a program, make suggestions for improvements, and indicate how useful the program is for their job, might be more motivated to transfer their learning than others who leave a program without providing input. Moreover, immediate posttraining questionnaires may be improved by assessing, in addition to utility reactions, the variables identified through the COMA model.

Learning

Although there are many types of learning outcomes that can be measured (Jonassen and Tessmer identify more than 10!), most training evaluations measure "declarative" learning.[18] In rare cases some evaluators also assess "procedural" learning. The contents of both the declarative and procedural learning measures are selected from the training content.

Declarative learning is by far the most frequently assessed learning measure. It refers to the acquisition of facts and information. **Procedural learning** involves the organization of facts and information into a smooth behavioural sequence. Research has shown that declarative learning has only a minor effect on behaviours. Procedural learning, however, is more strongly related to a number of training outcomes including transfer of training.

Declarative learning is usually assessed with multiple choice or true-false type questions. Students are quite familiar with these types of questions as they are most frequently found on university and college examinations. Table 10.4 presents an array of these options. The test items listed in Part A are termed objectively scored tests because there is only one correct answer possible. Part B gives some examples of subjectively scored test items. Test items that are considered subjective are essay questions, oral interviews, journals, and diaries. Here, several answers might be acceptable, and markers have some latitude in their interpretation of the correctness of the answer.

Declarative learning

Refers to the acquisition of facts and information and is by far the most frequently assessed learning measure

Procedural learning

Refers to the organization of facts and information into a smooth behavioural sequence

TABLE 10.3

Reactions Rating Form

Course or Session: _____

Instructor: _____

Content:

Please answer the following questions using the scale below:

1. disagree strongly 2. disagree 3. neither disagree nor agree 4. agree 5. strongly agree

_____ The material presented will be useful to me on the job.

_____ The level of information was too advanced for my work.

_____ The level of information presented was too elementary for me.

_____ The information was presented in manageable chunks.

_____ Theories and concepts were linked to work activities.

_____ The course material was up to date and reliable.

Instructor:

Please rate the instructor's performance along the following dimensions:

_____ Needs improvement

_____ Just right, or competent, effective

_____ Superior or very effective performance

The Instructor:

_____ Described the objectives of the session.

_____ Had a plan for the session.

_____ Followed the plan.

_____ Determined trainees' current knowledge.

_____ Explained new terms.

_____ Used work and applied examples.

_____ Provided opportunities for questions.

_____ Was enthusiastic about the topic.

_____ Presented material clearly.

_____ Effectively summarized the material.

_____ Varied the learning activities.

_____ Showed a personal interest in class progress.

_____ Demonstrated a desire for trainees to learn.

Perceived Impact:

_____ I gained significant new knowledge.

_____ I developed skills in the area.

_____ I was given tools for attacking problems.

_____ My on-the-job performance will improve.

Please indicate what you will do differently on the job as a result of this course.

Overall Rating:

Taking into account all aspects of the course, how would you rate it?

_____ Excellent _____ Very Good _____ Good _____ Fair _____ Poor

Would you take another course from this instructor?   _____ Yes _____ No

Would you recommend this course to your colleagues? _____Yes _____ No

Procedural learning, however, is rarely measured because the development of such measures is much more complex. Desjardins developed a procedural learning measure for "protecting a crime scene" course given to police officers.[19] The police officers learned the do's and don'ts when called to a crime scene. She interviewed task experts that demonstrated the proper actions and proper sequence of behaviours required and then summarized these steps, added some unnecessary and incorrect steps, and shifted the order of the steps. Trainees had to 1) distinguish between the required and erroneous steps and 2) reposition them in the correct order. Completing this task successfully requires procedural understanding of the training content.

Cheri Ostroff used another approach to develop a measure of procedural learning.[20] Education managers were instructed on how to interact with parents more effectively in tense situations. Different situations were drawn from real experience and presented to trainees along with four different ways of handling each situation. The four options were carefully constructed. Trainees who had acquired a basic comprehension of the principles of conflict management would tend to select one option while those with sophisticated comprehension levels would select another. The intermediate choices reflected comprehension levels between these extremes.

Procedural learning measures can also involve simulations conducted in realistic situations. For example, a pilot could be tested in a virtual-reality airplane. The skills of a drug counsellor could be tested using actors as drug addicts. A test could be conducted as a role play (for negotiation skills) or a practice session (for tennis certification). These tests are usually called performance tests or work sample tests.

Learning measures also vary in terms of when they are administered. For example, some researchers have divided learning measures into three subcategories: (1) immediate posttraining knowledge, which measures trainee learning immediately after a training program, (2) knowledge retention, which measures trainee learning sometime after a training program, and (3) behaviour or skill demonstration, which measures trainees' ability to perform the training task during the training program.

Learning measures are useful for a number of reasons besides determining if trainees have learned the training material. For example, a testing hurdle anticipated at the end of a course increases trainee motivation to learn the material.[21] Trainees at General Dynamics took this hurdle seriously. Employees were not allowed access to the manufacturing resource planning software until they had passed a competency test.

The information that learning tests provide to trainers is invaluable. In cases of accidents and litigation, the employer can prove that the employee was trained to the necessary levels. Furthermore, if trainees consistently score low on some aspect of the course, the trainer is alerted to the fact that this component needs to be revised. More information may be required or exercises might have to be added to ensure that learning does occur. At General Dynamics, trainers became extremely motivated because the trainees had to learn and could not be brushed off by hinting that they could "always learn misunderstood material back on the job." However, the trainer cannot

TABLE 10.4

Declarative Learning Test Formats

Part A: Objectively Scored Tests
True or False
1. A test is valid if a person receives approximately the same result or score at two different testing times. True _____ False _____

Multiple Choice
2. The affective domain of learning refers to

   _____ skills
   _____ attitudes
   _____ knowledge
   _____ all of the above
   _____ 2 and 3

Matching
3. For each of the governments listed on the left, select the appropriate responsibility for training and place the letter next to the term.

   _____ 1. federal   a. displaced workers
   _____ 2. provincial   b. language training
   _____ 3. municipal   c. student summer work

Short Answer
4. Kirkpatrick identified four types of evaluation. These are:

Part B: Subjectively Scored Tests
Essay
5. Describe how and why the process of needs analysis is a critical step in the measurement of the effectiveness of a training program.

Oral
6. The measurement of training has many potential benefits. Identify these benefits. Discuss the reasons why, given these advantages of measurement, most trainers do not evaluate training.

Observation Checklist
The customer service representative
   _____ greeted the customer
   _____ approached the customer
   _____ offered to help

Rating Scale
8. Indicate the degree to which you agree or disagree with the statements below:

   Scale: 1= strongly disagree 2 = disagree 3 = agree 4 = strongly agree
   During a selection interview, the interviewer
      used behavioural-based questions   1 2 3 4
      looked for contrary evidence   1 2 3 4
      used probing questions   1 2 3 4

Diaries, Anecdotal Records, Journals
9. In your journal, write about your experiences working with someone from a different culture. Record the date, time, and reason for the interaction. Describe how you felt and what you learned.

assume that scoring well on tests necessarily means doing well on the job. It is on the job where the real measurement of the payoff of training begins.

Behaviour

Behaviour refers to the display of the newly learned skills or competencies on the job. This is also what we have referred to in Chapter 9 as "transfer of training" and is arguably the most important of all training effectiveness criteria.[22] The behaviours assessed should be those identified by the training objectives (see Chapter 5). Behaviours can be measured using three approaches:

   a. *Self-reports*: The trainee indicates how often he or she has used the newly trained behaviours on the job.
   b. *Observations*: Others observe and record whether and/or how often the trainee has used the newly trained behaviours on the job. Typically it is supervisors that provide these observations but depending on the opportunity to observe the trained person, trainers, subordinates, or even clients can provide this information.
   c. *Production indicators*: The trainee's objective output is assessed through productivity records, such as sales or absenteeism.

A recent review found that *self-reports* are the most frequently used measures of behaviours.[23] However, the main problem with the use of such measures is that their accuracy can be problematic. How do we know that people are accurately reporting their own behaviours? Research conducted in the field of absenteeism has shown that self-reports may not be accurate but they may still be valid. The distinction between accuracy and validity is important. Studies comparing self-reports of absenteeism with company records of absence show that in general, people tend to report fewer absences than they actually have taken (low accuracy). However, people who are more absent tend to self-report more absences than those who have fewer absences (validity).

Observations by others (mainly supervisors) are also sometimes used to measure behaviour. Typically, the observer rates whether or not the person has used the behaviour and/or how often that has occurred. As with self-reports, the issue of accuracy is of significance here. Moreover, the person's opportunity to observe the behaviour is very important. Observational data is more useful when there is strong evidence to suggest that the observer has extensive contacts with the trainee thus enabling frequent observations.

For both self-report and observational data, it is important that the measure focus on specific behaviours (how many times in the last month has the trainee used the new machine) as opposed to general ones (has the trainee applied the skill on the job?). The more specific the behaviour the more likely that the data will be valid and accurate.

Performance indices (sometimes called "objective" measures) are a third type of behaviour data that might be gathered in an evaluation of behaviour. Performance indicators, such as sales performance, can often be obtained directly from company records. They are more frequently used when the evaluator is interested in measuring the impact of training on job performance.

In some cases, performance records can provide highly precise data on specific behaviours. For example "the number of times that a trainee has accessed a data base" can provide highly accurate behaviour data for evaluating a training program designed to train people in the use and application of a database. With the advent of computer technology, it is now increasingly easy to rely on this information to gauge training success. However, performance indices are not always the best measure as they sometimes contaminate individual performance with other events that impact performance. For example, one "objective" measure of a telephone operator might be the number of calls he or she has taken in an hour. However, that data might not lead to accurate conclusions as the number of calls an operator takes is also affected by the number of calls that are received. Similarly, the sales performance of a salesperson is influenced by external factors such as sales territory and competition in addition to the salesperson's behaviour.

Xerox uses many methods to ascertain behaviour, including postcourse observations of trainees performing their jobs, interviews with their managers, and a review of performance appraisal forms.[24] TD Bank uses a very simple approach. Participants in training programs are asked to describe three or four examples of when they used the new knowledge or skill on the job.[25]

Whatever approach is used, there must be time for trainees to become comfortable with newly acquired skills and to be given opportunities to demonstrate them on the job. The time lag for the assessment of behaviour can range from a few weeks to as much as two years, in the case of managerial skills. It is recommended that the measurement of behaviour take place at several points following a training program in order to determine the long-term effects of a training program.

Motivation

Training evaluators consider two types of motivation in the training context: Motivation to learn and the motivation to apply (transfer) the skill on the job. As described in Chapter 3, motivation to learn is a very important factor that influences training success. A number of scales have been designed to measure motivation to learn.[26]

Although there are no definitive and established methods to assess motivation to transfer, one important technique relies on expectancy theory that was described in Chapter 3. Three sets of items are used to measure the valence (the attractiveness of transfer outcomes), instrumentalities (the positive or negative consequences of transfer), and expectancies (the probability that transfer will result in successful performance). The principle is that trainees will be motivated to apply the training when they attach importance to the end result of training, that the attainment of that end result leads to positive consequences (or avoids negative ones), and that applying the training is likely to lead to the desired end result.

One example can be drawn from Haccoun and Savard. Trainees (supervisors) were trained to apply a new organizational policy designed to reduce employee absenteeism (amongst other things). Motivation was measured through three sets of questions. A) Valence: How important is it that absence be reduced in your work group, B) Instrumentality: If you reduce absence what would be the consequences (positive or negative) for you, and C) Expectancy: If you did apply the behaviours taught in training, how likely is it that absence levels would drop? Each question was rated on a five point rating scale. The product of the three sets of answers (Valence × Instrumentality × Expectancy) produces the transfer motivation score.

Self-efficacy

As described in Chapter 3, self-efficacy refers to the beliefs that trainees have about their ability to perform the behaviours that were taught in a training program. Self-efficacy assesses a person's confidence in engaging in *specific* behaviours or achieving specific goals.

Self-efficacy is measured relative to a specific behavioural target. Measures of self-efficacy vary but most tend to focus on assessing trainees' level of confidence for performing specific tasks and behaviours. In one option people would rate the likelihood of obtaining a certain result followed by ratings of the confidence they have in obtaining that result. For example, a measure of self-efficacy for an exam on training evaluation might read as follows: "Are you likely to obtain 50%; 60%; 70%; 80%; 90%; 100% on an exam on training evaluation" (Yes/No response). Next, the person rates how confident they are about obtaining the grade for each "Yes" response. The question might read: "How confident are you that you can obtain that grade" (0 = Not confident at all, 10 = Totally confident). Another, simpler method lists the key behaviours demonstrating transfer and asks trainees to rate each on a confidence scale such as: "How confident are you that you will obtain at least 70 percent on the training evaluation exam?" The response scales would range from totally confident to not at all confident. Although 10-point rating scales are common, scales employing a smaller number of points are also frequently used.

Perceived and/or Anticipated Support

As indicated in Chapter 9, the support provided to trainees as they return to work is a very important component of transfer and training effectiveness. Two important measures of support are perceived support and anticipated support. **Perceived support** refers to the degree to which the trainee reports receiving support in his or her attempts to transfer the learned skills. **Anticipated support** refers to the degree to which the trainee expects to be supported in his or her attempts to transfer the learned skills.

The measurement of perceived and/or anticipated support can be easily constructed for any training program. Specific questions can be designed to include the source of the support (e.g., supervisor, co-workers, or the organization) and the support perceived or anticipated in terms of the training content in general as well as specific components of a training program.

For example, in a study on the effects of a training program that trained nurses on a model of nursing, questions about anticipated support included: "If I am having difficulty writing a nursing care plan, I know I can obtain (very little—very much) help from my supervisor if I ask him/her" and

Perceived support

The degree to which the trainee reports receiving support in his or her attempts to transfer the learned skills

Anticipated support

The degree to which the trainee expects to be supported in his or her attempts to transfer the learned skills

"Based on my previous experiences, I think I can count on (very little—very much) support from my co-workers in applying the training content to my job." These items can easily be reworded to measure perceived support following a training program.

Notice that the former item refers to a specific component of the training program (i.e., nursing care plan) while the latter refers to the training program content in general. These two items also differ in terms of the source of support with the former being one's supervisor and the latter being co-workers. The respondents use a rating scale to fill in the blank spaces (1 = Very little, 5 = Very much). Similar items can be constructed to refer to key parts of a training program and then administered before training to measure anticipated support and then again once trainees have completed training and returned to work to measure perceived support.

Organizational Perceptions

Several researchers have designed scales to measure perceptions of the transfer climate and a learning culture. Transfer climate can be assessed via a questionnaire developed by Janice Rouiller and Irwin Goldstein. The questionnaire consists of a number of questions that identify eight sets of "cues" that can trigger trainee reactions that encourage or discourage the trainee to transfer the skill. The eight scales include: goal cues, social cues, task and structural cues, positive feedback, negative feedback, punishment, no feedback, and self-control. Trainees are asked questions about training-specific characteristics of the work environment such as, "In your organization, supervisors set goals for trainees to encourage them to apply their training on the job" (1 = Strongly disagree, 5 = Strongly agree).

In addition, a scale developed by J. Bruce Tracey, Scott Tannenbaum, and Michael Kavanagh has also been designed to measure if an organization has a continuous-learning culture. The questions measure trainees' perceptions, beliefs, expectations, and values with regard to individual, task, and organizational factors that support the acquisition and application of knowledge, skill, and behaviour. The Trainer's Notebook in Chapter 9 presents some of the items from this scale.

Organizational Results

Unlike all of the other variables we have discussed, results focus on the effects of training on the organization rather than on the trainee. Assessing the impact of training on organizational outcomes is the most difficult step in evaluating a training program. Results criteria are considered to be the "ultimate" criteria for training evaluation. They include quantifiable changes in areas important to organizations such as turnover, productivity, quality, profitability, customer satisfaction, accidents, and so on. In some instances, the objective is to cost the program and determine the net benefit. Chapter 11 is devoted to procedures for doing cost-benefit analysis.

Hard data
Results that can be measured objectively

Results information usually consists of **hard data** such as time (e.g., the time it takes to produce a product, serve a customer, etc.), outputs, inputs, and frequencies. In other words, anything that can be measured objectively. ACCO World Corp., a manufacturer of school supplies ranging from paper clips to binders, tracked the effect of training on new production hires. After training, new hires were able to produce vinyl binders at a 5 to 10 percent higher rate than tenured operators. The trainer then leveraged this result to continue the training and expand it to tenured operators.

In many cases, however, hard data are difficult to obtain or are simply not relevant to a training program. In these cases, trainers must use "soft data" measures. Examples of hard and soft data are summarized in Table 10.5.

Soft data are measures that consist of employees' perceptions and attitudes of organizational processes and include measures such as work climate, feelings and attitudes, and difficult-to-measure skills like decision making. The reasoning is that if employees can demonstrate a soft skill such as communication, this will ultimately have an impact on the organization's bottom line. However, it is difficult to assign a dollar value to this, or to prove that changes in attitude do make a difference.

In some cases it is difficult or impossible to adequately assess the impact of training directly. An alternative is to calculate **return on expectations**. Those who are involved in training decide exactly what they expect from the training. These expectations form the goals for training, and some time after the course, managers decide if the performance results are in line with their expectations.

For example, an organization that was restructured into product-performance teams was unable to place a dollar value on the cross-functional training employees had received, but managers were able to articulate improvements they noticed after the training. The numbers are not absolute, but managers are not only saying that time is being managed better, but that 95 percent of deadlines are being met. They feel that this anecdotal evidence does have an impact on the bottom line, and that profit improvements are noticeable.

There are several problems with measuring results. Not only does it take more time to collect results data, but the actual effect of the training program is more difficult to assess. For example, there are many things that influence an organization's productivity and sales thus making it difficult to know what effect a training program has on results criteria. In addition, the effects of a training program on organizational results can take months if not years. During that time, factors such as interest rates and competitor actions may have an impact on operating results and obscure the effect of training.

Some of these problems can be dealt with through the use of experimental research designs. In the next section, we discuss the different ways in which evaluators can design evaluation studies in order to isolate the effects of training on evaluation criteria.

Training Evaluation Designs

Training evaluation designs refer to the manner with which the data collection is organized and how the data will be analyzed. Training evaluation designs can be of three types: nonexperimental, experimental, and quasi-experimental.

Soft data

Results measures that consist of employees' perceptions and attitudes of organizational processes

Return on expectations

The measurement of a training program's ability to meet managerial expectations

Training evaluation designs

The manner with which the data collection is organized and how the data will be analyzed

TABLE 10.5

Examples of Hard Data and Soft Data

HARD DATA		SOFT DATA	
Output	• units produced • units sold • jobs completed • calls answered	**Work habits**	• absenteeism • lateness • safety infractions • turnover
Quality	• scrap and waste • product defects • customer complaints	**Work climate**	• grievances • complaints • job satisfaction • culture

Time	• downtime
	• overtime
	• time to completion
		Management	• quality of decisions
			• conflict resolution
			• successful
			  completion of
			  projects

Cost	• overhead • variable costs • accident costs • sales expenses • benchmarks		• implementation of new ideas using new skills

Source: Adapted from Phillips, J. (1996, April). How much is the training worth. Adapted from *Training & Development* magazine, American Society for Training & Development. 20–24. Copyright April 1996, adapted from *Training & Development* magazine, American Society for Training & Development. Reprinted with permission. All rights reserved.

All evaluation designs imply a comparison. When the comparison is made to a standard and not to another group of (untrained) people, the designs are deemed **nonexperimental**. When that comparison is to another group of people similar to those trained but that do not receive the training, the designs are known as experimental or quasi-experimental.

In **experimental designs**, the assignment of people to the trained (labelled the "experimental" or "treatment group") and to the nontrained group (labelled the "control group") is done randomly. In **quasi-experimental designs**, we also compare trained to untrained employees but the assignment to the groups is not done randomly. In that case, instead of speaking about a "control" group we refer to it as a "comparison" group.

Table 10.6 summarizes the uses and limitations of each type of design. In general, nonexperimental training evaluation designs cannot establish if trainee learning and behaviours were *caused* by a training program (with the exception

Nonexperimental designs

When the comparison is made to a standard and not to another group of (untrained) people

Experimental designs

When the trained group is compared to another group that does not receive the training and when the assignment of people to the training group and the nontraining group is random

Quasi-experimental designs

When the trained group is compared to another group that does not receive the training but when the assignment of people to the training group and the nontraining group is *not* random of the IRS strategy, which is discussed in Table 10.7). On the other hand, they are much less complex to organize and much more practical for use in organizations. Quasi-experimental and experimental designs are more complex but they do provide evidence of causality. Experimental designs provide stronger evidence of causality than is possible with quasi-experimental designs.

One of the reasons that experimental designs provide stronger evidence of causality is because one is able to have more confidence that any changes in trainees' learning and behaviour are due to the training and not to something else. To learn more about some of the other factors that might explain a change in trainees' learning and behaviour, see The Trainer's Notebook, "Understanding Pre-Post Differences."

Training evaluation designs were developed from the principles of experimental scientific research and there are many research designs within each of the three general types. Table 10.7 describes seven designs that are particularly relevant for training evaluation and Figure 10.1 shows you what they look like.

Designs A, B, and C are nonexperimental designs because the employees who are trained are not compared to untrained employees. Designs D, E, and F are causal models that compare trained and untrained people and, depending on subject assignment, they may be experimental or quasi-experimental. Finally, design G—the Internal Referencing Strategy—permits some of the conclusions made by the causal designs (D, E, F) while collecting data exclusively from trainees.

TABLE 10.6

Uses and Limitations of Nonexperimental, Quasi-Experimental, and Experimental Training Evaluation Designs

Experimental designs estimate the degree to which a training program has *caused* trainee proficiency. They are used to establish if the training program should be eliminated or expanded to other parts of the organization. The downside is that experimental designs are more difficult to use in organizational settings.

Quasi-experimental designs provide indications of cause but the proof is not definitive. However, because they do not require random assignment they are generally more accessible to organizations. Hence, quasi-experimental designs may be appropriate when experimental designs cannot be used and when the training manager is willing to live with some risk.

Nonexperimental designs *cannot* provide causal information (except for the Internal Referencing Strategy). Hence, such designs *cannot* be used to infer the quality of the training program. However, they are most practical and can provide useful information when the evaluator has an external standard against which trainee posttraining performance can be compared and when demonstrating that training caused that proficiency does not matter.

Understanding Pre-Post Differences

Suppose we wish to evaluate this chapter's effectiveness in teaching training evaluation. We select a pre-post design. Your class's knowledge of training evaluation is assessed using a multiple choice test administered on the first day of class (pretest) and on the last day (posttest). The mean score for the posttest is significantly higher than the pre-test scores. Can it be concluded that reading this chapter caused this gain in knowledge? Before jumping to conclusions, you should consider four alternative explanations:

History or Time: Events in the environment that coincide with this course and that have nothing to do with it may in fact have caused pre to post changes. For example, the class may have done better because many students saw a PBS program on training evaluation that was aired the week before the final exam.

Maturation: People mature and change over time. As the students are taking this course they are also taking other courses. Even if none of the other courses deal explicitly with training evaluation, they may have helped the students develop higher levels of reasoning and critical thinking skills. This growing general competence may translate into better performance on the post-test.

Testing: Taking the pre-test may have made it easier for students to perform better on the post-test. Some students may have remembered some of the questions asked on the pre-test, while others may have gained a better "feel" for the kinds of questions that are asked. Hence the post-test performance may be due, at least in part, with the mere experience of being pre-tested.

Mortality: Whereas most students that enrol in a course stay until the end, it is frequently the case that some students "drop" the course. Those that remain in the course and from whom post-test information will be available may be systematically different from those that dropped the course: They may be more interested in the subject matter, more motivated, more able than those that leave, and/or have more time to meet the course demands. These students may very well show large improvements in learning, shifting the average class performance on the post-test upward.

Source: Adapted from Cook, T.D. & Campbell (1979) Quasi-experimentation: Design and analysis issues for field settings. Skokie, IL: Rand McNally.

In general, all training outcome measures may be used irrespective of the training evaluation design chosen: affective, cognitive, or skill based as well as reactions and behaviours. *Hence, the choice of an evaluation design has less to do with the measures collected but much more to do with the inferences or decisions required about the training program relative to the original aims of the training program.*

TABLE 10.7

Different Types Of Evaluation Designs

Design A: **The single group post-only design.** This is the simplest and most common training evaluation design. Data is gathered once after training and only from those that have completed training. Each trainee is compared to a

continued

TABLE 10.7 *(Continued)*

pre-determined criterion of success and training is considered "effective" when the trainees meet that standard of proficiency. Three common examples of such programs include a college course on "organizational training," a course for new drivers, and the basic training program administered to new telephone operators.

The basic strength (and popularity) of this design is its simplicity. The two drawbacks to the design are that it cannot indicate if the trainees changed (e.g., trainees may have been proficient before training) or if the achieved outcome is a result of training (their observed proficiency may have been "caused" by some other experience coincidental to training).

Design B: The single group pre-post design. This is the second most frequently used evaluation design. Training outcome data is gathered from trainees both before as well as after training. Used to assess *changes* in trainees, this design infers training effectiveness when the posttraining data shows statistically significant improvement from pretraining. There are three main drawbacks of this design: a) When pre-post differences are noted, it is not possible to know if the differences resulted from training. Other events in the environment may have caused the difference rather than training (i.e., history effect); b) Because it is often the case that the same measure is used to assess pre- and posttraining knowledge and behaviours, improvements may be due to trainees remembering the questions asked on the pre-test (i.e., testing effect); and c) Pre-post improvements may be due to "maturation," the normal growth in experience and learning that occurs, irrespective of training.

Design C: The time series design. Principally used with "objective" measures of job performance, this design expands the single group pre-post design. It requires several data collection points before and after training (the pre-post design only requires one pre and one post measure). Training is considered effective when there is a clear and stable increase in post performance compared with pretraining. The use of several pre and several post measures is essential to this design because we wish to ensure that any pre-post differences are stable and persistent. Moreover, objective performance measures tend to move up or down due to many circumstances that may have little to do with the employee. Multiplying the measurement moments will tend to cancel out these fluctuations.

Take for example a course on "selling earthquake insurance." The analyst would retrieve for each trainee the number of earthquake policies sold during each of the four quarters prior to training and each of the four quarters after training. Training is considered effective when the number of policies sold is consistently higher following training. The *main advantage* of this design is its reliance on objective data. This is less disruptive because trainees do not need to answer questionnaires. The *main drawback* from this technique is that the quality of the conclusions depends on the number of times data is collected. The more data points the more valid the conclusion. Moreover, the statistical analyses required to evaluate the results are somewhat more complex than those required in the simpler single group pre-post designs.

Design D: The Single Group Design with Control Group. This is the simplest true experimental design. Posttraining data is collected from both trainees as well as a group of people who were not trained (i.e., control group) and assignment to groups is random. Effectiveness is inferred when those trained obtain higher scores on the training outcome than the untrained group. With this design, it is possible to state with considerable confidence that the training program caused the higher outcomes obtained by the trained group because random assignment ensures that both groups are initially equal. However, the statistical properties of randomness will equate the groups only when the number of people involved is large. This latter restriction is important because many training programs in organizations are administered to a limited number of people. When assignment to groups cannot be randomized (as is typical in organizational settings) the design becomes quasi-experimental and it cannot be categorically stated that the groups were initially equal. In that case the attribution of causality is more risky.

Design E: The Pre-Post Design with Control Group. Data is gathered from trainees both before and after training. Simultaneously, data is also gathered from a control group. This is a more complete training evaluation design because it allows one to examine the two most important questions about training programs: "Did the trainees change?" and "To what degree was the training program responsible for that change?" Training effectiveness is inferred when pre-post changes are greater for the trained group. The main drawback of this model is practical: rare are the cases where random assignment and multiple measurements can be conducted.

Design F: The Time-Series Design with Control Group. This design is identical to the time series design C except that additional data is simultaneously gathered from a control group. The addition of the control group allows for stronger conclusions about changes as well as about the role that the training intervention played in creating that change. Take for example the course on "selling earthquake insurance" described above (see design C). Suppose that shortly after the course is offered, an earthquake does occur. It is likely that selling earthquake insurance would become a lot easier and that all salespeople, whether or not they had taken the training would show a marked increase. Had we not had a control group, we would have falsely concluded that the training program was responsible for the pre-post changes.

Design G: The Internal Referencing Strategy. This quasi-experimental design was developed by Haccoun and Hamtiaux for use in those frequent cases where a

continued

causal inference is required but a control or comparison group is not available.[27] With this design, it is the outcome measure itself that forms the basis of the comparison.

The pre-test and the post-test measures need careful construction. Two types of test items—"relevant" and "irrelevant but germane"—are constructed. Relevant items are those that test the knowledge and behaviours that are covered in a training program. Irrelevant but germane items are those that could have been included in a training program but were not. For example, in testing the effectiveness of this chapter for teaching evaluation designs, one could ask questions about the Time Series design. One could also ask questions about the "Interrupted Time Series Design." Questions testing your knowledge of Time Series design would be "relevant" because the topic is covered in this chapter while questions testing your knowledge of the Interrupted Time Series would be "irrelevant but germane" because the chapter does not cover this design although it could have. Comparisons are then made between pre-post differences on the relevant and on the irrelevant but germane items. If the program was effective, the differences on the relevant items should be greater than those pre-post differences noted on the irrelevant but germane ones. This design can be used for a variety of learning, behaviour, and job performance outcomes and recent research has found it to be superior to quasi-experimental designs.[28]

FIGURE 10.1

Training Evaluation Designs

Legend:
- ● Trained
- ■ Untrained
- ▲ Training Relevant Items
- △ Training Irrelevant Items

A: **Single group post-only**
B: **Single group pre-post**
C: **Time series**
D: **Single group with control**
E: **Pre-post with control**
F: **Time series with control**
G: **Internal Referencing Strategy**

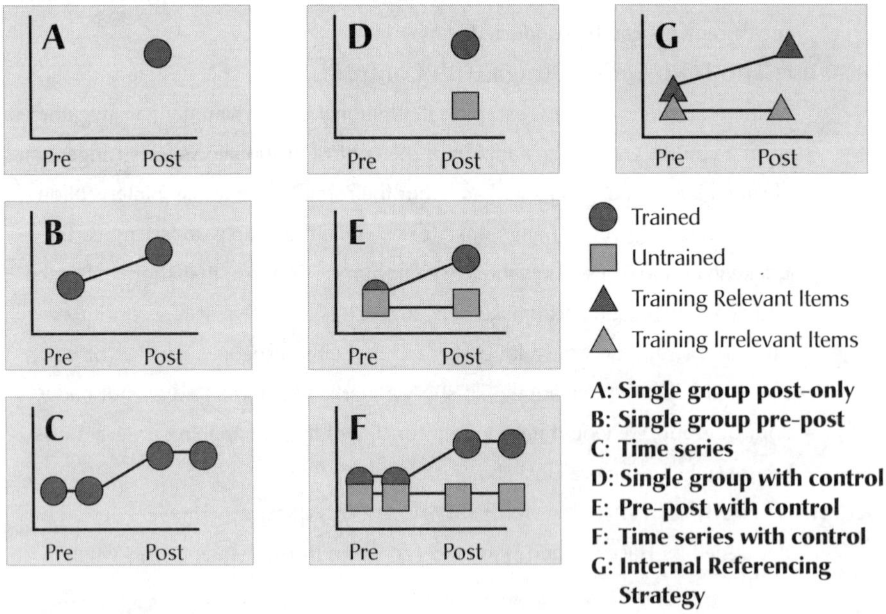

In summary, trainers have a variety of designs to choose from when evaluating a training program. These designs differ in terms of the time involved, the cost, the expertise required, and the kind of conclusions that one can derive from the evaluation. A trainer will have to weigh the importance of each of these factors when deciding on an evaluation design. Ultimately, what is most important is the question that the trainer must answer and the information that management desires.

Summary

This chapter reviewed the main purposes for evaluating training programs as well as the barriers that prevent training evaluation. Models of training evaluation were presented and contrasted. Although Kirkpatrick's evaluation model is the most common and frequently used, more recent evaluation models such as the COMA and DBE models that can provide more diagnostic and practical information were also discussed. We also described the variables to measure for an evaluation as well as some of the methods and techniques required to measure them. Finally, the main types of evaluation designs were described along with their advantages and disadvantages.

Key Terms

affective reactions (page 263)
anticipated support (page 270)
causal evaluations (page 257)
COMA (page 259)
decision-based evaluation (DBE) (page 260)
declarative learning (page 264)
descriptive evaluations (page 257)
experimental designs (page 273)
formative evaluations (page 257)
hard data (page 271)

nonexperimental designs (page 273)
perceived support (page 270)
procedural learning (page 264)
quasi-experimental designs (page 273)
return on expectations (page 272)
soft data (page 272)
summative evaluation (page 257)
training evaluation (page 253)
training evaluation designs (page 272)
utility reactions (page 263)

Weblinks

ACCO World Corp.: www.acco.com (page 272)
American Society for Training and Development (ASTD): www.astd.com (page 255)
General Dynamics: www.generaldynamics.com (page 266)
TD Bank: www.td.com (page 269)
Xerox: www.xerox.com (page 269)

Discussion Questions

1. Discuss the similarities and the differences between the evaluation models discussed in the chapter. In your discussion be careful to include the practical implications of preferring one model over another.

2. You have two training programs: a) a course designed to teach the use of a PC and b) a course to improve supervisory feedback to employees. Which evaluation design would you use in each case? What if you wanted to determine if training caused the outcome. Which design would you use?

3. One objection to training evaluations is that they require some of the training time be alloted to the evaluation activities, in particular, filling out end-of-training questionnaires. How would you defend the use of evaluation given this important constraint? Can you suggest alternatives when time is short?

Using the Internet

1. To find out how Canadian companies measure the results of training, go to Industry Canada at: **http://strategis.ic.gc.ca/epic/internet/incts-scf.nsf/vwGeneratedInterE/h_sl00007e.html**. Review the section on how companies measure the success of training and the case studies by clicking on "Explore the Case Studies." Write a brief report in which you describe how some of the companies featured in the case studies have evaluated and measured training success.

Exercises

1. Since you are reading this text, you are probably part of a course in training and development. Within teams, develop a reaction form that rates the effectiveness of the course, the instructor, the methods, the instructional technology, and so on.

2. Refer to the training evaluation models discussed in this chapter as well as Table 10.1. Describe how students are typically evaluated in university and college courses. What variables are most often used and how are they measured? Keeping in mind each model and the variables in Table 10.1, what other variables do you think should be included as part of the evaluation process? Design an evaluation form that you would like to see used to evaluate your performance in a course. For each variable you include, develop one sample question.

3. Refer to each of the evaluation designs described in the chapter (see Table 10.7). What design is most often used when evaluating students' performance in university and college courses? Given the design that is typically used, what kinds of conclusions can be made about the course and students' grades? Consider how some other designs might be used to improve the evaluation process? Develop an evaluation design that you think would improve the evaluation of students' performance.

4. Reflect on the most recent training program you have attended in terms of how it was evaluated. Refer to Table 10.1 and describe what variables were measured to evaluate the program. Also refer to Table 10.7 and describe what type of evaluation design was used. How effective do

you think the evaluation was in terms of the variables that were measured and the design that was used? How would you improve the evaluation in terms of the variables measured and the evaluation design?

5. Consider a situation in which you are the director of training and development in an organization that is going to deliver a very expensive training program. It is very important to find out how effective the training program is given the expense and the large number of employees that will be trained over the next several years. Your job is to develop a plan for the evaluation. Discuss what you will do in terms of the type of evaluation: What data should be gathered and analyzed? What is the purpose of the evaluation and should it be formative or summative? Should it be a descriptive or causal evaluation? Now consider the different types of evaluation designs in Table 10.7. What type of evaluation design do you think would be most appropriate? Consider the pros and cons of the various alternatives. Present your training evaluation strategy to the class.

Case

THE NORTH AMERICAN TRANSPORTATION COMPANY

The North American Transportation Company (NATC) is a very large organization that provides continent wide facilities for the shipping of goods from tonnes of wheat and iron ore to individual parcels. Headquartered in Canada, the company uses all forms of heavy equipment to load, transport, and deliver goods and materials for its clients.

In recent years, a number of accidents and near accidents had occurred. In some cases the accidents caused injuries to people (mainly employees though some injuries were sustained by bystanders). They also caused substantial material damage to property and/or the environment. In three cases in the last five years, people were killed.

Investigation of these accidents indicated that drug and/or alcohol abuse by company personnel was relatively common and that these may have been contributing factors to the accidents. This analysis also uncovered that absenteeism and job performance problems were also the result of drug/alcohol use by employees.

The CEO of the company asked the Human Resource department to solve the problem. In response, the department formulated a zero tolerance policy towards work place alcohol and drug abuse. The policy outlawed alcohol/drug use on the job and made the implementation and enforcement of the policy the direct responsibility of all supervisory personnel in the company. They further developed and implemented a training program to instruct all supervisors of the policy, the means to implement it, and the specific behaviours expected of them. This training program became known as the Alcohol/Drug Abuse Prevention Program (ADAPP).

The day-long training program explained that it was the responsibility of supervisors to be vigilant with respect to drug/alcohol use on the job and to act immediately when there is a problem.

The supervisors were required to do three major things: 1) Explain the policy to their employees as a group, 2) Observe their employees and note if employees show signs of being "under the influence." Were this to be the case, the supervisor was to individually meet the employee and direct him or her to the Employee Aid Program for further investigation and treatment, and 3) Immediately remove from the job any employee assigned to hazardous duties if the supervisor felt that the person was in no condition to do the work safely. Supervisors that failed to implement the procedure would face disciplinary actions including, in some cases, immediate dismissal.

The training program consisted of lectures and video presentations, followed by various role-playing exercises and discussions designed to help them learn the policy, to motivate supervisors into implementing it, and to enhance their confidence in their ability to do so.

Questions

1. Design a training evaluation for the ADAPP. The training evaluation must be both *summative* (has ADAPP led to an increase in the desired supervisory behaviours and has it led to a decrease in employee absence and workplace accidents and injuries?) and *formative* (what aspects of the training program, if any, should be improved?).
2. What model or models of training evaluation would seem appropriate in this case? Explain your answer.
3. What variables should be measured and how should this be done.
   a. Determine the main variables to measure.
   b. Determine the information to be collected to address program improvements.
4. What evaluation design or designs would you consider most appropriate for the evaluation? Explain your reasoning.

Running Case Part 6

VANDALAIS DEPARTMENT STORES

Several days before the structured employment interview training program for Vandalais Department Stores (refer to Chapter 5 for details on the training program), the director of human resources contacted the consultant who was hired to deliver the training program. She was concerned about being able to demonstrate the value of the training program to management. Following a lengthy discussion, the consultant agreed to conduct an evaluation of the training program.

1. Using the material in this chapter, develop a plan to evaluate the structured employment interview training program. In particular, you should provide specific details regarding each of the following issues:

    a. What variables will you measure and why?

    b. For each of the measures, describe exactly how you will measure them.

    c. How will you design your evaluation study? Consider each of the designs in Table 10.7. For each design, describe how you would use it to evaluate the structured employment interview training program and its advantages and disadvantages. Which design will you use to evaluate the training program and why?

References

[1]Sackett, P.R., & Mullen, E.J. (1993). Beyond formal experimental design: Towards and expanded view of the training evaluation process. *Personnel Psychology, 46,* 613–27.

[2]Twitchell, S., Holton, E.F. III & Trott, J.R. Jr. (2001). Technical training evaluation practices in the United States. *Performance Improvement Quarterly, 13*(3) 84–109.

[3]McMurren, D.P., Van Buren, M.E. & Woodwell, V.H. Jr. (2000). *The 2000 ASTD state of the industry report.* Alexandria VA: The American Society for Training and Development.

[4]Blanchard, P.N., Thacker, J.W. & Way, S.A. (2000). Training evaluation: perspectives and evidence from Canada. *International Journal of Training and Development, 4* (4), 295–304.

[5]Grider, D.T. (1990). Training evaluation. *Business Magazine 17*(1), 20–24.

[6]Kraiger, K., Ford, J.K. and Salas, E. (1993). Application of cognitive, skill based and affective theories of learning outcomes to new methods of training evaluation. *Journal of Applied Psychology, 78* (2) 311–28; and Colquitt, J.A., Lepine, J.A., Noe, R.A. (2000). Toward an integrative theory of training motivation: A meta-analytic path analysis of 20 years of research. *Journal of Applied Psychology, 85*(5), 678–707.

[7]Pace, R.W., Smith, C.P. & Mills, G.E. (1991). *Human resource development: the Field.* Englewood Cliffs, N.J. Prentice-Hall.

[8]Roullier, J.Z. & Goldstein, I.L. (1993). The relationship between organizational transfer climate and positive transfer of training. *Human Resource Development Quarterly, 4*(4), 377–90; and Tracey, J.B, Tannenbaum, S.I, Kavanagh, M.J. (1995). Applying trained skills on the job: The importance of the work environment. *Journal of Applied Psychology, 80*(2), 239–252.

[9]Quinones, M.A. (1995). Pretraining context effects: Training assignment as feedback. *Journal of Applied Psychology, 80,* 226–38; and Haccoun, R.R., Savard, P. (2003). Prédire le transfert des apprentissages à long terme Role de soutien anticipé et perçu, de la motivation et de l'efficacité personnelle. In Delobbe, G., Karnas, C., Vandenberghe, C. (ed) *Evaluation et développement des compétences au travail.* UCL : Presses Universitaire de Louvain, pp. 507–16.

[10]Montesino, M.U. (2002). Strategic alignment of training, transfer-enhancing behaviors and training usage: A posttraining study. *Human Resource Development Quarterly, 13*(1), 89–108.

[11]Worthen, B.R. & Sanders, J.R. (1987). *Educational evaluations: Alternative approaches and practical guidelines.* White Plains, N.Y.: Longman.

[12]Kirkpatrick, D.L. (1976). Evaluation of training. In R.L. Craig (Ed.) *Training and development handbook: A guide to human resource development* (2nd ed). New York: McGraw-Hill.

[13]Kraiger, K. (2002). Decision-based evaluation. In K. Kraiger (Ed.) *Creating, implementing, and managing effective training and development*: State-of-the-art lessons for practice, (pp. 331–75). San Francisco: Jossey-Bass; and Haccoun, R.R., Jeanrie, C. & Saks, A. M. (1999). Concepts et pratiques contemporaines en évaluation de la formation : Vers un modèle diagnostic des impacts. In Bouthilier, D. (Ed.) *Gérer pour la performance.* Presses de HEC, Montréal.

[14]Holton, E.F. III (1996). The flawed four-level evaluation model. *Human Resource Development Quarterly, 7.* 5–21. Alliger, G.M., Tannenbaum, S.L., Bennett, W., Traver, H., & Shortland, A. (1997). A meta-analysis on the relations among training criteria. *Personnel Psychology, 50,* 341–42.

[15]Haccoun, R.R. & Saks, A.M. (1998). Training in the 21st Century: Some Lessons from the Last One Invited Paper: Special Issue: Industrial Psychology at the Turn of the Century. *Canadian Psychology, 39* (1-2), 33–51.

[16] Morgan, R.B. & Casper, W. (2000). Examining the factor structure of participant reactions to training: a Multidimensional approach. *Human Resource Development Quarterly, 11.* 301–317.

[17] Alliger, G.M., Tannenbaum, S.L., Bennett, W., Traver, H. & Shortland, A (1997).

[18] Jonassen, D., & Tessmer, M. (1996-97). An outcomes-based taxonomy for instructional systems design, evaluation and research. *Training Research Journal, 2,* 11–46.

[19] Desjardins, D. (1995). Impact de la présentation d'un organisateur avancé sur l'apprentissage et le transfert en formation du personnel. Unpublished Master`s Thesis, Université de Montréal, Département de Psychologie.

[20] Ostroff, C. (1991). Training effectiveness measures and scoring schemes: A comparison. *Personnel Psychology, 44,* 353–74.

[21] Smith, J.E., & Merchant, S. (1990). Using competency exams for evaluating training. *Training and Development Journal, 44* (8), 65–71.

[22] Flynn, G. (1998). The nuts and bolts of valuing training. *Workforce, 17,* (11), 80–85; and Kozlowski, S.W.J. & Salas, E (1997). A multilevel organizational systems approach for the implementation and transfer of training. In J.K. Ford (ed) *Improving training effectiveness in work organizations* (pp. 247–87). Hillsdale, N.J: Erlbaum.

[23] Salas, E., & Cannon-Bowers, J.A. (2001). The Science of Training: A Decade of Progress. *Annual Review of Psychology 52,* 471–99.

[24] Olian, J.D., & Durham, C.C. (1998). Designing management training and development for competitive advantage: Lessons from the best. *Human Resource Planning, 21* (1), 20–31.

[25] Larin, N. (1998). Who understands return on investment better than a bank? *Canadian HR Reporter,* pp. 2–8.

[26] Noe, R.A. and Schmitt, N. (1986). The influence of trainee attitudes on training effectiveness: Test of a model. *Personnel Psychology, 39,* 497–523.

[27] Haccoun, R.R., Hamtiaux, T. (1994). Optimizing knowledge tests for inferring learning acquisition levels in single group training evaluation designs: The Internal Referencing Strategy. *Personnel Psychology, 47,* 593–604.

[28] Frese, M., Beimel, S., & Schoenborn, S. (in press) Action Training for Charismatic Leadership: Two Evaluation Studies of a Commercial Training Module on Inspirational Communication of Vision. *Personnel Psychology.*

Chapter 11

The Costs and Benefits of Training Programs

www.fedex.com

FEDERAL EXPRESS CANADA LTD.

Federal Express Canada Ltd. is ranked as one of Canada's 50 best companies to work for. The company has also been ranked as one of the 100 best companies to work for in the United States. Generous benefits and training and development are key to the company's success which includes one of the best tuition refund programs around.

Among the companies training programs is a two-week, 12-module basic training program for new courier van drivers. In an effort to determine the cost and benefits of the program, a study was conducted on groups of trained and untrained couriers. The trained group consisted of recent graduates of the basic training course—new employees who had completed the training and been on the job no more than 90 days before the study began. The untrained group consisted of new couriers sent to their job assignments without going through the training. Their managers were told to do no more or less on-the-job training than normal to prepare them for their new jobs. Managers typically ride with new couriers to familiarize them with their routes, teach them how to fill out an air bill, and generally show them the ropes. Also, the untrained group received defensive driving and dangerous-goods training. What they didn't get was the two-week training course.

The performance of the couriers was monitored daily, for 90 days, by their managers. The managers used checklists to track 18 performance indicators, determined by a task force of experts—namely, FedEx managers who oversee couriers. Some of the performance indicators were accidents, injuries, time-card errors, domestic air bill errors, international air waybill errors, pickup manifest errors, courier-caused wrong-day deliveries, customer complaints, and so on.

Ten of the 18 performance indicators were assigned dollar values in terms of the cost per error. The safety department, engineering, finance, and other groups supplied the figures.

In the category of accidents (meaning accidents involving vehicles), for instance, the average cost per accident was $1,600, according to the safety department. Given that figure and the data on the checklists turned in by supervisors at the end of the 90-day period, projecting the annual cost of accidents for couriers in each group becomes a simple exercise in arithmetic: Cost per error × number of errors = total cost of errors. Total cost of errors ÷ number of people in group = total cost per person. Multiply cost per person by four (because this was a 90-day study) and you have total cost per courier per year. They subtracted 25 percent from that total, reasoning that in the course of a year performance would improve somewhat with experience on the job. In other words, both the trained and untrained couriers would probably get better at avoiding accidents (and at completing waybills and manifests and delivery records) if they simply stayed on the job for a year. The training course should not get undue credit for producing performance differences that are apparent for 90 days but might diminish within six or nine months.

The cost of accidents per employee per year for a recently trained courier was $399 and for an untrained courier it was $1,920. Using the same formula with all 10 performance indicators that had dollar figures attached, the company determined that the annual cost of all errors per courier for each group was $2,492 for those who were trained and $4,833 for those who did not receive the training.

So what was the "value" of the two-week course? The difference in errors per year between a trained courier and an untrained courier is $2,341 ($4,833 – $2,492). The cost of the training program, per courier, is $1,890 (including hotel, meals, airfare, mileage allowance, instructor salary, courier salary while training, and "coverage" for the courier while in training—somebody else has to deliver those packages while this person is being trained). Thus, the net benefit for one courier during the first year on the job is $451 ($2,341 – $1,890) and for all 20 trained couriers it is $9,020. The return on investment or ROI is 1.24 ($2,341/$1,890). In other words, the training program resulted in a return of $1.24 for every dollar spent on training.[1]

Organizations have become increasingly concerned about the costs and benefits of their training programs. As you can see from the FedEx example, it is possible to calculate both the costs and benefits of training programs in monetary terms. This information is important for making decisions about whether or not to adopt a training program and as part of the training evaluation process. In fact, some experts consider the calculation of the return on investment (ROI) to be level 5 in Kirkpatrick's evaluation model.[2]

The purpose of this chapter is to describe the different approaches for calculating the costs and benefits of training and development programs and the calculation of return on investment (ROI) and utility analysis.

Training and the Bottom Line

In Chapter 10, we described the process of training evaluation. This often involves measuring trainees' reactions, learning, behaviour, and organization results. The intent is to show some improvement in employees' knowledge, on-the-job behaviour, and/or organizational outcomes. Typically, one would hope to see an improvement in employees' learning and on-the-job behaviour, and thrilled to see a positive effect on organizational outcomes.

But what about the cost of a training program? What if a training program is very expensive? That is, what if the cost is greater than the benefit?

Would improvements in employee behaviour and organizational outcomes still be significant? Would the training program be worth the cost?

Without any information on the cost of training and the monetary value of training benefits, one cannot adequately answer these questions. Clearly, the effectiveness of a training program also depends on its costs and benefits. Management might be pleased to know that a training program has improved customer satisfaction, but managers will be even more interested in knowing the financial value of an improvement in customer satisfaction.

Costing is a complex and time-consuming process that many training specialists traditionally have avoided. Some managers are skeptical about the theoretical underpinnings of costing, while others suggest, rightly, that in business not everything is quantifiable. Indeed, many managers suggest that some quality issues and processes—job satisfaction, communication techniques—make people feel good about themselves and the company they work for, and you just cannot put a dollar value on them.

However, there is increasing pressure for human resource specialists to demonstrate the financial value of their programs. Organizations increasingly want to know what the return is on their training investments.[3] Therefore, trainers and human resource specialists must increasingly be able to calculate and demonstrate both the costs and benefits of training programs. This not only helps to demonstrate the value of training programs to management and the organization, but it also helps to justify the training function's share of the budget and improve their credibility. Furthermore, other members of the organization are more likely to see training and development as an investment rather than a cost. Financial information about the benefits of training programs also places human resource and training specialists on an equal footing with other areas in an organization.

⓪ⓟⓒ

Costing

The process of identifying all the expenditures used in training

Costing Training Programs

Costing is the process used to identify all the expenditures used in training. This is an important procedure in both the design and evaluation of a training program. In Chapter 5, we noted that the trainer must prepare a budget that includes the costs of all of the expenses incurred in the design and implementation of a training program.

The calculation of the cost of a training program usually involves the assignment of various costs to a number of meaningful cost categories. Over the years, a number of approaches have been developed. One approach categorizes the costs of training according to the stages of the training process. For example, one might calculate the cost of needs analysis, training design, delivery, and evaluation. These costs are usually listed on a costing worksheet. One can then calculate and compare the cost of each stage as well as the total cost of a training program.

An example of this kind of costing worksheet is presented in Table 11.1. Note that in addition to the cost of the needs analysis, program development, delivery, and evaluation, this worksheet also includes a category for fixed costs (e.g., overhead, equipment) as well as the costs of revisions.

TABLE 11.1

Costing Worksheet

1. Fixed-cost factors

    i.   Overhead—AC/heat/light; space; rental/lease;

         communications; per input hour   _____

    ii. Supervisory allocation per input hour   _____

    iii. Equipment cost per input hour   _____

    iv. Administrative support cost per input hour   _____

    v.   Training unit fringe benefits cost per input hour   _____

         Total fixed costs per input hour   _____

2. Needs Analysis

    i.   Professional hours _____ @ $____/hour = cost   _____

    ii. Support hours _____ @ $____/hour = cost   _____

    iii. Transportation expenses   _____

    iv. Material   _____

    v.   Consulting fees   _____

    vi. Other costs   _____

         Total direct needs-analysis costs   _____

3. Program Development

    i.   Professional hours _____ @ $____/hour = cost   _____

    ii. Support hours _____ @ $____/hour = cost   _____

    iii. Material   _____

    iv. Consulting fees   _____

    v.   Subject-matter expert/management and staff input

         _____ hours @ _____/hour = cost   _____

    vi. Other costs   _____

         Total direct program-development costs   _____

4. Program Delivery

    i.   Administration hours   _____

         @ $_____/hour = costs   _____

    ii. Administrative support hours   _____

         @ $_____/hour = costs   _____

    iii. Presentation/delivery hours   _____

         @ $_____/hour = cost   _____

    iv. Technical support hours   _____

         @ $_____/hour = cost   _____   *continued*

TABLE 11.1 (Continued)

v.	Trainee materials costs	_____
vi.	Transportation/accommodations/meals	
	a. staff	_____
	b. trainees	_____
vii.	Facilities rental	_____
viii.	Equipment	_____
	Total direct program-delivery costs	_____

5. Evaluation

i.	Professional hours	_____
	@ $_____/hour = cost	_____
ii.	Support hours	_____
	@ $_____/hour = cost	_____
iii.	Management input hours	_____
	@ $_____/hour = cost	_____
iv.	Trainee input hours	_____
	@ $_____/hour = cost	_____
v.	Transportation costs	_____
vi.	Material costs	_____
vii.	Consulting fees	_____
	Total evaluation cost	_____

6. Revision Costs

i.	Professional hours ___ @ $____/hour = cost	_____
ii.	Support hours ____ @ $____/hour = cost	_____
iii.	Management/staff collaboration hours ____ @	
	$____/hour = cost	_____
	Total evaluation cost	_____

7. Total Program Cost

	1 + 2 + 3 + 4 + 5 + 6 = Total Cost	_____

Another approach to costing training programs is to categorize the costs according to the nature or kind of cost. A well-known example of this approach uses the following five cost categories: direct costs, indirect costs, development costs, overhead costs, and trainee compensation costs.

Direct costs are costs that are directly linked to a particular training program. This would include the trainers' salary and benefits, equipment rental,

Direct costs

Costs that are directly linked to a particular training program course materials, instructional aids, food and refreshments, and the cost of travel to and from the training site. These costs are so directly linked to a particular training program that they would not be incurred if a training program was cancelled.

Indirect costs are costs that are not part of a particular training program per se but they are expenses required to support training activities. Indirect costs include clerical and administrative support, trainer preparation and planning, training materials that have already been sent to trainees, and the cost of marketing training programs. These costs would still be incurred even if a training program were cancelled. In other words, unlike the direct costs, these costs cannot be recovered.

Developmental costs are costs that are incurred in the development of a training program. This would include the cost of doing a needs analysis, the cost of developing training methods such as videotapes, the design of training materials, and the cost of evaluating a training program.

Overhead costs refer to costs incurred by the training department but are not associated with any particular training program. Such costs are required for the general operation of the training function such as the cost of maintaining training facilities (e.g., heat and lighting) and equipment, and the salaries of clerical and administrative support staff. A portion of these costs must be allocated to each training program.

Trainee compensation refers to the cost of the salaries and benefits paid to trainees while they are attending a training program. This might also include the cost of replacing employees while they are in training. The logic behind this cost is simply that employees must be paid while they are not working and this is a cost of the training program.

Table 11.2 presents a costing sheet using this classification of training costs. The example is from a company that produces wood panels. The company has three problems that it wanted solved. First, it wanted to improve the quality of wood panels because they were experiencing a two-percent rejection rate each day due to poor quality. Second, they wanted to lower the number of preventable accidents, which was higher than the industry average. Third, they wanted to improve the housekeeping of the production area, which was considered poor and a cause of some of the preventable accidents. Visual inspections that used a 20-item checklist indicated an average of 10 problems in housekeeping each week.[4]

The solution was to train supervisors in performance-management and interpersonal skills. Forty-eight supervisors as well as seven shift superintendents and a plant manager attended a three-day behavioural-modelling skill-building training program. The main objectives of the program were to teach the supervisors how to discuss quality problems and poor work habits with employees; to recognize improvements in employee performance; to teach employees on the job; and to recognize employees for above-average performance.

The cost of the training program was calculated for each of the five cost categories. As shown in Table 11.2, the total cost of the training program was $32,564 or $582 per trainee. This was based on total direct costs of $6,507;

Indirect costs

Costs that support training activities and are not directly linked to a particular training program

Developmental costs

Costs that are incurred in the development of a training program

Overhead costs

Costs incurred by the training department but are not associated with any particular training program

Trainee compensation

The cost of the salaries and benefits paid to trainees while they are attending a training program indirect costs of $1,161; development costs of $6,756; overhead costs of $1,443; and compensation costs of $16,969.

It is important to recognize that the costing sheets presented In Tables 11.1 and 11.2 are only examples. They represent two approaches for categorizing training costs and they might need to be modified to suit an organization's unique circumstances. The idea is to identify the main costs of a training program and not to worry too much about the labels assigned to them. The trainer should be most concerned about how to design a costing approach that has credibility within an organization and that will be accepted by management.

Once the costs of a training program have been calculated, they can be used for at least two purposes. First, they can be used to prepare a budget for a training program and to compare and contrast the costs of different programs. This is important when making decisions about whether to adopt a particular training program. Second, they can be used along with benefit information to calculate a training program's net benefit and return on investment.

In the next section, we present examples of how to compare the costs of different training programs followed by a discussion of how to determine the benefits of training programs and the return on investment.

Comparing the Costs of Training Programs

While the costing of a training program is necessary for budgeting and reporting purposes, costing training programs is also necessary to determine the relative costs of different training alternatives. One of the foremost North American authorities on costing, Gary Geroy, uses the following simplified comparison worksheet:

Program _____	Analyst _____	Date _____
Option	1. _____	2. _____
Performance Value	$ _____	$ _____
Minus Cost	_____	_____
Net Benefit	$ _____	$ _____

To complete the analysis, Geroy then combines the program costs (see Table 11.3) with an estimate of the value of the program (performance value) to the organization.

To give you an example of how this type of cost-comparison works and how different organizations might require cost data at various levels of complexity and detail, consider the following situation.[5]

You are part of an organization that designs electronic systems. A recent reorganization has created a project-management division that places all lead engineers on projects in one group rather than being spread across several operations. The purpose of the reorganization was to allow the engineers to

TABLE 11.2

Training Cost Analysis for Wood Panel Plant

Direct costs. The travel and per-diem cost was zero, because training took place adjacent to the plant. Classroom space and audiovisual equipment were rented from a local hotel; refreshments were purchased at the same hotel. Because different supervisors attended the morning and afternoon sessions, lunch was not provided.

Direct Costs	
Outside Instructor	0
In-house instructor—12 days × $125 a day	$1,500
Fringe benefits—25 percent of salary	375
Travel and per-diem expenses	0
Materials—$60 × 56 participants	3,360
Classroom space and audiovisual equipment— 12 days × $50 a day	600
Refreshments— $4 a day × 3 days × 56 participants	672
Total direct costs	**$6,507**

Indirect costs. Clerical and administrative costs reflect the amount of clerical time spent on making arrangements for the workshop facilities, sending out notices to all participants, and preparing class rosters and other miscellaneous materials.

Indirect Costs	
Training management	0
Clerical and administrative salaries	750
Fringe benefits—25 percent of clerical and administrative salaries	187
Postage, shipping, and telephone	0
Pre- and post-learning materials— $4 × 56 participants	224
Total indirect costs	**$1,161**

Development costs. These costs represent the purchase of the training program from a vendor. Included are instructional aids, an instructor manual, videotapes, and a licensing fee. The instructor-training costs are for a one-week workshop the instructor attended to prepare for facilitating the training. Front-end assessment costs were covered by the corporate training budget.

Development Costs	
Fee to purchase program	3,600
Instructor training	
Registration fee	1,400
Travel and lodging	975
Salary	625
Benefits (25 percent of salary)	156
Total development costs	**$6,756**

Overhead costs. These represent the services that the general organization provides to the training unit. Because figures were not available, we used 10 percent of the direct, indirect, and program-development costs.

Overhead Costs	
General organization support, 10 percent of direct, indirect, top management's time and development costs	
Total overhead costs	**$1,443**

Compensation for participants. This figure represents the salaries and benefits paid to all participants while they attended the workshop.

Compensation for Participants	
Participants' salaries and benefits (time away from the job)	
Total compensation	**$16,969**
Total training costs	**$32,564**
Cost per participant	**$ 582**

TABLE 11.3

Simplified Comparison Worksheet

Program _____   Analyst _____   Date _____

_____Option name   1. _____   2. _____

Analysis:

Needs assessment _____   _____   _____

Work analysis _____   _____   _____

Proposal to management _____   _____   _____

Other _____   _____   _____

Other _____   _____   _____

Design:

General HRD program design_____   _____   _____

Specific HRD program design_____   _____   _____

Other _____   _____   _____

Other _____   _____   _____

Development:

Draft and prototype _____   _____   _____

Pilot test and revise _____   _____   _____

Production and duplication_____   _____   _____

Other _____   _____   _____

Other _____   _____   _____

Implementation:

Program management _____   _____   _____

Program delivery_____   _____   _____

Participant costs _____   _____   _____

Other _____   _____   _____

Other _____   _____   _____

Evaluation:

Program evaluation and report____   _____   _____

Performance followup _____   _____   _____

Other _____   _____   _____

Other _____   _____   _____

Total training program costs $ _____ $ _____

                                    (Option 1)   (Option 2)

have less hands-on technical activity and focus more on theory development, design, and management of others on projects. A manager from your firm with an outstanding record in project management now heads the management group. The group consists of 10 lead engineers. You have been experiencing an alarming rate of turnover in electronic engineers since this group was established. A needs analysis reveals that the engineer types who make up this management group are very unskilled in communicating directions, delegating, and handling people-crisis issues. Data from the exit interviews reveal that the inability of project managers to manage crises and the inability to transmit clear guidelines and directions have been the primary frustrations. Your needs analysis also confirms that the members of the organization and the management group itself feel that this reorganization was a good decision.

The crisis in the organization resulting from the high turnover rate is a financial one. Finding, hiring, and relocating an engineer with the appropriate credentials and experience costs the organization approximately $75,000. In the past nine months, your organization has replaced five engineers. At this rate you anticipate you will replace a total of six engineers before the year is complete. You have been asked to recommend a training program to address the management skills deficiencies in this group. The goal is to reduce the turnover rate to two engineers per year.

Your options are to send each project manager in the group to a management development institute identified by the president of the corporation, arrange for a vendor-delivered training program in-house, or develop a coaching program to help these managers acquire the necessary skills.

Your director has suggested that the last option might take 9 to 12 months to achieve the desired results. The probabilities are low to none that the managers will develop the skills needed on their own on the job. Your organization will not consider salaries or other normal employee maintenance costs as training expenses.

A budget of $7,000 will be provided for materials and $17,000 for consulting fees to support a coaching approach to solving the problem. The following information is provided to help you make your decision:

MANAGEMENT DEVELOPMENT INSTITUTE:

80-hour program delivered off site over a two-week period—$10,000 per trainee
(this includes airfare, lodging, food, and materials)

VENDOR-SUPPLIED PROGRAM:

15 four-hour sessions delivered on site over a six-month period—$15,000 per trainee

MATERIALS BUDGET TO SUPPORT COACHING OPTION: $7000

Needs Analysis	10%	
Work Analysis	5%	
Design	5%	
Development	15%	
Implementation	50%	
Evaluation	15%	
	100%	allocation

Table 11.4 shows the actual cost analysis worksheet used by the organization.

This example demonstrates a number of important aspects of costing and comparing training program alternatives:

1. It shows how the original costing sheet (Table 11.1) can be modified to meet an organization's needs. The substitution of a "maintenance of behaviour" category for the nebulous term "Performance follow-up," for example, makes this cost easier to sell. Also, there was no need to make a "proposal to management." The problem was well understood and immediate.

2. Management was not interested in a cost breakdown for either the institute or the in-house vendor program, hence the single cost entered in the "Delivery" column. In contrast, had this client been a government agency, a detailed breakdown of both bids might have been required.

TABLE 11.4

Cost Analysis Worksheet

	M.D. Institute	Outside Vendor	Coaching
Analysis:			
Needs Analysis	$	$	$ 10,700
Work Analysis	$	$	$ 4,350
Design:			
Program	$	$	$ 350
Instructional Aids	$	$	0
Development:			
Pilot Testing	$	$	$ 0
Formative Evaluation			
(during the HRD activity)	$	$	$ 0
Instructional Aids	$	$	$ 1,050
Implementation:			
Delivery	$ 100,000	$ 150,000	$ 3,500
Management	$	$	$ 0
Evaluation:			
Summative Evaluation	$	$	$ 3,000
Training Revision	$	$	$ 0
Maintenance of Trainee			
Behaviour	$	$	$ 1,050
(A) Total	$ 100,000	$ 150,000	$ 24,000
(B) Trainees	10	10	10
Cost Per Trainee (A)/(B) =	$ 10,000	$ 15,000	$ 2,400

3. As discussed previously, costs of salaries and benefits, overhead, and cost-productivity measures are not included. In this case, the problem had to be solved. Management was not interested in fine-tuning the costs.

4. Coaching, an on-the-job training method, is by far the cheapest option. Whether coaching will be the method chosen would require a benefit analysis. The important issue, however, is that a formal training program might not be the best investment. All appropriate training and development methods should be considered.

While this type of cost comparison analysis is useful for determining the costs of training programs and hence making sound choices and budgetary allocations, a decision should not be made without an estimate of the benefits likely to be received under each system. In the next section, we describe how to calculate the benefits of training programs and how to determine the return on training investments.

The Benefits of Training Programs

The benefits of a training program can be calculated in monetary or nonmonetary terms. When the benefit is calculated in monetary terms, it is referred to as cost-effectiveness evaluation. **Cost-effectiveness evaluation** involves comparing the monetary cost of training to the benefit of training in monetary terms.

Sometimes, however, it is not possible to determine the monetary value of training benefits or to express them in financial terms. As well, in some cases there might be important benefits of a training program that are not monetary benefits. This kind of evaluation is called cost-benefit evaluation.

Cost-benefit evaluation compares the cost of training in monetary terms to the benefits of training in nonmonetary terms. Nonmonetary benefits are similar to what was described as results or level 4 evaluation criteria in Chapter 10 and includes organization outcomes such as the rate of turnover, absenteeism, customer satisfaction, and so on. It is worth noting that such benefits might have a financial effect on the performance of an organization even though they might not be described in monetary terms.

For example, if a training program is expected to reduce the amount of scrap in the production of a product, then a cost-benefit evaluation would indicate how much the training program cost and the amount or percent reduction in scrap. On the other hand, a cost-effectiveness evaluation would calculate the monetary value of the reduction in scrap.

How benefits are calculated depends on the training situation, management needs, and the data available. Because of these differences, we present several examples of the calculation of cost-benefit and cost-effectiveness evaluation beginning with the example in Table 11.4.

Recall that the coaching option has the lowest cost ($24,000) compared to the other two options ($100,000 for the institute and $150,000 for the outside vendor). However, when the "Net Benefit Value Calculation Worksheet" (Table 11.5) is completed a different picture emerges.

Cost-effectiveness evaluation

A comparison of the monetary cost of training to the benefit of training in monetary terms

Cost-benefit evaluation

A comparison of the cost of training in monetary terms to the benefits of training in nonmonetary terms

First, we can calculate the cost-benefit by comparing the cost of each option to the nonmonetary benefit of the estimated reduction in turnover. As shown in Table 11.5, the reduction in turnover for the Management Development Institute is estimated to be 4.84; for the outside vendor the estimated reduction is 3.0; and for the coaching option it is 1.0. Thus, the Management Development Institute is estimated to result in the greatest amount of turnover reduction followed by the outside vendor and then coaching. Also note that the Management Development Institute is the most expensive option followed by the outside vendor and coaching option. In this case, if one were simply interested in the greatest turnover reduction, then the Management Development Institute would be the preferred option.

It is also possible to conduct a cost-effectiveness evaluation using data on the net benefit of each option. The **net benefit** of a training program refers to the estimated value of the performance improvement over the cost of improving performance. Thus, to conduct a net benefit analysis one simply subtracts the cost of a training program from its financial benefit.

For example, United Petroleum International wanted to evaluate the effectiveness of an e-learning program designed to improve the sales skills of engineers and managers. An increase in sales of $1,857,492 per year was realized and directly attributed to the training program. The cost of the program was $606,600 so the net benefit of the program was $1,250,400 ($1,857,492 – $606, 600).[6]

Returning to the example in Table 11.4, recall that finding, hiring, and relocating an engineer with the appropriate credentials and experience costs the organization approximately $75,000. Therefore, the financial benefit of each option is based on the reduction in turnover multiplied by $75,000 as follows: Management Development Institute is $363,000 (4.84 reduction × $75,000); the outside vendor is $225,000 (3.0 reduction × $75,000); and the coaching option is $75,000 (1 reduction × $75,000).

The final net benefit of each of the three training options is simply the financial benefit due to the reduction in turnover minus the cost of the program. These values are presented at the bottom of Table 11.5. The Management Development Institute is the most attractive option with a final net benefit of $263,000 ($363,000 – $100,000). In contrast, the net benefit of the vendor-supplied program is $75,000 ($225,000 – $150,000) and for coaching it is $51,000 ($75,000 – $24,000).

Does this mean that the organization should choose the Management Development Institute program? The answer to this question again depends on the criteria used to choose a training program. If one is simply interested in the final net benefit, then clearly the Management Development Institute is the best choice. If one is interested in the least expensive option, than coaching is the best choice.

Another approach for determining the benefits of a training program is the return on investment. **Return on investment (ROI)** involves comparing the cost of a training program relative to its benefits. The investment refers to the cost of a training program and the return refers to the financial benefits of a training program.

Net benefit

The estimated value of the performance improvement over the cost of improving performance

Return on investment (ROI)

A comparison of the cost of a training program relative to its benefits

A recent survey of HR trends by *Workforce* magazine found that 86 percent of responding organizations formally or informally measure the ROI of training.[7] For example, Cisco Systems calculates the ROI of e-learning by having employees complete a Web-based survey shortly after they have attended a training program. Employees are asked to select a percentage range that indicates the time savings or quality improvement in their performance since taking the course. The results are used to calculate the ROI of e-learning, which has been found to be 900 percent per course. In other words, every dollar the company spends on training results in a gain of $9 in productivity.[8]

The calculation of ROI is relatively simple and can be done using the following equation:

$$\text{Return on Investment} = \frac{\text{Net Program Benefits}}{\text{Cost of the Program}}$$

As an example, if a training program cost $100,000 and the financial benefit or return is $150,000, then the calculation of ROI would simply be $150,000/$100,000. The result is a 1.5 return on investment ratio. When the ROI is above 1 it indicates that the return of a training program is greater than the investment. A higher ratio of results to costs indicates a greater financial benefit to the organization. When the ROI ratio is less than 1 it indicates that the investment or cost is greater than the return. And when the ROI is 1, the return is equal to the investment and the training program breaks even.

A value of 1.5 is obviously a very good return on investment. It indicates that the organization would receive $1.5 for every $1.00 spent on training (1:1.5). The percentage return can also be calculated by simply multiplying the ratio by 100 so in this case, the return is 150 percent. This can also be described as a 50 percent return on investment (the gain of $50,000 is 50 percent of the $100,000 investment).

If we return to the net benefit and cost values presented in Table 11.5, we can calculate the ROI for each of the options. The ROI ratio for each of the options is as follows: the Management Development Institute is 3.63 ($363,000/$100,000); the outside vendor is 1.5 ($225,000/$150,000); and the coaching option is 3.12 ($75,000/$24,000). Thus, based on the ROI, the best option is the Management Development Institute. In other words, the organization receives the greatest return for each dollar spent ($3.63) on the Management Development Institute option. This is equivalent to a 363-percent return on investment, which is only slightly better than the return of the coaching option, which is 3.12 or 312 percent. However, if one is concerned about obtaining the highest return on one's training investment, the choice would be the Management Development Institute option, which also resulted in the greatest net benefit.

Few managers, however, would make the final decision based on these criteria alone. As previously suggested, there are qualitative concerns that become part of the analysis—reputation of the training institute, past experience, trainee perceptions of the options, the degree to which the training can be customized, and the time factor—all will be considered before a final decision is made. For

TABLE 11.5

Net Benefit Value Calculation Worksheet

	Institute Option 1	Vendor Option 2	Coaching Option 3
A. Data Required for Calculations			
(a) What is the desired performance as a result of worker training?	4 reductions per group	4 reductions per group	4 reductions per group
(b) What unit(s) of measure will be used to describe the performance?			
(c) What is the dollar value that will be assigned to each unit of measure?	$75,000	$75,000	$75,000
(d) What is the estimated training time to reach the goal?	.04 year	.5 year	1.0 year
(e) What is the current level of worker performance?	0 reduction	0 reduction	0 reduction
(f) How many workers will participate in the training?	10	10	10
B. Calculations to Determine Net Performance Value			
(g) What is the estimated performance level during training?			
Will trainee produce during training?	0	2	2
_____ No = 0			
_____ Yes = a + e / 2			
(h) What is the length of the period being evaluated (at a minimum this will be the longest "d" of all options under consideration)?	1.0 year	1.0 year	1.0 year
(i) What is the estimate of the total number of units (b) that will be achieved during training? [d × g]	0	1	2
(j) What is the estimate of the total individual performance (or the evaluation period [(h − d) × a] + 1)?	4.84 reduction	3.0 reduction	1.0 reduction
(k) What is the value for the total performance for the evaluation period? [c × j]	$363,000	$225,000	$ 75,000
(l) What is the net performance value gain? [k + (e × c × h)]	$363,000	$225,000	$ 75,000
(m) Do you want to calculate the total net performance value of all trainees?			
_____ Yes = 1 × f	$363,000	$225,000	$ 75,000
__X__ No = net performance value of 1 trainee			
Net Benefit	$363,000	$225,000	$ 75,000
Cost (from Cost-Analysis Worksheet)	$100,000	$150,000	$ 24,000
Final Net Benefit	*$263,000*	*$75,000*	*$ 51,000*

example, if time is a factor then one might choose the Management Development Institute since it has the lowest estimated training time to reach the goal while the coaching option has the longest estimated time. Thus, the preferred option will depend on the criteria used for selecting a training program.

For another example of the calculation of the net benefit and ROI, lets return to the wood panel plant. Recall that a supervisor training program that cost $32,564 was designed to improve the quality of wood panels by lowering the daily rejection rate; to improve the housekeeping of the production area; and to reduce the number of preventable accidents.[9] Table 11.6 shows how the benefits were measured in each of the three areas. The results in each area before and one year after training as well as the differences are shown. Before training, the rejection rate of wood panels was 2 percent per day or 1,440 panels. After training, this was reduced to 1.5 percent or 1,080 panels. The difference of .5 percent per day or 360 wood panels was calculated to be a saving of $720 per day or $172,800 per year. The housekeeping was measured in terms of a visual inspection using a 20-item checklist. Before the training there was an average of 10 defects per week while after training it was reduced to two defects. Thus, the training program resulted in a reduction of eight defects per week (this could not be calculated in monetary terms). The number of preventable accidents before training was 24 per year at a cost of $144,000. After training this was reduced to 16 per year or eight fewer accidents at a cost of $96,000 and a savings of $48,000.

By comparing this information to the cost information in Table 11.2, we can calculate the net benefit and the ROI of the training program. Recall that the total cost of the training program was $32,564. The total net benefit of the training program in monetary terms can be determined by adding the savings from the reduction in rejected wood panels ($172,800) with the savings from the reduction in preventable accidents ($48,000) and then subtracting the cost of the training program ($32,564). Thus, the final net benefit of the training program is: $220,800 − $32,564 = $188,236.

To calculate the ROI, we simply divide the monetary benefit of the program ($220,800) by the cost of the training program ($32,564): $220,800/$32,564 = 6.78. Therefore, the ROI for one year after training is equal to 6.78. It is worth noting that while this analysis is an example of cost-effectiveness evaluation, the results for housekeeping (i.e., a reduction of eight defects per week) is an example of cost-benefit evaluation.

While we have shown you how to calculate the ROI for one training program at a time, some organizations might want to know the ROI for all of its training programs. To find out how one company did just that, see Training Today, "The ROI of Training at Accenture."

In summary, this example as well as the previous example provides a good illustration of how the benefits of training programs can be measured in a manner that is consistent with the objectives of a training program (e.g., reduction in preventable accidents), and can then be translated into monetary terms and used to calculate a training program's net benefit and return on investment.

To learn more about how to convert benefits data into monetary values, see The Trainer's Notebook 1, "Converting Measures to Monetary Values."

TABLE 11.6

Operational Results for Wood Panel Plant

OPERATIONAL RESULTS AREA	HOW MEASURED	RESULTS BEFORE TRAINING	RESULTS AFTER TRAINING	DIFFERENCES (+ OR -)	EXPRESSED IN $
Quality of panels	percent rejected	2 percent rejected—1,440 panels per day	1.5 percent rejected—1,080 panels per day	.5 percent— 360 panels	$720 per day $172,800 per year
Housekeeping	Visual inspection using 20-item checklist	10 defects (average)	2 defects (average)	8 defects	Not measurable in $
Preventable accidents	Number of accidents	24 per year	16 per year	8 per year	$48,000 per year
	Direct cost of each accident	$144,000 per year	$96,000 per year	$48,000	

Total savings: $220,800

$$\text{ROI} = \frac{\text{Return}}{\text{Investment}} = \frac{\text{Operational Results}}{\text{Training Costs}} = \frac{\$220,800}{\$32,564} = 6.8$$

Net Benefit = $220,800 − $32,564 = $188,236

Training Today

The ROI of Training at Accenture

The consulting firm Accenture invests heavily in training its employees. Entry-level employees receive more than 750 hours of training during their first five years and during the next eight years they receive an additional 550 hours of training. But how much of a return does the company receive for all this training?

In an unprecedented move, the company analyzed the ROI of all training for 261,000 employees over the history of the company. They did this using a technique that begins with a comprehensive analysis of 261,000 employee records. The analysis factors out the effects of inflation, market cycle, experience, and employee level to isolate the training effect on a per-person margin.

This analysis enabled the company to determine that for every dollar invested in training, there was a return of $3.53 in net benefits. In other words, the overall ROI of all training over the history of the company was 353 percent.

On a per-person basis, they found that of the employees who take more training (the top 50 percent versus the bottom 50 percent), the top 50 percent are 70 percent more chargeable, have 20 percent higher bill rates, and stay with the company 14 percent longer.

Not surprisingly, with an ROI of 353 percent the company has decided that the per-person funding for training in 2003 will be 50 percent higher than actual spending in 2002 which was already one of the biggest training budgets around.

Source: Galvin, T., Johnson, G., & Barbian, J. (2002, March). The 2003 Training Top 100. *Training, 40*(3), 18–38. (2002, March). The 2002 Training Top 100. *Training, 39*(3), 42–60.

The Credibility of Estimates

We have been discussing the costs and benefits of training programs and how to calculate the return on training investments. However, it is important to realize that this is not an exact science. One must make some assumptions and judgments when estimating the monetary benefits of a training program. As a result, the process only works if managers and clients accept the assumptions that have to be made. The estimation of benefits is an inexact procedure and trainers should be concerned about professional credibility.

Credibility is a major issue in cost-benefits analysis and the data must be accurate and the process believable.[10] Consider the example of a large bank that was experiencing a high rate of turnover. A training program was designed to counter the turnover problem. The cost of employee turnover needed to be estimated to calculate the ROI. But actual cost calculation was difficult because of the many interacting variables—administrative costs, interviewing, testing, relocation, orientation, increase in supervisory time, initial less-than-optimal performance, on-the-job training—all make up the cost of replacing one person. As the bank did not want to devote the considerable resources necessary to developing a precise calculation, turnover was classified as a soft cost and a combination of approaches were used to derive an acceptable figure.

Initially, a literature search was used to determine that another institution in the same industry had calculated a cost of $25,000 per turnover. This figure,

The Trainer's Notebook 1

Converting Measures to Monetary Values

One of the most difficult aspects of calculating ROI is placing a monetary value on the benefits of training. Jack Phillips, one of the leading experts on the calculation of ROI, suggests the following five steps for converting data to monetary values.

Step 1: Focus on a single unit. Identify a particular unit of improvement in output (e.g., products, sales), quality (e.g., errors, product defects), time (to respond to a customer order or complete a project), or employee behaviour (e.g., one case of employee turnover).

Step 2: Determine a value for each unit. Place a value identified on the single unit identified in step 1. This will be easier for hard measures such as production, quality, and time because most organizations record the value of one unit of production or the cost of a product defect. It will be more difficult to do for softer measures such as the cost of one employee absence.

Step 3: Calculate the change in performance. Determine the change in performance following training after factoring out other potential influences. This change in units of performance should be directly attributable to the training.

Step 4: Obtain an annual amount. The industry standard for an annual performance change is equal to the total change in the performance data during one year.

Step 5: Determine the annual value. The annual value of improvement equals the annual performance change, multiplied by the unit value.

Source: Phillips. J. J. (1996, April). How much is the training worth? *Training & Development*, 20–24.

derived by an internal-audit unit and verified by a consulting specialist in turnover reduction, was used as a starting point. The application of this statistic to another (even though quite similar) organization, however, was in question. The training staff then met with senior executives "to agree on a turnover cost value to use in gauging the success of the program. Management agreed on an estimate that was half the amount from the study, $12,500. This was considered very conservative because other turnover studies typically yield statistics of greater value. Management felt comfortable with the estimate, however, and it was used on the benefits side of program evaluation. Although not precise, this exercise yielded a figure that was never challenged" (p. 337).[11]

The term "never challenged" is significant. Trainers must perform cost-benefit analyses, but they must do so from a position of strength. In this example, senior managers were brought on side when they were used as experts. It mattered little that the turnover cost was set at $12,500 rather than $25,000, because the benefit estimation produced from these data was credible and accepted by those with the power to make investment decisions.

Thus, despite the appearance of quantitative rigour, virtually all but the simplest cost-benefit designs are dependent to a greater or lesser extent on some assumptions and expert opinion.[12] Trainers must ensure that their clients and management agree on the cost factors and the measurement and estimation of benefits. Management and clients must perceive benefit estimates as credible, believable, and acceptable. It is therefore critical that trainers find out what management deems to be most important in terms of the benefits and expected results, and whenever possible, obtain cost estimates (e.g., the cost of turnover) from management.

It also helps to use internal and external experts to assist in making benefit estimates. Because they are experts who are familiar with the situation, they are likely to be seen as credible by management. For example, if one wanted to estimate the cost of employee grievances, a good expert would be a manager of labour-relations. Estimates might also be obtained from other sources who are close to the situation such as trainees and their supervisors.[13] For example, in the case of United Petroleum International, which was described earlier, the sales engineers and managers estimated that the training program was responsible for about 37 percent of the increase in sales and this estimate was used in the calculation of the monetary benefit of the training program.[14]

For some guidelines on how to increase the credibility of the estimates of training benefits, see The Trainer's Notebook 2, "Increasing the Credibility of Benefit Estimates."

RPC

Utility Analysis

As described in Chapter 10, in a typical training evaluation study the performance of a training group is compared to an untrained or control group that did not receive the training in order to determine how effective the training program was for improving job performance. While the results of this comparison might tell us that there is a significant statistical difference in the job performance between the two groups, it does not tell us the dollar value associated with the training program. Utility analysis, however, can do just that and it is another approach for determining the costs and benefits of training programs.

Utility analysis is a method for forecasting the net financial benefits that result from human resource programs such as training and development. Utility analysis involves procedures in which the effectiveness of a training program can be translated into dollars and cents.[15]

To calculate the utility of a training program, several key factors must be considered. One of the most important factors is the effectiveness of a training program. In other words, what is the difference in job performance between employees who are trained and those who do not receive training? This is sometimes referred to as the *effect size*. The larger the effect size, the more effective a training program will be and the greater its utility.

A second key factor is what is known as the standard deviation of job performance in dollars of untrained employees. This factor has to do with how much of a difference there is in the job performance of untrained employees and the monetary value of this difference. The standard deviation of job performance in dollar terms is an important factor because in jobs in which the contribution of individual employees to the organization is widely different, an effective training program will improve the performance of a greater number of employees and will, therefore, result in larger dollar gains. When individual contributions are relatively similar, an effective training program is less likely to result in large dollar gains. Therefore, it is necessary to know or estimate the value of the standard deviation of job performance of untrained employees to make estimates of utility. There are several approaches for doing this such as asking supervisors to provide an estimate of the dollar value of performance. The larger the standard deviation of job performance of the untrained group, the greater the utility of a training program.

Utility analysis

A method to forecast the net financial benefits that result from human resource programs such as training and development

A third factor is the number of employees trained. The more employees trained, the greater the utility. A fourth factor is the expected length of time that the training benefits will last. The longer the effects of training will last, the higher the utility of a training program.

Utility is equal to the multiplication of all of these factors minus the cost of the training program (cost per employee x number of employees trained). The following formula is used to estimate the utility of a training program:[16]

$$\Delta U = (T)(N)(d_t)(SDy) - (N)(C)$$

where

ΔU = utility, or the dollar value of the program

T = the number of years the training has a continued effect on performance

N = the number of people trained

d_t = the true difference in job performance between the average trained and untrained employee in standard deviation units (effect size)

SD_y = the standard deviation of job performance in dollars of the untrained group

C = the cost of training each employee

Consider a simple example. To increase the number of widgets produced in a factory, a training program is implemented and 50 of the plant employees attend. Compared to a group of workers who do not attend the training program, the performance of the 50 trained employees is found to be twice as high (e.g., they produce 100 widgets per day compared to 50 produced by untrained workers). We will assume that this equals an effect size of 2. We also assume that the standard deviation of job performance of the untrained employees is $100. The expected length of time that the training will last is estimated to be five years. The cost of the training program is $300 per employee. Using the utility equation above, we can calculate the utility of the training program as follows:

$$\Delta U = 5(50)(2)(\$100) - 50(\$300)$$
$$\Delta U = \$50,000 - \$15,000$$
$$\Delta U = \$35,000$$

Thus, the expected utility of the training program for the 50 employees trained is $35,000. This amount might be even greater if the training program lasts longer than five years or if the untrained employees learn how to improve their performance just working with and observing the trained employees. The ROI can also be calculated by dividing the utility by the total cost of the program: $35,000/15,000 = 2.33.

An interesting extension of the use of the utility formula is conducting a **break-even analysis** or finding the value at which benefits equal costs and utility is equal to zero.[17] This analysis can be done for any of the terms in the utility equation. However, it is most meaningful to conduct a break-even

Break-even analysis

Finding the value at which benefits equal costs and utility is equal to zero analysis for the effect size or the standard deviation. For example, what is the break-even effect size for the example presented above? This can be calculated by dividing the cost of the training program ($15,000) by the multiplicative function of the other factors; that is, $(N)(T)(SD_y)$ or $(50)(5)(100)$. The calculations are as follows:

$$d_t = 15{,}000/25{,}000$$
$$d_t = .6$$

Thus, a training program with an effect size of .6 will result in a utility of zero, and an effect size greater than .6 will result in a utility that is greater than zero. Therefore, a training program that is considerably less effective than the one in our example would still be likely to result in a financial gain so long as the effect size is greater than .6.

Break-even analysis can be very useful because it helps reduce the uncertainty associated with the estimates of the various parameters used to calculate utility. For example, to the extent that the break-even effect size is far below the actual effect size used to calculate utility, the greater the confidence one can have in the results.[18]

Supporting the Costing Function

Costing training programs involves more than simply working with costing sheets and measuring benefits. It also requires the support of a number of activities. In this section, we discuss a number of activities that support the costing function including cost-benefit tracking systems, accounting treatment of training costs, and record keeping.

Cost-Benefit Tracking Systems

One of the most important facets of a costing system is a database that can be used to measure the progress an organization is making toward meeting its objectives. In particular, historical data can be invaluable when costing new proposals or in negotiating for new funding.

The major weakness has been the difficulty in showing a training program's contribution to profits. Without a method of collating and reporting successes in financial terms, the training professional is reduced to a minor supporting role in the corporate enterprise.

Accounting Treatment of Training Costs

Once training costs have been identified, they have to be incorporated into the accounting system so that they can be included in the total cost of production or service rendered. There are three ways to administer training accounts.

1. *Allocation of costs.* Costs can be shared with other departments and may, for example, be allocated according to the number employed in

a department and its labour turnover or output. The main advantage of this method is its simplicity. Because of that simplicity, it is the most widely used method. However, this method has disadvantages:

- It is contrary to the principle that managers should not be held accountable for costs they do not control.
- It does not relate to actual use of the training facilities or services.
- It gives no incentive to the training unit or professional to reduce costs and to improve efficiency.

2. *Selling the service.* Under this system, the training unit is required to sell its services at competitive rates to the other departments, the aim being to cover the cost of the training department.[19] The main advantages of this method are:

- control over training costs (training costs have to remain reasonable or the training function will price itself out of the reach of consumer departments)
- a check on the relevance and efficiency of the training offered (training is carefully evaluated by the departmental managers who are required to pay for it)

The disadvantages arising from a fluctuating demand for training services and the consequent planning difficulties seem to outweigh the advantages of this method.

3. *Policy costs.* Under this system, training costs are regarded as company policy costs and are stated as such in the accounts. Training costs are accumulated and shown as a deduction from the gross profit of the business. This approach is simple but can mean that control over training expenditures is less rigorous than it should be. Use of the method can, however, be justified when training is designed to keep human resources available, irrespective of individual departmental needs, such as in a company-wide, management-development scheme.

Some form of joint responsibility for or division of costs appears to be the best solution. A fixed charge can be made to the departments according to the number of staff undergoing training and the duration and type of training given. This charge should be fixed in advance and be a realistic estimate of the expected cost of training an average employee. The departments utilizing the services know the amount in advance. The training department is treated as a profit centre in its own right; it is expected to show a profit on the fixed charges levied. In the company accounts, the training department's profit or loss is credited or debited, respectively, to the training account in the ledger, to which the total of the charges levied on the departments using the service is also debited. The balance on this training account is then incorporated in the final profit and loss account in the usual way.

Record Keeping

Record keeping is not done for its own sake, but as a communication tool. Evidence needs to be presented that a contribution from training is being made on a day-to-day basis, rather than at a once-a-year review before the next year's training plan is written.[20] In addition, historical and comparative data can be useful in the identification of opportunities. Even the humble flow chart can be used to advantage, to discourage "duplicate efforts and unnecessarily complicated procedures," and to prevent bottlenecks (pp. 132, 133).[21]

Summary

As organization investments in training and development increase along with the importance of training for organizational effectiveness, organizations want to know the financial benefits and ROI of their training and development programs. This chapter described the methods and approaches for estimating the costs and benefits of training programs. The differences between cost-effectiveness and cost-benefit analysis were described and examples of the calculation of the costs, net benefits, and ROI of training programs were provided. This information is not only important for budgeting purposes and for comparing the costs of training programs, but it is also important for training evaluation. Utility analysis was also described as an alternative approach to calculate the financial value of training programs. The importance of credibility in estimating the costs and benefits of training programs was also discussed as well as the activities required to support the costing function.

Key Terms

break-even analysis (page 306)

cost-benefit evaluation (page 297)

cost-effectiveness evaluation (page 297)

costing (page 288)

developmental costs (page 291)

direct costs (page 290)

indirect costs (page 291)

net benefit (page 298)

overhead costs (page 291)

return on investment (ROI) (page 298)

trainee compensation (page 291)

utility analysis (page 305)

Weblinks

Accenture: www.accenture.ca (page 302)

Cisco Systems: www.cisco.com (page 299)

United Petroleum International: http://www.itel.gr/upi/ (page 298)

Discussion Questions

1. Discuss the pros and cons of calculating the ROI of training and development programs. Should trainers always do this as part of a training evaluation?

2. What are some of the things a trainer might do to increase the credibility of his/her monetary estimates of the benefits of a training program?

3. What is the difference between cost-benefit evaluation and cost-effectiveness evaluation? What are some situations in which a trainer might want to calculate one or the other?

Using the Internet

1. To find out the latest about ROI and training, visit the website of the magazine, *Workforce*, at **www.workforce.com**. Then click on training and development and do a search for an article on training and ROI. Choose an article that interests you and write a brief review of the article to present to your class.
2. To learn about one approach for calculating the ROI of training, go to: **www.workplacebasicskills.com/frame/free_tools/roi/worksheet.htm** and find out about the Training ROI Worksheet. Think about the most recent training course you have taken in a current or previous job, and then calculate the ROI. Alternatively, ask a friend or family member about a recent training program they have attended and calculate its ROI. What is the ROI of the training program? Was the training program worth taking? What parameters would have to change in order to increase the program's ROI?

Exercises

1. In order to calculate the benefits of training programs, one has to develop measures that are consistent with a training program and its objectives. As well, some of these measures will need to be translated into monetary terms. For each of the following training programs, identify benefits that can be measured for the purpose of cost-benefit evaluation and cost-effectiveness evaluation:
   a. Sales training
   b. Management development
   c. Customer-relations training
   d. Health and safety training
   e. Quality training
   f. Sexual harassment prevention training
   To learn more about these training programs, refer to Chapters 12 and 13.
2. Consider a situation in which you, a trainer for an organization that manufactures sportswear, must present information on the costs and benefits of a training program to management who is about to decide if the program will be adopted organization-wide. You have already designed the training program and delivered it to one group of employees and you want to begin offering it to the rest of the organization. How will you present the information to management? Will you present information on the net benefit, ROI, and/or utility analysis?

Will you present cost-benefit information or cost-effectiveness information? What are the advantages and disadvantages of presenting information on each of these? Do you think that trainers should present financial information about the benefits of training to management? What are the advantages and disadvantages of doing so?

3. As the housing market began to heat up, the Renswartz Realty Company decided to capitalize by increasing the number of listings and sales on a monthly basis. In order to do this, the company president believed they would have to do two things. First, they would have to better market the company's superior customer service. Second, they would have to train all agents to improve their sales and customer service skills. Choosing an advertising company turned out to be much easier than choosing a training program. Two consulting firms were contacted to provide a proposal to design and implement a training program that would be attended by all 200 of the company's sales agents.

   The first consulting firm offered a five-day program that would consist of lectures on "how to get more listings," "how to improve your service," and "making the sale," and would involve videos and behavioural modelling. According to the consulting firm, research has shown that the sales performance of those who have attended the training is significantly better than those who have not; the effect size of the program is .35. The training is expected to last for two years and will cost $1,500 per employee.

   The second consulting firm offered a similar program with the exceptions that it would be for only two days and would consist of sessions on "how to improve your sales" and "providing excellent service." Research on the training program has found it to be highly effective with an effect size of .25. The effects have been found to last for one year at which time follow-up sessions are required. The cost of the training program is $450 per employee.

   Based on the current sales performance of all 200 sales agents at Renswartz Realty, the standard deviation of sales is $15,000.

   a. Calculate the utility of the training programs offered by each of the consulting firms.

   b. Calculate the break-even effect size for both training programs.

   c. What are the advantages and disadvantages of each training program?

   d. Which training program should the company purchase?

   e. What are the advantages and limitations of this approach for calculating the benefits of a training program?

4. Consider the costs and benefits of a university or college course such as the training and development course you are now taking. Using the five cost categories discussed in the chapter, identify the major costs of the course and try to come up with some estimates. Now consider the

benefits. What benefits would you include if you were to do a cost-effectiveness and a cost-benefit analysis? How would you determine the ROI and utility of your course? Consider the costs and benefits from the institution's perspective and the student's perspective.

Case

A Thousand Mistakes a Week

Herritta Humbolt, marketing manager for a large mail-order jewellery firm, looked over the error sheets: 5 percent—not bad when you're 95 percent right! A second look, however, pinpointed the problem. Her shipping department mailed out 20,000 orders every week. Five percent of 20,000 is 1,000, that's 1,000 unhappy customers every week, 4,000 every month, 48,000 every year. If everyone told 10 friends about Herritta poor service, 480,000 people could be struck off her potential customer list yearly. Obviously, Herritta had a big problem, especially since mail-order customers are a special breed. They get hooked on the bargains, each one tending to place at least three orders per year.

A thousand mistakes every week! What kind of mistakes? A quick analysis showed Herritta that wrong addresses and wrong picks (the wrong jewellery) made up 95 percent of the errors.

Herritta checked the stocking systems and the mailing procedures. Satisfied that nothing much could be done to improve shipping methods—a major systems analysis had been completed last year—she turned her thoughts to training.

A meeting of her three shift supervisors (the experts) set out the following performance criteria:

1. *Keyboarding* (order entry, inventory control) with no more than two errors per day
   - three shifts each with three shippers (266.6 orders per day per person)
   - 4,000 orders per week
   - 800 orders per day; 2 errors = 0.025 percent error rate
2. *Picking* correct goods to ship
   - 0 percent error rate acceptable
   - Proper order *packing* (no tangles, breakage)
   - 0 percent error rate acceptable
3. Proper *shipping* (directly related to keyboarding as address labels were produced automatically from order-entry document)
   - 0 percent error rate acceptable

Again, using her panel of experts, Herritta calculated that each error cost:

$ 1.00	wasted postage
$ 1.00	labour wasted shipping original order
$10.00	labour (management/shippers) to correct original mistake
$ 4.00	phone/fax charges
$ 9.50	to send replacement order by courier
$ 5.00	restocking inventory
$30.50	

Herritta wanted to add in a large amount for lost goodwill, but the general manager vetoed the idea, telling her to stick with the hard figures.

Herritta contacted a local consultant who agreed to design a training program. She estimated that 15 hours of specialized keyboard training, followed by five hours of in-house training in picking, packing, and shipping should be supported by 10 hours of general customer-service training. Her rate would be $160/contact hour for the initial training plus 10 hours at $100/hour for the evaluation. Additional costs would be $500/day for software rental (15 hours), and $16 per trainee for materials.

Although the training would take place at work on three consecutive weekends, seven computers would have to be rented at $80 per computer per weekend. Wages would have to be added in; average yearly wage was $25,000 + $12,000 in benefits. The shippers were promised time and a half (i.e., 1.5 times their regular wages). Salary costs for managers were set arbitrarily at $2000.

Additional costs included: record keeping in the personnel unit, invoicing, and extra payroll costs: $500 (an estimate); insurance on each of the rented computers at $12.50/day; lunch for 80 (three lunches) at $11.50 per person; coffee: $75 flat cost (three weekends); overhead (extra heat, lights, and so on): $500 (estimated for the entire course).

Questions

1. Using a costing worksheet, calculate the costs of the proposed training program.
2. Assuming that the objective of no more than two errors per day is reached, calculate the net benefit and the return on investment for the proposed training program.
3. What other factors besides the net benefit and ROI should Herritta consider in deciding whether or not to adopt the proposed training program?

Running Case Part 7

VANDALAIS DEPARTMENT STORES

Several months following the structured employment interview training program for Vandalais Department Stores (refer to Chapter 5 for details on the training program), the director of human resources contacted the consultant

Chapter 11: The Costs and Benefits of Training Programs

who designed and delivered the training program. She was upset because management did not receive the results of the evaluation very positively and she was concerned that they might not fund future training programs. The director thought that it would be a good idea to demonstrate the value of the training program in terms of its costs and benefits, and asked the consultant to help her determine the costs and benefits of the structured employment interview training program.

1. Identify all of the costs associated with the structured employment interview training program, and develop a costing worksheet that includes all of the cost categories.
2. How would you calculate the monetary benefits of the training program. What are the indicators of the training benefits, and how can they be translated into dollars and cents? How would you calculate a cost-effectiveness and cost-benefit evaluation?

References

[1]Gordon, J. (1991). Measuring the "goodness" of training. *Training, 27* (8), 19–25. Lopez-Pacheco, A., & Daly, J. (2002, January). The 50 best companies to work for in Canada: Fedex. *R.O.B.*, p. 52. Training: The Human Side of Business by Gordon, J. Copyright 1991 by V N U BUS PUBNS USA. Reproduced with permission of V N U BUS PUBNS USA in the format Textbook via Copyright Clearance Center.

[2]Phillips. J. J. (1996, February). ROI: The search for best practices. *Training and Development*, 42–47.

[3]Salas, E., & Cannon-Bowers, J. A. (2001). The science of training: A decade of progress. *Annual Review of Psychology, 52*, 471–99.

[4]Robinson, D. G., & Robinson, J. (1989, August). Training for impact. *Training & Development Journal,* 43(8), 34–42.

[5]Prepared by Dr. Gary D. Geroy, Colorado State University at Fort Collins. Reproduced with permission from his client organization.

[6]Lachnit, C. (2001, September). Training proves its worth. *Workforce*, 52–56.

[7](2002, May). Companies Continue to Invest in Training and Evaluate ROI. *Workforce* Online: www.workforce.com

[8]Gale, S. F. (2002, August). Measuring the ROI of E-Learning. *Workforce*, 74–77.

[9]Robinson, D. G., & Robinson, J. (1989, August).

[10]Bedinham, K. (1998). Proving the effectiveness of training. *Education & Training* 40 (4), 166–67. Phillips. J. J. (1996, April). How much is the training worth? *Training & Development*, 20–24.

[11]Phillips, J. J. (1991, Autumn). Measuring the return on HRD. *Employment Relations Today, 18(3)*, 329–342.

[12]Geroy, G.D., & Wright, P.C. (1988). Evaluation research: A pragmatic program-focused research strategy for decision makers. *Performance Improvement Quarterly, 1* (3), 17–26. Wright, P.C. (1990). Validating hospitality curricula within associated-sponsored certification programs: A qualitative methodology and a case study. *Hospitality Research Journal, 14* (1), 117–32.

[13]Phillips. J. J. (1996, April).

[14]Lachnit, C. (2001, September).

[15]Cascio, W.F. (1991). *Costing human resources: The financial impact of behavior in organizations.* Boston, MA: Kent.

[16]Schmidt, F.L., Hunter, J.E., & Pearlman, K. (1982). Assessing the economic impact of personnel programs on workforce productivity. *Personnel Psychology, 35*, 333–47.

[17]Cascio, W.F. (1991).

[18]Mathieu, J.E., & Leonard, R.L., Jr. (1987). Applying utility concepts to a training program in supervisory skills: A time-based approach. *Academy of Management Journal, 30*, 316–35.

[19]Long, R.F. (1990). Protecting the investment in people—Making training pay. *Journal of European Industrial Training, 14* (7), 21–27.

[20]Brown, M.G. (1992). The Baldrige criteria—Better, tougher, and clearer for 1992. *Journal for Quality and Participation, 15* (2), 70–75.

[21]Kaydos, W. (1991). *Measuring, managing, and maximizing performance.* Cambridge, MA: Productivity Press.

Chapter 12

Training Programs

Chapter Learning Objectives

After reading this chapter, you should be able to

- describe orientation training programs
- describe basic skills training and its importance to organizations
- describe technical skills training
- describe information technology training
- discuss WHMIS legislation and describe the type of information that should be included in health and safety training programs
- describe total quality management and quality training programs
- describe team training and the kinds of skills that team members require to work in teams
- describe sales training and the skills required to be effective in sales
- discuss customer service training and the skills that employees require to interact effectively with customers
- define sexual harassment and describe sexual harassment training
- describe diversity training and cross-cultural training and their use in organizations

www.eddiebauer.com

Organizations provide many different kinds of training to their employees. One of the most common and important types of training is new employee orientation training. Like Eddie Bauer, most companies today realize the importance of orientation training and the effect it can have on new employees. Inadequate orientation programs often leave employees feeling disconnected from their organization and more likely to quit within the first three months. Effective orientation programs, however, can shape corporate culture, increase new employees' speed-to-proficiency, and lower turnover.[2]

By now you should be familiar with the training and development process. We have covered all of the major steps in the development of a training program: needs analysis, training objectives, design, methods, delivery, transfer of training, and the evaluation and costing of training programs. At this point, you might be asking yourself, "What type of training programs do organizations design and deliver to their employees?" Obviously, the type of training program depends on an organization's training needs and objectives. However, we can still describe training programs in terms of specific kinds of training. The purpose of this chapter is to describe the major types of training programs that are designed and delivered by organizations today.

Types of Training Programs

During the last decade, organizations have made dramatic changes in response to an ever-changing work environment. New work arrangements combined with new technologies have led to a demand for skilled employees in both the manufacturing and service sectors. Whether employees are learning to operate a new computer system on the factory floor or how to provide customers with excellent service, some type of training program is invariably required.

Thus, it is not surprising that training and development has experienced dramatic growth in the last five years. In the United States, where 15 million employees participate in 17.6 million courses, one out of every eight American workers attends a formal training course each year.[3] It has been estimated that 54.2 billion was spent on formal workplace training in the United States in 2002.[4]

As indicated in Chapter 1, Canadian organizations spend approximately $5 billion a year on training and development. This figure translates into about 5.8 million Canadian adults enrolled in education and training activities, $850 spent per employee, and the average Canadian worker receiving about seven hours of training annually. As well, those companies rated as the 100 best to work for in Canada, spend the most per employee on training, and many Canadian organizations expect their training budgets to increase.

With so much money and effort being spent on training, you might be wondering what types of training employees are receiving. A recent study asked employees about the training they receive and found that nearly 80 percent of the employees reported that they had received some type of training in the past year.[5]

The most common types of training were job-specific and technical skills training followed by the use of new technology. Common types of soft skills training included teamwork, communication, problem solving, and customer service training. When asked if additional training would be useful to them, 99 percent of the respondents said yes; however, most indicated they wanted more of the same type of training they were already receiving. The exception to this was technology. In terms of training that is not provided by their organization but would be of value, 25 percent indicated computer training or some other type of current technology. If their organization offered it, nearly 75 percent said they would sign up for training on the use of new technology, communication skills to help them work better with other people, job-specific and technical skills, and management training.[6]

The amount and type of training varies by industry. For example, among manufacturing companies, more than 60 percent of employees receive training in specific job skills, followed next by quality and statistical analysis, group decision making, team building, multiple jobs, and leadership skills. During the past decade, the number of manufacturing organizations that have trained a majority of their workers in each training category has doubled or tripled.[7]

According to a recent survey by The Conference Board of Canada, the highest percentages of total training expenditures in Canadian organizations are for management/supervisory skills, technical processes, information technology skills, and professional skills (discipline or industry-specific). These four content areas combined account for 47 percent of the average overall expenditures on training and development by Canadian organizations. After these four, the next highest expenditures are spent on occupational health and safety training and new employee orientation training. Canadian organizations spend the least amount on basic skills training.[8]

Table 12.1 lists training type as a percentage of training expenditures in Canadian organizations for 14 training categories. Table 12.2 indicates the frequency that the different types of training described in this chapter are offered by organizations in the United States. Notice that new employee orientation tops the list with 98 percent of organizations providing this type of training followed by computer systems and applications training with 96 percent. In the remainder of this chapter, we will review each of the types of training programs listed in Table 12.2.

Orientation Training

Orientation training programs are programs that are designed to introduce new employees to their job, the people they will be working with, and the organization.[9] Formal orientation and training programs have become the main method used by organizations to socialize new employees. [10]

As noted in Table 12.2, new employee orientation is the most common type of training provided by organizations, with 98 percent indicating they provide it. This finding is consistent across a number of studies in different countries.

For example, a study of 100 major British organizations found that an overwhelming majority provided new hires with formalized, off-the-job induction training within four weeks of entry. Most of the organizations provided standardized programs that were designed and conducted by in-house human resource practitioners. The content of induction training was general in nature and pertained mostly to health and safety, terms and conditions of

TABLE 12.1

Training Type as A Percentage of Training Expenditures in Canadian Organizations

Management/supervisory skills	13.2
Technical processes	12.4
Information technology skills	10.9
Professional skills	10.8
Occupational health & safety/government mandated	9.1
New employee orientation	6.6
Product knowledge	6.5
Customer relations	6.0
Sales and dealer	5.9
Quality/competition/business practices	5.9
Interpersonal communication	5.0
Executive development	4.5
Other	2.1
Basic skills (literacy, numeracy, reading comprehension, writing)	1.1

Source: Harris-Lalonde, S. (2001). Training and development outlook. Reprinted by permission of *The Conference Board of Canada*. Ottawa.

TABLE 12.2

Percentages of Organizations Providing Common Types of Training in the United States

TYPE OF TRAINING	% PROVIDING*
New hire orientation	98
Computer systems, applications	96
Communication skills	89
Technical training	89
Customer service	87
Sexual harassment	87
Team training	84
Health and safety	81
Interpersonal communication	80
Diversity, cultural awareness	72
Sales training	52
Quality/process improvement	67
Basic life, work skills	36

*Percent of all organizations with 100 or more employees that provide these types of training.

Source: Galvin, T. (2002, October). 2002 Industry Report. *Training 40*, pp. 24–73.

employment, organizational history and structure, specific training provisions, and human resource management policies and procedures.[11]

Like Eddie Bauer, many companies today realize the value and importance of orientation training programs. Starbucks, for example, has a comprehensive orientation and training program. New employees receive 24 hours of training in their first 80 hours of employment. CEO Howard Schultz greets new hires via video and they learn about the company's history and obsession for quality and customer service.[12]

This first phase is followed by classes during the next six weeks on topics such as "Brewing the Perfect Cup," "Retail Sales," "Coffee Knowledge," and "Customer Service." Employees are also taught relaxation techniques and guidelines for on-the-job interpersonal relations. [13] According to CEO Howard Schultz, "For people joining the company we try to define what Starbucks stands for, what we're trying to achieve, and why that's relevant to them" (p. 126). [14]

Research has shown that orientation training has a positive effect on the attitudes and adjustment of new hires. According to Daniel Feldman, "the overall training program plays a major role in how individuals make sense of and adjust to their new job settings" (p. 399).[15]

One of the authors of this text examined the training of entry-level accountants in Canadian accounting firms and found that the amount of training received was positively related to their ratings of training helpfulness, and both the amount and helpfulness of training were positively related to job attitudes and negatively related to turnover. [16] Not surprisingly, the turnover rate at Starbucks is around 60 percent, which is considerably less than the average rate of 150 percent in the specialty-coffee industry.[17]

In a recent study on a voluntary new employee orientation training program, employees volunteered to attend a three hour orientation program that was designed to help them feel more a part of the organization; learn more about the organization's language, traditions, mission, history, and structure; and better understand the organization's basic workplace principles. The program consisted of an introduction and overview; a videotaped welcome from the company president; a game/exercise to familiarize employees with the company's traditions and language; a videotape and discussion about the mission, history, and structure of the organization; and a lecture/discussion of the organization's basic workplace principles.[18]

The results indicated that employees who attended the orientation training program were more socialized in terms of their knowledge and understanding of the organization's goals and values, history, and involvement with people. Furthermore, employees who attended orientation also had higher organizational commitment as a result of their greater socialization. The authors concluded that orientation training can help employees become more socialized and result in greater organizational commitment.[19]

In summary, the orientation and training of new employees is one of the most common types of training. In order for new hires to learn their jobs and adjust to the organization, they require knowledge and information about their job-related tasks, work roles, group processes, and organizational attributes (e.g., organizational goals, values, history, etc.). Research has shown that newcomers' knowledge in these areas is positively related to their job satisfaction, organizational commitment, and adjustment. Knowledge about one's tasks and role is especially important for successful socialization. Thus, orientation training programs should be designed to provide new hires with information and knowledge about their job, role, work group, and organization. The orientation and training received by new hires can have a lasting effect on their job attitudes and behaviours.[20]

Basic-Skills Training

At one time, it was possible to find a job that paid well and that did not require a high-school education. Those days are gone. The ability to read, write, and understand mathematics is now required for an increasing number of jobs. The number of factory workers who have a college education has been steadily rising over the past decade.[21] For young people, this means that a high-school diploma is the minimum amount of education they must have to acquire a good job in today's workplace.

But what about the workers who don't have a high-school education and whose jobs are changing and will require them to read, write, and understand arithmetic? Unfortunately, far too many workers in Canada fall into this category. A recent survey by Statistics Canada found that 48 percent of Canadian adults have some trouble with everyday reading, writing, or arithmetic, and for 22 percent the problem is severe.[22]

Literacy and numeracy are not only issues for immigrants or seniors. Forty percent of native-born Canadians between the ages of 16 and 65 have problems reading and 15 percent are in the lowest literacy category, meaning that they have serious difficulty with any printed material, including understanding a newspaper article or using a bus schedule.[23]

Table 12.3 shows the five literacy levels used by Statistics Canada to describe adult literacy. It is estimated that there are 4.5 million Canadian adults in the lowest literacy category. This statistic is particularly alarming when you consider that these people will make up the bulk of the labour force for decades to come. The survey also found that the literacy skills of 20 percent of recent high-school graduates were too low for entry-level jobs. Statistics Canada concluded that the literacy problem in Canada is so serious that it threatens Canada's economic future and global competitiveness.

The problem is just as serious in the United States where it is estimated that up to 20 percent of the workforce is functionally illiterate. In a recent survey, 63 percent of the respondents indicated that their employees have serious basic-skills deficiencies. The skill deficiencies, beginning with the highest percentage of respondents indicating a deficiency, were basic job skills, basic math skills, basic written skills, understanding of diagrams or drawings, technical skills, verbal communications skills, computer skills, and teamwork skills. In addition, it has been reported that many job applicants for manufacturing jobs have inadequate reading, writing, and communication skills, and a deficiency in employee skills is the reason why one in five manufacturing companies are unable to expand.[24]

The implications of the skills gap are enormous. For example, "In everyday work life, this deficiency translates into secretaries who can't write letters free of grammatical errors, workers who can't read instructions that govern the operation of new machinery, and bookkeepers who can't manipulate the fractions necessary to compute simple business transactions" (p. 71).[25]

It is estimated that the lack of basic skills in the workforce costs American organizations $60 billion in lost productivity as a result of mistakes, workplace accidents, and damage to equipment.[26] Organizations will have difficulty implementing new programs and new technology and staying competitive if their workforce does not have a basic education. Many companies are discovering this. They implement a new program such as statistical-process control and then discover that employees do not have the ability to synthesize the information.

It is becoming increasingly clear that organizations must provide their workforces with basic-skills training if they are to compete and survive in a global and high-tech workplace. Evidence suggests that without first providing trainees with basic-skills training, other programs and initiatives will not succeed.[27] Consider the following example in which managers did not feel that basic-skills training had any value for their organization:

> These managers soon found that when hourly employees, many of whom spoke little English, were put through quality or team training without first receiving basic-skills training, nothing on the manufacturing floor changed—no up-line communication, no

TABLE 12.3

Levels Of Literacy

Statistics Canada slots adults into five levels of literacy skills based on how well they handle everyday tasks that range from locating plant-care information in an article about impatiens to checking out a newspaper weather chart.

Level 1: Nonreaders who have serious difficulty with any printed material.

Level 2: Poor readers who can read only simple printed material containing no complex tasks.

Level 3: Average readers who can handle everyday printed material. This level of skill is needed for entry-level jobs.

Levels 4 and 5: High-end readers, from managers through professionals to academics. The passing grade to move up a level is 80 percent, meaning someone with a 75 percent probability of successfully completing the average Level 3 task is still slotted into Level 2 and labelled as having low literacy.

Source: Calamai, P. (1999, August 28). The literacy gap. *Toronto Star*, p. J2. Reprinted with permission–Toronto Syndication Services. Excerpt from an article originally appearing in the *Toronto Star*, August 1999.

consensus decision making, no team meetings. The managers who opposed basic-skills training were unable to comprehend what had gone wrong (p. 77).[28]

As Kuri notes, "What these companies failed to recognize was that improved literacy skills among the workforce could reduce waste and improve productivity—and increase earnings" (p. 77). Many companies have met the rigorous quality standards of the International Standards Organization and received ISO 9000 certification only after implementing basic-skills training programs.[29]

Basic-skills training programs are designed to provide employees with critical literacy skills and improve their ability to read things such as change orders, to make numerical calculations, to enter data for tracking, and to use the correct technical vocabulary. **Literacy** has been defined as "an individual's ability to read, write, and speak English, compute and solve basic math problems, and develop one's knowledge and potential through listening skills" (p. 71).[30]

As shown in Table 12.4, there are four primary types of basic skills or remedial training: reading, basic math or arithmetic, English as a second language, and writing. Reportedly, the most popular way of teaching basic skills to manufacturing employees is on-the-job training. An increasing number of organizations are realizing that it is imperative that employees receive basic-skills training. Motorola Inc., for example, spent $40 million to train 8000 of its employees in basic skills.[31]

Organizations that have implemented basic-skills training have not only experienced an improvement in productivity, efficiency, and quality, but some also report a decrease in absenteeism and the number of workers' compensation claims made, and an improvement in cross-cultural communication and morale. Basic-skills training also has several advantages for employees. Not only does the training improve their skills, self-esteem, and self-efficacy, but it also improves their chances of remaining employed. The percentages of employees who receive basic-skills training and remain employed or are promoted are higher than employees who do not receive training.[32]

In the banking and financial services industries, meeting math requirements has become a major problem for career advancement. The major banks have become involved in more complex lines of business that require employees to provide financial counselling. Employees must understand more than just adding, subtracting, multiplying, and dividing. This so-called math gap means that employees throughout the financial services industry must upgrade their math skills.[33]

Organizations cannot expand their services or implement new technologies if their employees do not have basic literacy skills. Providing basic-skills training is a critical requirement for surviving in an increasingly competitive and global environment.

As noted earlier, Canadian organizations spend very little on basic skills training, an under-investment that The Conference Board of Canada has described as "troubling" particularly in light of their own research, which has

Basic-skills training

Training programs that are designed to provide employees with critical literacy skills such as reading and arithmetic that are required to perform their job

Literacy

An individual's ability to read, write, and solve basic math problems found that employees who improve their basic skills are more likely to learn new job-related skills more quickly and accurately; make fewer mistakes; work more efficiently; and be less resistant to change.[34]

Technical Skills Training

Technical skills training

Training in specific job skills that all employees need to perform their jobs

Technical skills training is training for job specific skills that all employees need to perform their jobs. As noted previously, among manufacturing firms, specific job skills was the category for which the largest percentage of firms provided training to more than 60 percent of employees. As well, note that in Table 12.2 technical training was provided by 89 percent of organizations.

These figures should not be surprising given the changes in the workplace that have occurred over the past two decades. With increasing global competition, organizations have had to find new ways to stay competitive

TABLE 12.4

Remedial Training By Organization Size

NUMBER OF EMPLOYEES	% OF ORGANIZATIONS SPONSORING REMEDIAL/BASIC EDUCATION
100–499	17
500–999	14
1,000–2,499	24
2,500–9,999	33
10,000 or More	36
All Sizes*	18

TYPES OF REMEDIAL TRAINING PROVIDED[†]

Reading — 40%

Basic math/arithmetic — 50%

English as a second language — 51%

Writing — 52%

*Refers to U.S. organizations with 100 or more employees.

†Of organizations that do some type of remedial training, percent that teach these topics. Based on 803 responses.

Source: Industry Report (1997, October 10). Training technology. *Training 34*, p. 58. Training: The Human Side of Business by Industry Report. Copyright 1997 by V N U BUS PUBNS USA. Reproduced with permission of V N U BUS PUBNS USA in the format Textbook via Copyright Clearance Center.

and to survive, often by adopting new technologies and the redesign of work arrangements and systems. As a result, employees have had to undergo a considerable amount of technical skills upgrading and training. Nowhere is this more apparent than in the manufacturing sector, where low-skilled employees have had to become highly skilled employees to keep their jobs and for their organizations to survive.[35]

During the mid-1980s, companies such as Corning, Motorola, and Xerox began a trend toward high-skills manufacturing. Rote assembly-line workers were replaced with workers who needed to learn new skills to operate new technology and think while they worked. These innovative practices became mainstream in the 1990s as they spread throughout the manufacturing sector. Not only did these organizations realize that investments in training can boost productivity, but that training employees to improve their skills was essential to being competitive. As a result, factory workers in North America are now being trained to improve their technical skills to the level Japanese and German workers have already attained.[36]

Consider the case of Acme Metals Inc., a specialty steel maker in the United States. Faced with increased competition, the company spent $400 million to redesign their mill with a new high-tech German caster that converts molten steel into two-inch thick bands. Employees took an exhaustive battery of exams to test for reading, math, technical, and communication skills. Based on the results, 750 employees were chosen to be part of a new team-oriented system. However, this selection was just the beginning. Employees then spent nine months in training to upgrade their skills, doing everything from studying metallurgy, math, and computers to completing a piece-by-piece study of the new machinery, at a cost of $8 million.[37]

As organizations change to remain competitive, they are likely to continue to increase their use of new technologies thus making technical skills training a regular and continuous part of the job for manufacturing workers.

Information Technology Training

Information technology training refers to computers and computer systems training. As shown in Table 12.2, 96 percent of organizations indicated that they provide computer systems and applications training. Information systems training has been ranked as one of the top 10 issues of critical importance and is known to be a key factor in the successful implementation of information systems technology.[38] Research has shown that technological failures in the workplace are most often the result of training issues rather than the technology.[39]

Information technology training usually involves either introductory computer training programs in which trainees learn about computer hardware and software, or applications training in which trainees are instructed on specific software applications to be used within the organization.[40] Applications training is required whenever an organization upgrades its computer systems.

With the growing use of computers and computer technology in the workplace, workers increasingly require training in applications. For

Information technology training

Training programs that focus on the use of computers and computer systems

Chapter 12: Training Programs

example, factory workers must now learn to use computer controls to operate new equipment and to read computer-generated information in areas such as inventories, suppliers and customers, costs and prices.[41] It is not surprising that many computer users need training for computer-related job skills.[42]

One of the most common types of information technology training is computer software training. "**Computer software training** refers to the planned, structured, and formal means of delivering information about how to use a specific computer software application" (p. 271).[43] Computer software training has been shown to increase trainees' ability to use the system and their motivation to use software.

Information technology training is likely to continue to be a critical area of training given the rapid pace of change in computer technology and the increasing use of computers in the workplace. This means that trainers will have to increasingly provide computer-related training to employees. As discussed in Training Today, trainers must pay special attention to older trainees who might not be comfortable using computers.

Computer software training

Training programs that focus on how to use a specific computer software application

Health and Safety Training

Workplace health and safety has become an increasing concern in Canadian organizations. The costs of work-related injuries and illnesses are on the rise and present a serious threat to employees and their organizations. Approximately 423 000 workers in Canada are injured on the job each year. Workplace injuries result in 15 million lost workdays per year at a cost of $4 billion in compensation payments. The cost rises to between $8 and $10 billion when indirect costs are included.[44]

Preventing accidents and injuries and improving workplace health and safety is an important concern of workers, governments, unions, and organizations. Occupational health and safety should begin with preventative and corrective actions that eliminate or reduce accidents and injuries. Safety training is one of the most important ways to deal with accidents before they occur by educating employees in safe work methods and techniques. Employees should also be trained to recognize the chemical and physical hazards in the workplace so that they are prepared and capable of taking corrective action in the event of an accident.

As noted in Table 12.1, health and safety training accounts for 9.1 percent of the average overall expenditures on training and development by Canadian organizations. In the United States, 81 percent of the organizations surveyed indicated that they provide health and safety training. These high figures indicate the importance of health and safety training along with the fact that for many organizations it is government mandated.

An effective health and safety training program should include the following:[45]

- the organization's safety rules, practices, and accident and injury reporting procedures
- the duties of the employer, supervisor, and the worker as specified in the Occupational Health and Safety (OHS) legislation

Computer Training for Older Workers

In recent years, an increasing number of mature adults have been re-entering the workforce in unprecedented numbers. Older workers offer employers advantages such as strong work ethic, high productivity, a wealth of experience, and low absenteeism and turnover rates. But seniors usually are not regarded as computer savvy enough to help ease the high-tech labour shortage.

In fact, many employers and trainers assume that older workers can't—or won't—learn to use computers at all. But those who specialize in teaching older learners contend that this impression is dead wrong. Training departments attempting to teach computer applications to older learners often fail to consider their special needs.

For example, an insurance company decided to hire some older workers for its call centre because, it believed, its many elderly customers would relate better to a voice that had some years behind it. So the company recruited and trained a group of mature adults, and then ran them through the same computer training everyone else received. The company's new "old" workers had a high attrition rate during training and substandard performance afterward. The company concluded that hiring seniors was a mistake and that older people couldn't do the job.

But the fault didn't lie with the employees or the material but with the trainers. Trainers often do not think about how to accommodate the needs of an older audience. After adjusting the time allotted for its computer training, the same insurance company tried the experiment again and found that older employees' performance after training was on par with younger employees.

Those who specialize in training seniors suggest teaching them in smaller classes of people roughly the same age. A few seniors may find it a challenge to try to keep up with younger trainees, but most will be left behind and won't ask questions if the rest of the class seems to be faster on the uptake. Most experts recommend training seniors in small classes of six to ten. Computer training for older employees can also be improved by slowing it down; using mature trainers from the same peer group as the trainees who can allude to experiences they understand; conducting the training in a learning environment that is comfortable for older learners; and understanding that older learners have some particular problems with computers such as how to use a mouse and line-of-sight problems caused by bifocals. Most importantly, the trainer must adjust his/her instructional style to the needs of an older audience.

Source: Excerpted from Filipczak, B. (1998, May). Old dogs, new tricks. *Training, 35* (5), 50–58. Training: The Human Side of Business by Filipczak, B. Copyright 1998 by V N U BUS PUBNS USA. Reproduced with permission of V N U BUS PUBNS USA in the format Textbook via Copyright Clearance Center.

- the importance of strict compliance with warning and emergency signs and signals
- the types and use of emergency equipment (e.g., extinguishers or spill retainers)
- the use, care, and acquisition of personal protective equipment
- the organization benefits
- the known hazards and safeguards against them
- the importance of reporting other hazards (e.g., defective equipment) and the mechanism for doing so
- the emergency and evacuation procedures for dealing with things such as fires and explosions, spills, toxic exposure, and so on
- the need for good housekeeping
- courses in first aid, CPR, and defensive driving where applicable

Workplace Hazardous Materials Information System (WHMIS)

Legislation to ensure that workers across Canada are aware of the potential hazards of chemicals in the workplace and are familiar with emergency procedures for the clean-up and disposal of a spill

An important component of health and safety training involves the handling of hazardous materials and chemicals. The **Workplace Hazardous Materials Information System (WHMIS)** legislation is designed to ensure that workers across Canada are aware of the potential hazards of chemicals in the workplace and are familiar with emergency procedures for the clean-up and disposal of a spill. An important component of WHMIS legislation is employee training. Training in WHMIS is designed so that employees can identify WHMIS hazard symbols, read WHMIS supplier and workplace labels, and read and apply the information on material safety data sheets (MSDS), which outline the hazardous ingredient(s) in a product and the procedures for the safe handling of that product.[46]

Besides including health and safety education as part of the orientation and training of new employees, organizations should provide it on an ongoing basis, such as through safety meetings during working hours, especially when new procedures or equipment are introduced into the workplace. In addition, all levels of management and supervision should receive training in health and safety. Trained employees are the best deterrent to injuries, material damage, and health problems.[47]

Quality Training

In the 1980s, North American manufacturing organizations found themselves challenged by the high quality of foreign goods. Given the emphasis on quantity and economies of scale in North America, quality was viewed as simply an inspection of goods at the end of the line.[48]

To remain competitive, however, this approach had to change. In response, organizations in North America began to invest in new programs aimed at building quality into the production process. Today, quality programs can be found in many organizations.[49] The best example of this is total quality management (TQM).

Total quality management (TQM)

A systematic process of continual improvement of the quality of an organization's products and services

Total quality management is a systematic process of continual improvement of the quality of products and services. In addition to an emphasis on quality and continual improvement, TQM also involves teamwork and a customer focus.[50] Because TQM requires the involvement of all stakeholders in an organization, the concept moves far beyond piecemeal approaches to quality improvement, which often are limited to inspection and quality-control methods carried out by a specialized department. Although this search for quality is not a new concept, TQM can require major organizational changes.[51]

TQM places the training function in a pivotal position, as the process often requires significant changes in employees' skills and the way employees work. TQM literature, however, typically contains only superficial information about new approaches to training and development. Fortunately, some training professionals have had to become involved in TQM, and have provided some guidance on how to transform traditional practices into TQM.[52]

For example, employees are empowered by having the decision-making power driven down to those who can do the most for quality improvement. TQM requires that employees at lower levels share managerial responsibility, moving away from conventional command-and-control procedures to a more participative style of management. With empowerment, the roles of employees change and they assume more responsibility. In addition, they are required to work in teams that share decision-making and problem-solving responsibilities.

Most TQM advocates emphasize the importance of training and development.[53] Without proper employee training, the act of empowerment in TQM is meaningless.[54] Training and development are primary methods of reinforcing employee commitment to the consistent delivery of high-quality products and services. Accordingly, leading TQM companies invest heavily in training and development at all levels. In the absence of proper training, many TQM systems that are excellent at identifying and quantifying the cost of performance problems are ultimately unsuccessful because there is no way of changing the behaviours that caused the deficiencies in the first place.[55]

Because quality initiatives such as TQM involve substantial changes to employees' work roles and responsibilities, comprehensive and extensive training is required in a number of areas. Harper and Rifkind have provided the following outline for TQM training:[56]

1. *Overview of the state of the organization.* This overview provides information about the health of the organization and why it is planning to implement TQM.
2. *Statement from the head of the organization.* The best way to communicate the support of top executives for TQM is for a statement by the head of the organization to be delivered in person as part of training.
3. *Overview of TQM.* Employees need to be informed about what TQM involves including the use of teams, continual improvement, customer focus, employee empowerment, and plans for implementation.
4. *Team training.* Employees need to be trained on how teams function, such as the difference between a team and a committee, rules for team formation, the composition of teams, and team responsibilities.
5. *Training in the use of tools.* TQM involves the use of a number of statistical tools such as Pareto charts, fishbone diagrams, affinity programs, and interrelationship diagrams as part of the problem-solving and decision-making processes. Employees will need to be trained on how to use each of these tools.

Although the name of quality programs might differ depending on the approach, a focus on quality will continue to be one of the major initiatives critical to organizational competitiveness and survival. The success of quality initiatives, however, depends on training programs to provide employees with the knowledge and skills required to function in a quality-oriented work system. Quality training is related to quality outcomes, and is considered to be a critical factor in an organization's strategy and ability to achieve a competitive advantage.[57]

Nontechnical Skills Training

Although a great deal of emphasis has been given to technical skills, soft or nontechnical skills have also become an increasingly important set of skills for many jobs. **Nontechnical or soft skills** are skills that are required to work and interact effectively with other people, such as communication skills, interpersonal skills, conflict management skills, negotiation skills, problem-solving solving, and so on. Many of the changes taking place in organizations such as the increased use of teams has resulted in an increasing awareness of the importance of nontechnical skills.

Nontechnical skills have even become important in areas where traditionally they were not seen as relevant as technical skills. For example, in addition to technical skills upgrading required for many factory workers, new work arrangements often require factory employees to work in teams. As a result, they require nontechnical skills to work effectively with other team members and to make decisions and solve problems as part of a team. In addition to technical skills training, many factory workers now also receive training in areas such as conflict resolution, problem solving, and customer and supplier relations.[58]

As indicated in Table 12.1, several nontechnical skills training programs such as communication skills, interpersonal communication, and customer service are provided by a majority of organizations today. Although there are many types of nontechnical skills training, some of the most common are team training, sales training, customer service training, sexual harassment training, cultural diversity training, and cross-cultural training. In the remainder of this chapter, we describe each of these training programs.

Team Training

In recent years, many organizations have implemented team-based work systems. An estimated 80 percent of organizations with 100 or more employees now use some form of teams, and more than 50 percent of all organizations in the United States are exploring team-based work systems.[59] The reasons for this vary but in many cases it is an attempt to improve efficiency, quality, customer satisfaction, innovation, and the speed of production.

Levi Strauss & Co. explored team-based work systems in 1992 as part of a solution for dealing with overseas, low-cost competitors and the need to increase productivity and reduce costs. Levi's employees had previously worked on their own, operating machines on which they performed a single, specific, and repetitive task such as sewing zippers or belt loops on jeans, and were paid a set amount for each piece of work completed. Once the teams were implemented, groups of 10 to 50 workers shared the tasks and were paid for the total number of trousers that the group completed.[60]

However, top performers began to complain that their less skilled and slower teammates caused their wages to decline while the wages of lower skilled workers increased. Threats, insults, and group infighting became a regular part of daily work as faster workers tried to rid their group of slower workers. Top performers responded to their lower wages by reducing their productivity and employee morale began to deteriorate.

Because the groups had limited supervision, they had to resolve group problems on their own, and they also divided up the work of absent members themselves. In some plants, team members would chase each other out of the bathroom and nurse's station. Slower teammates were often criticized, needled, and resented by their group. Some couldn't take the resentment and simply quit. In one group, a member was voted off of her team because she planned to have hand surgery.

Unfortunately, the team system did not help Levi's accomplish its objectives. Profit margins declined as competitors began offering private-label jeans at two-thirds the price of Levi's, and Levi's market share of men's denim-jeans in the U.S. fell from 48 percent in 1990 to 26 percent in 1997. In 1997, the company closed 11 factories in the United States and laid off 6395 workers. In February of 1999, the company let go another 5900 employees, or 30 percent of its workforce of 19 900 in the U.S. and Canada, and announced that it will close 11 of its remaining 22 plants in North America.[61]

What went wrong with the team approach at Levi's? One of the answers to this question is the lack of team training. Employees received only brief seminars on team building and problem solving. Although workers were given time to learn unfamiliar machines, many felt that they had inadequate training on issues such as balancing workflows and spotting quality problems. Furthermore, although workers were now part of a team system, management was not given guidance on how to implement the system. The lack of training was an important factor in the failure of teams at Levi Strauss.

As this example illustrates, teams often do not work. There are many other examples of failed teams that have had disastrous consequences including a United Airlines plane crash in 1978 in which a breakdown in teamwork was found to be the primary cause of the accident.[62] These examples clearly indicate that teams are not always effective and team training is an essential and critical requirement for teams to function effectively.

Team training programs are designed to improve the functioning and effectiveness of teams in areas such as communication, coordination, compensatory behaviour, mutual performance monitoring, exchange of feedback, and adaptation to varying situational demands.[63] According to Bottom and Baloff, team training is an "attempt to improve a group's process through the use of interventions targeted at specific aspects of the process such as effective communication" (p. 318).[64] Group processes are usually the focus of team training, however, because team members are often expected to perform a variety of the group's tasks, they often must also receive technical training to become multiskilled.

Thus, team training focuses on two general types of skills: *taskwork skills* refer to skills that are required to perform the team's tasks, and *teamwork skills* are skills that team members require in order to interact, communicate, and coordinate tasks effectively with other team members. Both types of skills need to be incorporated into the design of team training programs, and it is recommended that team members first master taskwork and technical skills before they are trained on teamwork skills.[65]

Team training

Training programs that are designed to improve the functioning and effectiveness of teams in areas such as communication and coordination

Team training is one of the most popular types of human resource development interventions. However, team training programs have not always been effective primarily because of a lack of a diagnosis of all the relevant factors. For team training to be effective, a comprehensive diagnosis must first be conducted on group input, task, and process variables in order to determine the appropriateness of team training, and to tailor interventions to the needs of the group.[66]

Furthermore, once it has been determined that team training is necessary, a team task analysis as described in Chapter 4 must be conducted. The objective of a team task analysis is to identify the team competencies including the knowledge, skills, and attitudes that are required to perform team tasks effectively and to function as a team member.[67]

Training is a critical factor for the successful implementation of teams. In addition to providing team members with both taskwork and teamwork skills training, managers and supervisors must also receive training on how to implement teams, and on their role as a team coach and facilitator rather than as a traditional manager. When team training interventions are based on a comprehensiveness diagnosis and team task analysis, there is evidence that they can improve group processes and team effectiveness.[68]

Sales Training

If you have ever seen the movies *Tin Men* or *Glengarry Glen Ross*, then you have a good idea of what salespersons used to do. That is, they aggressively sold their wares by telling customers what they needed and their training focused on the hard sell approach. Today, shorter product cycles, finicky customers, more complex sales channels, and global competition has changed the sales profession and made it much more demanding and challenging.[69]

Sales professionals have to do much more than just sell. They need to develop relationships with their customers by listening to them, understanding their needs and problems, and helping them develop solutions. This process involves changing from an order-taking mentality, in which an organization competes primarily on price, to more of a business-partnership mentality, in which organizations compete by selling service rather than just commodities.[70] When Jack Welch was CEO of General Electric, he stated that GE is going to start to focus on customers by providing lower costs and more consistent service, and that the company-wide goal is to transform GE from a products provider to a provider of "productivity solutions."[71]

Sales professionals must develop a different set of skills to be successful in today's competitive sales environment. They need to be more knowledgeable about their products and their business, as well as their customers' business. As a result, sales training has become more than simply sending the sales troops off to a motivational pep rally.[72]

Today, sales training programs are being designed to upgrade sales professionals' skills and help them deal with new competitive challenges. At the centre of these new training initiatives is an emphasis on "relationship-based" sales training. Sales professionals are being trained to develop more strategic and complex relationships with clients, and to create relationships across client functions. They are also being trained to become knowledgeable about their customer's business needs, and to develop customized sales strategies. Rather than just selling a commodity, integrated teams of people from sales, support, and service are learning to sell solutions that combine support and service agreements.

Unlike traditional sales training, these new approaches require a high level of management support and commitment since they represent a cultural change in the way an organization conducts its business. However, there is evidence that this new approach can increase sales effectiveness. For example, Sprint Canada attributes an increase in revenues to its sales training program that includes training on developing strategic relationships with clients.[73]

Canadian telecommunications company TELUS determined that its sales force needed a fundamental change in its selling strategy that involved a shift in focus from a "product-based" sales approach to a strategic "solutions-based" sales approach. The sales force and sales managers had to develop selling strategies and skills to interact with and sell to CEO/COO level clients. They also had to learn to seek out opportunities and identify solutions for potential clients.[74]

In order to meet these new objectives, the entire sales force participated in a three-day realistic selling simulation that allowed them to experience first-hand the new selling environment. Sales teams had to compete against each other in order to win an account. This required understanding the client's needs and developing solutions. In addition to the simulation, which was meant to increase awareness of change initiatives, the sales force also took part in classroom-based workshops and a comprehensive assessment process. The workshop focused on new approaches to client relationship building and selling skills, and the assessment was used to develop performance goals and plans for the sales staff.[75]

The result for TELUS has been an increase in sales calls, sales opportunities, and new business that will lay the foundation for growth and success. Thus, the company's change in its approach to sales required an effective sales training program that was a key part of the change process and the implementation of the new strategy.

Customer Service Training

An organization's front-line employees play a key role in representing the organization to its customers. Good customer service and customer satisfaction are the keys to ensuring that customers return, so it is critical that front-line or customer-contact employees have the skills and abilities necessary to interact and communicate effectively with customers and provide them with excellent service. For many organizations, this requires extensive training in customer service.

Companies with a strong commitment to customer service such as L.L. Bean, Federal Express, Marriott, and Disney invest heavily in training their employees. For example, employees at L.L. Bean receive 40 hours of training before they deal with customers and at British Airways all employees attend two days of training called "Putting People First."[76]

At Delta Hotels and Resorts, employees are trained and empowered to provide customers with excellent service such as settling a disputed minibar charge or offering a complimentary room if a guest has a reasonable complaint. According to Bill Pallet, Delta's senior vice president of people and quality, "The name of the game isn't customer satisfaction, it's customer loyalty. It costs more to go out and get new customers than retain your current customers." As part of its training program, Delta has produced an award-winning training video and promises employees a certain amount of training every year. Delta's employee turnover rate has dropped, morale has improved, and occupancy rates have risen without having to drop prices to be competitive. As well, Delta is talking with other service companies and the medical sectors about its program.[77]

According to Schneider and Bowen, "The fundamental issue in training, whether it be training of individuals or training of teams, is to ensure that when customer meets employee, the encounter unfolds in ways that yield a sense of seamlessness for the customer" (p. 132).[78] They describe the experience this way:

> By seamlessness, we mean that the service, in all of its dimensions and characteristics, is delivered without a hitch. It is *simultaneously* reliable, responsive, competent, courteous, and so forth, and the facilities and tools necessary for it are all put into play smoothly and without glitches, interruptions, or delay. The same applies to responses to system failures and special requests. Seamless service is something all customers expect (p. 8).[79]

Customer service training can be either informal or formal. Informal training might involve pairing new hires with the organization's best employees in terms of customer service behaviour and philosophy. The kind of formal training required will depend on the type of service business that an organization is in and its service strategy. In other words, the training program must be tailored to an organization's strategy and characteristics as well as its customers.[80]

According to Schneider and Bowen, employees must be motivated and able to meet the following customer expectations for service quality:[81]

1. *Reliability:* dependability and consistency of performance (e.g., performing the service at the designated time).
2. *Responsiveness:* the willingness and readiness of employees to provide service (e.g., giving prompt service).
3. *Competence:* the required skills and knowledge to perform the service (e.g., research capability of the organization).

4. *Access:* approachability and ease of contact (e.g., convenient hours and location).
5. *Courtesy:* politeness, respect, consideration, and friendliness (e.g., clean and neat appearance).
6. *Communication:* keeping customers informed and listening to them (e.g., assuring customers that a problem will be handled).
7. *Credibility:* trustworthiness, believability, and honesty (e.g., personal characteristics of employees).
8. *Security:* freedom from danger, risk, or doubt (e.g., confidentiality).
9. *Understanding or knowing the customer:* making an effort to understand the customers' needs (e.g., providing individualized attention).
10. *Tangibles:* physical evidence of the service (e.g., appearance of personnel).

In addition to these quality expectations, employees must be able to deal with service failures, perform beyond customer expectations, and satisfy customer expectations for special requests. Employees must also ensure that customers feel secure, have their self-esteem enhanced, and are treated justly. Finally, service employees must also be able to act as supervisors or co-workers in those situations in which they are involved with customers in co-producing a service.[82]

Service employees must have both the *ability* and *motivation* to perform effectively. Because you cannot always hire people with the required abilities or motivation, you must be able to train them. Many organizations that have reputations for superb customer service are successful because of their commitment to training. Organizations that provide the best service also provide the most training. The key to service quality and competitiveness is customer service training.

Sexual Harassment Training

In recent years, a number of high-profile sexual harassment cases have made the news headlines and brought increased attention to sexual harassment in the workplace. In addition to the numerous cases of sexual harassment reported in the military, many organizations, including Mitsubishi, Astra, Sears & Roebuck, and Del Laboratories have found themselves embroiled in costly litigation cases.[83] The failure of these organizations to effectively respond to charges of sexual harassment has cost them millions of dollars in settlements not to mention lower productivity, increased absenteeism, and higher turnover.

Sexual harassment in the U.S. army is reported to cost $250 million a year in lost productivity, absenteeism, and the replacement and transfer of employees.[84] The effects of sexual harassment on employees can include decreased morale and job satisfaction, as well as negative effects on psychological and physical well being.[85] Men who perceive their workplace as hostile toward women and minorities also report lower job satisfaction and trust for their employer.[86]

Sexual harassment

Unwelcome sexual advances, requests for sexual favours, and verbal or physical conduct of a sexual nature that is a condition of employment, interferes with work performance, or creates a hostile work environment

Sexual harassment is defined as "unwelcome sexual advances, requests for sexual favours, and other verbal or physical conduct of a sexual nature ... when submission to requests for sexual favours is made explicitly or implicitly a term or condition of employment; submission to or rejection of such requests is used as a basis for employment decisions; or such conduct unreasonably interferes with work performance or creates an intimidating, hostile, or offensive work environment" (p. 401).[87]

There are two kinds of sexual harassment. *Quid pro quo* refers to explicit requests for sexual favours as a condition of employment. A *hostile environment* refers to a work environment in which language or actions or both create an uncomfortable and offensive work environment that interferes with job performance.[88]

With the number of litigation cases and costly settlements on the rise, organizations have become more concerned about sexual harassment. The most effective way for organizations to prevent sexual harassment is to develop sexual harassment policies and procedures for filing complaints and to provide training programs that educate employees about sexual harassment and the organization's policies and procedures.[89]

Training is especially important because the definition of what constitutes sexual harassment is not always clear or understood, and problems have occurred in situations in which employees and managers were unaware of an organizations' sexual harassment policy or did not know how to report it and proceed with a complaint. In the United States, sexual harassment training programs have become a popular way to ward off lawsuits.[90]

Organizations that are responsive to complaints of sexual harassment not only have policies and procedures in place, but, among other things, they have comprehensive education and training programs.[91] For example, E.I. Du Pont de Nemours has developed a sexual harassment awareness program called "A Matter of Respect" that includes interactive training programs, peer-level facilitators who are trained to meet with employees who want to talk about sexual harassment, and a 24-hour hotline. As the company has become more international, so has its training on sexual harassment, which is now provided in Japan, China, Mexico, and Puerto Rico.[92]

With increasing incidents of sexual and racial harassment in the workplace, organizations must develop policies to deal with complaints and provide comprehensive education and training programs. Not surprisingly, many organizations are now doing this. As indicated in Table 12.2, 87 percent of organizations reported providing sexual harassment training.

Diversity Training

There has been a rapid rise in the percentage of ethnic, cultural, language, and religious minorities in Canada that has resulted in a considerable change in the ethnic and racial origins of employees working in Canadian organizations. Visible minorities now represent approximately 11.2 percent of the Canadian population and are expected to increase to 18.3 percent by the year

2006.[93] Thus, the composition of the Canadian workplace is changing and becoming more diverse.

Because of this diversity and differences in attitudes and values across cultures, it has become increasingly important for organizations to manage diversity in the workplace. The effective management of diversity can have economic and competitive consequences for organizations, and is becoming part of many organizations' business strategy.[94] At IBM, diversity is embedded in the overall strategy, business goals, and policies toward employees, and every new manager is exposed to diversity training as part of the leadership development curriculum.[95]

Diversity training programs are one of the most common and effective ways for organizations to manage diversity and achieve a competitive advantage. **Diversity training** programs are designed to address the differences in values, attitudes, and behaviours of individuals with different backgrounds. The objectives are to increase awareness and understanding of cultural diversity, and to improve interaction and communication among employees with different backgrounds. Diversity training is reported to be one of the most widely used strategies for managing diversity in the workplace and there has been a dramatic rise in diversity training programs in the last decade.[96]

According to Noe and Ford, "The goal of diversity training programs is to eliminate barriers such as values, stereotypes, and managerial practices which constrain employee contribution to organizational goals and personal development" (p. 357).[97]

Diversity training has three main objectives: (1) increase awareness about diversity issues, (2) reduce biases and stereotypes, and (3) change behaviours to those required to work effectively in a diverse workforce.[98] Some diversity training programs are designed to change people's attitudes by creating an awareness of diversity and an understanding of differences in values and behaviours. The expectation is that, by creating an awareness and understanding of these differences, people will change their behaviour and overcome any stereotypes they might hold. Another approach to diversity training is to change behaviour. This approach emphasizes learning new behaviours that might then lead to changes in attitudes.[99]

A recent study on diversity in the workplace found that diversity experts rated training and education programs as one of the best strategies for managing diversity. According to the experts, training and education was considered to be important for the following reasons:[100]

1. building awareness and skills
2. helping employees understand the need and meaning of valuing diversity
3. providing education on specific cultural differences and how to respond to those differences
4. providing the skills required to work on diverse work teams
5. improving employee understanding of the cultural diversity within the organization
6. learning about the culture and community that the organization serves

Diversity training

Training that focuses on differences in values, attitudes, and behaviours of individuals with different backgrounds

7. providing skills and activities to assist diverse groups to integrate within the organization, perform their jobs effectively, and increase opportunities for advancement.

In addition, the study noted that diversity training should focus on increasing *awareness* of what diversity is and why it is important; providing *skills* required to work effectively in a diverse workforce; and *application* strategies to facilitate the use of diversity awareness and skills to improve work performance, interactions, and communication. The study also indicated that effective diversity training programs have the following components: commitment and support from top management, inclusion as part of the organizational strategic plan, programs that meet the specific needs of the organization, qualified trainers, association with other diversity initiatives, mandatory attendance, inclusive programs (i.e., include all individuals and groups), and evaluation.[101]

In one of the most comprehensive studies on diversity training, human resource professionals responded to questions about diversity programs in their organizations. The results indicated that the majority of diversity programs lasts one day or less and uses less than 10 percent of the training budget. As well, more than 80 percent reported that they evaluate participants' reactions immediately after training, but less than one third conduct any long-term evaluation. In terms of success, half of the programs were described as having a neutral effect, 18 percent were described as largely or extremely ineffective, and slightly more than 30 percent judged their training to be quite or extremely effective. The adoption and success of diversity training was strongly influenced by top management support as well as other organizational context factors such as organizational size and diversity-supportive policies.[102]

With the increasing diversity in the Canadian workplace, managing diversity and diversity training are likely to become more relevant and important than ever. For example, as part of their commitment to become more diversified, the Toronto Police Force has implemented a recruitment strategy to hire more minorities.[103] The Bank of Montreal has a Workplace Equality Program that includes training courses on the benefits of a multicultural workforce.[104]

BC Hydro has an "Aboriginal Cross-Cultural Awareness Program" that focuses on building relationships. BC Hydro's transmission lines cross more than 500 aboriginal reserves so employees need to be aware of aboriginal rights, customs, and laws protecting their lands. Employees learn how diversity can affect their work in a particular community. Aboriginals serve as subject matter experts for the training program, which includes face-to-face meetings. Training takes place in a traditional setting within a particular community and has included dancing and singing.[105]

Organizations are realizing that managing cultural diversity is not only the right thing to do, but that it also makes good business sense.[106] Furthermore, diversity training is one of the most effective strategies for providing employees with the skills required to perform effectively in a diverse workplace. As noted by Wentling and Palma-Rivas, "Organizations need to provide employees with the most important skills for operating in a multi-cultural environment so that they understand their own as well as others' cultures, values, beliefs, attitudes, behaviours, and strengths and weaknesses. Employers must invest constantly in all employees by providing training and improving competencies if they are to work most effectively in a diverse workplace" (p. 243).[107]

See The Trainer's Notebook to find out more about how to design an effective diversity training program.

Cross-Cultural Training

One of the implications of international business and a global marketplace is that workers, or *expatriates* as they are called, must work in different countries around the globe and interact with people from different cultures. Although middle managers are sent on overseas assignments most often, senior managers, sales staff, engineers, IS programmers, scientists, and other professionals are also sent.[108] Canada sends hundreds of technical advisors each year to developing countries as part of its international development assistance programs.[109]

A foreign assignment can last for years and involve contact and interactions with persons who differ from Canadians in terms of culture, values, and language. For an organization to succeed in its international business operations, it requires individuals who can function and work effectively in different cultures.

Unfortunately, both Canadian and American expatriates have typically not performed very well on foreign assignments. During the past two decades, North American expatriates who were assigned to work overseas for their organizations have tended to have a much higher failure rate than European or Japanese expatriates. In other words, they either perform poorly and/or they return home early.[110]

In the United States, it is estimated that 20 percent of U.S. expatriates fail in their global assignment.[111] A study on Canadian technical advisors working in developing countries found that only about 20 percent were highly effective in terms of their ability to transfer skills and knowledge to their counterparts in the host country, 65 percent had little impact, and 15 percent were highly ineffective.[112] The cost of failure is high, costing multinational companies millions of dollars each year. In North America, an estimated $2 to $2.5 billion is wasted when overseas assignments fail.

One of the main reasons for the high failure rate of North American expatriates is the culture shock they and their families experience living in a foreign culture. The study of Canadian technical advisors working in developing countries found that more than 50 percent experienced culture shock, and a major reason for their lack of effectiveness was the inability to interact effectively with their counterparts in the host country.[113] In addition, a major reason for failure is the inability of the expatriate's spouse and family to adjust to the foreign culture.[114] This inability to adjust stems in large part from a lack of cross-cultural training or pre-departure training for the expatriates and their families.

How to Design an Effective Diversity Training Program

Here are some key steps to follow in the design and implementation of an effective diversity training program:

1. **Obtain top-level leadership support**: The support and involvement of a company's CEO and top leadership team is a key factor in predicting the success of diversity programs. Leaders must clearly communicate the importance of diversity as a business value and goal and demonstrate their commitment to diversity initiatives.

2. **Conduct a needs analysis**: Conduct a needs analysis to determine the nature of diversity problems and issues in your organization. A needs analysis allows one to tailor a diversity training program to meet the specific needs of an organization and helps to determine the goals and objectives of a diversity program and the most appropriate training content and methods.

3. **Focus on three levels of learning**: Diversity training programs should be designed around three levels of learning: awareness, skill building, and action planning. *Awareness* involves learning about diversity issues, cultural differences, and bias in the workplace. *Skill building* refers to learning new skills such as new ways of communicating with persons with different backgrounds or managing diversity conflict. *Action planning* involves contributing to a more positive work environment by committing to and applying the knowledge and skills acquired in diversity training on the job.

4. **Embed and integrate diversity in a larger framework**: Diversity issues should be addressed as part of corporate change and development initiatives and as an embedded component of recruitment, development, training, compensation, and promotion. Diversity training should be part of a larger diversity program that is integrated with other business processes and objectives. Diversity initiatives and goals should be long-term and factored into management appraisal, reward, and recognition systems and policies.

5. **Research best practices**: Research companies with successful diversity programs. For example, IBM and AT&T provide outstanding examples of how to design and implement diversity programs that integrate diversity goals into strategic planning and business goals, and take a holistic, systematic approach to embedding diversity themes and priorities into all operational areas at all organizational levels.

6. **Use diversity as a business advantage**: Ensure that your organization fully appreciates the diversity of its employees and the ways in which diversity can be leveraged to marketplace advantage.

7. **Design informational and transformational programs**: Diversity programs need to convey information about specific policies and organization initiatives as well as being transformational in design and content (e.g., why workforce diversity is critical to achieving business goals) in order to create synergy, trust, and greater workplace cooperation and understanding.

8. **Use various methods and media**: Role plays, storytelling, small-group discussions, videos, simulations, vignettes, and exercises should all be incorporated into the design of diversity training programs.

9. **Recognize your role**: As a trainer, take it upon yourself to educate your company's CEO and top leaders about how diversity as a value and business focus can help the organization reach new markets, foster an atmosphere of inclusiveness, and create a world-class workforce. Also make sure that you or the diversity trainer is qualified and capable of discussing sensitive issues about diversity and managing the emotions that often arise during diversity training.

Sources: Koonce, R. (December, 2001). Redefining diversity. *Training & Development*, p. 27 (How to create effective diversity training).

Chrobot-Mason, D., & Quinones, M. A. (2002). Training for a diverse workplace. In Kurt Kraiger (Ed.), *Creating, implementing, and managing effective training and development*. Jossey-Bass, San Francisco, CA.

"**Cross-cultural training** is designed to prepare employees for overseas assignments by focusing on developing the skills and attitudes necessary for successful interactions with persons from different backgrounds."[115] Some of the major types of cross-cultural training include:[116]

- environmental briefings about a country's geography, climate, housing, and schools
- cultural orientation to familiarize expatriates with cultural institutions and the value systems of the host country
- cultural assimilators that use programmed learning approaches to expose members of one culture to the concepts, attitudes, role perceptions, and customs of another culture
- language training
- sensitivity training to develop attitudinal flexibility, and
- field experience such as visiting the country where one will be assigned to see what it is like to work and live with people in a different culture.

Despite increasing awareness of the importance of cross-cultural training, only a minority of firms (30 to 45 percent) provide cross-culture training for expatriates and their families—a major contributing factor in expatriate assignment failure.[117] Furthermore, in the few organizations that do provide cross-cultural training, it is usually not very rigorous. In fact, it is often quite basic and brief and consists of viewing films and reading books rather than building cross-cultural skills. This is unfortunate because research has shown that cross-cultural training can improve an expatriate's cross-cultural skills, cultural adjustment, and job performance.[118]

A critical factor in the success of cross-cultural training is training rigour. According to Black, Gregersen, and Mendenhall, **training rigour** refers to "the degree of mental involvement and effort that must be expended by the trainer and the trainee in order for the trainee to learn the required concepts." (p. 97)[119]

Training rigour also refers to the length of time spent on training. Generally, cross-cultural training programs that are high on training rigour tend to be more effective. Cross-cultural training programs that are considered to have a high degree of rigour include interactive language training, cross-cultural simulations, and field trips. Programs with a moderate degree of training rigour include role plays, cases, and survival-level language. Cross-cultural training programs that are considered to be the lowest in terms of training rigour include lectures, films, books, and area briefings. More rigorous cross-cultural training programs require trainees to be much more active and involved in practising cross-cultural skills.[120]

The degree of cross-cultural training rigour required by an expatriate for a particular foreign assignment depends on three dimensions: cultural toughness, communication toughness, and job toughness. Cultural toughness refers to how difficult it is to adjust to a new culture. Generally speaking, cultural toughness will increase the greater the difference or distance between one's

Cross-cultural training

Training that prepares employees for working and living in different cultures and for interactions with persons from different backgrounds

Training rigour

The degree of mental involvement and effort that must be expended by the trainer and the trainee in order for the trainee to learn the required concepts own culture and the foreign culture. For example, cultural toughness will be much higher for a Canadian expatriate in the Middle East than one in the U.S. The Canadian expatriate on assignment in the Middle East will require more rigorous cross-cultural training. An exception to this is the degree of past experience that an expatriate has had living in a foreign culture. For example, a Canadian expatriate with considerable experience living in the Middle East will require less cross-cultural training than one who has never lived there.[121]

Communication toughness is a function of the extent to which the expatriate will have to interact with the locals of the host country. When an expatriate will be required to have frequent interactions with host nationals that will involve face-to-face, two-way, and informal communication, the level of communication toughness will be high, and more rigorous communication training will be required. Job toughness refers to how difficult the tasks will be for the expatriate compared to what he/she is used to doing. If the expatriate will be working in a new area and the demands of the job will be different and require new responsibilities and challenges, then the degree of job toughness will be greater. As a result, the expatriate will require more rigorous job-specific training.[122]

An expatriate will have the most difficulty adjusting to foreign assignments that have a high degree of cultural, communication, and job toughness. As the levels of these three dimensions increase, the type of cross-cultural training required will need to be more rigorous. In addition to pre-departure training, it is also important that the expatriates and their families also receive follow-up or in-country cross-cultural training in the host country.[123]

With the increasing pace of change and the ever-expanding global marketplace, more Canadian workers will be sent on foreign assignments that require them to work and interact with persons in different and diverse cultures. Given that an organization's competitive success in the global marketplace depends to a great extent on its people, it is crucial that expatriates perform effectively and adjust to foreign cultures.

Research on Canadian expatriates has found that interpersonal and intercultural adaptation skills as well as knowledge of the local culture and participation in that culture, are important predictors of overseas effectiveness. Furthermore, among Canadian technical advisors, learning the local language was a major factor in overseas effectiveness.[124]

To be successful, expatriates require cross-cultural training that not only informs them of the history and politics of a country, but also teaches them the language, values, and appropriate patterns of behaviour. Cross-cultural training helps employees withstand the culture shock of working abroad and improves their job performance and adjustment.[125]

Summary

This chapter has provided an overview of the different types of training programs that are designed and delivered by organizations today. You should now be familiar with orientation training, basic skills training, technical skills training, information technology training, health and safety training, quality training, team training, sales training, customer service training, sexual harassment training, diversity training, and cross-cultural training. These training programs are a direct result of the many challenges and issues facing organizations in today's rapidly changing environment. Many of these training programs have become key components of an organization's corporate strategy, and are major factors in their efforts to remain competitive.

While many organizations provide these types of training programs, it is important to remember that their relevance and effectiveness will depend on how well the program is designed, and the extent to which it is based on a rigorous needs analysis. It is also important that these programs be thoroughly evaluated to ensure that they are in fact achieving their objectives and having a positive effect on employees and the organization.

Key Terms

basic-skills training (page 323)
computer software training (page 326)
cross-cultural training (page 341)
diversity training (page 337)
information technology training (page 325)
literacy (page 323)
nontechnical skills (soft skills) (page 330)

sexual harassment (page 336)
team training (page 331)
technical skills training (page 324)
total quality management (TQM) (page 328)
training rigour (page 341)
Workplace Hazardous Materials Information
    System (WHMIS) (page 328)

Weblinks

BC Hydro: www.bchydro.com (page 338)
Levi Strauss & Co.: www.levi.com/canada (page 330)
Sprint Canada: www.sprint.ca (page 333)
Starbucks: www.starbucks.com (page 320)
TELUS: www.telus.ca (page 333)
WHMIS: www.hc-sc.gc.ca/hecs-sesc/whmis/index.htm (page 328)

Discussion Questions

1. Diversity training programs have been criticized for doing more harm than good. In fact, there is some evidence that they may be ineffective at best and harmful at worst. Why do you think this is the case? Do you think this is true and should organizations abandon diversity training or embrace it?
2. Why do you think Canadian organizations invest so little in basic skills training (see Table 12.1)? What are the implications of this for employees, organizations, and society? Should Canadian organizations be spending more on basic skills training? What are the advantages and disadvantages of doing so?
3. What would be your reaction if your employer wanted to send you on an overseas assignment? What would be your reaction if the assignment

was in: 1. England, 2. France, 3. China, or 4. the Middle East? Would you accept the assignment and if so, what training would you require? Describe the training you would need in terms of the content and methods.

Using the Internet

1. Human Resources Development Canada has an interactive training directory at **www.trainingiti.com**. Select a training course in an area that interests you (e.g., career exploration) and conduct a search for available courses in your area. Then refer to the page on "How to Screen Training Providers and Courses" and answer the following questions for each of the programs you have located.
   a. How effective is this guide for assessing the quality of a training program? b. Summarize your results in a report and discuss the availability, frequency, purpose, content, and effects of each type of training program.
2. To learn more about workplace literacy and basic skills in Canada, go to: **http://www.conferenceboard.ca/workplaceliteracy** and find out about the challenges that employers face and the solutions. Prepare a brief report in which you summarize the challenges and solutions for small, medium, and large businesses.
3. To learn more about the Workplace Hazardous Materials Information System (WHMIS) go to: **www.hc-sc.gc.ca/hecs-sesc/whmis/index.htm** and find out what is available for employers on this site. Write a brief report in which you outline employer obligations and requirements. To find out about WHMIS education and training go to: **http://www.ccohs.ca/oshanswers/legisl/whmis_education.html**. Find the answers to the following questions: a. What is WHMIS education and training? b. Do I have to be educated and trained in WHMIS? c. What is the purpose of WHMIS training? d. What, in general, is the content of a WHMIS training program? e. Can people in the same plant receive different training? and f. What are the criteria of a successful program?

Exercises

1. The extent to which organizations provide certain types of training programs is often driven by external and internal factors. In other words, social, political, and economic changes in the work environment, as well as internal changes to organizational systems and work arrangements, have a substantial influence on training activities. Choose several of the following training programs as required by your instructor, and discuss the role of external and internal factors and how these factors might influence the need and importance of each type of training.
   a. orientation training
   b. basic-skills training

c. technical training

d. information technology training

e. health and safety training

f. quality training

g. team training

h. sales training

i. customer service training

j. sexual harassment training

k. cultural diversity training

l. cross-cultural training

2. Assume that you are a training director for a large retail organization. To increase your training budget for next year, you have to make a persuasive argument to convince other members of the organization of your need for an increase in resources. An important part of your argument will involve proving the need for and importance of several training programs. For some of the training programs listed in exercise 1 (as indicated by your instructor), describe how you will argue that it is important, the impact it will have on employee attitudes and behaviour, the benefits it will have for employees and the organization, and how it can help the organization gain a competitive advantage.

3. Design a training program for one of the types of training discussed in this chapter. In designing your program, specify each of the following:

a. the training objectives

b. the training content

c. the trainer for the program

d. the trainees that should attend the program

e. the training methods to be used

f. the required training materials and equipment

g. the training site

h. the schedule for the training program

i. the lesson plan

j. the criteria you will use to evaluate the program

4. One way to find out more about the training programs discussed in this chapter is to ask trainers or Human Resource professionals and employees about the training provided in their organization. Choose a few of the types of training programs described in this chapter and then contact a human resource professional and ask them the following questions:

a. Does your organization provide this type of training?

b. What are some of the reasons why you do or do not provide this type of training?

c. What are the objectives of this type of training program?

d. What is the content of this type of training?

e. How is this training program designed (e.g., what methods, techniques, etc.) and who is the trainer?

f. What effect does this type of training have on employees' attitudes and behaviours?

g. What effect does this type of training have on the organization?

In addition, contact several employees who work in different organizations and ask them the following questions:

a. Have you ever received this type of training?

b. If yes, what was the reason why you attended the training program?

c. What were the objectives of the training program?

d. What was the content of the training program?

e. How was the training program designed (e.g., methods, techniques, etc.) and who was the trainer?

f. What effect did the training have on your attitudes and behaviours?

g. What effect did the training have on the organization?

5. Describe the orientation training you received in the most recent job that you held. Some of the things to consider are:

a. How long was the orientation training?

b. What content was included?

c. What methods were used?

d. What did you learn from it?

e. Were you satisfied with the program and did it help you perform your job?

f. What did you like about it and what did you not like?

g. How might the orientation training have been conducted to make it more effective?

6. Choose one of the types of training programs described in this chapter that you have attended in a current or previous job. Describe the content and methods used and how effective the training was for your learning and on-the-job behaviour. Based on the material in the chapter and your experience, how might the program be improved to be more effective?

7. Imagine that your employer has just informed you that you are to go on a foreign assignment for three years to a country that you have never been to and know nothing about. Furthermore, the culture is very different from your own. Your employer has informed you that you will be receiving some written information about the country and its culture as well as videotape to help you prepare for your assignment. Prepare a memo to your employer in which you evaluate the training they are offering you and describe the type of cross-cultural training that you require if you are going to accept the assignment.

8. Students often have to work in groups on course projects without any knowledge of how groups function and what it takes for them to be effective. Students often experience difficulties when working in groups and sometimes they just fall apart. Therefore, it might be helpful if stu-

dents receive team training. Your task is to design a training program for students to prepare them for working in groups. Describe the nature of your training program including the objectives, content, and methods.

MANAGING DIVERSITY AT DENNY'S

On April 1, 1993, the very same day that Denny's settled a federal suit for discriminating against African American customers in California, six black Secret Service agents at a Denny's restaurant in Annapolis, Maryland, waited nearly an hour for breakfast. While they were ignored, their white colleagues sitting at a nearby table downed second helpings of French toast, bacon, and coffee. When the black agents went public with their treatment, Denny's became, almost overnight, a national symbol of big-business bigotry.

The black Secret Servicemen filed the third discrimination suit in a year against Denny's. Just one week before, a group of black students, who entered a Denny's restaurant in San Jose, filed a lawsuit claiming they were subjected to a late-night prepayment policy, while white patrons were not.

When racial problems erupted at a Denny's on the West Coast, former CEO Jerry Richardson and his team wrote them off as isolated misunderstandings, inevitable for a chain that serves one million meals a day. But piles of court documents from customers and employees indicated something far more serious was going on. Sandy Patterson, a white waitress who worked at several Denny's in California, stated in her court declaration that use of the N word was "not uncommon," nor were the terms "them," "those people," or "that kind" in referring to blacks. "I was told by management that we did not want to encourage black customers to stay in the restaurant," she said.

Robert Norton, who is also white, says that when he began his new job managing a Denny's in San Jose, he observed staffers "routinely" closing the restaurant when "they were concerned about the number of black customers" entering. Says Norton: "Black-out" was used by Denny's management to refer to a situation where too many black customers were in the restaurant. Norton says that when he discontinued the policy, his district manager threatened to fire him.

Over the years, Denny's has come under siege from African-Americans and various civil-rights organizations, which accused the chain of refusing service to black customers and promoting a corporate culture of racial discrimination.

In May 1994, Denny's settled two class-action suits, one of which was consolidated with the case originally settled in 1993 with the U.S. government. By December 1995, Denny's had paid $54 million to 295,000 aggrieved customers and their lawyers, the largest public accommodations settlement ever. In the consent decree it signed with the plaintiffs, Denny's promised to treat all customers equally in the future. The consent decree also mandated that Denny's publicize its nondiscriminatory policies and train employees in diversity issues. An independent civil rights monitor was appointed to supervise Denny's for seven years and to investigate any further charges of discrimination.

However, three years later the company faced another discrimination lawsuit when 10 Syracuse University students claimed they were denied service, told to leave the restaurant, and then beaten up by a group of white patrons while Denny's security guards watched. The lawsuit was filed in U.S. District Court in the Northern District of New York. Among the plaintiffs were six Asian-Americans, three blacks, and one white.

At a news conference called by the New York City-based Asian American Legal Defence and Education Fund, lawyer Elizabeth OuYang said, "Denny's has not fully implemented and taken seriously what it needs to do." She was referring to the legal agreement that Denny's ensure that all its employees undergo anti-discrimination training as required by the 1994 settlement of a class-action lawsuit.

According to the *Wall Street Journal*, Denny's says the franchisee, Syracuse, New York-based NDI Foods Inc., fired all the management, staff, and security personnel involved in the incident on the same day an appointed civil-rights monitor's recommendation was received by the company. In addition, Denny's says it has implemented new procedures for monitoring nondiscrimination training of franchised Denny's restaurants.

Sources: "Denny's Changes Its Spots." *Fortune*, 1996, May 13.

"More discrimination hashed out by Denny's." *Workforce*, 1977, October.

"Denny's pays $54 to settle bias suits." *Nation's Restaurant News*, 1994, June 6.

"Turning Around Denny's." *60 Minutes* (1998, April 26).

Questions

1. How effective do you think the anti-discrimination training program as required by the 1994 settlement of a class-action lawsuit will be for solving discrimination and racial bias at Denny's? How effective will it be for managing diversity at Denny's?
2. Discuss the potential of a diversity training program as a way to address discrimination and racial bias at Denny's. In particular, if you were to design such a program, how would you proceed? Describe the objectives of the program, the trainees, training content, training methods, etc.
3. What criteria would you use to evaluate a diversity training program at Denny's? Describe how you would evaluate a diversity training program and how you would determine if it was effective.
4. What do you think Denny's should do to address its problems of discrimination and racial bias and to manage diversity? Is diversity training the answer?

References

[1]Schettler, J. (2002, August). Welcome to ACME Inc. *Training*, 36–43. Training: The Human Side of Business by Schettler, J. Copyright 2002 by V N U BUS PUBS USA. Reproduced with permission of V N U BUS PUBNS USA in the format Textbook via Copyright Clearance Center.

[2]Schettler, J. (2002, August).

[3]Swanson, R.A., & Falkman, S.K. (1997). Training delivery problems and solutions: Identification of novice trainer problems and expert trainer solutions. *Human Resource Development Quarterly, 8*, 305–14.

[4]Galvin, T. (2002, October). 2002 Industry Report. *Training*, 24–73.

[5]Schaaf, D. (1998). What workers really think about training. *Training 35* (9), 59–66.

[6]Schaaf, D. (1998).

[7]Baker, S., & Armstrong, L. (1996, September 30). The new factory worker. *Business Week*, pp. 59–68.

[8]Harris-Lalonde, S. (2001). Training and development outlook. *The Conference Board of Canada*. Ottawa.

[9]Klein, H. J., & Weaver, N. A. (2000). The effectiveness of an organizational-level orientation training program in the socialization of new hires. *Personnel Psychology, 53*, 47–66.

[10]Feldman, D.C. (1989). Socialization, resocialization, and training: Reframing the research agenda. In I.L. Goldstein (Ed.), *Training and development in organizations* (pp. 376–416). San Francisco: Jossey-Bass.

[11]Anderson, N.R., Cunningham-Snell, N.A., & Haigh, J. (1996). Induction training as socialization: Current practice and attitudes to evaluation in British organizations. *International Journal of Selection and Assessment 4*, 169–83.

[12]Gruner, S. (1998).

[13]Reese, J. (1996, December, 9). Starbucks: Inside the coffee cult. *Fortune*, pp. 190–200.

[14]Gruner, S. (1998).

[15]Feldman, D.C. (1989).

[16]Saks, A.M. (1996). The relationship between the amount and helpfulness of entry training and work outcomes. *Human Relations 49*, 429–51.

[17]Gruner, S. (1998).

[18]Klein & Weaver (2000).

[19]Klein & Weaver (2000).

[20]Ostroff, C., & Kozlowski, S.W.J. (1992). Organizational socialization as a learning process: The role of information acquisition. *Personnel Psychology 45*, 849–74.

[21]Baker, S., & Armstrong, L. (1996, September 30).

[22]Calamai, P. (1999, August 28). The literacy gap. *Toronto Star*, pp. J1, J2.

[23]Calamai, P. (1999, August 28).

[24]Hays, S. (1999). The ABCs of workplace literacy. *Workforce 78* (4), 70–74.

[25]Hays, S. (1999).

[26]Hays, S. (1999).

[27]Kuri, F. (1996, September). Basic-skills training boosts productivity. *HRMagazine 41* (9), 73–79.

[28]Kuri, F. (1996, September).

[29]Kuri, F. (1996, September).

[30]Hays, S. (1999).

[31]Hays, S. (1999).

[32]Kuri, F. (1996, September).

[33]Bankers grapple with math gap. (1999, March 5). *The Globe and Mail*, B25.

[34]Harris-Lalonde, S. (2001).

[35]Baker, S., & Armstrong, L. (1996, September 30).

[36]Baker, S., & Armstrong, L. (1996, September 30).

[37]Baker, S., & Armstrong, L. (1996, September 30).

[38]Harp, C.G., Taylor, S.C., & Satzinger, J.W. (1998). Computer training and individual differences: When method matters. *Human Resource Development Quarterly 9*, 271–83.

[39]Martocchio, J.J. (1992). Microcomputer usage as an opportunity: The influence of context in employee training. *Personnel Psychology 45*, 529–52.

[40]DeSimone, R.L., & Harris, D.M. (1998). *Human Resource Development* (2nd ed.). Fort Worth, TX: Dryden Press.

[41]Baker, S., & Armstrong, L. (1996, September 30).

[42]Harp, C.G., Taylor, S.C., & Satzinger, J.W. (1998).

[43]Harp, C.G., Taylor, S.C., & Satzinger, J.W. (1998).

[44]Montgomery, J. (1996). *Occupational health and safety*. Toronto: Nelson Canada.

[45]Montgomery, J. (1996).

[46]Montgomery, J. (1996).

[47]Montgomery, J. (1996).

[48]Kuri, F. (1996, September).

[49]Murray, B., & Raffaele, G.C. (1997). Single-site, results-level evaluation of quality awareness training. *Human Resource Development Quarterly 8*, 229–45.

[50]Dean, J.W., Jr., & Bowen, D.E. (1994). Management theory and total quality: Improving research and practice through theory development. *Academy of Management Review 19*, 392–418.

[51]Armitage, H.M. (1992, January). Quality pays. *CGA Magazine 96* (1), pp. 30–37.

Fine, C.H., & Bridge, D.H. (1987). Managing quality improvement. In Sepehri, M. (Ed.), *Quest for quality: Managing the total system* (pp. 66–74). Norcross, GA: Institute of Industrial Engineers.

[52]Cocheu, T. (1989). Training for quality improvement. *Training and Development Journal 41* (1), 56–62. Rossett, A., &

Krumdieck, K. (1992). How trainers score on quality. *Training and Development 46* (1), 11–16.

[53]Oakland, J.S. (1989). *Total quality management*. Oxford: Butterworth-Heinemann Ltd.

Schonberger, R.J. (1992). Total quality management cuts a broad swath—Through manufacturing and beyond. *Organizational Dynamics 20* (4), 16–28. Tenner, A.R., & DeToro, I.J. (1992). *Total quality management, three steps to continuous improvement*. Reading, MA: Addison-Wesley.

[54]Gandz, J. (1990). The employee empowerment era. *Business Quarterly 55* (2), 74–79.

[55]Kiess-Moser, E. (1990). International perspectives on quality. *Canadian Business Review 17* (3), 31–33. Regalbuto, G.A. (1992). Targeting the bottom line. *Training and Development 46* (4), 29–38.

[56]Harper, L.F., & Rifkind, L.J. (1994). A training program for TQM in the diverse workplace. *Human Resource Development Quarterly 5*, 277–79.

[57]Murray, B., & Raffaele, G.C. (1997).

[58]Baker, S., & Armstrong, L. (1996, September 30).

[59]Banker, R.D., Field, J.M., Schroeder, R.G., & Sinha, K.K. (1996). Impact of work teams on manufacturing performance: A longitudinal field study. *Academy of Management Journal 39*, 867–90. Guzzo, R.A., & Dickson, M.W. (1996). Teams in organizations: Recent research on performance and effectiveness. *Annual Review of Psychology 47*, 307–38.

[60]King, R.T., Jr. (1998, May 20). Levi's factory workers are assigned to teams and morale takes a hit. *The Wall Street Journal*, pp. A1, A6.

[61]Steinhart, D. (1999, February 23). Levi to shut plants in Cornwall, U.S. *Financial Post*, pp. C1, C9.

[62]Salas, E., Burke, C. S., & Cannon-Bowers, J. A. (2002). What we know about designing and delivering team training: Tips and guidelines. In K.Kraiger's (Ed.), *Creating, implementing, and managing effective training and development: State-of-the-art lessons for practice*, (pp. 234–59). San Francisco. CA: Jossey-Bass.

[63]Tannenbaum, S.I., & Yukl, G. (1992). Training and development in work organizations. *Annual Review of Psychology 43*, 399–441.

[64]Bottom, W.P., & Baloff, N. (1994). A diagnostic model for team building with an illustrative application. *Human Resource Development Quarterly 5*, 317–36.

[65]Salas, E., Burke, C. S., & Cannon-Bowers, J. A. (2002).

[66]Bottom, W.P., & Baloff, N. (1994).

[67]Salas, E., Burke, C. S., & Cannon-Bowers, J. A. (2002).

[68]Bottom, W.P., & Baloff, N. (1994).

[69]Stamps, D. (1997). Training for a new sales game. *Training 34* (7), 46–52.

[70]Stamps, D. (1997).

[71]GE's Welch focuses on customers. (1999, March 5). *The Globe and Mail*, B25.

[72]Stamps, D. (1997).

[73]Stamps, D. (1997).

[74]Connal, D. Baskin, C. (2002, November). Transforming a sales organization through simulation-based learning: a TELUS Communications case study. *Training Report*, 4–5.

[75]Connal, D. Baskin, C. (2002, November).

[76]Schneider, B., & Bowen, D.E. (1995). *Winning the service game*. Boston, MA: Harvard Business School Press.

[77]Delta promotes empowerment. (1999, May 31). *The Globe and Mail*, C5.

[78]Schneider, B., & Bowen, D.E. (1995).

[79]Schneider, B., & Bowen, D.E. (1995).

[80]Schneider, B., & Bowen, D.E. (1995).

[81]Schneider, B., & Bowen, D.E. (1995).

[82]Schneider, B., & Bowen, D.E. (1995).

[83]Peirce, E., Smolinski, C.A., & Rosen, B. (1998). Why sexual harassment complaints fall on deaf ears. *Academy of Management Executives 12*, 41–54.

[84]Seppa, N. (1997). Sexual harassment in the military lingers on. *APA Monitor 28* (5), 40–41.

[85]Schneider, K.T., Swan, S., & Fitzgerald, L.F. (1997). Job-related and psychological effects of sexual harassment in the workplace: Empirical evidence from two organizations. *Journal of Applied Psychology 82*, 401–15.

[86]Murray, B. (1998, July). Workplace harassment hurts everyone on the job. *APA Monitor 29* (7), p. 35.

[87]Schneider, K.T., Swan, S., & Fitzgerald, L.F. (1997).

[88]Ganzel, R. (1998). What sexual harassment training really prevents. *Training 35* (10), 86–94.

[89]Ganzel, R. (1998). Peirce, E., Smolinski, C.A., & Rosen, B. (1998).

[90]Ganzel, R. (1998).

[91]Peirce, E., Smolinski, C.A., & Rosen, B. (1998).

[92]Flynn, G. (1997). Respect is key to stopping harassment. *Workforce 76* (2), 56.

[93]Employment and Immigration Canada. (1994). *Employment equity availability data report on designated groups*. Ottawa: Author.

[94]Wentling, R.M., & Palma-Rivas, N. (1998). Current status and future trends of diversity initiatives in the workplace: Diversity experts' perspective. *Human Resource Development Quarterly 9*, 235–53.

[95]Koonce, R. (2002, December). Redefining diversity. *Training & Development*, 22–32.

[96]Chrobot-Mason, & Quinones, M. A. (2002). Training for a diverse workplace. In K. Kraiger's (Ed.), *Creating, implementing, and managing effective training and development: State-of-the-art lessons for practice*, (pp.117–59). San Francisco. CA: Jossey-Bass. Wentling, R.M., & Palma-Rivas, N. (1998).

[97]Noe, R. A., & Ford, J. K. (1992). Emerging issues and new directions for training research. *Research in Personnel and Human Resources Management, 10*, 345–84.

[98]Hanover, J.M.B., & Cellar, D.F. (1998). Environmental factors and the effectiveness of workforce diversity training. *Human Resource Development Quarterly 9*, 105–24.

[99]Noe, R. A., & Ford, J. K. (1992).

[100]Wentling, R.M., & Palma-Rivas, N. (1998).

[101]Wentling, R.M., & Palma-Rivas, N. (1998).

[102]Rynes, S., & Rosen, B. (1995). A field survey of factors affecting the adoption and perceived success of diversity training. *Personnel Psychology 48*, 247–70.

[103]Duncanson, J. (1999, March 6). Mostly white, mostly male: Why police are reaching out again. *Toronto Star*, pp. A1, A25.

[104]Workforce staff. (1997). Bank of Montreal satisfies customers by satisfying employees. *Workforce 76* (2), 46–47

[105]Allerton, H. E. (2001, May). Building bridges in Vancouver. *Training & Development*, 84–97.

[106]Koonce, R. (2002, December).

[107]Wentling, R.M., & Palma-Rivas, N. (1998).

[108]Halcrow, A. (1999). Expats: The squandered resource. *Workforce 78* (4), 42–48.

[109]Kealey, D.J. (1990). *Cross-cultural effectiveness: A study of Canadian technical advisors overseas.* Hull, QC: Canadian International Development Agency Briefing Centre.

[110]Noe, R. A., & Ford, J. K. (1992).

[111]Black, J.S., Gregersen, H.B., & Mendenhall, M.E. (1992). *Global assignments.* San Francisco, CA: Jossey-Bass.

[112]Kealey, D.J. (1990).

[113]Kealey, D.J. (1990).

[114] Black, J.S., Gregersen, H.B., & Mendenhall, M.E. (1992).

[115]Noe, R. A., & Ford, J. K. (1992).

[116]Tung, R. L. (1982). Selection and training procedures of U.S., European, and Japanese multinationals. *California Management Review, 25* (1), 57–71.

[117]McEmery, J., & DesHarnais, G. (1990). Culture shock. *Training and Development Journal 44* (4), 43–47.

[118]Black, J.S., Gregersen, H.B., & Mendenhall, M.E. (1992).

[119]Black, J.S., Gregersen, H.B., & Mendenhall, M.E. (1992).

[120]Black, J.S., Gregersen, H.B., & Mendenhall, M.E. (1992).

[121]Black, J.S., Gregersen, H.B., & Mendenhall, M.E. (1992).

[122]Black, J.S., Gregersen, H.B., & Mendenhall, M.E. (1992).

[123]Black, J.S., Gregersen, H.B., & Mendenhall, M.E. (1992).

[124]Kealey, D.J. (1990).

[125]Black, J.S., Gregersen, H.B., & Mendenhall, M.E. (1992).

Chapter

Management Development

Chapter Learning Objectives

After reading this chapter you should be able to

- define management and management development
- describe the main functions, roles, and critical skills of managers
- discuss emotional intelligence and its relevance for management
- describe the models of management skill development
- describe the content of management skills development programs
- discuss the different types of management development programs
- describe outdoor wilderness training programs and their effectiveness for management development
- define coaching and discuss the characteristics of great coaches, the five conditions that are necessary to ensure the development of managers, and the challenges of coaching

IBM

As an industry leader in training and development, IBM spends more than $1 billion a year on training. IBM is a world leader when it comes to the development of sophisticated training programs. Perhaps then it is no surprise that the company recently developed a new state-of-the-art management development program called Managing@IBM.

Managing@IBM consists of a learning experience that includes a blended program for leadership teams, performance support, and an on-line "e-coach" to guide managers in creating personal management development plans.

The program allows employees to manage their training using three "tracks" thanks to a sophisticated system called Edvisor.

In track one, employees can access more than 150 on-line best practice management-support modules. In track two, managers' learning activities are assessed as they prepare for a two-day, face-to-face workshop focused on improving organizational climate and coaching skills. Edvisor helps managers to master specific Web-based program modules that prepare them for the face-to-face learning.

In the third track, an "intelligent agent" analyzes a manager's 360-degree leadership survey feedback and online responses. Edvisor then provides leadership advice and assists managers in building a personalized management development plan that includes access to a customized list of management development programs.

Managing@IBM uses cutting-edge technology to provide managers with a new kind of learning experience. Launched in 2001, the program is already being used by more than 3,000 managers. In 2002, *Training* magazine ranked IBM 4th on its list of the Training Top 100 thanks to its Managing@IBM program.[1]

In Chapter 12, we described many types of employee training programs. These training programs are aimed primarily at employees at various levels throughout an organization. In this chapter, we focus on management development. As you can tell from the chapter-opening vignette, IBM takes management development very seriously. This is because, like many companies, they know that managers have an impact on a company's performance.

In this chapter, we focus on management development. In particular, you will learn about the roles, functions, and critical skills that make managers effective and the nature and types of programs that are used to develop managerial skills. But first, we explain the differences between management development and employee training.

means that managers must often interact with other people: their peers, subordinates, and superiors, as well as customers and in many cases, members of the general public.

Most human interactions have an emotional component and the success of these interactions often depends on how well emotions are managed. Moreover, because of the heavy responsibilities of the management role and the sheer number of tasks that managers must perform, they often must deal with emotional pressures and issues. Thus, they must be able to cope with conflict, performance pressures, and uncertainty. Because much of this involves emotions, managers must also be skillful in managing their own emotions and understanding those of others. The skills that people have in managing emotions—their own and those of others—are known as Emotional Intelligence or EI.[16]

Emotional intelligence has to do with the ability to manage your own and others' emotions and your relationships with others. This involves five sets of skills that foster better understanding of oneself and effective interactions with others:

1. *Self-awareness*. Being aware of and understanding oneself and one's emotions when interacting with others.
2. *Self-control*. Managing and regulating one's emotions (both positive and negative) that arise from encounters and events.
3. *Motivation or drive*. Channelling emotions and energies in support of one's goals.
4. *Empathy*. "Reading" and recognizing the emotions of others and responding to them appropriately.
5. *Interpersonal skills*. The ability to understand and manage others' emotions and to interact with them in an appropriate and effective manner.

Emotional intelligence
The ability to manage your own and others' emotions and your relationships with others

Notice that the components of EI (e.g., self-awareness, interpersonal skills, etc.) are listed as skills. That is, they are controllable and learnable behaviours rather than "fixed" character-like traits. Unlike intellectual intelligence (IQ) which is a relatively stable and enduring characteristic of people's cognitive abilities, EI is believed to be a learnable and changeable factor. In other words, through appropriate management development and training, emotional intelligence can be developed and improved.

The fact that emotional intelligence can be developed is extremely important because empirical research has shown that managers with higher levels of emotional intelligence are more effective and successful than managers with lower levels of EI. They are more likely to be promoted and to rise to the highest levels of management in their organizations. Furthermore, emotional intelligence has been found to be much more important than IQ or cognitive ability in predicting a manager's success, and to also predict organizational success. Futhermore, research has also shown that organizations prefer to hire, for management positions, persons with higher levels of the skills associated with emotional intelligence.[17]

Unlike project planning or other "hard skills" associated with management, emotional intelligence involves people-oriented skills that are often labelled as "soft skills." EI and "soft skills" tend to be developed indirectly, through enhanced skills in dealing with others. As people learn to receive and deliver feedback, to manage stress or to diffuse conflicts, they also simultaneously enhance their own levels of emotional intelligence.[18]

In summary, emotional intelligence involves the ability to manage one's own and others' emotions and relationships with others. Given that managers spend most of their time interacting and communicating with others and that the main functions and roles of management involve people, emotional intelligence is a critical factor in management development and effectiveness. Therefore, management development programs should include activities and experiences that assist managers in the development and improvement of their emotional intelligence. In the next section, we discuss models of management skill development.

Models of Management Skill Development

In order to understand how managers can learn and develop managerial skills, one can refer to models of management skills development. A number of management skill development models exist in the management literature.[19] Although some models specify a greater number of steps than others (e.g., Whetten and Cameron list five steps while Hunsaker lists 10—see The Trainer's Notebook), most models of management skill development share four basic commonalities.

First, they all recommend that management development programs include: a) initial skills assessment (where people are), b) skill acquisition (learning the basic principles associated with the specific skill of interest), c) skill practice (developing procedural learning by integrating the principles into smooth behavioural actions), and d) skill application on the job (applying the learned principles in job situations that require the skills).

a. *Skill assessment.* This process is used to identify the level of skill that a person possesses before skill development. Initial skill assessment is used to identify the strengths and weaknesses that managers hold relative to the specific skills to be trained and most importantly to help managers become aware of them. Skill assessment is a key component of IBM's Managing@IBM program.

Building self-awareness is critical because it is essential that people recognize a need for development before development can take hold. Moreover, initial skill assessment is also used to identify the learning and the basic behavioural styles that managers hold. There is general recognition that the purpose of management development is not to change individual personalities or styles, but rather, to help managers translate these modes of functioning into practices and behaviours that are effective in meeting the goals of the organization.

Although initial skill assessment is of importance to all training programs, it is especially critical for management development because "development" is a gradual process where *improvement* in skills is the main objective. Managers will need to practice and rehearse the skill before mastery can be achieved. Keeping managers motivated and confident in the development of the specific skills requires reinforcement. Skill assessment before and after the development experience can help managers perceive the changes that they have achieved in their level of skills mastery. Helping managers perceive improvements helps to build motivation and self-efficacy, thus encouraging managers to continue to exert the efforts that lead to mastery. Hence, skill assessment and growth is useful not only to the trainer (to know how things are going), but also to the motivation and self-efficacy of the learner.

b. *Skill learning.* This refers to the learning of the required principles and behaviours that form the core of the intervention. All training programs focus on learning. As contrasted with technical training where the trainee is taught specific procedures and steps required to accomplish a task, the managerial role is more diffuse requiring that managers learn how to recognize the need for the skill in a diverse number of circumstances. In management development, the purpose is to help managers learn managerial principles and processes that they can integrate with their personal styles and apply to the conditions they are likely to meet on the job.

c. *Skill practice.* As described in Chapter 5, practice is the key to learning how to do most things well. The practice of learned skills serves three fundamental purposes. First and most obvious is that practice reinforces learning and more formally, helps shift the learning from the declarative to the procedural learning stage (see Chapter 3). A second use of practice is to enhance the manager's beliefs in his or her ability to perform the skill. That is, practice contributes to the development of self-efficacy. Managers who feel more confident in their capacity to learn and display the skill on the job are more likely to learn and transfer that skill. Third, skill practice can take a variety of forms including role plays, simulations, and videotaped behaviour with feedback. These activities are inherently more active and can help maintain interest and help the manager trainee focus their attention on the learning task.

d. *Skill application* on the job (transfer). The final step in management development has to do with the transfer process (see Chapter 9). Follow-ups and additional coaching and reinforcement are important to ensure that managers practice and perform their new skills on the job.

In summary, models of management skill development focus on a number of important steps or stages in the development process. This usually begins with self-assessment and then proceeds to skill learning, practice, and application. To learn more about the process of management skills development, see The Trainer's Notebook on the TIMS procedure.

The TIMS (Training in Management Skills) Procedure

Phillip Hunsaker provides the following 10 step process to management development that he refers to as TIMS or Training in Management Skills.

1. Self-assessment.
2. Learn skill concepts.
3. Check concept learning.
4. Identify behaviours that define the skill.
5. Model the skill (i.e., observe others performing the skill).
6. Practice the skill during training (to build self-efficacy and to contribute to procedural learning).
7. Re-assess skills (to test for progress and to intervene when skill changes are insufficient).
8. Questions to assist in skill application (questioning trainees to ensure that they have a clear understanding of the situations in which the application of the trained skill is warranted, and to identify constraints and coping strategies for overcoming these constraints).
9. Exercises to reinforce skill application (as well as self-efficacy and procedural learning).
10. Planning for future development.

The TIMS model (as most other models) helps training developers and management trainers focus their efforts by providing a template of the activities required to increase the odds that managerial skill levels do improve as a result of training. Although the TIMS model is somewhat more detailed than some other models, it reflects the key dimensions common to most management development models: skill-assessment (steps 1 and 7), learning (steps 2 though 5), and practice and preparation for application on the job (steps 6, and 8 through 10).

Source: Hunsaker, P.L (2001). *Training in Management Skills.* Upper Saddle River: Prentice Hall. Adapted by permission of Pearson Education, Inc., Upper Saddle River, NJ.

The Content of Management Development Programs

Based on our earlier discussion of management skills, we can organize them into three general categories: conceptual, technical, and interpersonal skills. These three clusters of skills are not completely independent. For example, the mastery of technical skills often requires conceptual skills, and interpersonal skills often require specific technical skills. Nevertheless, this categorization provides a convenient way to organize management development programs.

In this section, we describe the content of management development programs used to develop some of these skills. More complete descriptions of management development programs may be found in various texts on management development (e.g., Whetten and Cameron or Hunsaker) as well as by consulting Internet sources such as those identified at the end of this chapter in the Using the Internet section.

Conceptual Skills

To accomplish the planning, organizing, and control functions of management, managers require various conceptual skills. We will limit the discussion to three especially important conceptual skills—problem solving and decision-making, planning, and performance management.

a. *Problem solving and decision-making skills.* Because managers are required to make a myriad of decisions—small and large—it is essential that they have the skills to do so. Many years ago, James March and Herbert Simon, in one of the most influential studies of managerial decision making, showed that most people are uncomfortable making decisions, and that they tend to adopt solutions to problems that are not optimal but "adequate." Typically, the first solution that minimally solves the problem is selected.[20]

   Contemporary decision-making programs are designed to specifically avoid this tendency. As a result, most programs are organized around four basic steps: 1) Defining the problem, 2) Generating alternative solutions, 3) Evaluating and selecting an alternative solution, and 4) Implementation and follow-up.

b. *Planning.* Planning is an essential requirement of the organizing function of management. Planning involves first the clarification and specification of the goals the manager wishes to achieve. Next, the manager is taught to scan the environment to ensure that the plans are relevant and have a high probability of being successfully implemented. This second step is referred to as a "SWOT" analysis. That is, the manager is taught how to identify the Strengths and Weaknesses of the unit managed (that is their capabilities and weaknesses) relative to the Opportunities and Threats that exist in the environment. Based on this analysis, the manager is taught to translate these strengths and weaknesses (SW), opportunities (O), and possible threats (T), into specific actions in order to establish the strategies and tactics required for implementation. Finally, managers learn the processes by which the success (or lack thereof) of the plan is evaluated.

c. *Performance management and goal-setting.* Almost all organizations in North America require managers to manage the performance of their units and the people in them. Performance appraisal involves two distinct steps: a) Assessing the performance of people (to ensure that rewards and sanctions are applied fairly), and b) Establishing goals and directions for future performance. Whereas these two steps are usually associated with a yearly formal review session, it is now widely acknowledged that managers need to review the performance of others on an ongoing basis. Providing feedback in a manner conducive to performance improvement is one of the key skills that successful managers possess. Goal-setting is an integral part of the process. As shown by Edwin Locke and Gary Latham, goals have strong motivational effects and are one of the most important mechanisms for managing one's own performance as well as the performance of others.[21] Goals focus and direct one's efforts and can be self-reinforcing by providing specific feedback information that allows people to evaluate their progress.

   However, in order for goals to be motivational, they must be SMART goals. That is, they must be Specific, Measurable, Achievable, Relevant, and their achievement is specified in Time.

Managers need to know how to structure such SMART goals. Moreover, goals are motivating and effective only when there is commitment to goal attainment. Most goal-setting training programs are structured to teach managers how to set goals with employees and how to provide feedback relevant to goal attainment.

Goal-setting, which was discussed in Chapter 3, is now an integral part of performance management and many managers are trained in this area in order to enable them to conduct performance appraisals, and to help their employees improve their performance.

Many Canadian organizations including Pricewaterhouse-Coopers, the National Research Council of Canada, and Bell Canada have provided their managers with performance management and assessment training courses that all include goal-setting as one of the core dimensions of the program.

Technical Skills

Managers of marketing departments know something about marketing, as research directors know something about research. Such knowledge and skills are generally acquired through university programs that may be general (such as a general MBA) or more specialized (such as a university program in Human Resource Management, Marketing, Statistics, or Accountancy). Additionally, technical skills can be further developed through targeted training courses and workshops as well as specialized readings.

For example, university professors tend to build technical skills by reading scientific journals and by attending conferences. As a further example, medical doctors and pharmacists in Canada are required to attend a certain number of conferences and workshops that instruct them on new research, treatments, or diagnostic procedures in their areas of practice. Accountants are also required to attend periodic specialized information sessions such as when there are changes to the tax laws or when changes in auditing standards are enacted.

Interpersonal Skills

Interpersonal skills refer to the manager's ability to interact with others in a constructive manner. This includes skills in communication, coaching (see the section on "Coaching" later in the chapter), and in managing conflict and stress. Although we limit our discussion to these skills in this chapter, it is important to note that other skills are also important. For example, there is a growing recognition of the importance for managers to develop "political" skills designed to help them gain power and influence. Moreover, as organizations move towards knowledge-based systems, they require that their members increasingly self-manage their behaviour and show initiative. Managers need to learn how to function in this new environment by learning how to empower and motivate their employees and to build effective teams.

a. *Communication.* Communication skills are central to most management positions because much of a manager's time involves gathering and disseminating information from the environment to the people in the unit and from the people in the unit to the environment. In communicating effectively, managers are taught to recognize their own *biases and styles* in "hearing" and in "speaking" with others. Hence, managers need to understand their *frame of reference* (knowing "where they are coming from"), how their interpretations of what they hear and communicate are affected by their *values*, and their *trusts* or distrusts of others. These in turn affect *selective listening* (hearing what we want to hear) and *filtering* (telling only that which others want to hear). In addition to alerting managers to these tendencies that obscure communication, most communication training programs teach managers the principles and the practice of effective communication. This involves *congruency* (ensuring that the message that is sent is in line with their own actions), *clarity* (using language that is appropriate for the listener), and most importantly to ensure comprehension by actively soliciting *feedback* from the listener.

b. *Managing conflict.* Managing conflict is an essential skill for managers because they are invariably competing for resources with other managers and because they may be involved in managing the competition and conflict between employees.

Conflict can be described as being of one of two types—conflict that is *interpersonal* (co-workers who may dislike one another) or *issue based* (people who may have conflicting views on a problem or its solution).[22] Conflict is not an inherently "bad" thing because issue based disagreements can often serve to enhance the quality of the final decision.[23] However, when conflict is not properly managed it can quickly create organizational problems.

There are five ways of managing conflict: *avoidance* (avoiding it); *accommodation* (giving in); *forcing* (getting your way); *compromise* (providing each party with some of the things they want); and *collaboration* (finding a solution together that gives both parties what they want).

Collaboration is the ultimate conflict resolution outcome but it is not always possible or appropriate. Which style is appropriate depends on the situation faced by the manager. Forcing, for example, may be appropriate when the resolution requires an unpopular decision and when gaining the commitment of people to that decision is not important. However, regardless of the style that successful conflict resolution requires, managers must pay attention to the emotional aspects of the conflict. To do so requires managers to a) treat the parties with respect, b) listen to the other party and ensure that they know that they have been heard and understood, and c) share his or her needs and feelings.

c. *Managing stress.* Considering the scope, time pressures (managers spend about nine minutes on each problem), difficulties, and responsibilities of managers, it is no surprise that managerial jobs tend to be stressful.

A stress reaction is a person's emotional and physical response to a perceived threat. Stress reactions, like pain are useful warning mechanisms that inform people that "something is wrong" and that they should do something about it. Stress reactions are a response to environmental events that may find their source in the work itself and the organization. For example, two well-known work-related stressors are role conflict and role ambiguity. *Role conflict* is associated with having contradictory task demands, and *role ambiguity* refers to not knowing what is expected.

Stressors that impact work behaviours might also find their source in nonwork events (a family or health problem). Managers need to recognize stress reactions both in themselves as well as in those they manage because stress reactions can be quite damaging to one's health and performance.

There are two basic ways to reduce stress. First, one can change the environment by removing or eliminating the stressors. Second, one can learn to cope with and manage stressors more effectively.

The second approach is more likely to be successful because individuals are in a better position to be proactive and manage themselves rather than change their environment. In learning how to cope with stress, the first and most important step is to know when one is in fact experiencing stress. That is, to recognize the signs of stress. Once a manager learns how to be aware of his/her own signs of stress (and training programs on stress management spend considerable time on this), the manager can learn how to be proactive in a way that will reduce the harmful effects of a stress reaction through appropriate planning and organizing.

In summary, management development programs are often designed with a focus on the development of conceptual, technical, and interpersonal skills. There are of course many different approaches and methods for developing these skills and in the next section, we discuss some of the most popular methods.

Management Development Programs

The development of managerial skills requires that managers first acquire information and knowledge. Thus, one element of management development can be described as informational. However, management development programs tend to focus more on the learning of skills and are therefore usually highly experiential.

Experiential learning refers to learning experiences that include skill practice exercises that actively engage and involve the learner. This is especially important for management development because the expectation is that managers will acquire new skills and behave differently as a result of training. Moreover, management skills are complex and are intertwined with the personal characteristics of managers. Thus, it is not simply a question of memorizing and applying a set of prescriptions. Rather, the goal is to help

Experiential learning

Learning experiences that include skill practice exercises that actively engage and involve the learner managers adapt principles and techniques in conformity with their personal styles and within the context in which they work.

There are three general approaches to management development: management education programs, management training programs, and on-the-job development.

Management Education Programs

The development of managers has typically involved management education. **Management education** refers to "those activities traditionally conducted by colleges and universities that focus on developing a broad range of managerial knowledge and general conceptual abilities" (p. 278).[24]

The best example of management education programs is the ever-popular MBA that most business schools offer. Executive MBA programs are especially desirable for individuals who are already in managerial roles and want to advance in their organization. These programs provide individuals with a general education in management and are highly informational although they usually include some experiential learning as well. Students not only learn about management concepts and theory, but they are also expected to develop managerial skills. In fact, many MBA programs have managerial skills courses that focus on the kinds of skills listed in Table 13.1.

Management education programs make use of a number of experiential methods such as role plays, games, simulations, and behaviour modelling that were described in Chapter 6. The case study method, however, is the most often used method to teach management skills in most MBA programs.

Management education
The acquisition of a broad range of managerial knowledge and general conceptual abilities

Management Training Programs

Management training refers to training programs that involve activities and experiences that are designed to develop specific managerial skills (e.g., communication, decision-making), which would be immediately applicable in a particular organizational setting (p. 280).[25]

Management training programs usually focus on specific topics or particular skills. Some management training programs take place in classrooms and consist of specialized workshops and seminars. These programs are usually of short duration and can be provided by educational institutions, professional associations, and consulting firms as well as in-house at a company's learning centre. Some companies have their own corporate universities for this purpose.

Management training programs can also take place outside of the classroom in any number of settings. A popular example of this is Outdoor Wilderness Training programs, which take place in the outdoors and are discussed later in the chapter.

Management training
Programs and activities designed to develop specific managerial skills

On-the-Job Management Development

On-the-job management development programs are designed to provide individuals with managerial learning experiences on the job. Two of the most common examples are job rotation and coaching, which were discussed in Chapter 7.

On-the-job management development
Programs designed to provide individuals with managerial learning experiences on-the-job

Recall that job rotation involves exposing an individual to different areas and experiences throughout an organization. In this way, the individual not only acquires new skills from working on different projects and interacting with people throughout an organization, but also learns about the organization itself.

Coaching was described as a process in which a manager works closely with an employee to plan opportunities for learning. Because of its importance as a method of management development, we provide some additional insight on its use as a way to develop managers on the job later in the chapter.

Outdoor Wilderness Training

During World War II, the Canadian and other allied Navies played a major role in shipping supplies to England and in protecting these convoys as they crossed the North Atlantic. The German Navy opposed these convoys through the use of well organized and efficiently coordinated attacks by U-boats. The submarine attacks took a heavy toll on men and ships. Hundreds of ships were torpedoed forcing thousands of sailors to abandon ship and to escape in rafts and lifeboats.

To survive, the sailors had to overcome the rigours of life in the open ocean with little protection from the elements. Freezing in winter, broiling in summer, in open boats with scant supplies, many sailors successfully escaped their burning ships only to die awaiting a rescue that would sometimes come days, weeks, and even months after the torpedo attack.

Casualty reports unveiled a curious fact. Although it was expected that the younger, better fit sailors would be most apt to withstand the intense demands of survival on the high seas it was, paradoxically, the older sailors who were more likely to live through the ordeal. Discussions held with survivors indicated that younger sailors were more likely to panic and to adopt survival strategies that were not successful. It was determined that older sailors had better survival rates because they benefited from greater "life experience" that allowed them to control their anxieties and to summon the resources and cool-headedness required by the extreme situation they faced.

After the war this experience spawned "Outdoor Wilderness Training" as a mechanism designed to help people develop greater levels of "life experience." Many companies sponsor individual managers and teams to attend wilderness training experiences offered by hundreds of companies and institutions in Canada as well as in other countries.

Outdoor wilderness training programs are typically organized around a series of outdoor tasks that expose individuals to physically and psychologically demanding activities such as rock climbing, white water rafting, or even winter camping experiences, in which the trainees have had little or no prior experience. Though outfitters are careful to provide instructors who are safety conscious, it remains that many of the activities are inherently dangerous. In many cases, the successful and safe accomplishment of these tasks requires self-reliance as well as team work, strong communication skills, and the development of trust in others. This in turn is expected not only to help enhance the

Outdoor wilderness training

Programs designed to help managers develop greater levels of "life experience" by participating in physically and psychologically demanding tasks and activities

Managing Performance Through Training and Development

individual skills of trainees—such as leadership skills—but also to improve the individual's ability to function collaboratively with others (team work).

A key question, however, is just how effective is wilderness training? Recent research on Outward Bound Australia trainees indicates that an overwhelming proportion of participants retain highly positive reactions to their training experience. Moreover, the research indicates that such training appears to have effects on a very wide set of variables from leadership ability and mood to social skills and well being, and that this effect may be very durable and long-lasting. Moreover, these programs appear to have their largest impact in increasing the participants' self-confidence and their ability to manage time.[26]

As these are important contributors to managerial success, it is possible that such programs do lead to improvements in job performance, though the research remains insufficient to draw a firm conclusion. Furthermore, the research shows that there is considerable variation between programs, some being more successful than others in creating these changes. There are some indications that shorter programs (one to three days) are less successful than longer ones, however, once again there is much variation between programs.

Coaching

In the last fifteen years or so, coaching has become an important on-the-job method of helping managers develop the knowledge and skills they need to improve their capacity to adapt and their effectiveness.

As described in Chapter 7, coaching is a training method in which a manager works closely with an employee to develop insight, motivate, build skills, and to provide support through feedback and reinforcement. Coaching involves a one-on-one individualized learning experience in which a more experienced and knowledgeable person is formally called upon to help another person develop the insights and techniques in the accomplishment of their job.

For example, a marketing manager was selected to head the Organizational Learning group in the Canadian operations of a multinational pharmaceutical organization. Her boss, the vice president of human resources asked her to develop a training plan for one of the divisions of the company. As the manager lacked direct experience and knowledge of "organizational learning," an external consultant, who was an expert in training and development with extensive experience in the pharmaceutical industry, was hired to coach the manager with the task.

The role of the consultant was not to produce the training plan for the department, but rather to help the manager develop the plan by informing her of "best practices" by discussing with her the types of obstacles likely to be encountered, and by helping her develop strategies for dealing with these obstacles.

In this case, the coach was an external consultant. However, in many organizations the coaching role may be assumed by another manager in the organization and as previously discussed, it is often the case that a manager may be coached by another while at the same time, serving as a coach for a more junior manager.

In the Canadian branch of PricewaterhouseCoopers, for example (as described earlier in Training Today), senior people in the organization are called upon to act as coaches for more junior managers in the organization. Hence, it is now recognized that managers must act as coaches as part of their job responsibilities. It is for this reason that it is important to understand what a coach needs to do to be effective.

David Peterson lists several characteristics of great coaches of which three stand out:[27]

1. *Goal orientation.* Great coaches are great listeners who empathize with the learner and who are honestly interested in helping people achieve their goals.
2. *Challengers.* Great coaches are able to "feel" the mood state of the learner and know when to listen and when to challenge the beliefs and thinking of the learner.
3. *Person focused.* Great coaches focus their efforts and attention on the learner. They do not try to impose their views on the learner by insisting that there is "One Best Way" to do things. Rather, they focus on helping the learner use his or her own previous knowledge and experience to develop their own perspective, understanding, and styles in dealing with the problems to be solved.

Peterson proposed the "development pipeline," a list of five conditions that are necessary to ensure the development of managers. Coaches are maximally helpful when they structure their efforts to help managers develop:

- *Insight.* Recognizing and understand their own strengths and weaknesses.
- *Motivation.* Understanding and caring about changing the ways in which they operate.
- *Capabilities.* Identifying resources and best practices for dealing with complex decisions and situations and by exploring alternative ways of dealing with them.
- *Real-world practices.* Identifying opportunities to implement, on a day to day basis, the little changes that should be made and to develop the critical perspective needed to assess what works, what does not, and why.
- *Accountability.* Encourage the manager to demonstrate the new skills and knowledge through commitment to specific actions.

To achieve these objectives, coaches face a number of important challenges. First and foremost, coaches must act to gain the trust of the "coachee." Confidentiality, discretion, and honesty are three of the key behaviours coaches must demonstrate. Coaches must use this developing trust to provide feedback to managers and to help them gain a clearer understanding of what is important to the person as well as to those that surround him or her. Coaches must also help the manager develop skills, either directly (by suggesting best practices for example) or by identifying other activities (such as

Managing Performance Through Training and Development

upcoming training courses or seminars). Successful coaches also need to focus their efforts on supporting managers.

Applying new skills is difficult and attempts to do so are often subject to obstacles and hurdles that can discourage the use of the new skills as described in Chapter 9. Coaches have a special responsibility to be attentive to these situations and to help managerial persistence.

Finally, coaches are sometimes in a position to actually intervene elsewhere in the organization to remove obstacles that are inhibiting the display of new skills. That is, successful coaches are sometimes proactive as opposed to strictly passive in their interventions.

A number of research studies have shown that coaching does help managers become more successful and more effective in accomplishing their tasks. Research has also shown that managers who received coaching experiences, as part of their executive education program in a university, also reported higher levels of self-confidence and improved skills in developing others.

While this evidence speaks highly of coaching, it is important to note that most of the research has relied on self-report measures and/or on the perception of superiors to assess the effectiveness of coaching as a management development technique. As with all other similar research, the reliance on self-reports as a criterion of success must be viewed with caution until more objective criteria are used to measure effectiveness.[28]

Summary

This chapter described the roles, functions, and critical skills of managers and how they are developed. Managers are responsible for planning, organizing, leading, and controlling the work of others in order to achieve organizational goals. To meet these fundamental obligations, managers engage in a number of interpersonal, informational, and decisional activities. This requires them to master and display conceptual, technical, and interpersonal skills, and to have emotional intelligence. Management development programs are designed to develop these skills. Models of management development involve skill assessment, skill acquisition, skill practice, and skill application. The content of management development programs was described in terms of conceptual, technical, and interpersonal skills. Management development programs involve both informational and experiential learning and include management education, management training, and on-the-job development. Management education programs such as an MBA provide individuals with a general management education. A popular example of management training is outdoor wilderness training. Examples of on-the-job development include job rotation and coaching.

Key Terms

core functions of management (page 356)

emotional intelligence (page 363)

experiential learning (page 370)

leadership (page 355)

management (page 356)

management development (page 355)

management education (page 371)
management training (page 371)
on-the-job management development
(page 371)

outdoor wilderness training (page 372)
skills (page 361)

Weblinks

Bell Canada: www.bell.ca (page 368)
National Research Council of Canada: www.nrc-cnrc.gc.ca (page 368)
Microsoft: www.microsoft.com (page 360)
PricewaterhouseCoopers: www.pricewaterhouse.com (page 359)

Discussion Questions

1. What are some of the differences between management development and employee training?
2. Imagine the CEO of a company who has read this chapter and the section on coaching. She decides that coaching is a good idea and sends a memo to all managers telling them to formally take on the role of coach for each of their subordinates. Is this a good idea? How likely is it to improve performance? If the CEO had consulted you prior to announcing her decision, what would you have suggested she do?
3. Compare and contrast management education, management training, and on-the-job development. What are the advantages and disadvantages of each of these approaches for management development? How effective do you think each approach is for teaching the skills listed in Table 13.1?
4. What is emotional intelligence and what does it have to do with management and managerial skills? Can managers be trained to improve their emotional intelligence? If yes, how can this be done?

Using the Internet

1. There are many Internet sources that describe the types of management training programs that exist for different levels of management. Visit some of these sites:
   www.business-marketing.com/store/assessment
   www.businesstrainingmedia.com/
   and for senior-level management go to:
   www.managementcourses.com/
   a. Once you have visited some of these sites, identify the types of programs that are most frequently proposed.
   b. How do these "popular" and frequently offered courses relate to the management roles, functions, and skills discussed in the chapter?
2. Coaching is one of the more important one-on-one management development techniques in today's business environment. Go to:

http://teragram.ca/coach_preassess_corp.html and answer the following questions:

    a) Suppose that you had to implement a coaching program for junior executives and a coaching program for senior managers. Would the content of a coaching training program be the same or different for these two groups. If they did differ, how would they and why?

3. Among the many sources available to find out about wilderness training in Canada are Outward Bound at **www.outwardbound.ca/instprof.asp** and the Banff Centre at **www.banffcentre.ca/departments/leadership/leadership.asp**. Prepare a brief report about the kind of programs offered at each site and the skills they focus on.

Exercises

1. In an article called "The smart-talk trap," Jeffrey Pfeffer and Robert Sutton (1999) described a phenomenon in organizations that they call the "knowing-doing gap." According to the authors, many managers are knowledgeable and very good at talking but not very good at doing or action. In other words, talk substitutes for action. An especially dangerous form of talk is "smart talk" where the speaker is particularly good at sounding confident, articulate, and eloquent. Unfortunately, smart talk tends to focus on the negative and is often unnecessarily complicated. As a result, it tends to result in inaction or what the authors call the "smart-talk trap." Problems are discussed and plans for action might be formulated, but in the end nothing is done. This can have serious negative consequences for organizations. The authors suggest that one of the main reasons for the knowing-doing gap and the smart-talk trap is that managers have been trained to talk.

    a. What do you think about the knowing-doing gap and the smart-talk trap? Do you think that this is a serious problem in organizations?

    b. The authors argue that one of the reasons for the existence of the knowing-doing gap and the smart-talk trap is because of the training that managers receive. Do you agree with this assertion? How can management training result in so much knowing and talking and so little doing?

    c. Discuss the knowing-doing gap and the smart-talk trap with somebody you know in a managerial position. Find out what they have to say about the prevalence of it in their organization, why it might or might not be a problem, and what can be done to avoid it.

    d. What advice would you give organizations about how to develop managers in order to avoid the knowing-doing gap and the smart-talk trap?

2. To find out more about management development, contact a human resource professional and ask about management development in their organization. To guide your discussion, consider the following issues:

a. Describe the main skills that are the focus of management development programs. What are these skills and why are they the focus of management development?

b. Describe the process of management development. What are the main steps involved in the process?

c. Describe the content of management development programs.

d. What types of management development programs are used and why? Does the organization use experiential learning approaches, and if so, what are they? Does the organization use management education programs, management training programs, job rotation, and/or coaching and how effective are they?

e. How effective is management development for improving managerial and organizational effectiveness?

In addition, contact several managers who work in different organizations and ask them questions about their own management development along the following lines:

i. Describe the extent to which they have been involved in management development programs in their organization. How often and to what extent have they participated in management development?

ii. What skills were the programs designed to improve and how effective were they?

iii. What kinds of management development programs have they participated in (e.g., management education, management training, job rotation, coaching)?

iv. What has been the content or focus of their management development programs and how effective have they been?

v. Has their participation in management development activities improved their managerial effectiveness? Why or why not?

Summarize your results in a report in which you discuss the extent and nature of management development in organizations, and the effectiveness of management development in terms of managerial and organizational effectiveness.

3. Think of a manager who you have had in a current or previous job. Keeping in mind his/her behaviour and performance, how effective do you think they were in their performance of the core functions and roles of management? What skills do you think they need to improve? What would you recommend your manager do to improve his/her performance and managerial skills?

4. If you were hired in a managerial position and you were told to design your own plan for development, what would you do? Refer to the section on models of management skill development, and for each step in the process develop a plan for your own management development. Be sure to indicate what you will do in each step.

5. As the new director of training, you have been asked to develop a program to improve the emotional intelligence of managers in your organization. Using the material in this chapter, indicate what content will be included in your program as well as the methods and programs of management development that will be used. Be sure to explain why you are including particular content areas as well as certain methods and programs of management development.

Case

MARKET RESEARCH INC.

Market Research Inc. is a firm that specializes in conducting surveys and interviews with members of the general public in Vancouver. The company has a number of different teams of people who work on many different projects for its many corporate clients. It is usually the case that several projects are conducted at the same time.

The company is composed of three departments: Production, Technical, and Marketing. The Marketing group is responsible for selling the company's services to corporate clients. The Technical Department is mainly composed of research personnel who are responsible for developing and analyzing the results of the surveys, focus groups, and interviewing studies for the clients. The Production Department is composed of several teams of interviewers. It is that department's job to conduct the data collection. They are responsible for identifying the customers who will be interviewed or surveyed, for enlisting their cooperation, and for interviewing them either personally, by phone or mail, depending on the project.

Market Research Inc. has a wide set of corporate clients who need to better understand customer needs and reactions to company products. This information is crucial to the clients because it helps them better understand how the products and services they sell are perceived by the customers. This information, in turn, can be used by the senior executives to devise strategies to improve products and/or improve the advertising tactics they rely on to promote their products.

Thomas Waterfall (Tom) is the manager of the Production Department. The department is responsible for ensuring that all of the data collection projects sold by Marketing and developed by the Technical Department are conducted in a professional and timely manner. More specifically, Tom is responsible for ensuring that there is always enough staff on hand to conduct each study (never too many nor too few), for hiring (or letting go) the interviewers, for training them on the specific project requirements, and for ensuring and controlling the quality of the work done by the Production Department. He must keep himself informed of the activities of the Marketing and Technical Departments to ensure that the Production Department can meet the demands of these other groups. Finally, the

Chapter 13: Management Development

Production Department is a high-pressure environment where tensions among interviewers and between interviewers and the Technical staff can sometimes flare up threatening the efficient and effective production of the studies. The Production manager must often act as an arbiter of disputes and act to soothe people when they get upset, a skill for which Tom is famous.

Mary Milend has been working for the last five years for Market Research Inc. She works in the Production Department of the company where she is an interviewer. Her job is to administer the surveys and to conduct focus groups and other interviews with consumers. She has been doing a remarkable job. She conducts her interviews with professionalism and competence, always meets her deadlines, and has never been the object of a complaint, either by consumers or by her co-workers. She has always shown great cooperation, often volunteering to help other interviewers with their tasks when they were submerged. Finally, in the tense atmosphere of conducting the data collection under tight deadlines, she has always maintained extremely good relationships with the Technical staff with whom the Production Department interacts routinely.

Tom, the manager of the Production Department has announced that he will be retiring next year. Because of her superb record as an employee and her extensive hands-on knowledge of the Production Department, the vice-president has offered to promote Mary to the job of Production Manager when Tom retires.

Mary is quite interested in the job, as this would mean a much higher salary, better benefits, vacations, and greater influence in the company. However, as Mary is a very honest person, she told the VP, when he offered her the promotion, that although she was keenly interested in the job, she was not sure that she was the best choice. She explained that she had never acted in a managerial role before and that she felt uncertain that she had the skills to do the job well. Impressed by Mary's honesty, the VP indicated to her that he would be willing to provide her with all of the training she requires to acquire the managerial skills that she will need to perform her new job.

Questions

1. What are the main skills that Mary will need to develop if she accepts the promotion?
2. What are some of the training experiences that might benefit Mary?
3. Should Tom be invited to play a role in Mary's development? If so, what could that role be?
4. How effective do you think each of the following programs would be for Mary's development: management education programs, management training programs (i.e., outdoor wilderness training), and on-the-job development (i.e., job rotation and coaching). What are the advantages and disadvantages of each, and which one(s) do you recommend and why?

References

[1]Schettler, J. (2002, March). Training top 100: IBM. *Training, 39*(3), pp. 48–49.

[2]Tannenbaum, S.I., & Yukl, G. (1992). Training and development in work organizations. *Annual Review of Psychology, 43*, 399–441.

[3]Fulmer, R.M. (1997, summer). The evolving paradigm of leadership development. *Organizational Dynamics*, 59–72.

[4]McCallum, J. (1993). The manager's job is still to manage. *Business Quarterly, 57* (4), 61–67; Brown, T.L. (1995). Leadership is everyone's business. *Apparel Industry Magazine 56* (9), p. 14.

[5]Baldwin T.T. and Patgett, M.Y. (1994). Management development: a review and commentary. In Cooper, C.L. and Robertson, I.T. (Eds) *Key reviews in managerial psychology*. New York: Wiley.

[6]Marquardt, M.J., Nissley, N., Ozag, R., & Taylor, T.L. (2000). International briefing 6. Training and development in the United States. *International Journal of Training and Development 4*:2. 138–49; Mabey, C. & Thomson, A. (2000). Management development in the UK: a provider and participant perspective. *International Journal of Training and Development, 4*:4. 272–86; Cornuel, E., Kletz, P. (2001). An empirical analysis of priority sectors for managers' training. *Journal of Management Development, 20*, 5, 402–13; Agut, S. & Grau, R. (2002). Managerial competency needs and training requests: The case of the Spanish tourist industry. *Human Resource Development Quarterly, 13*, 1, 31–51; and Analoui, F. & Hosseini, M.H. (2001). Management education and increased managerial effectiveness. The case of business managers in Iran. *Journal of Management Development, 20*, 9, 785–794.

[7]Kouzes, J.M., & Posner, B.Z. (2002). *Leadership Challenge* (3rd edition). San Francisco: Jossey-Bass. (3rd edition); London, M. (2002). *Leadership development*: Mahwah, N.J: Lawrence Erlbaum Associates; Tichy, N.M., Cardwell, N. (2002). *The cycle of leadership: How great leaders teach their companies to win*. New York: HarperCollins Publishers. (3rd edition); Ketz de Vries, M (2001). *The leadership mystique*. London: Prentice-Hall; and Whetten, D.A. & Cameron, K.S. (2002). *Developing management skills*. Upper Saddle River, N.J.: Prentice Hall (5th edition).

[8]Robbins, SP., De Cenzo, D,A. Condie, J.L, & Kondo, L. (2001). *Supervision in Canada today*. Toronto: Prentice-Hall (3rd edition).

[9]Kouzes, J.M. & Posner (2002).

[10]Orth, C.D., Wilkinson, H.E. and Benfari, R.C. (1987). The manager's role as coach and mentor. *Organizational Dynamics*, Spring, 67–74.

[11]Mintzberg, H (1973). *The nature of managerial work*, New York, N.Y., Harper and Row; and Mintzberg, H (1975) The manager's job: Folklore and fact. *Harvard Business Review, 53*(4), 49–61.

[12]Whetten, D.A. & Cameron, K.S. (2002).

[13]Luthans, F., Rosenkrantz, S.A. & Hennesy, H.W. (1985). What do successful managers really do? An observation study of managerial activities. *Journal of Applied Behavioral Science, 21*, 255–70.

[14]Camp, R., Vielhaber, M., & Simonetti, J.L. (2001). *Strategic interviewing: How to hire good people*. San Francisco: Jossey-Bass.

[15]Cameron, K. & Tschirhart, M. (1988). Managerial competencies and organizational effectiveness, Working Paper, School of Business Administration, University of Michigan.

[16]Goleman, D. (1998). *Working with emotional intelligence*. New York: Bantam.

[17]Pfeffer, J. (1998). *The human equation: Building profits by putting people first*. Boston: Harvard Business School Press.

[18]Ryan, A.M., Brutus, S., Greguras, G.J. and Hakel, M.D. (2000). Receptivity to assessment-based feedback for management development. *Journal of Management Development, 19*, 4, 252–76.

[19]Hunsaker, P.L (2001). *Training in Management Skills*. Upper Saddle River: Prentice Hall.

[20]March, J.G., & Simon, H.A. (1958). *Organizations*. New York: Blackwell.

[21]Locke, E.A. & Latham, G.P. (1990). *A theory of goal setting and task performance*. Englewood Cliffs, N. J., Prentice-Hall.

[22]Eisenhardt, K.M. Kahwajy, J.L. & Bourgeois, L.J. III (1997). How management teams can have a good fight. *Harvard Business Review*. July-August, 77–85.

[23]Haccoun, R.R. & Klimoski, R.J. (1975). Negotiator status and accountability source: A study of negotiator behavior. *Organizational Behavior and Human Performance*. 14, 342–59.

[24]Wexley, K.N., & Baldwin, T.T. (1986). Management development. *Journal of Management, 12*, 277–94.

[25]Wexley, K.N., & Baldwin, T.T. (1986).

[26]Hattie, J., Marsh, H.W., Neill, J.T. & Richards, G.E. (1997). Adventure Education and Outward Bound: Out-of-class experiences that have a lasting effect. *Review of Educational Research, 67*, 43–87.

[27]Peterson, D. B. (2002). Management development: Coaching and mentoring programs. In K. Kraiger's (Ed.), *Creating, implementing, and managing effective training and development: State-of-the-art lessons for practice*, (pp.160-191). San Francisco. CA: Jossey-Bass.

[28]Peterson, D. B. (2002).

Chapter

14

Challenges and Best Practices

Chapter Learning Objectives

After reading this chapter, you should be able to

- describe how the role of the trainer has changed and evolved
- discuss the role of ethics in training and development
- describe the challenges faced by organizations and the implications and trends for training and development
- discuss the main reasons why training programs fail and the best practices to make them effective

www.telus.com

TELUS

TELUS Corporation is one of Canada's leading telecommunications companies. With a national sales force of more than 500 employees, TELUS provides a full range of communications products and services.

In order to increase shareholder value and sustainable growth in the highly competitive telecommunications sector, the company determined that it needed to adopt a fundamental change in its selling strategy. A shift in focus from a tactical, "product-based" sales approach to a more strategic "solutions-based" sales approach was needed. This shift would require the sales force to learn selling strategies and skills that focus on engaging "C"-level customers (CEO/COO-level clients) in meaningful, reciprocal dialogue.

In order to achieve this goal, the sales force and sales managers had to acquire the skills and confidence to interact with "C"-level customers. The following objectives were set as part of the change strategy: Assess the strengths and weaknesses of the sales force interacting with C-level customers; provide a safe environment to learn and practice C-level selling skills; allow the sales force to experience what will realistically be expected of them as they move forward; and identify high-priority skill gaps that would become the basis for a targeted development plan.

The solution involved simulations, classroom-based workshops, and a comprehensive assessment process. First, the entire sales force participated in a three-day complex and realistic simulated selling environment. The objective was to show the sales force what the new selling environment looked like, allow it to experience it first-hand, and provide a basis to build a longer-term, change-management and performance improvement program.

The objective of the selling simulation was also to enable the sales force to apply new behaviours and skills in an authentic and realistic business environment. A full-scale actual replication of the new environment was established that included a fictitious client corporation with actual office locations, audited financials, a corporate website, press releases, and an executive assistant. The company was staffed with real-life executives who role-played specific C-level positions in the fictitious company.

The simulation was set up as a competition in which four sales teams in each session competed against each other to win the account. The teams actually made sales calls to executives and had to uncover business needs. The team that demonstrated that it understood the client's needs and presented the most appropriate solution in the most professional manner won the business.

The classroom workshops involved guided, consultative sessions focused on self-exploration in which facilitators provided perspectives on change and new approaches to client relationship building and selling skills. Assessments were also conducted throughout the simulation by sales managers/directors and trained observers, and feedback from the executives on each participant's performance was also obtained. In addition, the sales force performed self-assessments and peer-assessments.

The assessments were then used to provide on-the-job support as well as performance goals and plans for sales staff. The assessment information was also used to develop future training and coaching programs.

The results for TELUS have been a marked increase in sales calls at the C-level and new sales opportunities and business. It also led to the identification of high-priority development needs and new programs to address them.[1]

TELUS is a good example of how changes in the environment led to the development of a new business strategy that had direct implications for training and development. It is also a good example of how best practices are used in the design and delivery of a training program.

In this final chapter of the text, we review four key areas that represent challenges and trends in training and development. First, we will discuss how the role of the trainer has been changing and evolving. Next, we provide a brief review of ethics, an increasingly important topic in organizations with implications for training and development. We then discuss the challenges facing organizations today and their implications for training and development. The chapter concludes with an overview of the main reasons why training programs fail and the best practices for the design and delivery of effective training and development programs.

The Changing Role of the Trainer

As you know from reading this text, a trainer's primary responsibilities revolve around the design, delivery, and evaluation of training and development programs. To get a better idea of what the job of a training manager involves, see Table 14.1.

In recent years, however, the trainer's traditional status as a staff employee of the HR area has begun to change. Trainers have begun to move out of the training department to work with management in solving organizational problems and creating and facilitating learning opportunities. This reflects a movement or evolution of the trainer from a staff employee to a strategic partner.

TABLE 14.1

Job Description for a Training Manager

Position Title: Training Delivery Manager

Department: Training

Reports to: Director of Training

Supervises: Four Skill Trainers and Two Management Trainers

Position Objective: To manage the training delivery services of the department and implement all scheduled training courses.

Responsibilities:

1. Manages training delivery services within approved budget.

2. Implements all training courses as scheduled.

3. Supervises employees reporting to her/him to ensure they meet performance standards.

4. Creates individual development plans for each employee reporting to him/her.

5. Serves as an active member of the Training Department's management team.

6. Assists the Training Director in developing annual budgets and plans.

7. Works with the Training Development Manager to create new courses and evaluate existing ones.

8. Recommends necessary revisions to existing training courses and possible areas requiring training courses.

The time has come according to some experts for trainers to relinquish their staff status by accepting assignments in specific departments and working directly with line personnel as part of a management team so that training better reflects organization needs.[2] Ron Zemke went one step further, reporting on a successful training approach in which at least half the staff were not professional trainers but line managers cycling through the training department as part of their career development plan.[3]

Involvement with line managers gives the training function and the trainer a broader mandate. Trainers will take a much broader approach that focuses on performance improvement, accepting the necessity to train only as part of an overall commitment to improve performance.

In one large bakery, for example, cakes came down a conveyer on the operator's right, the operator picked up a cake, decorated it, and placed it on a quality-check conveyer on the left. As efficient as that may sound, the left-hand conveyer was too high—the operator tended to throw the cakes onto the higher finished-goods conveyer to avoid standing up each time. The impact on quality was predictable. Successive attempts by management to train the operators failed, and there was constant friction between the production and quality control departments. In this case, money spent lowering the conveyer would not only improve quality, but would create a better work climate as well.

There are many similar situations in both the private and the public sectors. Coping with them requires an adaptation of the trainers' role to that of internal consultant with a mandate and a budget to search out and improve performance in any way possible.

As an **internal consultant,** the role of the trainer is not just to provide training and development, but to provide solutions to performance problems. Ideally, an internal consultant would have to prove that his or her services were cost-effective. Funds would be directed to areas of greatest potential benefit. If this area happened to be training, training would be conducted. If other activities promised greater returns, funds would be steered away from the training function.[4]

Internal consultant
Responsible for providing solutions to performance problems

How can a consulting focus affect the traditional training department? The answer depends on the environment and on the skills of the trainer. If training is found to be a necessary part of improving performance, or if training is obviously necessary to organizational survival, a consulting focus might have little effect on the training function. If the trainer has sufficient knowledge and prestige to work as a consulting specialist, however, he or she can play a vastly more important role in the organization. Conversely, should training professionals not be able to cope with this broader definition of productivity improvement, they could well find themselves redundant to the organization's needs.[5]

In essence, the trainer's role will evolve toward counselling management on managing change and solving performance problems. It will entail working with line managers at all levels as a facilitator, identifying key individuals, and creating links that bring about significant change, leading to measurable productivity and/or quality improvements. In HR terms, the task will become one of more effectively integrating the members of the organization in pursuit of the organization's mission and objectives. Whether training is involved will be irrelevant.

Finally, given the increasing importance of life-long learning and the concept of the learning organization, the role of the trainer will increasingly shift from training to learning and the many forms that it might take. Thus, the role of the trainer will be to facilitate and create learning opportunities throughout the organization, and to help organizations manage the transition to a learning organization. In fact, we are already seeing changes in the job titles of the most senior person responsible for training in Canadian organizations. Job titles such as "Learning and Development Consultant," "Manager, Learning and Organizational Development," and "Learning and Development Specialist" to name just a few reflect this new role.[6]

In summary, the traditional role of the trainer as a staff person responsible for training and development has been evolving into a much larger role based on the management of learning, change, and performance. This involves forming a strategic partnership with management to solve organizational problems and to achieve organizational objectives. It also means a greater focus on learning throughout the organization.

Ethics and Training and Development

Ethical dilemmas in our society range from large-scale corporate scandals to day-to-day management situations. Recently, the unethical conduct of senior management at major corporations like Enron and WorldCom has made the headlines. But what do we mean by ethics and what are the ethical dilemmas faced by trainers?

Ethics involves systematic thinking about the moral consequences of one's actions and decisions on various stakeholders. Stakeholders refer to persons inside or outside of the organization who might be affected by one's actions and decisions. In organizations, ethics often takes the form of standards of conduct that indicate how one should behave according to an organization's values and principles. For training professionals, ethics would involve following a set of standards and principles in the design, delivery, and evaluation of training and development programs. But what kinds of dilemmas are training professionals likely to face?

Trainers face many ethical dilemmas and they must monitor not only how they train, but what they train as well. For example, the Internal Revenue Service in the United States has been accused of abusing the taxpayer. No doubt, IRS trainers have performed well in training tax specialists in the art of collecting taxes according to a set of impersonal standards, but should the focus have been on these particular standards?[7]

Indeed, the zealous application of these "standards" has led the agency into disrepute.[8] Are trainers behaving in an ethical fashion if their training gradually destroys the organization's reputation? This is an example of one of the broader ethical questions faced by trainers.

A more everyday dilemma arises when trainers are asked to conduct training, often by powerful senior managers that might not be in the best interests of employees or the organization. For example, should stress management courses be provided, even though the trainer knows that the sources or causes of the stress have not been addressed? Suppose a senior manager insists on courses in the latest fad-of-the-month management technique. What is the ethical response?

Faced with these challenges and the normal concern for self-preservation, many trainers will relent and deliver the courses without comment. Indeed, they might have no other choice, but the damage to the training function and to the organization can be severe.

If the training function has been placed at or near the top of the organization, however, then the trainer can approach these dilemmas differently, pointing out that training effectiveness is likely to be limited and the costs substantial. By appealing to good business sense (i.e., the effect on performance and on profitability), many of these inappropriate requests can be rejected.

By having input into an organization's strategy and mission, trainers can help to guide corporate direction and they can design the training and development function with ethical implications in mind. Given the widespread interest in business ethics, and in ethical management practices and employee conduct, can business ethics be taught to managers and employees (i.e., can behaviour be changed through training)?

Although many Canadian organizations have codes of ethical conduct, only 39 percent provide ethics training. Furthermore, ethics training programs are usually limited to about one hour per year. Thus, there is clearly a need for trainers to increase the awareness of ethical issues and dilemmas in their organizations and in teaching employees how to deal with them.[9]

Ethical dilemmas and moral problems can be complex. Ethics courses, then, should not advocate one best way to approach specific ethical problems, nor should they promote formulas for thinking through problems. Instead, ethical training can add value to the moral environment of a firm and to relationships in the workplace by:

- developing a match between company and employee values
- helping employees to deal with potential unethical behaviour of superiors or colleagues
- enabling employees to deal with systems, either formal or informal, that encourage unethical behaviour

The teaching of business ethics should not promise to provide solutions to complicated problems involving morality and ethical behaviour; employees can be made aware of the boundaries between behaviour that is ethically correct and behaviour that is not. As well, the trainer can help employees to search out unintentional ethical blind spots and to establish forums in the workplace for discussing morality and corporate social responsibility.[10]

Ultimately, however, training professionals themselves must adhere to a set of ethical principles that guide their own behaviour and serve as role models of proper ethical conduct to the rest of the organization. These standards can be set by organizations and associations.

For example, the Bank of Montreal has made changes to its ethical standards in HR areas such as training.[11] An association called The Academy of Human Resource Development developed a code of ethics and integrity called the Standards on Ethics and Integrity. It was developed to establish desired standards of behaviours and to bring an increased sense of professionalism to those who do research and practice human resource development.[12] It provides principles and guidance to cover different situations encountered by training professionals such as issues concerning competence and expertise, privacy and confidentiality, and relationships with and responsibilities to others to name just a few. The Canadian Society for Training and Development (CSTD) also has a code of ethics that sets standards of practice and professionalism for its members.

To learn more about the kinds of ethical standards that are important for trainers, see The Trainer's Notebook 1, "Ethical Guidelines for Trainers."

Challenges and Trends

The field of training and development is undergoing a revolution of a kind it has never seen before. This revolution is in response to the many changes in the nature of work and in organizations. In this section, we briefly describe the challenges that organizations are facing and the implications for training and development. We have categorized the challenges into the following four

The Trainer's Notebook 1

Ethical Guidelines for Trainers

Trainers must conduct themselves according to a set of ethical guidelines and standards as follows:

1. **Voluntary consent:** Trainers should not implicitly coerce unwilling or skeptical participants into self-revealing or physical activities.
2. **Discrimination:** Age, sex, race, or handicaps should not be used as barriers to determine who receives training.
3. **Cost effectiveness:** Training activities should be based on demonstrated utility, should show a demonstrated benefit vis-à-vis costs, and should not be undertaken simply to spend a training budget.

4. **Accurate portrayal:** Claims for the benefits of training need to be accurate; training should be consistent across time and trainers; training materials should be appropriately depicted.
5. **Competency in training:** Teaching methods that do not work, such as talking down to audiences, should be avoided.
6. **Values:** Trainers should believe in the value of what they teach.

Source: Lowman, R.L. (1991). Ethical human resource practice in organizational settings. In D.W. Bray (Ed.), Working with organizations. New York: Guilford.

areas: 1. Changes in the Environment, 2. Changes in the Workforce, 3. Changes in the Nature of Work, and 4. Changes in Organizations.

Changes in the Environment

Many of the changes in the environment that impact organizations have to do with increased competition, new technology, and changes in the economy. However, there is perhaps no better example of how a change in the environment can impact training and development than the effect of the terrorist attacks in the United States on September 11, 2001.

We have already noted some of the effects this had on training such as the new guidelines for the training of baggage screeners and flight crews (see Chapter 1), how Canadian cities have begun sending police, fire and medical staff for counterterrorism training at CFB Suffield (Chapter 4), and the impact of the attacks on the use of technology-based training methods (Chapter 8).

The terrorist attacks have had a major impact on the topics and content of training programs (e.g., security) and the methods used to provide training. It created an immediate need for information about new security procedures, anthrax contamination, bioterrorism, and building evacuation, to name a few. As a result, the use of technology in all its forms (e.g., satellite broadcasts, video conferencing, CD-ROMs) became key to getting the information to employees as soon as they needed it.[13]

The worldwide concerns about more terrorist attacks, bioterrorism, personal safety, and emergency preparedness are likely to continue to have a profound effect on training and development. This is going to force training departments not only to update the content of their training programs on a regular basis, but to use technology more than ever to ensure that employees receive the information and training they need to stay informed and prepared all the time. Thus, the impact of the terrorist attacks is likely to have a permanent and lasting effect on the training function, especially in terms of the increased use of technology.[14]

To learn more about the effects of terrorism on training, see Training Today, "The Effect of Terrorism on Training."

Changes in the Workforce

There are a number of changes in the composition of the workforce that will have an effect on the type of training provided as well as the way that training is designed and delivered.

First, the Canadian workforce is getting older. As the baby boomers approach their fifties, the Canadian population in general is aging. This, combined with the fact that there are fewer young people entering the workforce, skill shortages in many areas, and the tendency for people to work beyond the traditional retirement age, means that there will be an increasing number of older workers in Canadian organizations.

What are the implications of this for training and development? There are a number of factors that are associated with the aging process that need to be considered for the purpose of training. In particular, a slowing of basic cognitive processing as well as a decline in the senses are associated with the aging process. On the other hand, long-term memory and quantitative knowledge increase during adulthood. Thus, older workers are most likely to have difficulties when they encounter rapidly changing and unfamiliar job requirements rather than jobs that depend on existing knowledge.[15] Therefore, training programs for older workers must consider these differences.

Training Today

The Effect of Terrorism on Training

A survey of training professionals conducted by the American Society of Training and Development, found that the most common mentioned changes following the terrorist attacks on training and development were:

- a shift to distance technologies and e-learning
- travel either stopped or significantly reduced (for trainers and trainees)
- different training topics rising to the forefront, including diversity, security, stress management, and change management

- budget restrictions, business slowdowns, and lay-offs
- development of security and evacuation plans
- assistance to victims and families

Source: (2002, February). ASTD survey results: The effect of terrorism on training. *Training & Development*, p. 28. Copyright August 1989, adapted from *Training & Development* magazine, American Society for Training & Development. Reprinted with permission. All rights reserved.

For example, providing older workers with extra time for learning, self-pacing, and various job aids are likely to improve their learning. As well, training materials might have to be designed to account for declines in hearing and sight (see Training Today, "Computer Training for Older Workers" in Chapter 12).

Another important change in the workforce is the increasing diversity. In Canada, visible minorities are the fastest growing segment of the population and it is estimated that two-thirds of entrant's into the labour force are women, visible minorities, aboriginal people, and persons with disabilities.[16] The Canadian population and the labour force is becoming more diverse, multicultural, and multiethnic. This has a number of implications for training and development.

First, trainers will need to be aware of and sensitive to cultural differences. Differences in values and expectations across cultures will have implications for how training programs are designed and delivered. For example, the effectiveness of training methods can vary across cultures. Outdoor or experiential training that requires participants to work together doing things such as rock climbing and white water river rafting, has been found to be more effective for Canadians and Americans than British and German managers who are uncomfortable with the displays of emotion and the so-called "huggy-feely-touchy-stuff."[17] Thus, to be most effective, training programs will need to consider the cultural values of trainees in both the design and delivery of training. This also means that a blended approach that uses a variety of training methods, as described in Chapter 6, is probably the best approach for training a culturally diverse workforce.

A second implication is the need for diversity training. As noted in Chapter 12, diversity training is one of the most widely used approaches for managing diversity in the workplace. Diversity programs address cultural differences in values, attitudes, and behaviours in order to improve interactions and communication among employees with different backgrounds. Unfortunately, diversity programs are usually implemented without a needs analysis and they are seldom evaluated. As a result, it is not known to what extent they are effective or what aspects of them are most important. Given the increased need for diversity training programs, it will be necessary for trainers to conduct a needs analysis prior to implementing diversity programs and to also rigorously evaluate them following the guidelines presented in Chapter 10.

Changes in the Nature of Work

The nature of work has been undergoing major changes during the last decade and this is likely to continue. Jobs have become increasingly complex and most jobs now require at least a high-school education. The increasing use of computers and technology such as advanced manufacturing techniques has increased the cognitive demands of jobs and the education and training required to perform them.[18]

In addition to the increasing complexity of jobs, the frequency with which people change jobs has also increased. This has been particularly apparent in organizations that have downsized and reengineered. Many workers have had to deal with changes in their jobs as well as increasing workloads and responsibilities. Thus, jobs and work are not only becoming more complex, they are also being enlarged.

Another important change in work has been the increasing use of teams and group work. As noted in Chapter 12, it is estimated that 80 percent of organizations with 100 or more employees now use some form of teams. This not only requires workers to perform many if not all of the tasks performed by the team, but they must also have good social and interpersonal skills in order to interact, coordinate their efforts, solve problems, manage conflict, and communicate effectively with each other.

The type of work is also shifting away from manufacturing to the service sector. This is noteworthy because the skills that are required for service sector jobs are quite different from traditional manufacturing jobs. Service jobs involve much more interaction and contact with customers and as a result, they require workers to have good social, interpersonal, and communication skills.[19] These are skills that many people do not have and they are skills that are also more difficult to acquire than technical skills.

What are the implications of changes in the nature of work for training and development? Clearly, organizations are going to have to provide a great deal of retraining over the next decade in order to prepare employees for jobs that require new skills and continual upgrading. This means that many of the training programs discussed in Chapter 12 such as team training, nontechnical skills training, and customer service training to name a few, will become extremely important as the nature of work and jobs continue to change.

Changes in Organizations

It is now common knowledge that change is a frequent and necessary part of organizational life. Organizations today operate in turbulent environments that are highly competitive. The increasing uncertainty and turbulence in the external environment means that organizations must constantly change and adapt in order to remain competitive and survive. This might mean a change in strategy such as the change in selling strategy at TELUS, or new approaches to management.

Organizational change programs such as total quality management, reengineering, job redesign, team work arrangements, and so on require changes in the tasks and jobs performed by employees. As a result, employees require new knowledge, skills, upgrading, and training as organizations change. The more organizations change, the more employees require training.

For example, many organizations have begun to focus on the quality of their goods and services. This often involves programs such as total quality management, ISO 9000, and six sigma. In order for these programs to be effectively implemented and effective, employees must receive extensive training in the use of statistical tools, teamwork, and other quality practices. Thus, training is key to the success of quality programs.

For other organizations, the creation of high-performance work systems has been the key to remaining competitive. High-performance work systems involve self-managed teams, flat organizational structures, and flexible technologies. This usually leads to enriched jobs and employees who are empowered and multiskilled. As a result, employees require extensive training not only in technical skills, but also in nontechnical skills such as interpersonal, problem-solving, and team skills.

Global competition has also forced organizations to expand their operations to other countries and cultures. This means that many Canadian workers will increasingly find themselves living and working in other countries with very different cultures and values. Unfortunately, Canadian and American workers have tended to have a higher failure rate on overseas assignments compared to Japanese and European workers.

As indicated in Chapter 12, employees are more likely to succeed on overseas assignments when they have received cross-cultural training that prepares them to live and work in foreign countries. Thus, training is critical for overseas business success and for being globally competitive.

Finally, as discussed in Chapter 2, many organizations have become learning organizations. That is, they consciously gather, organize, share, and analyze knowledge to further their goals. Learning organizations are able to transform themselves by acquiring new knowledge, skills, and behaviour. Learning is required in order to make improvements in work systems, products, services, teamwork, and management practices. Organizational learning is the process of creating, sharing, diffusing, and applying knowledge in organizations. Learning organizations depend on employee knowledge and skills and therefore support and encourage continuous learning. Employees are expected to continuously learn new ways of doing things and to apply what they learn in order to improve products and services.

Although training and development as well as informal learning are integral parts of this process, the shift towards learning organizations will have an impact on the way in which organizations structure the learning experiences of their employees. While most organizations will retain the methods to train employees described in this text, many have also started to use new tools and methods to enable employees to create and share knowledge and information.

In summary, organizations face many challenges today that threaten their competitiveness and survival. A key part of meeting these challenges is the provision of training and development programs that provide employees with new knowledge and skills that they require in order to perform new tasks, and to continuously improve how they work and how they perform their jobs.

We have noted how the different challenges will lead to an increased need for specific kinds of training programs (e.g., diversity training, nontechnical skills training, team training, cross-cultural training, etc.) as well as changes in how training programs are delivered (e.g., technology-based methods). These challenges also mean that training programs must be highly effective and available when they are needed. We will now address these issues in the final section of the chapter.

Best Practices and Just-in-Time Learning

In addition to the challenges described in the previous section, trainers have been facing increasing pressure to demonstrate the value-added of their programs. As organizations invest more heavily in training and development and human capital, they expect to see a significant return on their investments. Thus, as described in Chapter 11, estimating training costs, benefits, and return on investment is becoming increasingly important. It also means that training programs must be more effective than ever.

Trainers are also facing pressure to deliver training programs at an increasingly rapid pace. Given the rapid pace of change in organizations today, trainers often do not have very much time to design and deliver a training program. Employees increasingly need to obtain new knowledge and skills immediately as was the case following the terrorist attacks of 9/11. This means that trainers must find ways of providing learning opportunities on demand or what has become known as "just-in-time learning."

Just-in-time (JIT) learning refers to the capability to provide learning and training opportunities when they are needed and where they are needed. The terrorist attacks of 9/11 made it clear that the need for just-in-time learning has never been more important and urgent. To meet this need, trainers will have to find new and innovative ways to design and deliver training. This will further impact the role of the training professional, which will continue to evolve into more of a knowledge structuring and learning facilitation and support role.[20]

Related to JIT learning is the use of technology. As we noted earlier, the ability to provide knowledge and information immediately following the terrorist attacks of 9/11 was largely due to the use of technology. Furthermore, as organizations find that they need to provide training more often to increasing numbers of employees, they will continue to look for approaches that are timely and cost effective. Thus, the use of technology-based training methods and blended approaches are likely to become more frequent and widespread in the years ahead.

Much of what you have read in this text represents best practices for the design and delivery of training programs. However, as a final review and conclusion, we present The Trainer's Notebook 2 with an overview of the main reasons why training programs sometimes fail along with best practices to make them highly effective. As well, the chapters where these practices are described in the text are also indicated.

Just-in-time (JIT) learning
The capability to provide learning and training opportunities when they are needed and where they are needed

Summary

This chapter began with a review of the changing role of the trainer as well as the importance of ethics in training and development. We noted how the trainer's role is shifting to that of an internal consultant who is responsible for identifying and facilitating solutions to performance problems. The chapter also discussed the increasing importance of ethics and ethical conduct and professionalism in training and development. As well, some of the major challenges facing organizations today and their implications for training and

Main Reasons for Failure and Best Practices

1. **Lack of Alignment with Business Needs**. Training programs often fail because they are not linked to business and organizational needs.

   Best Practices: Effective training programs begin with a needs analysis that links organizational needs to training programs. Needs must also be translated into clear objectives and evaluation criteria.

   Chapter: Chapter 4, "The Needs Analysis Process."

2. **Failure to Recognize Nontraining Solutions**. Training is often implemented with the intention of improving a performance problem even though it is not always the best solution.

   Best Practices: There are many possible solutions to performance problems that might be more effective and less costly than training and development. It is therefore important to use a model like the one presented in Chapter 4 to determine the best solutions to performance problems.

   Chapter: Chapter 4, "The Needs Analysis Process."

3. **Lack of Objectives to Provide Direction and Focus**. Training programs sometimes fail because they lack clear objectives.

   Best Practices: Training objectives serve a number of purposes for trainers, trainees, and the organization. Training objectives set the stage for training design and indicate the criteria that should be included for training evaluation. Training objectives for most training programs should be set at multiple levels (i.e., reactions, learning, behaviour, results, and ROI).

   Chapter: Chapter 5, "Training Design and Delivery."

4. **The Solution is too Expensive**. Although a training program's ROI is an important measure of effectiveness, a negative ROI does not mean that a training program has failed. There are often many intangible benefits of training programs that add value to an organization.

   Best Practices: Training programs do not have to be expensive to be effective. It is important to estimate the costs and benefits of training programs before making a decision. It is also important to be clear about the main criteria to use when comparing training alternatives.

   Chapter: Chapter 11, "The Costs and Benefits of Training Programs."

5. **Regarding Training as an Event**. When training is treated as a separate or isolated event, it is likely to fail.

   Best Practices: Training programs have to be considered as part of a larger process and organizational system that requires on-going attention and support not only during training, but before and after training.

   Chapter: Chapter 9, "Transfer of Training."

6. **Participants are not Held Accountable for Results**. When employees are only expected to attend a training program without any responsibility for what they learn or do after training, they are not likely to show any change in behaviour or improvement in job performance.

   Best Practices: Trainees must be held accountable for what they learn in training and how they will apply it on the job. Managers must also be accountable and responsible for their employees' learning and transfer as well as organizational results.

   Chapter: Chapter 9, "Transfer of Training."

7. **Failure to Prepare the Job Environment for Transfer**. Barriers in the job environment that can undermine the success of an otherwise effective training program.

   Best Practices: Needs analysis information can be used to identify transfer barriers and remove them before a training program is implemented. Facilitating the transfer of training can involve activities before, during, and after training and include trainers, trainees, and management.

   Chapter: Chapter 9, "Transfer of Training."

8. **Lack of Management Reinforcement and Support**. If management does not support, encourage, and reinforce the use of new knowledge and skills on the job, training programs will not be effective.

   Best Practices: It is extremely important that management be involved with trainees before and after training. Managers need to know how critical their role is and how they can provide support and reinforcement.

   Chapter: Chapter 9, "Transfer of Training."

9. **Failure to Isolate the Effects of Training**. It is especially difficult to be able to demonstrate that changes or effects in employees and the organization are due to a particular training program and not something else. Failure to isolate the effects of training might leave some wondering about the need and value of training and development.

   Best Practices: The traditional way of isolating the effects of training is to conduct an experiment with a training group and a control group. Unfortunately, this type of design is often difficult to implement and is more often the exception than the rule. Therefore, alternative approaches need to be used such as the internal referencing strategy described in Chapter 10. Other techniques for isolating the effects of training include trainee, supervisor, and management estimates of the impact, as well as estimating the impact of other factors.

   Chapter: Chapter 10, "Training Evaluation."

10. **Lack of Commitment and Involvement from Executives**. Training and development programs are doomed to fail without the commitment and involvement of senior executives. Their commitment is critical for the effectiveness of training and development programs.

    Best Practices: Executives can demonstrate their commitment to the training function by providing resources for programs, and they can become involved by their presence and participation at training sessions.

    Chapter: Chapter 9, "Transfer of Training."

11. **Failure to Provide Feedback and Use Information about Results**. Training programs cannot be improved and are not likely to reach their expectations if the various stakeholders do not receive feedback and information about the results of training. Feedback and information is necessary to make training programs effective for all of the major stakeholders.

    Best Practices: Trainers need to know if their training programs are achieving the objectives; trainees need to know if they have acquired new knowledge and skills; and management needs to know if training has had an impact on business results.

    When training programs are evaluated, it is possible to provide feedback to all of the key stakeholders. Feedback can be used by trainees for learning and performance improvement. Trainers can use feedback to improve the design and delivery of training programs. Management can use feedback to make decisions about future programs and actions needed to solve an organization's problems and improve results.

    Chapter: Chapter 5 "Training Design and Delivery" and Chapter 10, "Training Evaluation."

Source: Phillips. J. J., & Phillips, P. P. (2002, September). 11 reasons why training and development fail...and what you can do about it. *Training*, *39* (9), 78–85. Training: The Human Side of Business by Phillips, J.J. & Phillips, P.P. Copyright 2002 by V N U BUS PUBNS USA. Reproduced with permission of V N U BUS PUBNS USA in the format Textbook via Copyright Clearance Center.

development were presented. These challenges will have a direct effect on the type of training provided and the way in which training is delivered. The chapter concluded with a review of the major reasons why training programs fail and the best practices for making training and development programs effective.

Conclusion

It should now be clear to you that training and development is an important part of the management of performance in organizations. Training and development can play a critical role in helping organizations meet today's and tomorrow's challenges. Unfortunately, training programs sometimes fail and limit an organization's ability to remain competitive and to survive. The good news is that the science of training, as described in this text, contains practical information on how to design, deliver, and evaluate training programs. By following the theories, concepts, and principles described in this text, it is possible to design and deliver training programs that are effective and beneficial for individuals, organizations, and society at large. You now know the science of training; it is up to you to translate training science into practice.

Key Terms

ethics (page 388)
internal consultant (page 387)
just-in-time (JIT) learning (page 395)

Web Links

Academy of Human Resource Development: www.ahrd.org (page 389)
Bank of Montreal: www.bankofmontreal.ca (page 389)
Canadian Society for Training and Development: www.cstd.ca (page 389)

Discussion Questions

1.   What is the responsibility of training professionals for ethics in their organizations? Do trainers bear some of the responsibility for unethical behaviour in organizations such as Enron and Arthur Andersen?
2.   How has the role of the trainer changed over the years and what future roles might trainers play?
3.   What are some of the challenges facing organizations today and what are the implications for training and development?
4.   Why do training programs sometimes fail and how can they be more effective?

Using the Internet

1.   To find out about ethics training in Canada, visit the website of the Ethics Practitioners' Association of Canada (EPAC) at **www.epac-apec.ca** and click on the Inventory of Education and Resources. Find out what kinds of education resources are available in your province and what kind of training resources are available in Canada. Write a brief report in which you describe the kinds of ethical education programs and training programs available.
2.   To learn about ethical standards of practice for training professionals, visit the website of the Canadian Society for Training and Development (CSTD) at **www.cstd.ca** and click on "About Us" and then "Member Code of Ethics." Review the ethical standards and describe how they apply to the different stages of the training and development process and to training research, practice, and consulting.

Exercises

1. Contact the training director in an organization to find out how his/her role has changed and how it will change in the future. What was the trainer's role five years ago? What is the trainer's role today? What will the trainer's role be in five years? What skills and experiences do trainers need in order to perform their current and future roles, and how has this changed over the last five to 10 years?

2. Review The Trainer's Notebook 2, "Main Reasons for Failure and Best Practices," and then contact a manager or director of training in an organization and ask him/her about the success and failure of training and development programs in his/her organization. Make up a question for each of the 11 reasons for failure to find out how the organization deals with them (e.g., Are training programs in your organization based on a needs analysis and linked to business needs?) and if best practices are used in the design and delivery of training and development programs.

3. If an organization wanted to hire a training professional today, what would they look for? Find several job advertisements for a training manager or director in your local newspaper. Bring the advertisements to class and summarize the main tasks and responsibilities of the position. Describe how the job matches the traditional role of a trainer as well as more current roles and expectations.

4. Consider the ethics of the most recent training experience you have had either in a current job or in a previous job. Review the six ethical guidelines listed in The Trainer's Notebook 1, "Ethical Guidelines for Trainers," and determine how well they stand up against your most recent training experience. Based on your analysis, was the trainer and the training program ethical? Be prepared to explain and defend your answer.

5. Review the chapter-opening vignette on TELUS and then comment on how each of the 11 main reasons for failure and best practices described in The Trainer's Notebook 2, "Main Reasons for Failure and Best Practices" apply to the TELUS training program. Comment on each of the reasons for failure and best practices as they apply to the sales training program. Are there any reasons why the sales training program might fail? What best practices have been used in the design and delivery of the sales training program?

Case

CHANGING EMPLOYEES' MINDS

For many employees, the chance to attend a training course is a wonderful opportunity. SaskTel employees were excited about a six-week training course to prepare them to be part of a team and to learn about process re-engineering to redesign business processes and improve company performance. However, instead of re-engineering training, these employees were part of a social engineering experiment after which half of the 24 participants required psychological counselling or stress leave.

The employees claimed that they were brainwashed. The union claims that this training program was one more reason why SaskTel had its first general province-wide strike in 88 years.

What went wrong? The company included this training as part of a $2-million corporate makeover to make it more competitive. At the outset, the managers believed that they were simply implementing courses that would tap the potential of employees and enable them to become more productive.

SaskTel was not the only company trying to capitalize on the human potential movement, which meant designing ways to tap the values and beliefs of employees to increase performance effectiveness. But the techniques of changing belief systems are not well established, and it is more an art than a science. Other Canadian firms found themselves unknowingly buying training programs from religious cults.

TransAlta paid a consulting company $24 million to train 1500 employees. These employees were subjected to daily sayings that ended with employees saying "amen," and to supervisors conducting daily mood checks so that inappropriate emotions could be monitored and changed. Public criticisms of employees were encouraged in an effort to improve performance, but these public humiliations left employees in tears, and some quit the company.

After employees leaked news of this abusive treatment to CBC-TV, the CEO placed ads in newspapers, and sent letters to all workers apologizing for their distress.

The re-engineering program at SaskTel proved more damaging than that at TransAlta. Windows were papered over to prevent people seeing in or out. Employees were discouraged from communicating with each other. There was a lot of jargon (terms such as "blue-skying," "thinking outside the box"), and employees felt that they were trapped in a 1984 Orwellian nightmare. The original program, scheduled to last six weeks, was continually extended. The consultants were highly aggressive, and employees were told to play the game or get out. Fearing for their jobs, the employees played the game, at great personal costs.

Source: Kay, E. (1996, November). Trauma in real life. *The Globe and Mail: Report on Business Magazine*, pp. 82–92. Reprinted by permission of Edward Kay.

Questions

1. Was the training described in the case ethical? Do organizations have a right to provide this kind of training? Do employees have a right to refuse to attend such training programs?

2. The training sessions were designed to change employee's attitudes. Does management have the right to do this? Under what circumstances? What are the legal and ethical issues? Should employees give

informed consent? Do these types of training programs violate individual rights?

3. What is the role of an organization's training professionals in allowing the kind of training programs described in the case to take place? From an ethical perspective, what is their responsibility?

4. Review The Trainer's Notebook 1, "Ethical Guidelines for Trainers," and conduct an ethical audit of the consultant trainers and the training programs described in the case. Based on your audit, how ethical or unethical were the consultants and their training programs? How ethical were the managers of the organizations that hired the consulting firms to provide the training?

5. If you were a trainer in an organization in which management required employees to attend the kind of training described in the case, what would you do? As a trainer, do you have any ethical responsibility for training that has been approved by management?

Running Case Part 8

VANDALAIS DEPARTMENT STORES

Refer to the Vandalais Department Stores case described in Chapter 5 and answer the following question.

1. Refer to The Trainer's Notebook 2, "Main Reasons for Failure and Best Practices." Review each of the reasons for failure and discuss how they apply to the structured employment interview training program. In particular, identify any reasons that might lead to the failure of the structured employment interview training program as well as how best practices might be applied to ensure its success.

References

[1]Connal, D. Baskin, C. (2002, November). Transforming a sales organization through simulation-based learning: a TELUS Communications case study. *Training Report*, 4–5. http://www.telus.com.

[2]Harrison, R. (1997). Financial giants taking training into big league. *People Management*, 3, (13), 47.

[3]Zemke, R. (1987). Bill Yeomans: Making training pay at J.C. Penney. *Training*, 24 (8), 63–64.

[4]Wright, P.C., & Geroy, G.D. (1991). *Experience, judgement, and intuition: Qualitative data-gathering methods and aids to strategic planning.* Bradford: MCB University Press.

[5]Wright, P., & Kusmanadji, K. (1994). The strategic application of TQM principles to human resources management. *Training for Quality*, 1(3), 5–14.

[6]Harris-Lalonde, S. (2001). Training and development outlook. *The Conference Board of Canada.* Ottawa

[7] Nilson, C. (1998). Research summary. In Nilson, C. (Ed.), *Training and development yearbook, 1998* (pp. 4.48–4.49). Paramus: Prentice Hall.

[8]Broder, J.M. (1997, October 11). Clinton presents proposals to improve IRS. *New York Times*, p. A9.

[9]Adams, C. (2002, October). Organizational ethics' exponential growth. *The Training Report*, pp.11–12.

[10]Weiss, J.W. (1998). *Business ethics.* Orlando: Harcourt Brace & Company.

[11]Alaton, S. (2003, June 2). HR seen as "moral guardian" for firms. *The Globe and* Mail, B17.

[12]Hatcher, T., & Aragon, S. R. (2000). A code of ethics and integrity for HRD research and practice. *Human Resource Development Quarterly, 11*, 179–85.

[13]Caudron, S. (2002, February). Training in the post-terrorism era. *Training & Development*, 24–30.

[14]Caudron, S. (2002, February).

[15]Thayer, P. W. (1997). A rapidly changing world: Some implications for training systems in the year 2001 and beyond. In M. A. Quinones & A. Ehrenstein (Eds.), *Training for a rapidly changing workplace*. Washington, DC: American Psychological Association.

[16]Kanungo, R. N. (1998). Leadership in organizations: Looking ahead to the 21st century. *Canadian Psychology, 39*, (1-2), 71–82.

[17]French, C. (1996, August 20). When cultures collide. *The Globe and Mail*, C1.

[18]Thayer, P. W. (1997).

[19]Thayer, P. W. (1997).

[20]Caudron, S. (2002, February).

Index

job instruction training, 175–78, 179
job redesign, 184
job rotation, 180–81, 371–72
just-in-time
    learning, 395
    training, 208–9

Kavanagh, Michael, 271
Kirkpatrick, Donald, 118, 127, 130, 258
knowledge
    declarative knowledge, 56, 148
    defined, 32
    interpretation of, 38–39
    knowledge acquisition, 36–37
    knowledge compilation, 56–57
    knowledge dissemination, 39–40
    knowledge management/infra-
        structure, 34, 35–36, 41, 42
    procedural knowledge, 57
    retention of, 40–41
    shared knowledge, 38, 39, 40–41
    types of, 32–33
knowledge of results, 123
    See also feedback
Knowles, Malcolm, 62
Kolb, David, 63–64
Kouzes, J.M., 358
KPMG, 206
Kraft General Foods, 41
Kraiger, K., 260
Krispy Kreme, 112
Kuri, F., 323

Labatt Brewing Co. Ltd., 9
labour market, and training and
    development, 14
Latham, Gary, 367
Law 90, 9
leadership, 355–56
leading function, of management, 358
learning
    Canadian organizations and,
        31–32
    culture, 89, 230
    defined, 55
    disciplines of, 29
    facilitation strategies for, 44
    feedback and, 123–24
    firm performance and, 30
    learning measures, 264, 266–68
    learning organizations, 28–32, 394

mental models and, 38
modes of, 63
multilevel systems approach,
    42–44
outcomes, 55–56
overlearning, 123
part learning, 123
social dimension of, 38–39
stages of, 56–57
styles of, 63–65
whole learning, 123
See also knowledge
learning goals, 70, 122
learning theories, 57–65
    Adaptive Character of Thought
        (ACT) theory, 56–57
    adult learning theory, 61–64
    conditioning theory, 58–59
    social learning theory, 59–61
lecture method, 147–49
lesson plan, 130–32
Levi Strauss & Co., 330–31
literacy
    defined, 323
    levels of, 322
    problems of, 150, 321
    See also basic skills training
literature, academic and
    practitioner, 119
L.L. Bean, 334
Locke, Edwin, 367
locus of control, 71

Mager, R.F., 96
maintenance, in transfer of
    training, 225
management
    core functions of, 91, 356–59
    defined, 356
    managerial roles, 359–60
    skills, 361–62, 366–70
management development
    content of development pro-
        grams, 366–70
    defined, 355
    education programs, 371
    investment in, 355
    models of skill development,
        364–65, 366
    on-the-job development, 371–72,
        373–75

outdoor wilderness training,
    372–73
training programs, 371
mandatory courses, 235
March, James, 367
Maslow, Abraham, 66–67
massed practice, 122
mastery goals. See learning goals
maturation, and posttraining results,
    275, 276
MBA programs
    management education, 371
    online, 206
McDonald's Canada, 173–74
McMaster University, 62
media, 128, 134, 136
mental maps, 38
mental models, 29, 38
mentoring, 60
    choice of mentors, 187
    mentor-protégé match, 188
    online mentors, 40, 187
    on-the-job training, 181, 185–88
    purposes, 186
metacognition, 121
metacognitive strategies, 121
Microsoft, 33, 360
Mintzberg, H., 359
Mitsubishi, 335
Morgan, R.B., 261
mortality, and posttraining
    results, 275
motivation
    and computer-based training,
        212–13
    defined, 65
    evaluation of, 263, 269–70
    goal setting, 69–70, 98–99, 367
    insecurity and, 175
    to learn, 71–72
    as managerial skill, 363
    theories of, 65–70
    training motivation, 71–72,
        234–35
    to transfer, 238, 259, 269–70
Motorola, 37, 38, 202–3, 210,
    323, 325
motor skills, 55
multilevel systems approach, to
    organizational learning, 42–43
multimedia, 201

practice
  active practice, 120–21
  conditions of, 122–24, 125
  defined, 121
  prepractice conditions, 121–22
  skill practice, 365
  and transfer of training, 239–40, 241
pragmatic barriers, to training evaluation, 255
preferred learning styles, 65
preparation phase, of job instruction training, 175, 176–77
preparatory information, 122
pre-post design, 275, 276–77
preparatory briefs, 122
pressure point, 84–85
PricewaterhouseCoopers (PwC), 359, 368, 374
private training companies, 116
procedural knowledge, 57
procedural learning, 264, 266
process theories, 66
  expectancy theory, 68–69
  goal setting theory, 69–70
production environment, 213
production indicators, 268–69
productive responses, 120
productivity, and standard of living, 8
professional membership, 184–85
psychological fidelity, 159
psychological states, analysis of, 257
psychosocial support roles, 185
punishment. See penalties and punishment

quality, focus on, 328–29, 393
quasi-experimental designs, 273, 274
Quebec, training legislation in, 9
Quebecor World Inc., 2
questions
  of learners, 134, 135
  phrasing of, 135
  time for, 148
quid pro quo, sexual harassment, 336

reaction measures, 261–64, 265
readiness to learn/trainability, 233–34
recall of prior knowledge, 133
record keeping, 308
recruitment and retention, employee

training and development and, 6–7
reflective observation (RO), learning mode, 63
reinforcement, 58–59
  supportive attitude, 177–78
relapse prevention, 240–41
relatedness needs, 67
relationship capital, 34–35
renewal capital, 34
repositories, knowledge, 40–41
resource analysis, 88
return on expectations, 272
return on investment (ROI), 298–303, 306
Revans, Reginald, 159
rewards
  for correct performance, 124
  intrinsic and extrinsic benefits, 7
  See also penalties and punishment; reinforcement
Rifkind, L.J., 329
role ambiguity, 370
role conflict, 370
role play, 154–56
Rothschild PLC, 41
Rouiller, J.Z., 271
Royal Bank, 37
Royal Bank Financial Group of Canada, 158

safety considerations, 176, 177, 190
Saks, A.M., 259
sale-of-service accounting method, 308
sales training, 332–33, 384–85
Sanders, J.R., 257
satellite television, 201, 208
scheduling, of training program, 129–30
Schneider, B., 334
Schultz, Howard, 320
Scotiabank, 9, 208
Sears & Roebuck, 335
security needs, 66
self-actualization needs, 67
self-awareness, 363
self-control, 363
self-development, 203
self-directed learning (SDL), 202–3, 204
self-efficacy, 270
  evaluation of, 263, 270

and motivation, 71
  in social learning theory, 60–61
self-management
  in social learning theory, 61
  transfer interventions, 241–43
self-paced training, 120
self-reports, 268
Senge, P.M., 28, 29, 38
sequence approach, 174
sexual harassment training, 116, 335–36
shaping, 59
shared vision, 29
Simon, Herbert, 367
simulations, 157–59
single group design with control group, 277
single group post-only design, 275–76
single group pre-post design, 276
Skandia, 35
skills
  application, 365
  assessment, 364
  in collaboration, 157
  conceptual skills, 366–68
  in critical thinking, 149
  defined, 361
  interpersonal skills, 149, 154, 160, 361–62, 363, 368–70
  leadership skills, 157
  management skills, 361–62
  planning, 367
  practice, 365
  in problem solving, 151, 153, 366–67
  skill learning, 365
Skinner, B.F., 58
Sloman, M., 178
small business, and on-the-job training, 174
SmartForce Publishing Ltd., 187
SMART goals, 367–68
socialization. See orientation training
social learning theory, 59–61
societal benefits, of training and development, 7–8
soft data, 272
soft skills
  cross-cultural training, 339, 341–42

effect of terrorism on, 12, 199,
390–91
environmental context of, 12–14
global competition and, 12, 394
informal learning, 29, 37
investment in, 8–10, 44–45,
317–18, 319
model of training effectiveness,
72–73
organizational context of, 14–16
performance, 3–4
as subsystem, 12–16
technological change and, 14, 395
trends and challenges, 393–95
training content, 118–19
training design. *See* design, training
Training in Management Skills
(TIMS), 366
training inputs, 227–30
training materials and equipment,
128, 134, 136, 238
evaluation of, 257
training methods
blended delivery approach, 120,
161, 163, 190, 214
choice of, 161–63, 190
cost consideration, 162
management support and, 162–63
objectives and, 161
productive responses, 120
trainee preferences and, 162
See also off-the-job training
methods; on-the-job training
training plan, 128

training programs
compulsory programs, 127–28
health and safety training, 326–28
information technology training,
325–26, 327
nontechnical skills training,
330–42
orientation training, 318, 320–21
quality training, 328–29
reality-based programs, 146
technical skills training, 324–25
train the trainer programs, 126
types of, 317–18
training site, 128–29
training step approach, 174
training transfer climate, 89, 230, 271
TransCanada PipeLines Ltd, 240
transfer, job, 99
transfer climate. *See* training transfer
climate
transfer of training
actual extent of transfer, 226
barriers to transfer, 227
defined, 225
evaluation of, 268–69
management, role of, 229–30,
233–36, 237–38, 293–94
model of effectiveness, 243–44
pretraining activities, 231, 233–36
process, 226–67
trainee characteristics and, 227–28
training activities, 237–38
training design and, 228–29
training inputs, 227–230

transfer enhancement procedures
(TEPs), 240–41
trial-and-error approach, 176
trouble-shooting, 360
trust, in employee–coach relationship, 185, 374
Tschirhart, M., 361–62

utility analysis, 304–6
utility reactions, 263

valence, 68–69, 269–70
Vanderstoop, Nick, 49
verbal information, 55
vertical transfer, 225–26, 243–44
video conferencing, 207–8
viewed performance/feedback, 174

Web-based training, 120
Welch, Jack, 332
Wentling, R.M., 338–39
Western Gas Marketing, Ltd., 240
Whetten, D.A., 356, 364
Whirlpool Corp, 146
whole learning, 123
Workplace Hazardous Materials
Information System
(WHMIS), 328
Worthen, B.R., 257

Xerox, 37, 239, 269, 325

Zemke, Ron, 386
zero transfer, 225